D1795675

World Yearbook of Education 2015

This latest volume in the *World Yearbook of Education Series* focuses on educational elites and inequality, focusing particularly on the ways in which established and emergent groups located at the top of the social hierarchy and power structure reproduce, establish or redefine their position.

The volume is organized around three main issues:

- analyzing the way in which parents, students and graduates in positions of social advantage use their assets and capitals in relation to educational strategies, and how these are different for old and new and cultural and economic elites;
- studying how elite institutions have adapted their strategies to take into account changes in the social structure, in policy and in their institutional environment and exploring the impact of these strategies on educational systems at the national and global levels;
- mapping the new global dynamics in elite education and how new forms of 'international education' and 'transnational cultural capital' as well as new global educational elite pathways shape elite students' identities, status and trajectories.

Making use of a social and an institutional approach as well as a focus on practices and policies, the volume draws on research conducted on secondary schools and on higher education. In addition, the global contributions within the book allow for a comparison and contrast of situations in different countries. This results in a comprehensive picture of common processes and national differences concerning advantage and excellence and a thorough examination of the impact of globalization on the strategies, identities and trajectories of elite groups and individuals alongside more general cultural and economic processes.

Agnès van Zanten is Senior Research Professor at the Observatoire Sociologique du Changement at Sciences Po, Paris.

Stephen J. Ball is Karl Mannheim Professor of Sociology of Education at the Institute of Education, University of London.

Brigitte Darchy-Koechlin holds a PhD in sociology and works at the Department of Research Development, Innovation and Experimentation of the French Ministry of Education, Higher Education and Research.

World Yearbook of Education Series
Series editors: Terri Seddon, Jenny Ozga, Gita Steiner-Khamsi and Agnès van Zanten

World Yearbook of Education 1989
HEALTH EDUCATION
Edited by Chris James, John Balding and Duncan Harris

World Yearbook of Education 1990
ASSESSMENT AND EVALUATION
Edited by Chris Bell and Duncan Harris

World Yearbook of Education 1991
INTERNATIONAL SCHOOLS AND INTERNATIONAL EDUCATION
Edited by Patricia L. Jonietz and Duncan Harris

World Yearbook of Education 1992
URBAN EDUCATION
Edited by David Coulby, Crispin Jones and Duncan Harris

World Yearbook of Education 1993
SPECIAL NEEDS EDUCATION
Edited by Peter Mittler, Ron Brouilette and Duncan Harris

World Yearbook of Education 1994
THE GENDER GAP IN HIGHER EDUCATION
Edited by Suzanne Stiver Lie, Lynda Malik and Duncan Harris

World Yearbook of Education 1995
YOUTH, EDUCATION AND WORK
Edited by Leslie Bash and Andy Green

World Yearbook of Education 1996
THE EVALUATION OF HIGHER EDUCATION SYSTEMS
Edited by Robert Cowen

World Yearbook of Education 1997
INTERCULTURAL EDUCATION
Edited by David Coulby, Jagdish Gundara and Crispin Jones

World Yearbook of Education 1998
FUTURES EDUCATION
Edited by David Hicks and Richard Slaughter

World Yearbook of Education 1999
INCLUSIVE EDUCATION
Edited by Harry Daniels and Philip Garner

World Yearbook of Education 2000
EDUCATION IN TIMES OF TRANSITION
Edited by David Coulby, Robert Cowen and Crispin Jones

World Yearbook of Education 2001
VALUES, CULTURE AND EDUCATION
Edited by Roy Gardner, Jo Cairns and Denis Lawton

World Yearbook of Education 2002
TEACHER EDUCATION: DILEMMAS AND PROSPECTS
Edited by Elwyn Thomas

World Yearbook of Education 2003
LANGUAGE EDUCATION
Edited by Jill Bourne and Euan Reid

World Yearbook of Education 2004
DIGITAL TECHNOLOGY, COMMUNITIES AND EDUCATION
Edited by Andrew Brown and Niki Davis

World Yearbook of Education 2005
GLOBALIZATION AND
NATIONALISM IN EDUCATION
Edited by David Coulby and Evie Zambeta

World Yearbook of Education 2006
EDUCATION RESEARCH AND
POLICY: STEERING THE
KNOWLEDGE-BASED ECONOMY
Edited by Jenny Ozga, Terri Seddon
and Tom Popkewitz

World Yearbook of Education 2007
EDUCATING THE GLOBAL
WORKFORCE: KNOWLEDGE,
KNOWLEDGE WORK AND
KNOWLEDGE WORKERS
Edited by Lesley Farrell and Tara Fenwick

World Yearbook of Education 2008
GEOGRAPHIES OF KNOWLEDGE ,
GEOMETRIES OF POWER:
FRAMING THE FUTURE OF
HIGHER EDUCATION
Edited by Debbie Epstein, Rebecca
Boden, Rosemary Deem,
Fazal Rizvi and Susan Wright

World Yearbook of Education 2009
CHILDHOOD STUDIES AND THE
IMPACT OF GLOBALIZATION:
POLICIES AND PRACTICES AT
GLOBAL AND LOCAL LEVELS
Edited by Marilyn Fleer, Mariane
Hedgaard and Jonathan Tudge

World Yearbook of Education 2010
EDUCATION AND THE ARAB
WORLD
Edited by André E. Mazawi and Ronald
G. Sultana

World Yearbook of Education 2011
CURRICULUM IN TODAY'S
WORLD: CONFIGURING
KNOWLEDGE, IDENTITIES, WORK
AND POLITICS
Edited by Lyn Yates and Madeleine
Grumet

World Yearbook of Education 2012
POLICY BORROWING AND
LENDING IN EDUCATION
Edited by Gita Steiner-Khamsi and
Florian Waldow

World Yearbook of Education 2013
EDUCATORS, PROFESSIONALISM
AND POLITICS: GLOBAL
TRANSITIONS, NATIONAL
SPACES AND PROFESSIONAL
PROJECTS
Edited by Terri Seddon and
John Levin

World Yearbook of Education 2014
GOVERNING KNOWLEDGE:
COMPARISON, KNOWLEDGE-
BASED TECHNOLOGIES AND
EXPERTISE IN THE
REGULATION OF
EDUCATION
Edited by Tara Fenwick, Eric Mangez
and Jenny Ozga

World Yearbook of Education 2015
ELITES, PRIVILEGE AND
EXCELLENCE: THE NATIONAL
AND GLOBAL REDEFINITION OF
EDUCATIONAL ADVANTAGE
Edited by Agnès van Zanten and
Stephen J. Ball with Brigitte
Darchy-Koechlin

World Yearbook of Education 2015

Elites, Privilege and
Excellence: The National and Global
Redefinition of Educational Advantage

**Edited by
Agnès van Zanten and Stephen J. Ball
with Brigitte Darchy-Koechlin**

Routledge
Taylor & Francis Group

LONDON AND NEW YORK

First published 2015
by Routledge
2 Park Square, Milton Park, Abingdon, Oxon OX14 4RN

and by Routledge
711 Third Avenue, New York, NY 10017

Routledge is an imprint of the Taylor & Francis Group, an informa business

© 2015 Agnès van Zanten, Stephen J. Ball and Brigitte Darchy-Koechlin

The right of the editors to be identified as the authors of the editorial
material, and of the authors for their individual chapters, has been
asserted in accordance with sections 77 and 78 of the Copyright, Designs
and Patents Act 1988.

All rights reserved. No part of this book may be reprinted or reproduced
or utilised in any form or by any electronic, mechanical, or other means,
now known or hereafter invented, including photocopying and recording,
or in any information storage or retrieval system, without permission in
writing from the publishers.

Trademark notice: Product or corporate names may be trademarks or
registered trademarks, and are used only for identification and
explanation without intent to infringe.

British Library Cataloguing in Publication Data
A catalogue record for this book is available from the British Library

Library of Congress Cataloging in Publication Data
A catalog record for this book has been requested

ISBN: 978-1-138-78642-4 (hbk)
ISBN: 978-1-315-76730-7 (ebk)

Typeset in Minion
by Book Now Ltd, London

Printed and bound in Great Britain by
TJ International Ltd, Padstow, Cornwall

Contents

List of Illustrations   xi
Notes on Contributors   xiii
Series Editors' Introduction   xxi

Introduction   1

**Educating Elites: The Changing Dynamics and Meanings
of Privilege and Power**   3
AGNÈS VAN ZANTEN

PART I
Class and Family Educational Strategies   13

1   **Elites: Some Questions for a New Research Agenda**   15
    CLAIRE MAXWELL

2   **A Family Affair: Reproducing Elite Positions and Preserving
    the Ideals of Meritocratic Competition and Youth Autonomy**   29
    AGNÈS VAN ZANTEN

3   **Elite Schools in Buenos Aires: The Role of Tradition and School
    Social Networks in the Production and Reproduction of Privilege**   43
    VICTORIA GESSAGHI AND ALICIA MÉNDEZ

PART II
Elite Institutions in National and Local Contexts   57

4   **Changes in Elite Education in the United States**   59
    SHAMUS RAHMAN KHAN

 5 The Changing Strategies of Social Closure in Elite
    Education in Brazil   71
    ANA MARIA F. ALMEIDA

 6 Germany's Hesitant Approach to Elite Education: Stratification
    Processes in German Secondary and Higher Education   82
    ULRIKE DEPPE, WERNER HELSPER, REINHARD KRECKEL,
    HEINZ-HERMANN KRÜGER AND MANFRED STOCK

 7 The Boundaries of Privilege: Elite English Schools' Geographies
    and Depictions of a Local Community   95
    RACHEL BROOKS AND JOHANNA WATERS

PART III
The Impact of Globalization on Institutional
and Student Identities   109

 8 Globalization and Elite Universities in China   111
    TIEN-HUI CHIANG, FAN-HUA MENG AND XIAO-MING TIAN

 9 The Discourse of "Asia Rising" in an Elite Indian School   126
    FAZAL RIZVI

10 National and International Students' Definitions of Merit in
    French *Grandes Écoles*   140
    BRIGITTE DARCHY-KOECHLIN, HUGUES DRAELANTS
    AND ELISE TENRET

11 Globalizing Femininity in Elite Schools for Girls:
    Some Paradoxical Failures of Success   153
    JANE KENWAY, DIANA LANGMEAD AND DEBBIE EPSTEIN

PART IV
Elite Institutions, Elite Positions and Elite Jobs   167

12 Elite Universities, Elite Schooling and Reproduction in Britain 169
    PAUL WAKELING AND MIKE SAVAGE

13 Paths to the Elite in France and in the United States   185
    JULES NAUDET

14 Contextually Bound Authoritative Knowledge: A Comparative
    Study of British, French and Norwegian Administrative Elites'
    Merit and Skills   201
    MARTE MANGSET

15 **Higher Education, Corporate Talent and the Stratification of Knowledge Work in the Global Labour Market** 217
PHILLIP BROWN, HUGH LAUDER AND JOHNNY SUNG

Conclusion 231

Elites, Education and Identity: An Emerging Research Agenda 233
STEPHEN J. BALL

Index 241

Illustrations

Figures

4.1 Professional composition of the 1 percent   61
8.1 The distribution of economic development in China   118
8.2 The geographic locations of the 211 Project universities   120
8.3 The geographic locations of the 985 Project universities   120
8.4 Average expenditure of students on education   121
12.1 Percentage of graduates in NS-SEC1 and Elite by university
       'mission' group/type, GBCS (respondents aged 25–65 only)   176
12.2 Percentage of RG graduates in NS-SEC1 and Elite by
       institution, GBCS   177
12.3 Percentage membership of Elite/NS-SEC1 classes by category
       of school last attended, GBCS   178
12.4 Pathways to the Elite for GBCS respondents aged 30–49
       (selected categories only)   179
13.1 Indices of differentiation of the academic courses of study
       (external differentiation) and vocational specialization of
       education (vocational orientation index) for the educational
       systems of 31 countries   192

Tables

12.1 Reported economic capital for graduates of RG institutions –
       institutional means, GBCS   174
12.2 Mean cultural capital scores for graduates of RG institutions,
       by institution, GBCS   175
12.3 Elite membership by social/educational pathway for GBCS
       respondents aged 30–49 (selected categories only)   181
13.1 Distribution of the directors of CAC 40 by type of training in 2007   194

Contributors

Ana Maria F. Almeida is Associate Professor of Education at the University of Campinas, Sao Paulo, Brazil. She has researched extensively on education and inequalities and elite education. She is the author of *As Escolas dos Dirigentes Paulistas* (2009), and co-edited *A Escolarização das Elites* (Vozes 2002) and *Circulação Internacional e Formação Intelectual das Elites Brasileiras* (2004). She has been a visiting professor at the École des Hautes Etudes en Sciences Sociales in Paris, at the Facultad Latinoamericana de Ciencias Sociales (FLACSO) in Buenos Aires, and Visiting Scholar at the Center for Latin American Studies in Stanford, USA. She holds a fellowship at the Conselho Nacional de Desenvolvimento Científico e Tecnológico (CNPq) and is the editor-in-chief of *Pro-Posições*.

Stephen J. Ball is Karl Mannheim Professor of Sociology of Education at Institute of Education, University of London. His main areas of interest are in education policy analysis and the relationships between education and education policy and social class. He brings to bear on these issues the tools and concepts of 'policy sociology' and in particular the methods of Michael Foucault and Pierre Bourdieu. In 2008, he was involved in launching the BERA Social Theory and Education SIG. His most recent books are: *How Schools do Policy* (2012), *Global Education Inc.* (2012), *Networks, New Governance and Education* (with Carolina Junemann) (2012), and *Foucault, Power and Education* (2013). He has two current research projects (British Academy and Leverhulme Foundation) which explore the spread and impact of a global education policy network on Africa and India. He is also working on an international study of philanthropy and education policy with Antonio Olmedo of University of Roehampton.

Rachel Brooks is Professor of Sociology and Head of the School of Social Sciences at the University of Surrey. She is also editor of *Sociological Research Online* and an executive editor of the *British Journal of Sociology of Education*. She has conducted research on a wide variety of topics within the sociology of education, including the higher education choices of young people; the experiences of higher education students with dependent children, and international student mobility. Her recent books include *Contemporary Debates in the Sociology of Education* (co-edited with Mark McCormack and Kalwant

Bhopal) and *Ethics and Education Research* (co-authored with Meg Maguire and Kitty te Riele).

Phillip Brown is a Distinguished Research Professor in the School of Social Sciences, Cardiff University. He worked in the auto industry in Cowley, Oxford before training as a teacher. His academic career took him to Cambridge University and the University of Kent at Canterbury before joining Cardiff University in 1997. He has been a Visiting Professor at the University of British Columbia, Sciences Po in Paris, and the University of Turku. He has written, co-authored and co-edited sixteen books, including *The Global Auction: The Broken Promises of Educations, Jobs and Incomes* (2011) (with Hugh Lauder and David Ashton).

Tien-Hui Chiang is a Professor of Education teaching at the Department of Education, National University of Tainan, Taiwan. He has published extensively and is a well-known scholar in Taiwan, Mainland China and Japan. He is currently President of the Taiwan Association for Sociology of Education. His areas of expertise cover a wide range of fields, including teacher training, education policy, globalization and education and the sociology of education.

Brigitte Darchy-Koechlin holds a PhD in sociology and works at the Department of Research Development, Innovation and Experimentation of the French Ministry of Education, Higher Education and Research. The topic of her dissertation was the internationalization of the French model of excellence approached through the experience of foreign students' elites. In addition to articles (with Hugues Draelants) on the education of elites in the *British Journal of Sociology of Education* and *French Politics*, she edited with Agnès van Zanten a special issue on the education of elites for the *Revue Internationale d'Education* in 2005.

Ulrike Deppe, Doctor of Philosophy, has been Research Associate in the key project of the German Research Foundation (DFG)-funded research unit 'Mechanisms of Elite Formation in the German Education System' at the Centre for School and Educational Research (ZSB) at the Martin-Luther-University Halle-Wittenberg (MLU) in Germany since 2011. Dr Deppe studied education science at the MLU Halle between 2003 and 2008. Her research is based mainly on qualitative and biographical methods. Her main fields of research are childhood, youth and peer groups, as well as schools, especially in relation to social inequality and, more recently, elite education.

Hugues Draelants is Associate Professor at the Université Catholique de Louvain and member of the Interdisciplinary Research Group in Socialization, Education and Training (GIRSEF). He was previously a Research Fellow with the Fonds de la Recherche Scientifique (F.R.S.-FNRS) in Belgium and Post-doctoral Researcher at the Centre National de la Recherche Scientifique (CNRS) in France. His research focuses on educational policies and organizations, the training and socialization of elites and new forms of inequalities in school systems. He has published articles on elites and education (with Brigitte Darchy-Koechlin and Hélène Buisson-Fenet) in *Social Science Information, Higher Education, Research Papers in Education, British Journal of Sociology of Education* and *French Politics*.

Debbie Epstein is Professor of Cultural Studies in Education at the University of Roehampton, UK. Her research is concerned with in/equalities and how the dominant stays in place. Her publications include the jointly written books *Towards Equality: Gender and Sexuality in South African Schools in the Time of HIV and AIDS* (2009), *Silenced Sexualities in Schools and Universities* (2003) and *Schooling Sexualities* (1998). Her most recently jointly edited book is *The World Yearbook of Education 2008. Geographies of Knowledge, Geometries of Power: Facing the Future of Higher Education* (2008). She is a co-investigator on the 'Elite Independent Schools in Globalising Circumstance: a multi-sited global ethnography' project.

Victoria Gessaghi is Assistant Researcher at the National Scientific and Technical Research Council (CONICET) in Argentina. She is a professor and senior researcher at the Anthropology and Education Program, in the Department of Anthropology at the University of Buenos Aires, Argentina. She is also Senior Researcher at the Centre of Studies on Elites and Inequality (NEEDS) at the Department of Education in the Latin American Faculty of Social Science (FLACSO). Her PhD dissertation (University of Buenos Aires) examined the relation between elites and education in Argentina. In addition to her edited collection *La formación de las elites en Argentina*, she has published several articles and book contributions on education and social inequality, elite education and educational ethnography.

Werner Helsper is Professor of School Research and General Didactics at the Institute of School Pedagogy and Didactics in Primary Schools at the Martin-Luther-University Halle-Wittenberg (MLU) in Germany. Since 2011, he has been Vice-Chairman of the German Research Foundation-funded research unit 'Mechanisms of Elite Formation in the German Education System'. Since 2012, he also been Vice-Chairman of the review board of the Research Council for Education Science of the German Research Foundation (DFG). His main fields of research are school and youth research, theory of school and school culture, theory of professions and qualitative research methods.

Jane Kenway is a Professorial Fellow with the Australian Research Council, in the Education Faculty at Monash University, Australia, and elected Fellow of the Academy of Social Sciences, Australia. Her research expertise is in socio-cultural studies of education in the context of wider social and cultural change, focusing particularly on matters of power and politics. Her more recent, jointly written books are *Haunting the Knowledge Economy* (2006) and *Masculinity Beyond the Metropolis* (2006). Her most recent jointly edited book is *Globalising the Research Imagination* (2009). She currently leads an international team conducting a multi-national five-year research project called 'Elite Schools in Globalising Circumstances: a multi-sited global ethnography'.

Shamus Rahman Khan is Associate Professor of Sociology at Columbia University. He is the author of *Privilege: The Making of an Adolescent Elite at St. Paul's School, The Practice of Research* and two forthcoming books, *Exceptional: The Astors, The New York Elite, and the Story of American Inequality*, and *Approaches to Ethnography: Modes of Representation Analysis in Participant Observation.* He works in the areas of elites, inequality and cultural sociology.

Reinhard Kreckel is Professor Emeritus of Sociology at the University of Halle-Wittenberg (Germany). Until his retirement in 2010 he was Director of the Institute of Higher Education Research (HoF) in Wittenberg. He held previous appointments in the Universities of Munich, Aberdeen (Scotland) and Erlangen-Nuremberg, and was Visiting Professor at New School University (New York), Dalhousie University (Halifax), the Institut d'Études Politiques (Paris) and the Institute for Advanced Studies (Vienna). Between 1996 and 2000, he served as Rector (Vice-Chancellor) of the University of Halle-Wittenberg. With Manfred Stock, he has been co-director since 2011 of the DFG-funded project 'Elite Formation and Universities' within the research unit 'Mechanisms of Elite Formation in the German Education System'. His main fields of research are theoretical macrosociology, especially social inequality, and higher education research, especially comparative research on the academic profession.

Heinz-Hermann Krüger is Professor of General Education Science at the Institute of Pedagogy at the Martin-Luther-University Halle-Wittenberg (MLU), Germany. From 2004 to 2012, he was Member and Chair of the review board of the Research Council for Education Science of the German Research Foundation (DFG). He has also been Chair since 2008 of the graduate school in 'Education and Social Inequality' and, since 2011, of the DFG-research unit 'Mechanisms of Elite Formation in the German Education System'. His main fields in research are theories and methods of education, research on childhood and youth, as well as school and higher education research.

Diana Langmead is a Project Officer with the 'Elite Independent Schools in Globalising Circumstances: a multi-sited global ethnography' project at Monash University, Australia. She has been involved in a variety of sociology of education research projects, ranging from analyses of higher education marketing materials for international students to investigating best practices for dealing with homophobic bullying in schools. Her publications focus on feminist and social justice issues. She returned to research in 2011, after a period in small business ownership.

Hugh Lauder is Professor of Education and Political Economy at the University of Bath (1996– to present) and Acting Director, The Institute for Policy Research. He specialises in the relationship of education to the economy and has for over 10 years worked on comparative studies of national skill strategies and more recently on the global skill strategies of multinational companies with Phillip Brown. His most recent books are: Brown, P., Lauder, H., Ashton, D. (2011) *The Global Auction: The Broken Promises of Education, Jobs and Incomes*; Lauder, H., *et al.* (eds.) (2012) *Educating for the Knowledge Economy: Critical Perspectives*. He is Editor of the *Journal of Education and Work and* has been a Visiting Professor at the Institute of Education, London, The University of Turku (Finland) and currently at the University of Witwatersrand (South Africa).

Marte Mangset is a Postdoctoral Research Fellow at the Centre for the Study of Professions, Oslo and Akershus University College. She holds a joint doctoral degree from Sciences Po Paris and the University of Bergen, and the title of her thesis is *The Discipline of Historians: a comparative study of historians' constructions of the discipline of history in English, French and Norwegian universities.* She specialises in international comparative qualitative studies in the sociology of knowledge, education and power and is currently working on a comparative study of the knowledge and skills which legitimises bureaucratic elite power in Britain, France and Norway.

Claire Maxwell is a Reader of Sociology of Education at the University College London. Her main areas of research include: elite and private education, with a focus on England; processes of elite formation within families and through education; and examining how gender shapes privileged and elite identities. Between 2009 and 2013 she was the Principal Investigator of a study examining the experiences and aspirations of young women being educated in four elite schools in one area of England. Her recent books, both co-edited with Peter Aggleton, include *Privilege, Agency and Affect* (2013) and *Elite Education: International perspectives on the education of elites and the shaping of education systems* (2015).

Alicia Méndez is Senior Researcher at the University of Buenos Aires (UBA). She has been visiting scholar at the Institut de Recherche Interdisciplinaire sur les Enjeux Sociaux (IRIS), École des Hautes études en Sciences Sociales (EHESS). She is Professor in Creative Writing and Anthropology and Elites at the University of Buenos Aires. At the Latin American Faculty of Social Science (FLACSO), she is Post-Graduate Professor in Academic Writing. In her PhD dissertation she examined the educational model of elite education at the Colegio Nacional de Buenos Aires. She has published several articles on the formation of elites and a book *El Colegio. La formación de una elite meritocrática en el Nacional Buenos Aires* (2013).

Fan-Hua Meng is Dean of the School of Education and Pro Vice-Chancellor of Capital Normal University, Beijing, China. He is an evaluation expert for the National Social Science Fund, a recipient of the State Council Special Allowance and has won many prizes such as Distinguished Scholar of the National Talents

Project, and Top Scholar of National Teaching Achievement His areas of interest and expertise include educational polices, educational administration, globalization and education.

Jules Naudet is Research Fellow and Head of the 'Politics and Society' division of the Centre de Sciences Humaines in New Delhi, India (MAEE-CNRS). He is a former student of Sciences Po Paris and of the INALCO (Hindi) and holds a doctorate degree in sociology. His doctoral research focused on a comparative analysis of the experience of upward social mobility in France, India and the United-States. His postdoctoral research at the Centre Maurice Halbwachs (EHESS/ENS/CNRS) focused on a comparison of upper-class neighbourhoods in Paris, São Paulo and Delhi and he is now studying Indian elites. He is the author of *Entrer dans l'élite. Parcours de réussite en France, aux Etats-Unis et en Inde* (2012) and of *Grand patron, Fils d'ouvrier* (2014). He also co-edited *Justifier l'ordre social* with Christophe Jaffrelot (2013).

Fazal Rizvi is Professor of Global Studies in Education at the University of Melbourne in Australia, and Emeritus Professor at the University of Illinois at Urbana-Champaign in the United States. He has written extensively on issues of identity and culture in transnational contexts, as well as on theories of globalization and education policy. His recent books include *Globalizing Education Policy* (2010) and *Encountering Education in the Global* (2014). He is an elected member of the Australian Academy of the Social Sciences and serves on the advisory board of Asia Education Foundation.

Mike Savage is the Martin White Professor of Sociology and Head of Department at the London School of Economics. He is one of the Directors of the BBC's Great British Class Survey, and has conducted extensive research on the sociology of class and stratification. His recent books include *Identities and Social Change in Britain since 1940: the politics of method* (2010), and *Culture, Class, Distinction* (with Tony Bennett, Elizabeth Silva, Alan Warde, Modesto Gayo-Cal and David Wright, 2009).

Manfred Stock is Professor of Sociology of Education at the Martin-Luther-Universität Halle-Wittenberg in Germany. Since 2002, he has been a senior scientist at Wittenberg Institute for Research on Higher Education, Martin-Luther-Universität Halle-Wittenberg. With Reinhard Kreckel, he has been since 2011 co-director of the DFG-funded project 'Elite Formation and Universities' within the research unit 'Mechanisms of Elite Formation in the German Education System'. His main research areas are the sociology of education and higher education.

Johnny Sung is Professor of Skills and Performance, and is currently Principal Research Fellow at the Institute for Adult Learning (IAL) in Singapore. Upon taking up this appointment in 2011, he established the Centre for Skills, Performance and Productivity (CSPP) within IAL, specialising in skills utilisation, adult competencies and the sectoral approach to skills development as new areas of workforce development research in Singapore. He is also honorary professor at Cardiff University and has just completed a book on *Skills in Business: the role of business strategy, sectoral skills development and skills policy* (with David Ashton).

Elise Tenret is Assistant Professor at the Université Paris Dauphine, member of the Institut de Recherche Interdisciplinaire en Sciences Sociales (Irisso) and Associate Researcher at the Observatoire Sociologique du Changement (Sciences-Po/CNRS). She works on students' perceptions of social inequality and on the belief in meritocracy. She has published several articles and books on these subjects, including *L'école et la méritocratie. Représentations sociales et socialisation scolaire* (2011).

Xiao-Ming Tian is a Professor and doctoral supervisor in psychology, and Pro-Vice-Chancellor of Soochow University. He is the Vice-Chairman of the Industrial Psychology Committee, Chinese Psychological Society, Vice-Chairman of Jiangsu Psychological Association, Deputy Director of the Industrial Psychology Specialized Committee and Vice- Chairman of Suzhou Psychological Association. He has presided over three projects of the National Natural Science Foundation and the National Social Science Foundation. His research expertise is in organizational behaviour and higher education management. He has published several books, including *A Research on Psychological Problems Caused by Unemployment*, and participated in the compilation of *Management Psychology*. His articles have been published in academic journals, such as *China Social Science* and *Psychological Science*.

Paul Wakeling is Senior Lecturer in the Department of Education, University of York. He has research interests in the sociology of education, particularly higher education and social stratification and mobility. He has conducted extensive research on access to graduate education and is currently working with the UK Economic and Social Research Council and Higher Education Funding Council for England on a multimillion-pound programme to develop and research graduate education.

Johanna Waters is Associate Professor of Human Geography at the University of Oxford, attached to both the Department for Continuing Education and the School of Geography and the Environment. She is also a Fellow of Kellogg College. She researches transnational mobilities and the internationalisation of education, and household experiences of international migration. She is also interested in the reproduction of social advantage through education. She is author of numerous articles on these issues, and of several books, including *Education, Migration and Cultural Capital in the Chinese Diaspora: transnational students between Hong Kong and Canada* (2008) and (with R. Brooks) *Student Mobilities, Migration and the Internationalization of Higher Education* (2013).

Agnès van Zanten is Senior Research Professor at the Observatoire Sociologique du Changement at Sciences Po, Paris. Her main research areas are class, elites and education, school segregation and school choice, transition to higher education, widening participation and educational policies. She has published widely on these topics, including her books *Choisir son école* (2009), *L'école de la péripherie* (2nd ed., 2012) and *La formation des élites* (2015, forthcoming). She is presently conducting two research projects on 'Transition to Higher Education: the role of institutions, markets and networks' and 'Accountability and New Modes of Governance of Educational Systems'. She is Co-Director of the group on Educational policies at the Laboratoire Interdisciplinaire d'Evaluation des Politiques Publiques at Sciences Po, and directs the series 'Education et société' at Presses Universitaires de France.

Series Editors' Introduction

This volume of the *World Yearbook of Education Series*, like its predecessors since 2006, responds to changes at the global, national, local and institutional scale that have prompted debate and discussion in the field of education. The topic of this volume – elite education – largely disappeared from view during the last thirty years. However, in the contemporary context, elite education is once more a very dynamic research area. Since 2000 a number of important qualitative studies have been conducted in various countries and yet others are underway at the time of writing. This renewed interest indicates a concern to understand how elites are positioned in relation to education in the shifting and fluid global context, where elites themselves may be changing, and what counts as elite education is also subject to change.

Despite the recent growth of interest in the topic, whose transnational character is evidenced in multi-sited and comparative research projects, most existing studies have been carried out by researchers working independently of one another and in some cases with no knowledge of similar endeavours being simultaneously conducted in other contexts. This observation tends to support the hypothesis that the emergence of these new studies is largely due to global trends affecting all countries, but not in the same way. In countries undergoing economic crises elite education is influenced by new questions about the responsibility, recruitment and training of political leaders and the CEOs of national firms. In rising economies, in contrast, the focus is on how to train highly skilled professionals and build national elite universities. These different national contexts, as well as sometimes conflicting or competing transnational interests, produce very varied reconsiderations of what constitutes 'elite education', as well as different approaches to creating or enlarging educational elites.

These developments also unfold against a background of growing global competition among universities for 'world class' status that has generated diverse national policies aiming to create and reward 'excellence' – with significant effects on the reconfiguration of higher education. During the same period, international assessments of the effectiveness and equity of educational systems have prompted educational reforms intended to increase the proportion of national 'educational elites' – students showing the highest mastery of the skills and knowledge – or to widen participation into selective educational institutions. At the same time, other, possibly contradictory, policies have encouraged parental and school strategies that tend to preserve elite status through 'segregation at the top'.

Higher education, indeed, has provided a focus for a number of volumes of the *World Yearbook of Education Series*, and features here through contextual material that deals with the substantial effects on education systems and societies generated by a small number of prestigious national institutions. However, *Elites, Privilege and Excellence: The National and Global Redefinition of Advantage*, moves beyond conventional discussions of change in higher education in globalising conditions and the impact on elite education to address two themes that connect directly to the series' fundamental concerns. The first is the issue of education inequalities, considered here not from the perspective of the disadvantaged but from that of the winners of educational competition; the second is globalisation understood through a focus on the globalised and globalising strategies of elite parents, students and schools as well as those of employers of elite graduates.

In addressing these two key themes, the volume stresses the importance of looking closely at the actors involved in elite education. Students are the subjects of several analyses that focus on the objective returns of an elite education in terms of the kinds of positions and occupations that graduates achieve but also with a perspective on students' subjective experiences and identities. The picture that emerges from the intersection of these two approaches is an interesting one. At first sight it may seem that there is nothing new under the sun as students from elite families continue to have much easier access to elite institutions than do students from disadvantaged families, while graduates from these institutions in turn continue to represent a very large share of occupants of prestigious positions and highly paid jobs. However, elite students are currently valued by schools, administrations and firms not only for their 'old money' and family connections, but also for their embodied knowledge, qualities and skills. On the other hand, analyses of educational establishments show that there is now a wide variety of elite schools catering not only for different established elite families but also for groups vying for elite status through the education of their children.

Many of the schools competing for both old and new elites suggest that they will equip students for a global job market, although often a wide gap remains between what is taught and learned in these highly segregated and confined spaces and the reality of work in transnational companies. The volume shows how these different dynamics, as well as family strategies and education policies, are creating new dividing lines between social groups and between educational institutions, divisions that are frequently legitimated by discourses emphasising students' merit and institutional quality.

This important and innovative volume captures a snapshot of elite education in the process of change, characterised by tensions and contradictions, and offering varied responses to globalising pressures, as old elites attempt to retain their positions, and newer elites challenge their hold on educational privilege. While many dimensions of change and continuity in elite education remain to be explored, this collection offers a selection of material from leading scholars in the field, who reveal current developments in different national contexts and raise important questions about their content and their effects in ways that will stimulate new research and debates in this area.

Julie Allan, *Birmingham*
Terri Seddon, *Melbourne*
Gita Steiner-Khamsi, *New York*

Introduction

Educating Elites

The Changing Dynamics and Meanings of Privilege and Power

Agnès van Zanten

After a period of relative oblivion since the 1980s, the study of the educational practices of elite groups and institutions has gained new momentum since the turn of the century (van Zanten 2009). The United States is possibly an exception to this trend as the analysis of continuities and changes in the admission procedures of elite colleges (Kamens 1974; Karen 1990; Karabel 2005; Stevens 2009), as well as in the institutional routes leading to them (Falsey and Heyns 1984; Attewell 2001; Espenshade *et al.* 2005; LeTendre *et al.* 2006), has been systematically pursued for several decades by a small group of scholars, alongside many studies exploring the effects of policies aiming at increasing the racial and ethnic diversity of prestigious universities (Bowen and Bok 1998; Charles *et al.* 2009; Espenshade and Radford 2009). Only recently, however, did two major ethnographic studies by Gaztambide-Fernandez (2009) and Khan (2011) extend the findings and interpretations offered by Cookson and Persell (1985) in their research on American elite boarding schools conducted thirty years ago.

In France and Britain, there are several recently completed and ongoing research projects which have focused on elite students (Maxwell and Aggleton 2010; Draelants and Darchy-Koechlin 2011; Allan and Charles 2013; Daverne and Dutercq 2013) and elite schools (Lingard *et al.* 2012; Darmon 2013; Brooks and Waters 2014; van Zanten 2015). Furthermore, there have been additional studies examining admissions processes at Oxbridge (Soares 1999; Zimdars 2010) and the curriculum and socialisation processes of French *grandes écoles* (Lazuech 1999; Abraham 2007). These analyses have revisited some of the questions addressed in previous studies by Wakeford (1969) and Walford (1986), as well as in the seminal study by Bourdieu (1996) examining how elite tracks drive the reproduction of the French 'state nobility'. As illustrated by the contents of this volume, studies on the education of elites have also flourished more recently in many other countries in Europe as well as in Latin America, in Asia and in Australia where, with a few exceptions, there was no tradition of research in this area. Some of these later studies are part of a multi-sited global ethnography project on elite schooling, examining the historical legacy of the British Empire's 'public' schools model and the effects of globalisation (Epstein *et al.* 2013).

Such developments are indicative of changes in the educational research agenda driven both by the internal dynamics of ideas and by the perception of significant shifts in education, society and the economy. After having devoted considerable attention to the study of the education of the disadvantaged in the 1960s and 1970s and then to middle-class students and parents in the 1980s and 1990s, researchers are now interested in 'studying up' again (Aguiar 2012). This tendency has been strongly encouraged by the observation of persistent and new inequalities in educational systems.

The education of elites has traditionally been associated with the transmission of privilege (understood as the specific advantages granted to (or seized by) particular individuals or groups) and of power (the authority and capacity to affect other people's lives in significant ways). Concepts of privilege and power continue to lie at the heart of many contemporary analyses within the field (Khan 2011, Maxwell and Aggleton, 2013b); it therefore seems relevant to adopt them in this introduction to examine some of the main changes witnessed within elite education, as explored through the chapters of this volume. Privilege and power will be understood here as objective phenomena, which influence and, in turn, are influenced by what goes on in elite institutions. However, critical to our analysis and to those of several contributions is also how educational institutions contribute to the subjective redefinition of these two terms.

The Objective Circulation of Privilege and Power

A classic way of analysing privilege and power as objective phenomena is to equate them with the possession of resources allowing for the hoarding and monopolisation of desired positions, opportunities and honours (Weber 1921; Parkin 1974; Tilly 1998). From this perspective, two key questions can be posed with regard to the education of elites. The first is the extent to which educational institutions traditionally considered 'elite' have become more open to non-elite groups. Does a historical legacy of having trained future economic, cultural and political leaders and/or being associated with elite groups having used these particular school or universities to secure their positions guarantee the longevity of their elite status? That is to say, are these schools still reserved for a small circle of 'eligibles' who possess a particular combination of valued resources (Maxwell this volume), or has the importance of elite markers for acceptance into these institutions diminished over time? The second central question research must explore is how certain privileges are granted to the alumni of elite educational institutions and the role these institutions play in 'propelling' their former students into positions of power. Are graduates from these institutions still guaranteed easy access to highly paid and prestigious jobs as well as important positions in key political and administrative organisations and private firms or do these elite graduates find themselves increasingly in competition with those from other institutions?

Significant for the development of elite education in the last half a century has been the widening participation policies that have affected secondary and higher education almost everywhere. Many elite schools no longer see their role as erecting a 'class wall' in order to separate old privileges from upstarts (Soares 1999). As they have become more 'meritocratic' – if meritocracy is equated with academic selectivity – they have, in principle, become open to 'deserving' students from all social classes. Nevertheless, while these schools and universities have to some extent unsettled the previous monopoly of established elites and made way for members of other groups vying for elite status (Khan 2011 and this volume), the proportion of students from disadvantaged groups entering these institutions has not risen dramatically, and has even decreased in some countries such as France (Euriat and Thélot 1995).

There are various reasons why the elites and other well-resourced groups have managed to continue successfully hoarding educational opportunities despite increasing competition from other groups. Two crucial ones were identified by Bourdieu and Passeron (1977) several decades ago: the fact that evaluations of scholastic merit are related to particular understandings driven by the culture of dominant groups in society and the fact that parents from these dominants groups are able to further use their cultural assets and to transform their economic capital into cultural capital in order to help their children comply with school expectations and enjoy successful school careers.

Concerning the first dimension, recent research by Zimdars and colleagues (2009) has shown for instance that, in addition to students' merit' as measured by grades and results at examinations, students' cultural capital acquired at home and at school still plays a role at admissions at Oxford. The second dimension appears even more important today than in the 1960s. As shown by van Zanten (this volume), elites seem indeed to have developed new and very powerful ways of securing educational advantages for their children through their skilful use of both economic and private resources. While early (and late) parental intervention at home remains crucial, the buying of private tuition for example offers now more than in the past a 'safety net' (Johnson 2006) to prevent children from elite families from falling behind and provides them with competitive advantages at key transition points in the educational system.

Another crucial dimension in restricting the openness of elite tracks is school choice (Ball 2003). School choice is heavily shaped by access to economic resources (allowing families to live in residential neighbourhoods near the most desired schools and to buy entrance into private schools in their home countries or abroad) and cultural resources, necessary to gather, analyse and use relevant information on schools, their children and educational systems (Felouzis *et al.* 2013). School choice is also highly effective in terms of access to elite higher education institutions not only because differences between schools due to their school mix and effectiveness affect children's results ('merit') but also because selection panel members in some of the national contexts studied here use information on the school the students attended to interpret and judge their results (Zimdars 2010; van Zanten 2015). These dynamics help understand why the elite schools analysed in this volume tend to recruit their majority of students from elite and well-to-do families, although scholarships and outreach programmes provide some opportunities for the educational mobility of a small number of 'deserving' disadvantaged students.

If we turn now to the types of elite education that are chosen by those who are able to do so, we observe that some of the old distinctions remain. For instance, as shown by Gessaghi and Méndez in their chapter in this volume, different elite fractions choose elite private or public schools according not only to their economic resources and expectations in terms of financial returns but also to social, religious and political factors. However, a new significant dividing line becoming visible in some European countries (Weenink 2009) but much more marked in 'rising' Latin American, African and Asian countries (as underscored in the chapter on India by Rizvi in this volume), is that between elite schools that exhibit a strong international profile with respect to both the characteristics of their student body and of their curricular provision, and those schools that attempt to cater more for 'domestic-oriented' elite groups. While the former, as we point out in the next section, are trying to educate new 'global' professionals and citizens, the later still conceive their role as 'propelling' graduates into national positions of privilege and power.

To what extent are elite institutions still focused on producing graduates with nationally oriented ambitions for the future and also to what extent are employers looking for those types of graduates? The chapter by Wakeling and Savage (in this volume) on the perspectives of graduates from British elite universities shows that although access to elite positions is not monopolised by them, and that an elite education no longer guarantees membership to the elite, significant differences still exist between graduates from elite institutions and those from other institutions with respect to both the types of future positions occupied and the earnings they command. Similarly, the chapter by Naudet makes reference to French studies showing that the highest positions in French private firms are still monopolised by graduates from a small number of *grandes écoles*, this being also true for the highest positions within the state administration. By contrast, the chapter by Brown, Lauder and Sung shows that in Singapore, where the national economy is highly dependent on the presence of transnational companies, employers tend to favour graduates from America or English universities considered 'world class' (Brown *et al.* 2011) rather than national elite higher education institutions.

The Subjective Construction of Privileged and 'Empowered' Individuals

A second, significant research approach to understanding the links between elite education, privilege and power is to examine the framing and content of students' socialisation experiences in elite institutions and map out how they come to think of themselves and be perceived by others as privileged and 'empowered' individuals. Two traditional characteristics associated with elite institutions are small size and physical closure, which contribute to distinctiveness as well as inclusiveness (Wakeford 1969). These two elements were important characteristics that distinguished many elite schools and colleges around the world but appear now less significant.

While small size is still important for boarding schools and for some exclusive liberal arts colleges in the United States, as well as for the most prestigious *grandes écoles* in France, in fact many elite higher education institutions, especially American universities, are now huge organisations. For many of them it has become imperative to grow in size, by recruiting not only students from a small local elite, but other 'deserving' students from across a nation or beyond, in order to remain economically valuable and competitive on a global scale.

Moreover, elite institutions are now expected to face outward in various ways. In their chapter, Brook and Waters illustrate how elite schools in England, both private and public, are now much more engaged with their local communities and particularly the local schools around them. Similar dynamics are at work in both English and French elite higher education institutions, as widening participation policies have pushed these organisations to engage with a broader range of schools, frequently chosen among those geographically close to them (van Zanten 2010; Allouch 2013). These changes have not reduced privilege or power though, but rather redefined them. On the one hand, while elite establishments continue to focus on a small proportion of the overall population of students, they now have a much wider recruitment pool from which to drawn them, which is important in sustaining their legitimacy in meritocratic societies; on the other hand, their prestige and power are enhanced by the services they now seem to provide to other, frequently disadvantaged, schools and communities.

The chapters in this volume also highlight continuities and changes in the curricula of elite schools. The preeminent focus on excellence and hard work is a shift away from the model of the traditional English 'public schools' (and elite private schools in the United States and elsewhere where this model was imitated) which traditionally emphasised well-roundness and accomplishment in a variety of physical and cultural activities, reflecting the gentlemanly lifestyles and aristocratic values of the nineteenth-century 'leisure class' (Anderson 2007). Contemporary elite schools of this type are still characterized by their offer of a wide breath of sports, arts, music and drama activities, but are now increasingly focused on teaching a variety of academic subjects in which students are expected to engage and excel.

The co-existence of social and academic requirements can either provoke tensions for students and families, or integrate harmoniously into a single model of excellence (Forbes and Lingard 2013), but in either case, it has profound effects on how privilege and 'entitlement' (Lareau 2011) are conceived. The focus is now less on inherited symbolic resources and more on modelling 'accomplished' boys or girls (Maxwell and Aggleton 2013a) and encouraging them to become 'the best of the best' in many areas (Gaztambide-Fernandez 2009) although, as Khan reminds us, given the weight given to academic excellence, it is particularly important to be 'the best and brightest' (2012, this volume).

Underscored by Khan (2011) but also by Pasquier (2005) in the French context, other important changes relate to the redefinition of legitimate culture by young elite generations. While elites, especially in France, have for a long time been char-acterised by their attachment to 'high brow' aristocratic and bourgeois culture, involving intimate acquaintance with valued cultural works, there is now a growing tendency for young elite groups to become more 'omnivorous' consumers. Critical to maintaining elite status is the ability to move almost effortlessly between an appreciation of classical literature to comic books, from classical music to rap songs. This does not mean that the cultural gap between these students and students from disadvantaged groups engaging mainly and frequently exclusively with popular culture is being reduced but that it is being subtly reconfigured (Coulangeon 2013).

Linked to such cultural openness is an orientation to social openness. The new global elites being produced by some of the elite institutions studied by Kenway *et al.* (Kenway and Fahey 2014; Kenway *et al.* this volume) are expected to become 'cosmopolitan' in traditional ways, that is knowledgeable about other (elite) cul-tures and habits (Wagner 2007), but also in new ways which imply being able to interact with people from different cultural origins occupying a range of social positions across local and global contexts. This again is not a move towards the 'democratisation' of elites but another way of redefining power and advantage in a globalised world.

Students educated in these institutions have been shown to embody a high degree of assuredness and self-confidence (Maxwell and Aggleton 2013a; Forbes and Lingard 2013) and a strong 'sense of entitlement' (Lareau 2011, Gaztambide-Fernandez 2009) to their elite status. One might wonder, however, how these young people can dissociate their own merit from the resources provided by their family when making sense of their elite status. One explanation is that the relative homogeneity of elite institutions encourages the development of very limited frames of reference within which young people can position themselves, so that small differences in degrees of accomplishment and merit between them and close peers loom larger than wider social differences (Maxwell and Aggleton 2010; Darchy-Koechlin *et al.*, this volume; Kenway *et al.* this volume). A second, equally important reason is that these students' parents, while devoting considerable resources to their education in and out of schools, also expend a lot of effort in hiding this investment to emphasize their children's achievements and thus sus-tain the belief in their meritocratic legitimacy to occupy future elite positions (van Zanten 2015 and this volume).

The existing literature shows the importance of these embodied qualities, atti-tudes and skills. The chapter by Mangset in this volume shows, for instance, that despite their varying degrees of specialisation in different university disciplines, administrative elites across various European countries tend to believe that they are entitled to occupy positions of responsibility because they are 'intelligent', 'confident' and 'ambitious' and possess other very general communication skills rather than because of their technical training. Similarly, the employers inter-viewed by Brown, Lauder and Sung (this volume) are not only looking for highly specialized professionals but also for graduates exhibiting 'soft skills' such as lead-ership, ability to communicate and capacity to build effective networks, that they associate to training in specific elite institutions.

Conclusion

Many of the chapters in this volume discuss significant changes in the ways in which elite status is now reproduced and understood. Four main trends should be highlighted: the increasing power of money which can directly or indirectly buy membership into elite institutions; the diversification of elite institutions, now catering for different groups of elites as they vie for elite positions on a national and/or international scale; the importance of academic merit both as a requisite for access to elite institutions and as the main expected outcome of an elite education; and the subjective redefinition of elite status which sees the importance of family history and resources being pushed into the background and personal accomplishments and merit being foregrounded in understandings of the self and of the ways in which elite establishments create new generations of leaders.

The focus of most of the chapters in this volume are on the families, students, teachers and employers who are directly involved in the education and recruitment of elites. What fewer studies in this volume do is consider in any great depth the broader consequences of elite education for other individuals and for educational and social systems. In other words, how are disadvantaged students affected by elite education tracks and what kinds of new social boundaries and new types of exclusionary closure strategies are being developed through the continuing status and influence of elite education systems (Lamont and Molnar 2002; Parkin 1974)? Naudet's chapter does discuss the 'cleft *habitus*' (Lee and Kramer 2013) that characterises, in France much more than in the United States, the few individuals from lower-class backgrounds that do get access to elite institutions or arrive through other routes to occupy elite positions. Some of the other chapters, especially those by Almeida, Deppe *et al.* and Tien-Shu *et al.*, do examine as well the effects of changes in the perspectives and actions of elite groups and elite educational institutions on the broader stratification of national educational and social systems. However, further research should help establish a more solid bridge and stimulating dialogue between studies of elite education and research focusing on educational and social inequalities allowing for a better understanding of the interaction between the experiences of different groups as well as between the social processes that condition and influence them.

References

Abraham, Y.M. (2007) 'Du souci scolaire au sérieux managérial ou comment devenir un "HEC" ', *Revue Française de Sociologie*, 48(1): 37–66.

Aguiar, L.L.M. (2012) 'Redirecting the academic gaze upward', in L.L.M. Aguiar and C.J. Schneider (eds) *Researching Amongst Elites: Challenges and Opportunities in Studying Up*, Farnham: Ashgate, 1–27.

Allan, A. and Charles, C. (2013) 'Cosmo girls: Configurations of class and femininity in elite educational settings', *British Journal of Sociology of Education*, 35(3): 333–532.

Allouch, A. (2013) *L'ouverture sociale comme configuration. Pratiques et processus de sélection et de socialisation des milieux populaires dans les établissements d'élite. Une comparaison France-Angleterre*, PhD dissertation, Sciences Po.

Anderson, R. (2007) 'Aristocratic values and elite education in Britain and France', in D. Lancien and M. de Saint-Martin (eds) *Anciennes et Nouvelles Aristocracies de 1880 à Nos Jours*, Paris: éditions de la Maison des Sciences de l'Homme.

Attewell, P. (2001) 'The winner take-all high school: Organizational adaptations to educational stratification', *Sociology of Education*, 74: 267–295.

Ball, S.J. (2003) *Class Strategies and the Education Market*, London: Routledge Falmer.

Bourdieu, P. (1996) *The State Nobility: Elite Schools in the Field of Power*, Stanford, CA: Stanford University Press.

Bourdieu, P. and Passeron, J.C. (1977) *Reproduction in Education, Society and Culture*, Beverly Hills, CA: Sage.

Bowen, W.G. and Bok, D. (1998) *The Shape of the River: Long-Term Consequences of Considering Race in College and University Admissions*, Princeton, NJ: Princeton University Press.

Brooks, R. and Waters, J. (2014) 'The hidden internationalism of elite English schools', *Sociology*. Advance online access.

Brown, P., Lauder, H. and Ashton, D. (2011) *The Global Auction: The Broken Promises of Education, Jobs and Income*, New York: Oxford University Press.

Charles, C.Z., Fischer, M.J., Mooney, M.A. and Massey, D.S. (2009) *Taming the River: Negotiating the Academic, Financial, and Social Currents in Selective Colleges and Universities*, Princeton, NJ: Princeton University Press.

Cookson, P.W. and Persell, C.H. (1985) *Preparing for Power*, New York: Basic Books.

Coulangeon, P. (2013) 'Changing policies, challenging theories and persisting inequalities: Social disparities in cultural participation in France from 1981 to 2008', *Poetics*, 41(2): 177–209.

Darmon, M. (2013) *Classes Préparatoires. La Fabrication d'une Jeunesse Dominante*, Paris: La Découverte.

Daverne, C. and Dutercq, Y. (2013) *Les Bons Elèves. Expériences et Cadres de Formation*, Paris: Presses Universitaires de France.

Draelants, H. and Darchy-Koechlin, B. (2011) 'Flaunting one's academic pedigree? Self-presentation of students from elite French schools', *British Journal of Sociology of Education*, 32(1): 17–34.

Epstein, D., Fahey, J. and Kenway, J. (2013) 'Multi-sited global ethnography and travel: Gendered journeys in three registers', *International Journal of Qualitative Studies in Education*, 26(4): 470–488.

Espenshade, T.J. and Radford, A.W. (2009) *No Longer Separate, not yet Equal: Race and Class in Elite College Admission and Campus Life*, Princeton, NJ: Princeton University Press.

Espenshade, T.J., Hale, L.E. and Chung, C.Y. (2005) 'The frog pond revisited: High school academic context, class rank and elite college admission', *Sociology of Education*, 78(4): 269–293.

Euriat, M. and Thélot, C. (1995) 'Le recrutement social de l'élite scolaire en France: évolution des inégalités de 1950 à 1990', *Revue Française de Sociologie*, 36: 403–438.

Falsey, B. and Heyns, B. (1984) 'The college channel: Private and public schools reconsidered', *Sociology of Education*, 57(2): 111–122.

Felouzis, G., Maroy, C. and van Zanten, A. (2013) *Les Marchés Scolaires. Sociologie d'une Politique Publique d'Education*, Paris: Presses Universitaires de France.

Forbes, J. and Lingard, B. (2013) Elite school capitals and girls' schooling: Understanding the (re)production of privilege through a habitus of 'assuredness', in C. Maxwell and P. Aggleton (eds) *Privilege, Agency and Affect*, Basingstoke: Palgrave Macmillan, 50–68.

Gaztambide-Fernández, R. (2009) *The Best of the Best: Becoming Elite at an American Boarding School*, Cambridge, MA: Harvard University Press.

Johnson, H.B. (2006) *The American Dream and the Power of Wealth: Choosing Schools and Inheriting Inequality in the Land of Opportunity*, New York: Routledge.

Kamens, D. (1974) 'Colleges and elite formation: The case of prestigious American colleges', *Sociology of Education*, 47(3): 354–378.

Karabel, J. (2005) *The Chosen: The Hidden History of Admission and Exclusion at Harvard, Yale and Princeton*, Boston, MA: Houghton Mifflin.

Karen, D. (1990) 'Toward a political-organizational model of gatekeeping: The case of elite colleges', *Sociology of Education*, 63(4): 227–240.

Kenway, J. and Fahey, J. (2014) 'Staying ahead of the game: the globalising practices of elite schools', *Globalisation, Societies and Education,* 12(2), 177–195.

Khan, S.R. (2011) *Privilege: The Making of an Adolescent Elite at St. Paul's School*, Princeton, NJ: Princeton University Press.

Khan, S.R. (2012) 'The sociology of elites', *Annual Review of Sociology*, 38: 361–377.

Lamont, M. and Molnar, V. (2002) 'The study of boundaries in the social sciences', *Annual Review of Sociology*, 28: 167–195.

Lareau, A. (2011) *Unequal Childhoods: Class, Race, and Family Life*, Berkeley: University of California Press.

Lazuech, G. (1999) *L'Exception Française. Le Modèle des Grandes Écoles à l'Epreuve de la Mondialisation*, Rennes: Presses Universitaires de Rennes.

Lee, E.M. and Kramer, R. (2013) 'Out with the old, in with the new? Habitus and social mobility at selective colleges', *Sociology of Education*, 86(1): 18–35.

LeTendre, G.K., Gonzalez, R.G. and Nomi, T. (2006) 'Feeding the elite: The evolution of elite pathways from star high schools to elite universities', *Higher Education Policy*, 19: 7–30.

Lingard, B., Forbes, J., Weiner, G. and Horne, J. (2012) 'Multiple capitals and Scottish independent schools: The (re)production of advantage', in J. Allan and R. Catts (eds) *Social Capital, Children and Young People: Implications for Practice, Policy and Research*, Bristol: Policy Press, 181–198.

Maxwell, C. and Aggleton, P. (2010). 'The bubble of privilege: Young, privately educated women talk about social class'. *British Journal of Sociology of Education*, 31(1): 3–15.

Maxwell, C. and Aggleton. P. (2013a) 'Becoming accomplished: Concerted cultivation among privately educated young women', *Pedagogy, Culture and Society*, 21(1): 75–93.

Maxwell, C. and Aggleton, P. (eds) (2013b) *Privilege, Agency and Affect*, Basingstoke: Palgrave Macmillan.

Parkin, F. (1974) *The Social Analysis of Class Structure*, London: Tavistock Publications.

Pasquier, D. (2005) *Cultures Lycéennes. La Tyrannie de la Majorité*, Paris: Editions Autrement.

Soares, J.A. (1999) *The Decline of Privilege: The Modernization of Oxford University*, Stanford, CA: Stanford University Press.

Stevens, M.L. (2009) *Creating a Class: College Admissions and the Education of Elites*, Cambridge, MA: Harvard University Press.

Tilly, C. (1998) *Durable Inequality*, Berkeley: California University Press.

van Zanten, A. (2009) 'The sociology of elite education', in M. Apple, S. Ball and L.A. Gandin (eds) *International Handbook of the Sociology of Education*, London: Routledge.

van Zanten, A. (2010) ''L'ouverture sociale des grandes écoles': Diversification des élites ou renouveau des politiques publiques d'éducation?', *Sociétés Contemporaines*, 78: 69–96.

van Zanten, A. (2015) *La Formation des Elites. Sélection et Socialisation*. Paris: Presses Universitaires de France.

Wagner, A.M. (2007) *Les Classes Sociales dans la Mondialisation*, Paris: La Découverte.

Wakeford, J. (1969) *The Cloistered Elite*, London: Macmillan.

Walford, G. (1986) 'Ruling-class classification and framing', *British Educational Research Journal*, 12(2): 183–195.

Weber, M. (1921/1978) *Economy and Society: An Outline of Interpretive Sociology*, Berkeley: University of California Press.

Weenink, D. (2009) 'Creating a niche in the education market: The rise of internationalised secondary education in the Netherlands', *Journal of Education Policy*, 24(4): 495–511.

Zimdars, A. (2010) 'Fairness and undergraduate admission: A qualitative exploration of admissions choices at the university of Oxford', *Oxford Review of Education*, 36(3): 207–323.

Zimdars, A., Sullivan, A. and Heath, A. (2009) 'Elite higher education admissions in the arts and sciences: Is cultural capital the key?', *Sociology*, 43(4): 648–666.

Part I

Class and Family Educational Strategies

Education systems are shaped by and in turn, shape the formation and practices of elite groups at local, national and global levels. Education itself is a significant resource that is drawn on to secure elite status – a system through which individuals, families and groups attempt to not only distinguish themselves but also to actively close off opportunities for others to pursue particular trajectories into the world of work and access to certain, influential social networks. This part of the volume begins by examining some critical theoretical, methodological and empirical questions which the study of elite education needs to engage with. This is then followed by an analysis of elite education processes in two, quite different, national contexts.

Claire Maxwell's chapter raises some fundamental questions about the concept of 'elites' and the ways various disciplines (politics, sociology, education, economics) have developed our understandings of these group of people and organizations. Calling for the study of elites to be positioned within the study of power, she suggests ways in which the nature of elites might be empirically studied to better understand the effect of elite practices on social relations. The ways in which families and education institutions work together to produce the next generation of elites is reviewed. The chapter concludes by discussing whether or not elites could be considered a distinct social class grouping.

Agnès van Zanten's chapter is focused on the strategies of upper-class families in France, and their engagement with elite preparatory classes. The author explores how families shape their children's school trajectories by drawing on a range of economic, cultural and social resources, while working hard to preserve the social illusion of the French system being built on the principle of meritocracy, which rewards intelligence and hard work. She also highlights the important consequences of elite parents' practices in terms of social closure and educational inequalities, as well as on how elites come to think of themselves as a 'class meritocracy' and the political implications of this belief.

In contrast to the French national education system, which claims to operate along universalist principles, Victoria Gessaghi and Alicia Méndez's chapter on Argentina helps to emphasize the broader point that the specific national configuration shapes the meanings attached to schooling by different fractions of the upper classes. The chapter shows in particular how members of traditional families tend to choose private schools that support the legitimacy of this group through 'nepotist' admission procedures, while other groups willing to work hard can attain a different kind of elite status by access to selective and intellectually demanding state-funded schools.

1 Elites

Some Questions for a New Research Agenda

Claire Maxwell

Introduction

This chapter offers an introduction to the field of elite studies, identifying questions that this academic field still needs to grapple with. While interest in the elites has experienced a resurgence, much theoretical and empirical work is still needed. One of the first questions must be how we define elites, which in turn will inform attempts to gain a greater understanding of what shapes the formation and main- tenance of these groups across local, national and global spaces. The second key area requiring further research and theorisation is whether and how the concept of elites can be integrated into our more developed understandings about social class structures and practices. Drawing on key writings in the field of elite studies, the chapter sets out in more detail the kinds of questions already engaged with by colleagues and the focus future enquiries should take. The chapter concludes with some questions scholars working on elite education should consider further.

The Study of Elites: A Brief History

A concerted focus on 'elites' emerged within social and political theory in the early twentieth century. Theorists were interested in where power was located and who held power within societies, focusing on 'the governing elite' (Pareto [1901] 1968) or 'ruling class' (Mosca 1939) of national political systems. Pareto offered an understanding of power as held by individuals and institutions. Power was made possible through the structural positions occupied by individuals and institutions, but crucially for Pareto, the governing elite were also powerful because they were seen by those outside the elite as possessing the qualities and talents that consti- tuted 'the elite of that practice' (Hearn 2012, p. 59). Pareto and Mosca's work can therefore be understood as an attempt to understand why a minority of people would govern a majority, but especially in Pareto's case, also as a treatise for explaining the necessity and value of an elite – as they represent those with the most talent in a society.

Work on elites was mainly concentrated in the USA after the Second World War, and began to focus on elites as 'the mark of a social problem' (Khan 2012, p. 364). Mills' (1956) work on 'power elites' argued that a small group of (white) men at the apex of the political, military and economic bureaucracies held significant power within US society. Thus, while Mills expanded our understandings of the power bases that structure society and what constitute the governing elite, he also found that the individuals within the power elites of post-war America came from a similar social class – the upper class(es). Mills' work appears therefore to both challenge the conception of a ruling class by suggesting that power bases for ruling society exist in three domains – industry/corporations, politics and the military – while at the same time supporting the idea of a 'ruling class' by demonstrating the shared social and educational histories of this group, which facilitated close working together. Subsequent work by Hunter (1953), Dahl (1961) and Domhoff (1967) continued to examine how America was governed.

While much work on elites was conducted in the USA during the mid- to late twentieth century, more recent work on elites has extended its focus and geographical reach. Thus, today research is being published that looks at elites within the economic spheres (Hartmann 2010, Maclean *et al.* 2010, Bühlmann *et al.* 2013, Ellersgaard *et al.* 2013, Tholen *et al.* 2013) and examines which groups shape political and economic decision-making (Dogan 2003b, Scott 2003, Denord *et al.* 2011, Bond 2012), including a focus on transnational elites (Rothkopf 2009, Buono 2012, Murray 2012). Within the field of education there is also a growing interest in the education of elites and the composition of elite education systems at a national and global level (Karabel 2005, Gaztambide-Fernández 2009, Brezis 2011, Khan 2011, Koh and Kenway 2012, McCarthy and Kenway 2014, van Zanten 2015).

Defining and Researching Elites

The study of elites should be about the study of power and how power operates within (nationally bounded) societies, but increasingly understandings also need to focus on the flows of power at a global level (Savage and Williams 2008). Both Pareto (1968) and Mills (1956) saw power as a zero-sum game (or 'fixed in quantity' – Scott 2008, p. 29), where elites had 'power over' others. This fits with Scott's (2003) definition of elites – 'social groups defined by hierarchies of authoritarian power' (p. 155) able to exert command and who have 'corrective influence' (Scott 2008, p. 30). Elites of this kind will use punishments and rewards to affect the actions of others – such as using force (a physical sanction) or manipulation (which can be a positive or negative sanction that will limit or facilitate access to certain resources).

However, Pareto and Mills also appear to conceptualise power as a form of hegemony (Gramsci 1971) shaping both social practices and discourse (see Lukes 2005 and Foucault 1988) – the 'power to' (Scott 2008 also defines this as 'persuasive influence', p. 30 – using argument and appeals to reason to influence the action of others). Theory suggests, therefore, that elites maintain their position because others have assessed them as excelling in performing a particular set of social practices that are seen as necessary and desirable (Pareto 1968) or because their strong similarity in backgrounds, characteristics and networks has the effect of making the exercise of power by these elite groups appear to be co-ordinated and natural (Mills 1956).

Thus, as Kahn (2012) emphasizes, to 'study elites, then, is to study the control over, value of, and distribution of resources' (p. 362). The kinds of resources that are valued and the ways these can be drawn on to exert power are socially and historically determined, arguably shaped by elites themselves if we draw on a 'power to' framework, which then shapes what, who and how 'power over' is practised.

Most research today acknowledges that globalisation and financialisation have had a significant effect on the more traditional bases of power found within political and bureaucratic structures – thereby reshaping the flows of power within, between and across nations (Savage and Williams 2008, Ball 2010). This makes the study of elites more challenging. If elites are 'those who have vastly disproportionate control over or access to a resource ... [or those] occupying a position that provides them with access and control or as possessing resources that advantage them' (Khan 2012, p. 362), then how can these individuals and groups be empirically identified? Is 'elite' a relational term – where certain groups are compared to average members of society (Bottomore 1993, Harvey 2011)? Many researchers define the 'elite' groups they are studying in terms of the positions they occupy – senior management and board-level positions (Griffiths *et al.* 2008, Harvey 2011, Ellersgaard *et al.* 2013). Such an approach within sociology, political science and business studies conflates eliteness with a particular position held. This seems too one-dimensional as an approach, and one that is not grounded within a strong theoretical framework, underscoring the centrality of the concept of power in the study of elites.

Recently, authors such as Maclean *et al.* (2010), Denord *et al.* (2011) and Flemmen (2012) drawing on a Bourdieusian-inspired approach, managed to maintain a close focus on power by drawing on the concept of 'field of power' (Denord *et al.* 2011, p. 86), understood as a social space where 'dominant agents' (Maclean *et al.* 2010, p. 328) within each field compete and struggle over resources. Using the notion of 'capitals', these authors collate data from large datasets to construct variables/indicators and perform Multiple Correspondence Analysis (Le Roux and Rouanet 2010). Such analyses identify particular individuals as dominant agents within a field as well as those who traverse or span several fields (arguably the truly elite) through identifying the particular resources and connections with others these elite individuals have (Carroll and Carson 2003, Savage and Williams 2008, Ball 2012).

There are, however, some ways in which these theorisations would benefit from further extension. This more recent research does engage with Savage and Williams' (2008) call to reconsider elites within 'present day capitalism' (p. 3), and acknowledges that power networks and configuration of elites (Dogan 2003a) have diversified, moving beyond the level of the nation state. However, more studies are needed to understand whether and how 'new' groups are taking the place of more established elite groups within local, national or international fields of power, and whether new fields of power are emerging within which new processes of elite formation are being developed.

Furthermore, within current research, the measures of 'power' are still relatively circumscribed – as they are required to be measurable indicators contained in large datasets or reducible to quantitative collation. Does such an approach miss some of the more subtle ways in which 'power over' and 'power to' can be under-stood and practised? I would suggest it does. These newer studies employ a theoretically coherent approach inspired by Bourdieu's work and also offer empirically operationalisable definitions of elites through the concept of capitals. However, they potentially fail to capture the range of practices (social, emotional, economic, educational, cultural) engaged in by individual members of elite groups or practices that constitute part of what makes a collection of people an elite group. A closer focus on 'practices' and discursive and affective contexts that shape and drive these practices (Maxwell and Aggleton 2014a) may be critical to better understanding how elites practice power over and power to. This will be examined in greater depth further below.

A Limited Circle of Eligibles or the Circulation of Elites?

Pareto (1968) was interested in examining how equilibrium was established (formed, maintained and re-formed) within societies. He identified two types of elite groups – the governing elite and the non-governing elite. These two elite groups displayed different orientations, with the speculators being more progres-sive, while the rentiers were conservative in approach. Pareto argued that these elite groups alternated in who governed society at a particular point in time. Thus, Pareto suggested that while a small minority ruled, elites groups did change over-time – the 'circulation of elites' (Pareto 1968). Speculators, in particular, recruited talented individuals from non-elite groups to rejuvenate their ranks – suggesting that merited social mobility would benefit society, as well as being critical for social stability. However, Pareto did recognise that some elite groups resisted the circula-tion of elites (usually the rentiers), which he believed explained why 'history is a graveyard of aristocracies' (1963, p. 1430). Furthermore, he acknowledged that sometimes individuals and groups were considered elite by virtue of being labelled so, without necessarily demonstrating that they were the most qualified to be gov-erning (i.e. that they were 'the best of the best' – Gaztambide-Fernández 2009).

Work in the USA in the second half of the twentieth century continued to explore the extent to which the elite groups were stable or circulating. Hunter (1953) and Domhoff (1967), for instance, have found, as Mills (1956) did, that a particular class of persons continue to hold political power within local and national systems in America. Dahl (1961), meanwhile, through his research in New Haven, found that the city moved from an elite system of governance to one where a range of groups controlled different resources and areas of power. Although Dahl recognised that it was still a relatively small group who 'governed', this group was continuously changing.

Dogan (2003a) usefully distinguishes between a horizontal circulation of elites which he terms 'elite interlock' or 'interpenetration' and Pareto's more vertical understanding of elite circulation which describes recruitment and movement into the elites. The degree to which elite groups are stable or more fluid in terms of composition, interlocking and 'cousinhood' (Dogan 2003a – narrow social base from which they are recruited) is still a source of debate. Authors such as Brezis

(2011) and Bond (2012) demonstrate considerable stability amongst the power elites, while Dogan (2003a) and Ellersgaard *et al.* (2013) argue that mechanisms for elite group formation are shaped by different national systems – political structures, education systems and the extent of separation between functional elite groups (within politics, finance/corporate sector, civil service and so forth) – with some national systems and some elite groups within these, showing greater stability than others.

How best are we to theorise processes which facilitate the circulation of elites and those that limit the 'circle of eligibles' (Parkin 1974, p. 44) in the formation of elites?

Preparing for Power

Drawing on Pareto's work, the extent of vertical circulation of elites will depend on who the current governing elite are – the spectulators or rentiers. But research suggests that a longer historical perspective is necessary to understand the kinds of broader societal commitments and structures that are in place to facilitate entry into elites of previously non-elite individuals or groups. France and Singapore, for instance, have education systems that are firmly grounded in the principle of meritocracy, where future elites are to be carefully selected based on their academic attainment and then educated separately either from the time of their secondary schooling (Singapore) or at the post-compulsory education stage, as in France (Koh and Kenway 2012, Koh 2014, van Zanten 2015). Meanwhile, the USA and England have longer histories of educating different social classes separately, so that future leaders were largely drawn from the upper classes (Levine 1980, Walford 1986, 2005, 2012, Joyce 2013).

Flemmen (2012) in his study of Norwegian elites, found that inherited economic and cultural capital was secured through education – concluding that educational credentials were critical to processes of reproduction for the upper classes in Norway. In what ways does education secure privilege for young people from elite/upper-class families, or for those who get onto an elite education track? Research has found strong links between the various elements that help to steer a trajectory into future elite positions – from access to elite schools for those from more highly resourced families (Gaztambide-Fernández 2009, van Zanten 2009, Draelants and van Zanten 2011); through close relationships between elite groups and schools, and elite universities (Karabel 2005, Stevens 2009, Allouch 2013, Parel and Adams 2013, Weis and Cipollone 2013); and through opportunities provided via internships, which are often secured via social networks and by having the resources to work without a salary (Bathmaker *et al.* 2013, Tholen *et al.* 2013).

Critically, however, research emphasizes that the kinds of knowledges and orientations (Bourdieu 1996, Howard 2008, Khan 2011, Maxwell and Aggleton 2014c), the high levels of accomplishment (Maxwell and Aggleton 2013) and the sense of connectedness, belonging and assured optimism (Forbes and Lingard 2013, Gaztambide-Fernández *et al.* 2013, Maxwell and Aggleton 2014a) that are secured through an elite education are critical for the production and reproduction of elite trajectories. Elite professions seek out new recruits with whom they share particular histories and cultural practices, that have been secured both within families and through the various educational institutions they attend (Cook *et al.* 2012, Kahn 2012). Bond (2012) powerfully demonstrates how one elite education institution alone – Eton College – shapes membership of particular social clubs and their close associations to political decision-making processes in England, for instance.

An emerging focus of research into the effects of elite education is whether these institutions are seeking to prepare their students to take up national positions of power or embody a more transnational identity. Power *et al.* (2013) found that students at the elite institution – the University of Oxford – demonstrated more global orientations to their future work lives than their French counterparts studying at the *grande école* – Sciences Po. Meanwhile, Maxwell and Aggleton (2014b) and Brooks and Waters (2014) highlight a more ambivalent connection to transnationality among the English elite schools they studied. Papers from the *Elite schools in globalising circumstances: a multi-sited global ethnography* project highlight that certain subjects are more likely to have a transnational orientation to their future; if they come from southern contexts and/or the schools they attend fiercely promote such an outlook (Fahey 2014, McCarthy *et al.* 2014, Rizvi 2014).

Less well understood are the processes of enculturation that occur within elite families. Maxwell and Aggleton (2014a) have argued that to examine processes that produce and reproduce positions of privilege, the family, school, and individual young people's 'projects of the self' need to be considered together to understand how practices and trajectories are shaped. Van Zanten (2015) explores in close detail how families sending their children to elite schools engage in processes of concerted cultivation to facilitate their futures. Not only can financial resources support access to elite tracks, but critically, it is the cultural knowledges, sensibilities and skills that allow affective attachments to be made to elite spaces, that compel people to be agentic and act (Forbes and Lingard 2013, Gaztambide-Fernández *et al.* 2013, Howard 2013, Maxwell and Aggleton 2014a), and therefore support the formation of a group of people socialised into particular orientations towards the self, others and broader society.

These processes of enculturation are then further extended beyond education, through the professional positions entered in the workplace (Cook *et al.* 2012), the social networks and social clubs joined (Bond 2012, Kahn 2012), marriage partners chosen (Baltzell 1987, Maxwell and Aggleton 2014c) and so forth. Thus, from this review of the literature, it would appear as if various institutions and social networks serve to arguably limit the circle of eligibles that can take up future elite positions and calls into question the idea of a vertical circulation of elites.

However, processes of reproduction are never seamless (Maxwell and Aggleton 2014a, 2014c) and little is known about how 'newer' elite groups, such as families who accrue significant resources over a generation or two, experience processes of social closure or openness in their movement into elite circles. How does wealth (in the form of money and/or property) potentially form the 'basis of significant power' (Scott 2008, p. 28), and subsequently shape the kind of symbolic value attributed to it? Just as the Industrial Revolution gave some newly wealthy families the opportunity to send their sons to some of the elite schools in England (Ringer 1979), so too, the economic elite that have emerged in countries such as Russia, China, India and so forth in the present day are now making education choices for their children with reference to the international field for their secondary and tertiary education (Brooks and Waters 2011, Kenway *et al.* 2013, Kenway and Fahey 2014).

Even within national borders, we need to understand how, and to what extent, the 'new economic elite' are negotiating access to elite tracks for their children. A study of two Norwegian elite groups – the economic and cultural elite – by Aarseth (2013) suggests that both groups have quite different orientations to schooling and futures. Furthermore, while work by Gaztambide-Fernández (2009), Reay *et al.* (2009) and Khan (2011) has examined the experiences of more marginalised young people (from working-class families or from minority ethnic backgrounds) in elite institutions, few longitudinal studies have followed these non-elite subjects into the future (for an exception see Power *et al.* 2003). Therefore, there remain a number of research priorities if we would like to facilitate a greater understanding of how future members of the elite are being 'prepared for power' (Cookson and Persell 1985).

Are Elites a Distinct Social Class?

While we have a growing understanding of the structures and resources which promote certain groups to replace or move into the current governing elites, what broader theoretical frameworks might be drawn on to understand elites and their relationship to other groups within societies? Earlier, I argued that work is still needed around the definition of elites. Currently Bourdieu's work is most prominently drawn on in the field – for the purposes of outlining what constitutes being elite, largely with reference to the concept of capitals (Caletrío 2012). Thus, people and groups who are the 'dominant agents' within their fields, who hold and manage resources and determine how these resources are valued, are labelled elite.

Khan (2012) argues that elites use various cultural institutions to 'construct themselves as a class' (p. 368) through a particular orientation to the self, others and what is valued. In this way, Khan suggests, elites are undertaking a process of 'differentiation and distinction' (2012, p. 368), as so often noted by social class theorists about the work being done by the middle classes in particular (Skeggs 2004, Lawler 2005). Yet, Scott (2008) suggests that social class and elite categorisations should be seen as analytically separate due to the mechanisms of power that are critical in defining elite membership and elite status. Scott warns that while characteristics and practices may appear similar across different elites (especially if they are drawn from a narrow section of society) they do not constitute a coherent social class as such. Thus, elite group practices are not distinguishable from other social class practices. If we take Scott's argument further, this would suggest that there is no significant effect of having the resources or being enabled by societal structures to have 'power to' and 'power over' on the orientations and practices of elite individuals and groups. Reflecting on the largely qualitative-based work done on elite education and how spaces of privilege shape practices, this seems unlikely (Maxwell and Aggleton 2013, Fahey 2014).

Social class theorists writing since the cultural turn within sociology (Ball 2003) examine power relations and seek to describe and understand how practices operate as forms of power (Skeggs 2004, Lawler 2005, Flemmen 2013). Many commentators (Lareau 2002, Vincent and Ball 2007, Crozier *et al.* 2011) have noted that social class position is reflected in, and driven by, practices of social and educational cultivation within families and schools. Examining such practices, in particular within families, but also over the lifecourse of people and groups identified as elite, will yield greater insight into (a) whether 'elites' are a distinct social grouping and why; and (b) the extent to which possibilities for social mobility are facilitated or limited by the boundary work (Lamont and Molnar 2002) occurring within and between various elite groups, and between the elites and their non-elite peers. Just as debates about the nature and cohesiveness of the middle classes have been a focus for sociological work, particularly in the last two decades (Butler and Savage 1995, Savage 2000, Power and Whitty 2002, Ball *et al.* 2004, Bennett *et al.* 2008, Ball 2010), it is necessary now to consider similar questions for the groups which are labelled 'elite'.

Lockwood (1995) suggests class formation should be considered according to economic, normative and relational dimensions to decide whether the group being studied is a 'well-formed class with its own distinct social identity' (p. 3). Thinking about the economic dimension and the ways categories of social class have traditionally been understood, we might ask – to what extent are members of elite groups found in particular employment sectors or found to be holding comparable positions across sectors? By virtue of their being elite, members should be concentrated at the top of the hierarchy within their fields – but seeking to identify CEOs, judges, senior politicians and so forth is not a comprehensive enough approach to the study of elites.

We need to differentiate between individuals and groups according to practices that exert power to and power over, and consider how we might conceptualise different elite fractions – by 'field' or according to the power these groups can command. A focus is also needed on the many less visible players who wield considerable power through the networks they are linked into to (Rothkopf 2009), as well as the key institutions sustaining and driving the development of particular cultural practices that may best characterise what is elite about the elites. Furthermore, if the truly elite are those who act as intermediaries connecting different spheres (Caletrío 2012), i.e. playing the role of dominant agents across fields, then while social network analysis can identify these individuals and points of connection between them, greater understanding is needed about what economic and affective motivations drive them to take on such roles – considering both the aspired to and actual outcomes of such power plays.

A focus is also needed on the relational and normative dimensions of elite groups. When examining for group cultures and identities (Ball 2010), greater attentiveness is needed to various factors that will shape these. Here I suggest five areas requiring further research and theorisation. First, the role of gender and ethnicity in driving practices and points of difference between groups needs to become a greater focus of enquiry. Parents (and especially mothers) will be actively shaping the processes of intergenerational transmission of status through efforts around cultivation and the consumption patterns of these groups. Second, the attachment to, and use of space may be another way in which we can identify whether or not the elites are a distinct social grouping (Savage 1995), with fractions being differentially characterised as urban-centred and the urban-fleeing (Butler 1995), and/or how particular elites are associated with the economies and cultural practices dominant in so-called global cities (Ball 2010). Third, understanding norms and practices around transnational mobility is also essential, as mobility is argued to be a key feature of being elite (Caletrío 2012). Fourth, a focus is needed not only on practices, but significantly, on the narratives that are articulated by individuals, families, educational institutions, social clubs and so forth about how particular groups come to understand themselves as elite or otherwise. Ball (2010) calls this gaining access to the 'social structures in their heads' (p. 140). Fifth, this kind of work is necessary at the national level, given Dogan's (2003a) and Ellersgaard *et al.*'s (2013) argument that elite groups are structured by the bureaucratic and educational systems within a country, but, critically, must also take a global approach, given the increasing diversification of sources of power (Savage and Williams 2008) and the supposed emergence of a transnational (Embong 2000) or superclass (Rothkopf 2009).

I suggest that we will be able to integrate the concept of an elite class – comprising various fractions – within social class theory, but that we currently do not yet have enough empirical data for such theoretical work. New data is needed to support further examination of how current understandings of elite groups' practices (family processes of cultivation and aspirations for their children, education choices, orientations towards transnational mobility, consumption of goods and culture, political and ethical engagement), make elites distinctive from those recorded within other social classes and the mechanisms of social closure being operated to sustain the boundaries which maintain class divisions.

Concluding Thoughts

While much research has identified the relative stability of various elite groups governing societies, most scholars acknowledge that the 'disorganized capitalist order ... has created the conditions for the emergence of new elites within new fields' (Caletrío 2012, p. 148). The field of elite studies is still relatively small and has only recently experienced a significant resurgence (Scott 2008, Aguiar 2012). A number of critical questions remain for scholars to tackle. First, a clearly articulated and coherent theoretical approach to the study of elites is needed. Second, such an approach must be consistently drawn on when examining how practices, and the narratives constructed to make sense of these can help us to understand whether or not elites are individuals and/or groups of individuals that are distinctive enough to be categorised as a social class in their own right.

I have argued that any definition of elites should take as its starting point that elites have 'power over' and 'power to'. Furthermore, attention should be paid to how power is made visible through the kinds of affective motivations and consequences of elite groups' practices, so as to consider what might make elites distinctive from non-elite groups. While some research has been done on consumption practices, social networks, mobility patterns, and the educational histories of elites, more in-depth data is needed on a wider range of practices that the elite individuals and groups engage in. Attention needs to be paid to how the various aspects of these practices may be shaping each other and what determines differences across practices identified within elite groups. Critically, we need to develop stronger understandings of how new generations of elites are being prepared for power, the extent to which elite group membership is stable or more fluid, and what drives the degree of stability or fluidity found across various sectors of society and at the global level.

With specific reference to contributions around elite education, future research should consider further what is 'elite' about local, national and global elite education systems. Work should also consider how the elite nature – the affective and discursive contexts, the groupings found within specific elite education institutions, the economic, social and cultural outcomes of such education, and the creation of certain forms of practice – differs across contexts and why this might be. If current and future research continues to grapple with these specific questions around elite education and the broader points that relate to elites more generally, the field of elite studies will be greatly enriched and our understandings of how power configurations organise societies deepened.

References

Aarseth, H., 2013. Family cultures and pedagogic practices in the cultural and economic elite in Norway. *Private and Elite Education: International Perspectives.* Institute of Education, University of London.

Aguiar, L. L. M., 2012. Redirecting the academic gaze upward. In: Aguiar, L. L. M. and Schneider, C. J. (eds) *Researching Amongst Elites: Challenges and Opportunities in Studying Up.* Farnham: Ashgate, 1–27.

Allouch, A., 2013. *L'ouverture sociale comme configuration. Pratiques et processus de sélection et de socialisation des milieux populaires dans les établissements d'élite. Une comparaison France-Angleterre* (Doctorate). Sciences Po.

Ball, S. J., 2003. *Class Strategies and the Education Market: The Middle Classes and Social Advantage.* London: Routledge Falmer.

Ball, S. J., 2010. Is there a global middle class? The beginnings of a cosmopolitan sociology of education: A review. *Journal of Comparative Education,* 69(1), 137–161.

Ball, S. J., 2012. *Global Education Inc.: New Policy Networks and the Neo-liberal Imaginary.* London: Routledge.

Ball, S. J., Vincent, C., Kemp, S. and Pietikainen, S., 2004. Middle class fractions, childcare and the 'relational' and 'normative' aspects of class practices. *The Sociological Review,* 52(4), 478–502.

Baltzell, E. D., 1987. *The Protestant Establishment: Aristocracy and Caste in America.* New Haven, CT: Yale University Press.

Bathmaker, A.-M., Ingram, N. and Waller, R., 2013. Higher education, social class and the mobilisation of capitals: Recognising and playing the game. *British Journal of Sociology of Education,* 34(5–6), 723–743.

Bennett, T., Savage, M., Silva, E., Warde, A., Gayo-Cal, M. and Wright, D., 2008. *Culture, Class, Distinction.* London: Routledge.

Bond, M., 2012. The bases of elite social behaviour: Patterns of club affiliation among members of the House of Lords. *Sociology,* 46(4), 613–632.

Bottomore, T., 1993. *Elites and Society.* 2nd edition. London: Routledge.

Bourdieu, P., 1996. *The State Nobility.* Cambridge: Polity Press.

Brezis, E. S., 2011. The effects of elite recruitment on social cohesion and economic development. *International Conference on Social Cohesion and Development.* OECD Conference Centre, Paris.

Brooks, R. and Waters, J., 2011. *Student Mobilities, Migration and the Internationalization of Higher Education.* Basingstoke: Palgrave.

Brooks, R. and Waters, J., 2014. The hidden internationalism of elite English schools. *Sociology.* doi: 10.1177/0038038514525517.

Bühlmann, F., David, T. and Mach, A., 2013. Cosmopolitan capital and the internationalization of the field of business elites: Evidence from the Swiss case. *Cultural Sociology,* 7(2), 211–229.

Buono, R. A. D., 2012. Transnational elites and the class character of Latin American integration. *Critical Sociology,* 38(3), 373–380.

Butler, T., 1995. The debate over the middle classes. In: Butler, T. and Savage, M. (eds) *Social Change and the Middle Classes.* London: Routledge, 26–36.

Butler, T. and Savage, M., 1995. *Social Change and the Middle Classes.* London: Routledge.

Caletrío, J., 2012. Global elites, privilege and mobilities in post-organized capitalism. *Theory, Culture and Society,* 29(2), 135–149.

Carroll, W. K. and Carson, C., 2003. The network of global corporations and elite policy groups: A structure for transnational capitalist class formation. *Global Networks,* 3(1), 29–57.

Cook, A. C. G., Faulconbridge, J. R. and Muzio, D., 2012. London's legal elite: Recruitment through cultural capital and the reproduction of exclusivity. *Journal of Environment and Planning A,* 44(7), 1744–1762.

Cookson, P. W. and Persell, C. H., 1985. *Preparing for Power: America's Elite Boarding Schools.* New York: Basic Books.

Crozier, G., Reay, D. and James, D., 2011. Making it work for their children: White middle-class parents and working-class schools. *International Studies in Sociology of Education,* 21(3), 199–216.

Dahl, R. A., 1961. *Who Governs: Democracy and Power in an American City.* New Haven, CT: Yale University Press.

Denord, F., Hjellbrekke, J., Korsnes, O., Lebaron, F. and Le Roux, B., 2011. Social capital in the field of power: The case of Norway. *The Sociological Review,* 59(1), 86–108.

Dogan, M., 2003a. Introduction: Diversity of elite configurations and clusters of power. *Comparative Sociology,* 2(1), 1–15.

Dogan, M., 2003b. Is there a ruling class in France? *Comparative Sociology,* 2(1), 17–89.

Domhoff, G. W., 1967. *Who Rules America Now?* New York: Simon & Schuster.

Draelants, H. and Darchy-Koechlin, B., 2011. Flaunting one's academic pedigree? Self-presentation of students from elite French schools. *British Journal of Sociology of Education,* 32(1), 17–34.

Draelants, H. and van Zanten, A., 2011. Sélection et canalisation à l'entrée en «prépa». In van Zanten, A. (ed.) *La formation des élites.* Paris: Presses Universitaires de France.

Ellersgaard, C. H., Larsen, A. G. and Munk, M. D., 2013. A very economic elite: The case of the Danish top CEOs. *Sociology,* 47(6), 1051–1071.

Embong, A. R., 2000. Globalisation and transnational class relations: Some problems of conceptualisation. *Third World Quarterly*, 21(6), 989–1000.

Fahey, J., 2014. Privileged girls: The place of femininity and femininity in place. *Globalisation, Societies and Education*, 12(2), 228–243.

Flemmen, M., 2012. The structure of the upper class: A social space approach. *Sociology*, 46(6), 1039–1058.

Flemmen, M., 2013. Putting Bourdieu to work for class analysis: Reflections on some recent contributions. *British Journal of Sociology*, 64(2), 325–343.

Forbes, J. and Lingard, B., 2013. Elite school capitals and girls' schooling: Understanding the (re)production of privilege through a habitus of 'assuredness'. In: Maxwell, C. and Aggleton, P. (eds) *Privilege, Agency and Affect*. Basingstoke: Palgrave Macmillan, 50–68.

Foucault, M., 1988. Technologies of the self. In: Martin, L., Gutman, H. and Hutton, P. (eds) *Technologies of the Self: A Seminar with Michael Foucault*. London: Tavistock.

Gaztambide-Fernández, R., 2009. *The Best of the Best: Becoming Elite at an American Boarding School*. Cambridge, MA: Harvard University Press.

Gaztambide-Fernández, R., Cairns, K. and Desai, C., 2013. The sense of entitlement. In: Maxwell, C. and Aggleton, P. (eds) *Privilege, Agency and Affect*. Basingstoke: Palgrave Macmillan, 32–49.

Gramsci, A., 1971. *Selections from the Prison Notebooks of Antonio Gramsci*. London: Lawrence & Wishart.

Griffiths, D., Miles, A. and Savage, M., 2008. The end of the English cultural elite? *Sociological Review*, 56(Supplement 1), 187–209.

Hartmann, M., 2010. Achievement or origin: Social background and ascent to top management. *Talent Development and Excellence*, 2(1), 105–117.

Harvey, W. S., 2011. Strategies for conducting elite interviews. *Qualitative Research*, 11(4), 431–441.

Hearn, J., 2012. *Theorizing Power*. Basingstoke: Palgrave Macmillan.

Howard, A., 2008. *Learning Privilege: Lessons of Power and Identity in Affluent Schooling*. New York: Routledge.

Howard, A., 2013. Negotiating privilege through social justice efforts. In: Maxwell, C. and Aggleton, P. (eds) *Privilege, Agency and Affect*. Basingstoke: Palgrave Macmillan, 185–201.

Hunter, F., 1953. *Community Power Structure: A Study of Decision Makers*. Chapel Hill: University of North Carolina Press.

Joyce, P., 2013. *The State of Freedom: A Social History of the British State Since 1800*. Cambridge.

Karabel, J., 2005. *The Chosen: The Hidden History of Admission and Exclusion at Harvard, Yale and Princeton*. Boston: Houghton Mifflin.

Kenway, J. and Fahey, J., 2014. Staying ahead of the game: The globalising practices of elite schools. *Globalisation, Societies and Education*, 12(2), 177–195.

Kenway, J., Fahey, J. and Koh, A., 2013. The libidinal economy of the globalising elite school market. In: Maxwell, C. and Aggleton, P. (eds) *Privilege, Agency and Affect*. Basingstoke: Palgrave Macmillan, 15–31.

Khan, S. R., 2011. *Privilege: The Making of an Adolescent Elite at St. Paul's School*. Princeton, NJ: Princeton University Press.

Khan, S. R., 2012. The sociology of elites. *Annual Review of Sociology*, 38, 361–377.

Koh, A., 2014. Doing class analysis in Singapore's elite education: Unravelling the smokescreen of 'meritocratic talk'. *Globalisation, Societies and Education*, 12(2), 196–210.

Koh, A. and Kenway, J., 2012. Cultivating national leaders in an elite school: Deploying the transnational in the national interest. *International Studies in Sociology of Education*, 22(4), 333–351.

Lamont, M. and Molnar, V., 2002. The study of boundaries in the social sciences. *Annual Review of Sociology*, 28, 167–195.

Lareau, A., 2002. Invisible inequality: Social class and childrearing in black families and white families. *American Sociological Review*, 67(5), 747–776.

Lawler, S., 2005. Disgusted subjects: The making of middle-class identities. *Sociological Review*, 53(3), 429–446.

LeRoux, B. and Rouanet, H., 2010. *Multiple Correspondence Analysis*. London: Sage.

Levine, S., 1980. The rise of American boarding schools and the development of a national upper class. *Social Problems*, 28(1), 63–94.

Lockwood, D., 1995. Marking out the middle class(es). In: Butler, T. and Savage, M. (eds) *Social Change and the Middle Classes*. London: Routledge, 1–12.

Lukes, S., 2005. *Power: A Radical View*. 2nd edition. Basingstoke: Palgrave Macmillan.

McCarthy, C., Bulut, E., Castro, M., Goel, K. and Greenhalgh-Spencer, H., 2014. The Argonauts of postcolonial modernity: elite Barbadian schools in globalising circumstances. *Globalisation, Societies and Education*, 12(2), 211–227.

McCarthy, C. and Kenway, J., 2014. Introduction: Understanding the rearticulations of privilege over time and space. *Globalisation, Societies and Education*, 12(2), 165–176.

Maclean, M., Harvey, C. and Chia, R., 2010. Dominant corporate agents and the power elite in France and Britain. *Organization Studies*, 31(3), 327–348.

Maxwell, C. and Aggleton, P., 2013. Becoming accomplished: Concerted cultivation among privately educated young women. *Pedagogy, Culture and Society*, 21(1), 75–93.

Maxwell, C. and Aggleton, P., 2014a. Agentic practice and privileging orientations among privately educated young women. *The Sociological Review*. Published online 14 August 2014.

Maxwell, C. and Aggleton, P., 2014b. Creating cosmopolitan subjects – the role of families and elite schools in England. *Transnational Capital and Transformation of the Elites*. Université de Paris 1 Panthéon-Sorbonne.

Maxwell, C. and Aggleton, P., 2014c. The reproduction of privilege: Young women, the family and private education. *International Studies in Sociology of Education*, 24(2), 189–209.

Mills, C. W., 1956. *The Power Elite*. New York: Oxford University Press.

Mosca, G., 1939. *The Ruling Class: Elemenzi di scienze politica*. London: McGraw-Hill.

Murray, G., 2012. The new fractionation of the ruling class. *Critical Sociology*, 38(3), 381–387.

Parel, K. and Adams, R., 2013. Oxford University data shows private school A-level pupils' advantage. *The Guardian*, 15 August.

Pareto, V., 1963. *The Mind and Society: A Treatise on General Sociology*. New York: Dover.

Pareto, V., 1968. *The Rise and Fall of Elites: An Application of Theoretical Sociology*. Totowa, NJ: Bedminster Press.

Parkin, F., 1974. *The Social Analysis of Class Structure*. London: Tavistock Publications.

Power, S. and Whitty, G., 2002. Bernstein and the middle class. *British Journal of Sociology of Education*, 23(4), 595–606.

Power, S., Edwards, T., Whitty, G. and Wigfall, V., 2003. *Education and the Middle Class*. Buckingham: Open University Press.

Power, S., Brown, P., Allouch, A. and Tholen, G., 2013. Self, career and nationhood: The contrasting aspirations of British and French elite graduates. *British Journal of Sociology*, 64(4), 578–596.

Reay, D., Crozier, G. and Clayton, J., 2009. Strangers in paradise'? Working-class students in elite universities. *Sociology*, 43(6), 1103–1121.

Ringer, F. K., 1979. *Education and Society in Modern Europe*. London: Indiana University Press.

Rizvi, F., 2014. Old elite schools, history and the construction of a new imaginary. *Globalisation, Societies and Education*, 12(2), 290–308.

Rothkopf, D., 2009. *Superclass: The Global Power Elite and the World They are Making*. London: Abacus.

Savage, M., 1995. Class analysis and social research. In: Butler, T. and Savage, M. (eds) *Social Change and the Middle Classes*. London: Routledge, 15–25.

Savage, M., 2000. *Class Analysis and Social Transformation*. Buckingham: Open University Press.

Savage, M. and Williams, K. (eds), 2008. *Remembering Elites*. Oxford: Blackwell.

Scott, J., 2003. Transformations in the British economic elite. *Comparative Sociology*, 2(1), 155–173.

Scott, J., 2008. Modes of power and the re-conceptualization of elites. In: Savage, M. and Williams, K. (eds) *Remembering Elites*. Oxford: Blackwell, 27–43.

Skeggs, B., 2004. *Class, Self, Culture*. London: Routledge.

Stevens, M. L., 2009. *Creating a Class: College Admissions and the Education of Elites*. Cambridge, MA: Harvard University Press.

Tholen, G., Brown, P., Power, S. and Allouch, A., 2013. The role of networks and connections in educational elites' labour market entrance. *Research in Social Stratification and Mobility*, 34, 142–154.

Vincent, C. and Ball, S. J., 2007. 'Making up' the middle-class child: Families, activities and class dispositions. *Sociology*, 41(6), 1061–1077.

van Zanten, A., 2009. *A choisir son école. Stratégies parentales et médiations locales*. Paris: Presses Universitaires de France.

van Zanten, A., 2015. *La formation des élites. Sélection et socialisation*. Paris: Presses Universitaires de France.

Walford, G., 1986. *Life in Public Schools*. London: Methuen.

Walford, G., 2005. *Private Education: Tradition and Diversity*. London: Continuum.

Walford, G., 2012. *Privatization and Privilege in Education*. London: Routledge.

Weis, L. and Cipollone, K., 2013. 'Class work': Producing privilege and social mobility in elite US secondary schools. *British Journal of Sociology of Education*, 34(5–6), 701–722.

Wetherell, M., 2012. *Affect and Emotion: A New Social Science Understanding*. London: Sage.

2 A Family Affair

Reproducing Elite Positions and Preserving the Ideals of Meritocratic Competition and Youth Autonomy

Agnès van Zanten

Introduction

As discussed in the introduction to this volume, and reflected in its chapters, there has been an important renewal of research on the education of elites since the turn of the century. Yet very few of the new analyses have focused on the role that families play in the (re)production of elite status. It could be argued that this absence in the literature is compensated by the significant number of studies published in the last 15 years that examine the educational strategies of (upper-) middle-class families (Lareau 1989, 2011; Devine 2004) and the school choices they make (Power *et al.* 2003; Ball 2003; van Zanten 2009a, 2013a; Reay *et al.* 2011). However, although this research provides relevant insights into what these parents do and the values and resources that inform their practices, empirical work has not focused on the most privileged families.

Moreover, although some of these studies, and particularly Lareau's (2011) rich ethnographic study, directly address the question of how parents' pedagogical models influence their children's views of themselves, they only briefly touch on the key question examined here. In this chapter we consider in depth how privileged families draw on resources, shape their children's desires, and influence their choices around education, while at the same time managing to preserve the social illusion that access to future elite positions is based on individual merit and the autonomous decisions and actions of their children.

In order to explore this question, the chapter draws on a recently completed study – 'Elite education in France: selection and socialisation'[1] – and, more specifically, on observations from 'open days' at two elite preparatory classes,[2] as well as on 20 interviews with parents.[3] The two preparatory classes – one public and one private – are among the most prestigious in France. Their reputation has been secured through their success in producing the future generations of French elites. Graduates from these preparatory classes represent the largest share of students who succeed at the *concours* which determine entry into the most prestigious *grandes écoles*. These preparatory classes are also considered prestigious because they have always been associated with the upper classes and perceived as central to these social actors' strategies to reproduce their elite status (Bourdieu 1996).

The chapter is organised in three sections. The first two sections describe and analyse the ways in which upper-class parents are able to make plans for their children's education and use their diverse resources (economic, cultural and social) to manage their children's educational careers, including gaining access to elite higher education tracks. More specifically, these sections will consider the conditions that allow these families' diverse resources to be activated in both domestic and institutional contexts (Stefansen and Aarseth 2011; Lareau and McCrory Calarco 2012). The third section of this chapter will examine what strategies are (un)consciously used by these upper-class parents to solve the quandary they experience when actively engaging in processes of 'concerted cultivation' (Lareau 2011) yet seeking to perpetuate the family and wider social myth that attributes their children's educational success solely to their intelligence, effort, commitment and capacity for self-direction.

Successful Educational Careers: Activating Diverse and Cumulative Resources

The group of families studied here comprises a significant number of established elite families and a smaller number of 'pretenders' seeking elite status for their children. These first are characterised by the volume and diversity of their resources. They have very important financial resources, frequently comprising inherited capital and financial investments, as well as highly educated and networked extended families. They also live in privileged neighbourhoods and have access to a wide social network of equally educated and wealthy people. 'Pretenders', on the other hand, lack some of these resources (their financial resources come only in the form of salaries, their own parents are not as highly educated and/or they live in more socially mixed areas).[4] Despite these differences all these families are intensively engaged in promoting the educational careers of their children through the most effective use of available resources.

Our research found that economic resources are critical in explaining access to elite education tracks. First, money can buy location and location is increasingly crucial in building successful educational careers (Butler and Robson 2003; Johnson 2006; Ball and Vincent 2007). High salaries and private investments, inherited money and/or financial help from affluent grandparents allowed many of our interviewees to live in expensive and exclusive areas of Paris and its western suburbs. This, in turn, gave them access to prestigious public schools that recruit their pupils based on local catchment areas, or facilitated access to prestigious private schools, which are generally located in privileged neighbourhoods. Additionally, a variety of institutions, associations and clubs offering cultural and sporting activities are often located in the same neighbourhoods, offering opportunities for building other types of cultural capital. Geographical segregation in these privileged areas also maintained and extended the social capital of these parents and their children through relationships in and out of the school with people who shared similar aims, values, tastes and practices.

Second, money can also buy time, a crucial condition for enabling the activation of both cultural and social resources (van Zanten 2009b). In a significant number of cases in our sample, the time bought was that of mothers themselves. Although French women are less likely to stop working after having children than women in other Western countries, in our small sample, one-third had never worked or had stopped working to take care of their children, and at least a further third worked part-time or had organized their work hours in such a way so as to maximize the time spent with children either at home or in transporting them to various cultural and sporting extracurricular activities. This was made possible by the fathers' high salaries and sometimes by inherited wealth, but was typically presented by the mothers themselves as the result of pure 'devotion' (Blair-Loy 2003):

And you, you don't work?

I stopped working to take care of the children. I worked in advertising. At one point, I had three babysitters to take care of them. And in the end, I stayed with them.

And you didn't regret it?

No. If I had to do it all over, I would do it again. There is such an intense relationship between a mother and her children. It's spectacular. It's an opportunity.

So you stopped working to take care of them?

Yes. I was there for logistics. That's why it happened so well. We are with our children all the time. I did what I felt was right. It worked.

(Mrs Kramarz)

Third, money also makes it possible to buy other people's time: babysitters when the children were young, as in the case of Mrs. Kramarz, but also later on, private tutoring, as well as experienced professionals who supported their children in their various cultural, physical and social extracurricular activities. Money was also crucial in allowing these parents to pay for language courses in France or abroad and, in many cases, to provide a private education in private schools that were not subsided by the state.

The cultural resources of these parents were also extremely important in facilitating their children's journey to the top of the educational ladder. Many of the parents interviewed, especially those from 'established elites', were 'cultural inheritors' (Ferrand *et al.* 1999), meaning that not only were they highly educated themselves, with several holding degrees from prestigious *grandes écoles*, but their siblings and cousins and, to a lesser degree but not unusually, their own parents, aunts and uncles were also highly educated and had themselves often followed elite higher educational tracks.

This familial 'institutional cultural capital' (Bourdieu 1986b), which usually comes with other types of cultural capital acquired by these individuals through diverse cultural engagements and activities, does not remain passive. It is activated through the many opportunities that exist for interaction between adults and children of the extended family, during, for instance, family meetings in country homes over weekends and holidays. Many of the families studied, as is frequently the case among the bourgeoisie (Pinçon and Pinçon-Charlot 2000), considered it essential to maintain strong ties with their relatives and to include their children from a very young age in this family circle. This is crucial for the 'osmotic' transmission of aspirations, values and tastes.

However, the close interaction within the nuclear family between highly educated parents, especially mothers, and children plays the more critical role. Rendered possible by time, and the money that buys it, continuous and informal interactions include and bring together expressive and instrumental dimensions (Bernstein 1977). Although some of the mothers may have idealized their relationship with their children, many declared how much they enjoyed the close intimacy they had with them (Stefansen and Aarseth 2011). This intimacy, which has been described by some authors as a form of 'emotional capital' (Reay, 2000), allows mothers to engage in frequent discussions with their children and progressively, not only transmit expectations, values and knowledge, but also boost their children's self-confidence, sustain or further develop their ambitions and orient future choices.

The instrumental nature of the interaction between parent/mother and child was most apparent in the way in which these parents transformed every activity into in a learning opportunity. Such a framing corresponds to the normative vision of education as 'concerted cultivation' (Lareau 2011) that is typical of mothers who are teachers or university professors and who where well represented in our small sample (6 out of 20):

Did you help out during her schooling?

Not directly, no, because she was always so independent. But I would say indirectly, yes, meaning I made it so that she was interested in many things. We went to museums when she was young. We told her lots of stories. I always tried to stimulate her, get her interested in many things. When we would watch a film, we would talk about it. I always tried to get as much as possible out of what we did together. I am a teacher, too. It's true that . . . I think that even if I didn't directly help her with her work, because she did it by herself, I tried to interest her, since she was really young, in a lot of things.
(Mrs Labro)

As illustrated by Mrs Labro, who characterizes many of the mothers interviewed, a wide range of cultural activities are engaged with from when the children are young. Mothers read, play games and watch TV with them at home and take them to different cultural places and events such as museums, concerts and plays, in addition to more mainstream leisure activities such as theme parks and the cinema. As the children grew older, parents explained that they clearly encouraged them to participate in regular cultural activities and sports. Not all of them claimed that these activities had a direct impact on their children's schooling but several mentioned the fact that they considered them important in their children's acquisition of certain qualities that they judged intrinsically valuable but also important for school success, such as discipline and following the rules, rigour and precision, patience and tolerance.

By contrast, these parents tended to minimize their direct investment in their children's schooling, especially when discussing helping them with homework. Some parents strongly insisted that they had never helped their children or paid for private tutoring. Others acknowledged that they had helped them but 'only for poem recitations in primary school' or only with subjects that they themselves mastered well or liked, and that they paid for 'just a few extra lessons' or 'only when (the child) had a small problem with maths'.

Parents, however, were more open about the ways in which they drew on their cultural capital and their 'internal social capital' to select schools for their children. Prestigious public or private schools were chosen because, as parents explained, they had good academic results and they allowed their children to associate with similar children, which would sustain the family's social status (Podolny 1993). The latter criteria particularly motivated families who had sent their children to private schools. Likewise, school subjects and curriculum tracks were chosen because they were thought to be useful for opening up particular higher education choices or for ensuring that their child got into a class where the majority of children were high achieving. Particular subjects such as Latin were also favoured because they were conceived as central to a distinctive bourgeois culture (Bourdieu 1986a).

This 'internal social capital' of parents was also used to promote their children's school careers on a daily basis. In particular, these parents expected and – probably by activating the strong 'sense of entitlement' that characterizes members of the upper class (Lareau 2011; Lareau and McCrory Calarco 2012) – frequently obtained support and input from teachers and headteachers in resolving any schooling issues their children were experiencing.

Accessing Elite Tracks: Capitalising on and Extending Previous Investments

Throughout their school careers, students from these families continuously capitalised on the investment of their parents, alongside the efforts they themselves made, to obtain good academic results and succeed at their other cultural endeavours. The transition to elite higher education tracks remains, nevertheless, a critical moment when activity is heightened in efforts to transform parents and students' personal resources into fully institutionalised educational capital (Bourdieu 1986b). The selection process to gain access to preparatory classes is presented as the first stage of a 'meritocratic contest' (Turner 1960) culminating with the *concours* two or three years later that gives students a place in a *grandes écoles*. Yet, our research re-emphasizes that the French elite education system is characterised by strong family sponsorship directly and indirectly, through the schools chosen for the children by their parents (van Zanten 2015).

The members of the selection panel determining entry into the preparatory classes are looking for 'excellent' students. Although they only have access to limited information when making their decisions – students' files from the last two years of *lycée*, including their grades, class rank, teachers' comments, a general note by the headteacher and their results of *baccalauréat* subject examinations, this information is used as a summary of students' entire school trajectories, which in most of the cases considered here are 'faultless'. After a 'head start', a phenomenon observed in 18 of the 20 children we focused on, who started their first year of formal schooling at age 5 rather than age 6, the vast majority of these students appear to effortlessly move up a grade each year. Their academic results are usually outstanding, frequently being ranked among the top 10 per cent of their class. All of the students obtained a general *baccalauréat*, most with honours, at the very young age of 16 or 17.

Because it is very difficult to distinguish between the independent effects of parental action and a student's own qualities and efforts, as they are so closely intertwined, children and external observers (like the selection panel members) are likely to consider that such excellent school profiles essentially reflect individual merit. However, in addition to the fact that they are strongly influenced by direct parental sponsorship of the children's educational careers, these profiles are also strongly dependent on the schools these children attended previous to selection into a preparatory class. Most of them went to schools, private or public, located in privileged neighbourhoods and carefully chosen by their parents. Due both to their school mix and the strong focus on results, in these schools all students pass the *baccalauréat*, in many cases with honours, and the great majority intend to pursue higher education studies, frequently following elite tracks.

These schools are in fact part of an unofficial 'high-status track' (Kingston and Lewis 1990), which further advantages their students in two main ways. First, the teachers and headteachers in these schools are keenly aware of the importance of grades and teacher comments during the selection process for preparatory classes (Darmon 2013) and therefore strategically calculate the former and carefully word the latter to increase the chances of those students they believe to have the highest potential. Second, members of these panels tend to trust the student evaluations written by teachers from these particular schools, while they are more likely to distrust or question teachers' grades and comments on students from more disadvantaged schools (Zimdars 2010; van Zanten 2015).

Parental involvement in children's curricular choices also increases their chances of being selected into these preparatory classes. Many of these parents encouraged their child to pursue the scientific track, which keeps a number of future education tracks open as opposed to the economic or literary track. Having followed specific classes specialising in 'Europe' or music or having taken Latin or Greek as optional subjects which was strongly recommended and sometimes imposed by parents on children, also acts as a signal to selection panel members of a student's academic disposition and indirectly of her or his social background.

Given the characteristics of the admission procedures for public preparatory classes in France, selection panel members are unable to incorporate into their assessments the cultural skills and interests of those students who, in addition to being top educational performers, are frequently very accomplished in a range of cultural subjects, largely due to their parents' intense efforts to 'cultivate' them (Lareau 2011). For instance, many of these students speak English fluently, through having been exposed to English-speaking babysitters or au pairs, having taken English language courses in France or abroad, and in some cases having studied for longer periods in England or the United States. A significant number of young people also play music, dance or do a range of sports. However, students applying to private preparatory classes are allowed to write a 'motivation letter' where they can outline these kinds of accomplishments and the values and qualities attached to them (Karabel 2005; Stevens 2007). From interviews with parents, it is clear that they encourage their children to use this letter to distinguish themselves in this respect:

> She highlighted the fact in the letter that she is bilingual French–English because we lived in the United States for four years. I know that at Sainte-Marie they like bilingual people because a significant number of people there are foreign.
>
> (Mrs Sémichon)

> Clémence presented herself as someone who is rather ambitious, who works quickly, who likes sports, who likes her friends, so it was very honest. And I want to say that if she is there, she wasn't accepted by mistake. It's simply that the letter showed who she is, someone who is happy when she is challenged and has a very full schedule.
>
> (Mrs Godard)

Parents support their children's desire and efforts to enter elite higher education tracks in other ways too. Economic capital once again plays an important role. While some parents did discourage their children from applying to private preparatory classes because of the expense, many did not see this as a hindrance or explained they were willing to make other sacrifices. Public preparatory classes are not without cost either, as students may need to board if families do not live nearby, or want their children to live independently.

Parents' cultural capital is also, once more, drawn upon during regular discussions with their children about the advantages and disadvantages of different higher education choices they should consider. Parents talk about their own experience but also share an impressive amount of information they have gathered through reading and discussions with educational professionals and others in their social networks. Rankings of the various preparatory classes are perused, curricular contents considered and employment destinations assessed to inform these discussions.

An important activity that triggers these discussions are 'open days' organised by many higher education institutions and especially preparatory classes, that parents and children often attend together. Not only do these visits allow students and their parents to gain additional factual information on the different tracks and institutions, but they also provide two other important types of knowledge that become crucial for determining the students' final choices. The first is knowledge about a student's chances of being accepted into that particular preparatory class. Students usually bring their school files with them and these are carefully examined by the professors, who evaluate the extent to which their profile matches institutional expectations (and sometimes use this activity to start pre-selecting outstanding and motivated candidates before the official selection process begins). The other type of knowledge gained is more intuitive. It involves the 'feel' of schools based on students and parents' class-based expectations and tastes (Bourdieu 1986a; Reay *et al.* 2005):

> A year ago, he told me: 'If I am accepted at Thiers or Mazarin [the two most prestigious public preparatory *lycées* with preparatory classes], I don't want to go to those establishments because it seems like there is an enormous pressure on the students [there]. The teachers call the parents when [their child] is not doing well'. I wanted him to go to a good prep class and so I was a bit disappointed because he had the potential. But at the open door days, I was happy because we went to visit the different prep classes together. [...] He saw what Thiers was like. It gave him a bit of direction. And he was pleasantly surprised by Thiers, and he also talked with someone at Mazarin. And then he told me: 'I absolutely must go to Thiers or Mazarin'.
> (Mr Thomas)

Preserving Students' Merit and Leaving Room for Autonomy: Subtle Strategies

The parents studied here are thoroughly involved in the construction of their children's educational careers. Their intervention must nevertheless be rendered as invisible as possible. This is necessary, first, in order to maintain the social fiction of meritocratic mobility within the educational system, critical for the French elite education system's social and political legitimacy (Dubet 2004; van Zanten and Maxwell 2015), and thereby preserve the self-esteem of their own sons and daughters through sustaining the belief that their achievements are essentially rooted in their own talents and efforts. Second, because such intensive mothering (Hays 1996), and at later stages 'fathering' as well, contradicts social ideals of the importance of youth autonomy, parents develop (un)conscious rhetorical and practical strategies that conceal the extent of control they exert over their children, their schooling and their education choices.

A main rhetorical strategy displayed is an insistence on children's innate qualities which both justify parental intervention and still maintains children's sense of achievement. All the parents interviewed spontaneously mentioned how 'brilliant' their children were. Many other intellectual qualities such as the capacity to obtain results without much effort, to work quickly, or that children were interested in many different subjects were mentioned as well. These qualities legitimise for many parents their investment in their children's educational careers. Several families brought up, for instance, the fact that other children in their family were not as talented or as successful at school, implying that their investments were clearly differentiated according to each child's abilities. At the same time, the children we focus on in this chapter are also presented as being from an early age very independent and self-motivated with respect to school work. Therefore, although they hold great expectations for them, many parents explained that they did not have to spend a lot of time on homework, to pay for private tuition, or discuss their progress with teachers.

Parents also referred during the interviews to their children's personality when seeking to explain parental influence or lack of influence on their choices. Some parents depicted their children as 'headstrong' and 'determined'. For instance, according to Mr de Saint-Maur, his daughter 'has always had the upper hand on things and on her parents since she was born'. Thus, they never dreamt of opposing her desire to take a prestigious economy preparatory class, which 'fortunately' closely matched their own wishes for her. By contrast, others, frequently 'pretenders', insisted that their interventions were necessary because, despite being 'brilliant', their children were too modest to opt for a very prestigious and selective preparatory class:

He is relatively humble. He is reasonable and reasoned. Perhaps if we hadn't pushed him, he wouldn't have taken the chance.

He wouldn't have applied to Mazarin?

No, and yet, he passed his *baccalauréat* with distinction without working too hard, without killing himself. And if we had let him apply on his own, he wouldn't have chosen Mazarin and would have settled for Verlaine. Probably. We talked about it a lot.

(Mrs Klaus)

In fact, whether they depicted their children as lacking in ambition and uncertain about their future or as very determined and passionate about a specific area of study, the parents interviewed saw their role as helping their children seek out or affirm their particular qualities and projects (de Singly 1996; Lareau 2011). A parent's role was not to impose choices but to continuously provide stimulating discussions and activities to extend and enhance their children's natural interests and skills. Interestingly, parents often became so involved in these projects that several of them used the pronoun 'we' (or, more frequently, the French more impersonal 'on') when describing their children's decisions about higher education choices and practices engaged in to obtain information and advice, and to prepare applications for entry into preparatory classes. This was particularly evident when parents talked about the 'motivation letter' for private preparatory class selection:

We would discuss it from time to time. She would say to me, 'Hey, I'd like to talk about our experience abroad', the fact that she was born abroad, 'I would like to start with that'. So, I would jump on that. We talked about it but at one point she went into her room, closed the door and delivered ... I think she first wrote down some ideas over time. It's something she mulled over for several days or weeks and then she wrote it. I wouldn't have done it that way but, oh well, it worked! We talked about it but I also sometimes told her, 'I feel like you are determined. You should be able to highlight this quality of yours [your determination]. Or look, you're going non-stop. Saturday you have work and you have a game and you also want to see friends in the afternoon. That's the kind of person they are looking for. So, there you go, we tried our best. I might have helped her get to know herself better but she wrote it herself'.

(Mrs Godard)

Another less rhetorical but more practical strategy that these parents used to shape their children's higher education choices, while distancing themselves from seeking to actively influence these decisions, was 'externalisation'. Parents encouraged their children to talk to other people who had followed a similar educational path, held an employment position their child coveted, or had insider information about certain institutions, expecting that the opinions and advice of these chosen 'others' would closely match their own.

Where children had older siblings or cousins who were currently attending or who had already graduated from elite higher education tracks, parents encouraged them to seek out advice from these personal networks. Such advice was not only considered trustworthy, but could also be tailored by parents through asking family members to focus on particular aspects during these discussions. Similarly, requests were made of friends and the children of friends, especially if they had insider knowledge on a targeted institution or tracks. These parents also resorted to professional networks, most frequently the teachers working at the *lycée* attended by the children, but also in a few cases private psychologists and coaches.

By encouraging their children to listen to other people, these parents skilfully displace the extent of their own influence on their children's higher education choices. As they carefully engineer the exchanges and in many cases participate in them as well, the chances are very high that the 'external' views and advice that these 'relevant others' can provide, will complement or reinforce their own perspectives and desires. Moreover, these parents seldom seem to follow advice given by others blindly, especially if it contradicts their own wishes and opinions (Lignier 2012).

Conclusion

An important question this volume is considering is whether and how the educational practices that are sketched out in this chapter (and others) are common to all (upper-) middle-class parents or whether there are aspects which distinguish particular families as 'elite'. Although the two groups of families share many features, we would argue that the privileged families studied in this chapter, especially the 'established' (Elias with Scotson 1965) elites, exhibit some distinctive features and practices. Through a skilful combination of economic, cultural and social resources, these families are able to ensure 'flawless' trajectories for their children leading them to take up places at the best preparatory classes and within the most prestigious curriculum subject tracks, which, in turn, significantly increase their children's chances of success at the *concours,* and at securing their desired jobs in the future. Moreover, these families are clearly engaged in a more general process of social reproduction. By giving their children access to educational contexts characterized, not only by their excellence, but also by their social exclusivity, they are nurturing possibilities for future social connections; ties that will prove useful in many fields (Granovetter 1973). They are also securing the collective reproduction of their elite social status (Naudet 2013).

The actions of this group of parents are so effective because they have developed carefully thought out strategies, adapted to the different stages of their children's education career and drawing on a range of sophisticated and creative means to attain the goals they have set for themselves and their children. Although at first sight these parents seem to share the expressive orientation found in other upper and especially middle-class parents (van Zanten 2009b, 2013b), this study highlights how their practices are structured by specific goals related to status maintenance or improvement. The differences in the extent and depth of the resources they have access to, and their adeptness at manipulating situations to meet their own needs have been shown here to be crucial in determining the degree to which parents' strategies of reproduction are likely to be successful.

The chapter has also highlighted the extent to which parents and children feel a 'sense of entitlement' concerning their elite status. Significantly, it was only among the group of elite 'pretenders' that some parents mentioned encountering resistance from their children at their active strategies for securing their elite education, or where parents themselves expressed some doubts about successfully building the future they desired for their children.

The practices of these elite parents have important macro and micro consequences. From a macro perspective, the most significant is the crucial role they play in perpetuating educational inequalities through hoarding and monopolizing the kinds of educational opportunities and goods (Parkin 1974; Murphy 1988; Tilly 1998) that will later be converted into economic, cultural and social privileges (Bourdieu *et al.* 1973).

At a more micro-level, the psychosocial, sociological and political consequences of these parents' pedagogical approaches to educating and rearing their children are important too. Our analysis of students' own points of view highlights that due to the perceived meritocratic conditions of selection into elite tracks as well as the hard work expected of them at prestigious preparatory classes, the majority think of themselves as 'deserving educational elites' (Tenret 2011; Darchy-Koechlin, Draelants and Tenret this volume). Simultaneously, because these young people have been schooled in educational contexts that are not only extremely demanding but also socially exclusive, they have also learnt to associate legitimate access to elite status with membership of specific social groups. In other words, they become great proponents of the perceived meritocracy of the French elite education system while understanding it as a class meritocracy (Power *et al.* 2003). This has profound implications for these future leaders' political views and choices, not the least in the area of educational policies (van Zanten 2010).

Notes

1 This research was funded by the French National Agency for Research and was conducted by a team of 5 researchers, 4 doctoral students and a research assistant working under van Zanten's direction.
2 *Classes préparatoires* are taken by students for two or three years after their *baccalauréat* to prepare for the competitive examinations called *concours* that allow access to the higher education institutions known as the *grandes écoles*. They are officially viewed as a form of higher education taking place in secondary schools.
3 We interviewed 13 mothers, 4 fathers and 4 couples who had at least one child in a preparatory class.
4 Among the 12 'established' elite families, fathers either owned a firm (2), were managers (7) engineers (2) or professionals (1) and 8 of them had studied at a *grande école*. Mothers had more diverse professions and educational trajectories but many of them had higher education degrees earned after having taken preparatory classes. Among families of 'pretenders', fathers were managers (2) professionals (3) and researchers or professors (3) and held university degrees from less prestigious *grandes écoles* and universities. Mothers also held higher university degrees but frequently without having taken preparatory classes first. Most of the 'established' (10 out of 12) sent their children to the private preparatory classes and most of the 'pretenders' to the public preparatory classes. Although the location of families is influenced by that of the preparatory classes, it is also significant that among the 'established' 11 families out of 12 lived in the 16th or 7th districts of Paris or in cities to the West of Paris (Neuilly, Versailles and Rambouillet for instance) considered as 'bourgeois' enclaves', while 'pretenders' lived in the 5th and 6th districts, which are quite expensive and exclusive as well but still associated with an intellectual lifestyle.

References

Ball, S.J. (2003) *Class Strategies and the Education Market*, London: Routledge Falmer.
Ball, S.J. and Vincent, C. (2007) 'Education, class fractions and the local rules of spatial relations', *Urban Studies*, 44(7): 1175–1189.
Bernstein, B. (1977) *Class, Codes and Control*, Vol. 3. London: Routledge & Kegan Paul.
Blair-Loy, M. (2003) *Competing Devotions: Career and Family Among Women Executives*, Cambridge, MA: Harvard University Press.
Bourdieu, P. (1986a) *Distinction: A Social Critique of the Judgement of Taste*, London: Routledge.
Bourdieu, P. (1986b) 'The forms of capital', in J. Richardson (ed.) *Handbook of Theory and Research for the Sociology of Education*, New York: Greenwood, 241–258.
Bourdieu, P. (1996) *The State Nobility*, Cambridge: Polity Press.
Bourdieu, P., Boltanski, L. and de Saint-Martin, M. (1973) 'Les stratégies de reconversion', *Information sur les Sciences Sociales*, 12(5): 61–75.

Butler, T. and Robson, G. (2003) *London Calling: The Middle Classes and the Remaking of Inner London*, London: Berg.

Darmon, M. (2013) *Classes Préparatoires. La Fabrique d'une Jeunesse Dominante*, Paris: La Découverte.

de Singly, F. (1996) *Le Soi, le Couple et la Famille*, Paris: Nathan.

Devine, F., (2004) *Class Practices: How Parents Help Their Children Get Good Jobs*, Cambridge: Cambridge University Press.

Dubet, F. (2004) *L'École des Chances: Qu'Est-Ce Qu'une École Juste?*, Paris: Le Seuil.

Elias, N. with Scotson, J.L. (1965/1994) *The Established and the Outsiders*, London: Sage Publications.

Ferrand, M., Imbert, F. and Marry, C. (1999) *L'Excellence Scolaire: Une Affaire de Famille?*, Paris: L'Harmattan.

Granovetter, M. (1973) 'The strength of weak ties', *American Journal of Sociology*, 78(6): 1360–1380.

Hays, S. (1996) *The Cultural Contradictions of Motherhood*, New Haven, CT: Yale University Press.

Johnson, H. (2006) *The American Dream and the Power of Wealth: Choosing Schools and Inheriting Inequality in the Land of Opportunity*, New York: Routledge.

Karabel, J. (2005) *The Chosen: The Hidden History of Admission and Exclusion at Harvard, Yale and Princeton*, Boston, MA: Houghton Mifflin.

Kingston, P. and Lewis, L. (eds) (1990) *The High-Status Track: Studies of Elite Schools and Stratification*, New York: SUNY.

Lareau, A. (1989) *Home Advantage: Social Class and Parental Intervention in Elementary Education*, London: Falmer Press.

Lareau, A. (2011) *Unequal Childhoods: Race, Class and Family Life. Second Edition. A Decade Later*, Berkeley: University of California Press.

Lareau, A. and McCrory Calarco, J. (2012) 'Class, cultural capital, and institutions: The case of families and schools', in Friske, S. and Hazel, M. (eds) *Facing Social Class*, New York: Russell Sage Foundation.

Lignier, W. (2012) *La Petite Noblesse de l'Intelligence. Une Sociologie des Enfants Surdoués*, Paris: La Découverte.

Murphy, R. (1988) *Social Closure: The Theory of Monopolization and Exclusion*, Oxford: Clarendon Press.

Naudet, J. (2013) 'Par-delà les spécificités nationales: comprendre les expériences de mobilité sociale en France, aux Etats-Unis et en Inde', *Sociologie du Travail*, 55(2): 172–190.

Parkin, F. (1974) *The Social Analysis of Class Structure*, London: Tavistock Publications.

Pinçon, M. and Pinçon-Charlot, M. (2000) *Sociologie de la Bourgeoisie*, Paris: La Découverte.

Podolny, J. (1993) 'A status-based model of market competition', *American Journal of Sociology*, 98(4): 829–872.

Power, S., Edwards, T., Whitty, G. and Wigfall, V. (2003) *Education and the Middle Class*, Buckingham: Open University Press.

Reay, D. (2000) 'A useful extension of Bourdieu's conceptual framework? Emotional capital as a way of understanding mothers' involvement in their children's education', *The Sociological Review*, 48(4): 568–585.

Reay, D., David, M. and Ball, S. (2005) *Degrees of Choice: Social Class, Race and Gender in Higher Education*, London: Trentham Books.

Reay, D., Crozier, G. and James, D. (2011) *White Middle Class Identities and Urban Schooling*, London: Palgrave Macmillan.

Stefansen, K. and Aarseth, H. (2011) 'Enriching intimacy: The role of the emotional in the "resourcing" of middle-class children', *British Journal of Sociology of Education*, 32(3): 389–405.

Stevens, M.L. (2007) *Creating a Class: College Admissions and the Education of Elites*, Cambridge, MA: Harvard University Press.

Tenret, E. (2011) *L'École et la Meritocratie. Représentations Sociales et Socialisation Scolaire*, Paris: Presses Universitaires de France.

Tilly, C. (1998) *Durable Inequality*, Berkeley: California University Press.

Turner, R.H. (1960) 'Sponsored and contest mobility and the school system', *American Sociological Review*, 25(6): 855–867.

van Zanten, A. (2009a) *Choisir Son École. Stratégies Parentales et Médiations Locales*, Paris: Presses Universitaires de France.

van Zanten, A. (2009b) 'Le travail éducatif parental dans les classes moyennes et supérieures: Deux modes contrastés d'encadrement des pratiques et des choix des enfants', *Informations Sociales*, 154(4): 80–85.

van Zanten, A. (2010) '"L'ouverture sociale des grandes écoles": Diversification des élites ou renouveau des politiques publiques d'éducation?', *Sociétés Contemporaines*, 78: 69–96.

van Zanten, A. (2013a) 'A good match: Appraising worth and estimating quality in school choice' in Beckert, J. and Musselin, C. (eds) *The Constitution of Quality in Markets*, Oxford: Oxford University Press.

van Zanten, A. (2013b) 'La compétition entre fractions des classes moyennes supérieures et la mobilisation des capitaux autour des choix scolaires', in Coulangeon, P. and Duval, J. (eds) *Trente ans après La Distinction*, Paris: La Découverte.

van Zanten, A. (2015) (ed.) *La Formation des Elites. Sélection et Socialisation*, Paris: Presses Universitaires de France (in press).

van Zanten, A. and Maxwell, C. (2015, in press) 'Elite schooling and the French state: Durable ties and new challenges', *British Journal of Sociology of Education*, 36(1).

Zimdars, A. (2010) 'Fairness and undergraduate admission: A qualitative exploration of admissions choices at the University of Oxford', *Oxford Review of Education*, 36(3): 207–323.

3 Elite Schools in Buenos Aires

The Role of Tradition and School Social Networks in the Production and Reproduction of Privilege

Victoria Gessaghi and Alicia Méndez

This chapter intends to document, for a specific national configuration, Argentina, the active work schools carry out in the construction of diverse elite groups. Throughout the twentieth century, the Argentinean education system experienced a comparatively early democratization with respect to other Latin American countries. However, in the context of gradual expansion and massification of primary, and later secondary education, diverse groups appropriated and colonized different educational institutions as a strategy for the production and reproduction of privilege. In this chapter, our main goal is to highlight gaps and continuities in the contribution of school institutions to the (re)production of privilege of specific social groups, through the construction and appropriation of social networks and the use of heterogeneous traditions. We begin by presenting existing research and by describing the current consensus in terms of elite formation in Argentina. We then proceed to analyse the ways in which subjects and families within middle and upper classes construct meanings regarding school and schooling attached to seemingly opposed values, such as meritocracy and family, through the analysis of families that enrol their children in two different educational segments: traditional schools and 'university' schools.

Research on Elite Education in Argentina

In Argentina, research on society's more privileged sectors has been erratic and dependent on social and political impetus at specific historical periods. Early research in the field during the 1960s reconstructed the trajectories of individuals who occupied 'the highest institutionalized positions' in society, aiming to analyse their power, prestige and diverse status situations (De Imaz 1964). Regarding this debate, several years later a key author asserted that after 1890, there was not a monolithic elite but several elite groups influential in the fields of economy, politics and ideas entertaining relationships that were not always harmonious (Halperín Donghi 1992). Land ownership, belonging to a certain social stratum, ancestry in the country (Germani 1965), occupation and educational level of parents (Cantón 1966), 'family traditionalism' and economic activity (Halperín Donghi 1992; Sigal and Gallo 1971) and manners (De Imaz 1964) were all requirements for accessing positions of privilege that over the century became more porous or remained restricted to limited spaces depending on historical circumstances.

Research during the 1970s and 1980s focused more on the relationship between these social groups and the important issues of those decades: development, dependency, democracy. Through class analysis, structural relationships between different social groups were established (O'Donnell 1977; Portantiero 1973) as well as their links with democratic institutions (Sábato 1988). Other studies analysed the trajectory of the Argentinean bourgeoisie (Azpiazu 1996; Basualdo 1997).

After these initial studies, it was only at the turn of the century that researchers from different disciplines (history, sociology, anthropology, education) showed a renewed interest in elite education. The most productive effect of the 2001 crisis – the main expression of change in the accumulation model characteristic of the past thirty years of Argentinean history – was the re-interrogation of existing representations regarding Argentinean society and the emergence of new debates over the values that were assumed in the past to organize it. Not only was the illusion that previous governments had managed to integrate all social sectors shattered, but the 'equality' that allegedly characterized Argentina as a country was also contested (Tiramonti 2007).

This new awareness brought about a series of studies[1] analysing the practices of 'dominant sectors', 'elites' or the 'ruling classes'.[2] Within the field of education, the diagnosis of high levels of educational inequality brought about new analyses of the education of our society's most privileged groups, their development and constitution as well as their transformation over the last quarter of the twentieth century (Tiramonti 2004b; Tiramonti and Ziegler 2008). These new studies highlighted, in the first place, the difficulty of formulating a conclusive definition of elites in Argentina due to the fact that egalitarian discourses, the lack of previous solid hierarchies and the fluidity of social structure undermined the legitimacy of any social group to claim a stable position at the top of the social hierarchy.

Second, these studies also pointed out that Argentina does not have an organized elite production system. In contrast to other national contexts (De Saint Martin 2008, van Zanten 2009), Argentina does not have a 'circuit' of State-supported institutions that guarantees access to elite positions, although there have been attempts to promote it. Indeed, there are no direct links between attending certain schools and occupying positions of leadership and power within the State or in other sectors.

However, although the State did not 'certify' the creation of educational spaces reserved for a happy few, it did not dissuade or regulate them either: it delegated in fact the consecration of elites to free competition between groups and institutions. Although the most privileged sectors had to adjust their educational trajectories to the early democratization of the Argentine education system, these groups did create – with unequal intensity throughout the twentieth century – a network of institutions that guaranteed socialization among peers. While the expansion of schooling and its massification was taking place, these sectors 'colonized' certain institutions, thus contributing to the 'segregated democratization' of the educational system.

Currently segregation has increased to such an extent that many studies describe an actual fragmentation of the educational system (Tiramonti 2004b). In each 'fragment' it is possible to observe the influence of the resources and values of different social groups who use them to select and evaluate schools. Some studies have shown that family and institutional strategies vary among different elite 'fragments' (Ziegler 2004; Villa 2005; Rodriguez Moyano 2012; Fuentes 2012; Méndez 2013). Schools operate differently according to the dimensions that their representatives and users see as necessary requisites for access to, and consolidation of, the positions of privilege they strive to occupy (Ziegler 2007).

These studies about 'elite fragments' have identified different institutional configurations serving different audiences. There are schools that 'educate for competition', schools that 'educate in and for the conservation of Christian values' and schools that educate for 'intellectual distinction' (Ziegler 2004). The first two ideal types include private schools and the last type includes only state-funded schools, the so-called university schools. Thus, it must be noted that in Argentina, contrary to other countries, the dividing line is not between private and state schools but between state and private schools for the poor, and those, state or private, that target the narrow strip of the most privileged social sectors (Neufeld and Thisted 2005).

In the following sections we will examine the socialization processes of youth from elite sectors using the results of two ethnographic studies.[3] We will distinguish between two types of elite institutions: those that 'educate for conservation' and those that 'educate for intellectual distinction', and will analyse the ways in which each type of school selects and recruits its student body, its value system and its contribution to the production and reproduction of elite social groups.

Traditional Schools

Argentina's upper class is composed of a network of kinship groups whose surnames are associated with the 'founding elite of the homeland' and the land itself, as they mainly operate in the agriculture and cattle-farming industry. Many of these families inhabited Argentina before the wave of massive overseas immigration at the beginning of the twentieth century. Surname, ancestry in the country, links to land and national history are resources deployed by these groups in their disputes over belonging to the upper class (Gessaghi 2011). School is a central part of the formation process of this social group. It is decisive in the construction of relations of recognition between 'traditional families'. Subjects affirm that their school belongs to 'their social milieu', to 'their class', and that 'everybody knows each other' there. A seventy-year-old woman who belongs to a family of judges, ministers and owners of land in the Province of Buenos Aires mentioned that she studied in a Catholic school in the neighborhood of Recoleta because 'there was no other option, my mother went there and they cared about the social dimension; it was not about the intellectual level, the social dimension meant that there were people like ourselves, good teaching did not matter'.

A Familiar Environment

Traditional families seek a well-known and familiar environment: 'people that know each other well' meet in school; in addition, students are related through kinship, as brothers and cousins, uncles and grandparents attend or have attended the same institution. Thus, families agglutinate in a network that fosters relationships among its members and gradually constructs a familiar atmosphere, through the process of creating, maintaining and preserving a social 'world'.

Schools themselves foster ties between families and school through their admission procedures: priority is given not only to siblings of current students, but also to anyone with relatives who were former students of the institutions. The student selection process takes a year. Candidates must first submit a form including information about their parents, the schools they attended, their surnames and their current job positions, as well as a photo of the family and data regarding the children. At a second stage, adults are evaluated through a personal interview. Finally, children must take exams in English, language and maths, as well as a psycho-educational test. It is only at the end of the year that families will receive a letter informing them whether their application was accepted or not. Justification of the final decision is never made public. Some institutions request the payment of an admissions fee when initiating primary school. This membership creates cohesion among the families 'that belong'.

The distinction of upper-class families lies mainly in their surname and their origin. However, the institutions where their members are educated are significant for the construction of social recognition. Interviewees agree: 'The first sign of belonging is the school you attend', they say, 'It is more important than your clothes, your house, more than everything'. School 'positions you, because it grants you specific codes'. At school – in addition to polishing whatever is necessary according to origin – subjects are infused by the institution and its members' ethos. A crucial part of the school's work is to build this mystique that erases differences among students and constructs distances with 'others'. Notwithstanding some controversy, participants agree that this shared system of values is what enables their mutual recognition as members of a community.

A past that extends into the present constructs significant symbolic differences: a traditional family is considered as such because it is composed of parents, grandparents and great-grandparents with a well-known history in the community. School is where several generations from the same lineage meet. By admitting each new generation, the institution continues the family's history. This work of linking generations enables inscription in the long term and establishes stable and a-temporal relationships. It contributes to making seniority the veiled principle of power hierarchies and to set obstacles to newcomers (Bourdieu 2013).

Schooling and Family Networks

These families assert their membership to the upper class not only through the possession of economic resources or of institutionalized positions of power but also from an alleged moral superiority granted to them by educational institutions recruiting and shaping 'good people that care for family'. The exclusivity of these schools does not derive from their tuition fees. Traditional schools are not the most expensive schools in Argentina. They are not chosen because of their alleged academic level but because of the moral education they provide. Neither does it seem necessary to obtain educational credentials in order to secure a position, to 'be someone' or for personal fulfilment. 'Most of them will work in family companies or on family property', says an interviewee, so the purpose of education is to acquire a 'general culture', for the pleasure of it, 'whether you'll work in that field or not'.

However, the meanings members of traditional families attach to education are not univocal. They combine meritocratic notions about school with membership to a traditional family. This perception varies according to individual trajectories and the trajectory of a family group within the upper class. Schooling plays a key role in the context of economic and symbolic erosion of the family network and is strategically used as an asset by the offspring of those who experience individual trajectories of downward or upward social mobility – either to integrate the workforce if they don't possess other capital or to acquire the cultural codes that their parents did not hold. In other cases, formal education is presented as relevant for those who want 'to be the best' as it allows them to marry the academic excellence granted by educational institutions and the legitimacy provided by birth to occupy an important position in the family business.

Family support and linage are resources held by members of the more established upper class that guarantee the social reproduction of its members and that they appreciate more than educational experiences in the formal education system. Schooling remains relevant but distinction lies in holding resources that cannot be acquired by all in school. The protection and support of the family makes strong expectations about school unnecessary.

Catholic or Secular?

The increase of the current fragmentation of the Argentinean education system should not conceal the fact that most of these families were never completely integrated into state schooling and part of the modernizing project of Argentinean society launched at the beginning of the twentieth century. Religious education was always a central concern for this group of families. The current consolidation of traditional schools does not involve a rupture with the socialization model that was previously carried out by the public sector as very early on, these families negotiated their integration within the education system in a form that allowed them to retain their traditions. While some members resorted to the Catholic and private schools, others –especially sons – were educated in national schools, which were for a long time highly socially segregated. After the massification of secondary schools, which started in 1930, these families took refuge in certain Catholic private schools.

The Colegio Nacional de Buenos Aires (CNBA)

The decisive impulse for the development of a local secondary public education system was given by the decree for the creation of national schools in several provincial capitals in 1863 (Dussel 1997). The first school, founded that same year, was the *Colegio Nacional de Buenos Aires* (CNBA). Despite its great visibility and para-digmatic character, it is not relevant to project its pedagogic model upon other national schools because each of them, founded at different historical periods, is embedded in a specific local history as well as in the complex interaction of the interests of the elites from Buenos Aires and those from the Litoral and the Interior of the country between 1862 and 1880 (Legarralde 1999).

Some of these schools' first students were the sons of traditional families. Others mainly recruited immigrants' children and even some girls; some were initially religious, others were secular; not all of them resorted to an entry exam to select their student body; and some persistently oriented their students toward university (given that at some point of their respective histories they became 'uni-versity schools'), while others also fostered trades and commerce as prospective work opportunities.

If we focus on the present, we can notice that the diversity of ways in which these schools resolve issues such as admission procedures, maintaining a certain academic level and relationships with other state agencies is the result of the work of students, parents, teachers, former students and education authorities. This work is undertaken in order to guarantee the existence of elite institutions in the context of Argentinean society where there is a strong pressure in favour of widening participation in the education system and of abolition of entry exams in secondary schools (Tiramonti 2004a; Southwell 2011; Del Piero 2013). At least since the mid 1950s, the perpetuation of selection has been a key factor in their recognition as elite institutions, as well as in the self-image of their stu-dents and alumni.

A Reference in Youth Education in Argentina

'*El Colegio*', as it is known among its students, was founded in the civic, religious and economic centre of Buenos Aires by Bartolomé Mitre, a politician, military, historian and translator who, as president, embodied *porteño*[4] interests and fos-tered a state project – that accounts for the existence of this school – to educate future 'government men' (Álvarez 1936, p. 146) and the nation itself: 'A modern, Western, republican and democratic nation, with an advanced economy' (Halperín Donghi 1994, p. 54). Throughout Argentina's turbulent history, the CNBA remained a reference for youth education: it trained a small number of notewor-thy representatives of the public and private top administration, liberal professions, the sciences and the arts who contributed to maintain the school's prestige with their professional achievements.[5] However, the student body between the end of the nineteenth century and the 1930s was socially quite heterogeneous. It com-prised children from traditional and influential families but the majority of students were of immigrant origin. Progressively these families became middle class and constituted the most important social group in the school alongside a few children either from very wealthy or very humble homes. The CNBA was effective in creating a sense of belonging and in providing significant cultural resources to its students. It instilled in them some key values, especially the importance of intellectual pursuits and efforts associated both with high culture and with political and moral traditions of secularism, tolerance and openness.

Transmission

The '*Colegio*' was successful in socializing students that were not inheritors of great family resources into the social and cultural traditions of the *porteño* notables. This took place through their admission and education at the institution and was extended through durable social relationships among former students and through their relation to society during their adult life.

Many former students have stated that they feel they have had good professional opportunities throughout their lives thanks to having made an important effort during their teenage years in taking the entry exam, made compulsory after 1957. Despite different procedural arrangements concerning the way this entry exam has been organized over time, feelings of suffering, fear, of having undergone an enormous trial, have shaped the way alumni see themselves and each other. This also seems to have transformed the way in which they perceive people who never carried out such a strenuous task, that is to say, those who are not 'exceptionaaaaaaal', as a former student[6] called them during an interview: neighbourhood friends, with more time for leisure; parents, who during examinations remained outside the school, 'on the other side of the iron bars, like in *The Planet of the Apes*' (a very famous children's TV show during the 1970s) said another.

Once this transition from a dominant family environment to that of *el Colegio* was accomplished through success at the entry examination, it was still an endeavour to remain there. Our interviewees told us about their fear of being rejected by an institution that was so difficult to access, or of not being able to adapt. These fears in turn were important in leading them to develop a new way of seeing others, to interiorize external standards such as time control, intellectual rigor and an institutional organization structured according to non-negotiable rules. Perhaps this common experience has influenced their willing acceptance of the CNBA as a meritocratic institution. In relation to the extent of realization of this justice model, today it might be said that the design put forward by the CNBA is the one described by historian Christophe Charle (1994) in *La Republica de los universitarios*: 'Meritocracy is about accessing the spaces no longer desired by the offspring of influential families'. It is also less clear that the CNBA currently is the instance that helps a significant number of students pass through what Pierre Bourdieu (2013) has called 'the big door', giving access to the most prestigious positions. However, as the political scientist Natalio Botana (1994) stated, its graduates 'perform with valour in international arenas' and access ministerial positions before the age of forty-five.

Regarding relations among classmates, peers strongly control extra-school intellectual activities, as well as ways of speaking, dressing and spending free time. These ways are also influenced by the intellectual, professional and political experiences and networks in which students participate as children, grandchildren or friends (Monjardet 1994). They are however collectively interpreted in a unique way that allows the different alumni generations of *el Colegio* to recognize each other as there are families where grandparents, parents, sons and daughters are 'ex CNBA'. Thus, some former students mentioned having been harshly judged by peers or confessed mocking or reprehending classmates for their readings, their political choices (sympathizing with Peronism at specific moments, for example, when it was considered an unsophisticated and therefore not a prestigious political stance) or for not making amusing or original comments.

Moreover, beyond the educational and social experience of day-to-day exchanges with classmates, the memories of suffering, fear and effort at the school have promoted ways of relating that persist over time. There are in Argentina large-scale professional networks based on the 'trust' that CNBA alumni have in other graduates they have never previously met. It seems that simply knowing that the other attended the school activates professional recognition. In addition, former students mentioned that years after graduating, they 'discovered' in former student meetings classmates with whom they had had practically no interaction in spite of having been part of the same classroom for over six years. These discoveries led to new friendships, joint professional projects or even marriages.

However, in this long-term social relation other feelings and practices also intervene. Once again, a sort of control takes place in different casual or strongly formalized exchanges in group settings: at meetings organized by former students of the same class, or organized by the school itself to celebrate key dates. During these gatherings ex-students construct a hierarchical inventory of who has had 'a good and fast career', or who 'is in CONICET'[7] or 'is top', 'good' or 'one of the bunch'.[8] Former students thus constantly compare their own position with the positions of their former classmates, hoping to come unscathed through the comparison, and at the same time confirm that their colleagues are successful enough to continue considering themselves part of that group and of that game. In a type of relationship 'between possible equal parties in the fields of social and moral hierarchy', as Ana Claudia Marques (2001) affirms, 'the other is the measure of the self'.

This is a type of social relation among people who remain connected to each other over time, sometimes aided or driven by other former students who have shaped high expectations about their professional future, where an idea about what it means to be successful is enacted, having as a point of reference the image of their most accomplished classmates. This idea of success is, on the one hand, incommensurable with regard to the standards of the broader society and, on the other hand, stratifies the group of alumni, given that only a small sample of them accesses what the group considers top positions. As pointed out by Marie Duru Bellat, there will never be as many good positions in the labour market as degrees handed out by elite institutions.[9] A former CNBA student posted the following comment on Facebook, in relation to an article about our book *El Colegio* that appeared in a Sunday newspaper magazine edition, predictably portraying relevant CNBA alumni from the areas of medicine, science, history but also media (that is, 'successful' people according to very different parameters): 'And what about the rest of us who remain cockroaches?' In fact, she held a philosophy degree and a master's from the London School of Economics.

Conclusion: The Contribution of Schools to the Production of Elites

The exercise of comparing meanings attached to schooling in different fragments of elite schools and the methods of selection and recruitment of these institutions and their values systems shows gaps and continuities in the contributions such schools make to the (re)production of specific social groups.

Both for the social groups that choose traditional schools and for CNBA alumni, school is a space that encourages the construction of collective strategies of collaboration, aspiration and self-control anchored in the construction and appropriation of school networks that operate as informal channels of access to highly valued positions in the professional and social world. The construction and/or strengthening of family and social ties among the diverse kin groups and different generations and between parents and students is part of the active job carried out by traditional schools in the production of the upper class. In contrast, in the CNBA – given its high academic selectivity and gratuitous character – individuals who bring relevant social capital with them coexist with others who construct and accumulate social capital through forms of sociability within the institution, and benefit from the existing social capital of their classmates.

Nevertheless, both fractions of the upper class, the established and the new, are included into an elite genealogy that involves and transcends them by their participation to specific school traditions. CNBA's students, because they are associated with an institution that values knowledge and intellectual endeavours, are part of an illustrated and secular tradition of notables. Students of traditional schools, on the other hand, reinforce at school their membership into the fraction of the elite associated with the founders of the homeland and the local farming economy.

The difference between both upper-class fractions lies in the use of family support as a strategy of social reproduction and as a principle to legitimize social position. Members of traditional families tend to choose schools that through their admission procedures, values and institutional culture recreate the dense familial networks which are the main supports of its legitimacy. In turn, national schools such as the CNBA, given their hyper-selective academic recruitment procedures and school socialization processes, target individuals that have already proven their ability to work hard and to 'survive' in a meritocratic context.

These families make use of specific primary and secondary schools – from a young age – and not only of school certification as such as evidence of social distinction: selecting and being selected by certain institutions is what grants a 'nobility title' (Bourdieu 2013). CNBA alumni – even though in some cases, several generations of a family have attended the school – claim their elite status within a system that guarantees the right to occupy positions based solely on personal merit proven in school competitions. According to Bourdieu, while some only demand of the education system that it certifies the good moral education and social distinction that specific schools can provide, offering them the minimum of necessary consecration to ratify their acquired situations, for others the school degree is the *sine qua non* requirement to access the field of power.

(2013, p. 410)

The study of different elite fractions highlights the work performed by educational institutions not only to reproduce elites but also to produce them. The way in which the different schools we have described in this chapter interact with the individuals (and families) that attend them, documents the diversity of the legitimization criteria – a mix of ancestry, kinship and meritocracy – for access to elite positions in contemporary societies.

Notes

1 In sociology, see Castellani (2002), Canelo (2002), Heredia (2005), Luci (2010) and Svampa (2001). Among historians, Hora (2002) and Losada (2008) examine, complete or discuss the classic analysis of Halperín Donghi (1992) and Botana (1994), among others. In addition, Argentinean anthropologists have also studied processes of elite participation (Badaró and Vecchioli 2009; Hernández 2010; Servetto 2010; Gessaghi 2011).
2 These terms are not equivalent. Each category refers to different theoretical frameworks corresponding to the different positioning assumed by each investigation.
3 The first investigation analysed the formative experiences of the Argentinean 'upper class' and involved the conduct and analysis of sixty-three in-depth interviews and observations in schools as well as the examination of secondary documents. The other investigation documented the social origin and sociability of alumni from the *Colegio Nacional de Buenos Aires*. It is based on over fifty interviews, analysis of autobiographies, a prosopographic study and the analysis of student files from 1897 to 1999 (Méndez 2013).
4 This term refers to the dwellers of the City of Buenos Aires and has been coined because of the city's proximity to the port, one of the main communication and exchange channels between Argentina and the World.
5 Among the CNBA alumni there are two Nobel Prize winners and three presidents.
6 For reasons regarding the length of this chapter, that also prevents us from illustrating the sociability of former students of the CNBA over different periods of time, in the rest of this section we will focus on the actors privileged during our doctoral research on the CNBA: men and women around forty years of age, who are immersed in their professional lives but have had at the same time opportunities to become part of broader sociability spaces than the ones that summon 'ex CNBA'.
7 Many graduates around age forty complained that attending alumni meetings was mainly to 'compare CV's', meaning to show off personal professional achievements, and control others'. CONICET is a state research funding agency. Entering CONICET as a professional researcher is a desired aim for academics, given the prestige as well as the economic and labour stability it provides.
8 This expression is from a former student who is very well known in his profession, comparing himself to someone with another specialty but with similar professional merit.
9 Conversation. Paris, May 2013.

References

Álvarez, J. (1936) *Las Guerras Civiles Argentinas y el Problema de Buenos Aires en la República*, Buenos Aires: La Facultad.

Azpiazu, D. (1996) 'Elite empresaria en la Argentina. Terciarización, centralización del capital, privatización y beneficios extraordinarios', working paper No. 2 at Privatización y regulación de la economía en Argentina, Buenos Aires: FLACSO-SECYT-CONICET.

Badaró, M. and Vecchioli, V. (2009) 'Algunos dilemas y desafíos de una antropología de las elites', *Etnografías Contemporáneas*, 4: 7–20.

Basualdo, E. (1997) *Notas Sobre la Evolución de los Grupos Económicos en la Argentina*, Buenos Aires: CTA.

Botana, N. (1994) *El Orden Conservador. La Política Argentina entre 1880 y 1916*, Buenos Aires: Sudamericana.

Bourdieu, P. (2013) *La Nobleza de Estado*, Buenos Aires: Siglo XXI Editores.

Braslavsky, C. (1985) *La Discriminación Educativa*, Buenos Aires: FLACSO-Miño y Dávila.

Canelo, P. (2002) *La construcción de lo posible. Identidades y política durante el menemismo*, Buenos Aires: FLACSO.

Cantón, D. (1966) *El Parlamento Argentino en Épocas de Cambio*, Buenos Aires: Editorial del Instituto.

Castellani, A.G. (2002) 'La gestion estatal durante los regímenes burocratico autoritarios. El caso argentino entre 1967–1969', *Sociohistórica*, 11–12: 35–68.

Charle, C. (1994) *La République des Universitaires (1870–1940)*, Paris: Seuil.

De Imaz, J.L (1964) *Los que Mandan*, Buenos Aires: Eudeba.

De Saint Martin, M. (2008) 'Les recherches sociologiques sur les grandes écoles: de la reproduction à la recherche de justice', *Éducation et Sociétés*, 21: 95–103.

Di Piero, M.E. (2013) 'Tensiones entre la inclusión y la selección en la escuela media: el caso de un grupo de instituciones tradicionales en la ciudad de La Plata', paper presented at 2ª Reunión Internacional sobre Formación de las Elites, NEEDS-FLACSO, Buenos Aires, October 2013.

Duru Bellat, M. and Kieffer, A. (2000) 'La démocratisation de l'enseignement en France: polémiques autour d'une question d'actualité', *Population*, 1: 51–79, vol. 55.

Dussel, I. (1997) *Curriculum, Humanismo y Democracia en la Enseñanza Media (1863–1920)*, Buenos Aires: EudeBA.

Fuentes, S. (2012) 'La educación del joven solidario en sectores de clase media alta y alta en Buenos Aires. Del campo a la reflexión etnográfica', paper presented at *Tercer Congreso Latinoamericano de Antropología*, Santiago de Chile, November.

Germani, G. (1965) *Política y Sociedad en una Época de Transición. De la Sociedad Tradicional a la Sociedad de Masa*, Buenos Aires: Paidós.

Gessaghi, V. (2011) 'Clase alta y educación: etnografía de una relación', unpublished thesis, Buenos Aires University.

Halperín Donghi, T. (1992) 'Clase terrateniente y poder político', in *Cuadernos de Historia Regional*, Universidad Nacional de Luján, 15: 11–46.

Halperín Donghi, T. (1994) 'Entrevista', in Hora, R. and Trímboli, J., *Pensar la Argentina*, Buenos Aires: El cielo por asalto.

Heredia, M. (2005) 'La sociología en las alturas. Aproximaciones al estudio de las clases/elites dominantes en la Argentina', *Revista apuntes de investigación del CECYP*, no. 10.

Hernández, V. (2010) 'Elites: elucidación antropológica de una práctica de poder', paper presented at the 1º Reunión Internacional sobre Formación de las Elites, FLACSO, October.

Hora, R. (2002) *Los Terratenientes de la Pampa Argentina: una Historia Social y Política, 1860–1945*, Buenos Aires: Siglo XXI.

Hora, R. and Trimboli, J. (1994) *Pensar la Argentina*, Buenos Aires, El cielo por as alto.

Legarralde, M. (1999) 'La fundación de un modelo pedagógico: los colegios nacionales entre 1862–1887', *Propuesta Educativa*, 10(21): 38–43.

Losada, L. (2008) *La Alta Sociedad en la Buenos Aires de la Belle Époque*, Buenos Aires: Siglo XXI.

Luci, F. (2010) 'L'intégration réussie à l'élite managériale: la constitution des dirigeants de grandes entreprises en argentine', unpublished thesis, EHESS.

Marques, A.C. (2001) *Intrigas e Questões. Vingança de Familia e Tramas Sociais no Sertão de Pernambuco*, Río de Janeiro: Relume-Dumará.

Méndez, A. (2013) *El Colegio. La Formación de una Elite Meritocrática en el Nacional Buenos Aires*, Buenos Aires: Sudamericana.

Monjardet, D. (1994) 'La culture professionnelle des policiers', *Revue Français de Sociologie*, 34: 393–411.

Neufeld, M.R. and Thisted, J.A. (2005) 'Investigadores implicados: la investigación educativa en espacios barriales de la Ciudad de Buenos Aires', paper presented at the VI Reunión de Antropología del Mercosur, Montevideo.

O'Donnell, G. (1977) 'Estado y Alianzas en la Argentina 1956–1976', *Desarrollo Económico*, 16(64): 523–554.

Portantiero, J.C. (1973) 'Clases dominantes y crisis política en la Argentina actual', in Braun, O. (ed.), *El Capitalismo Argentino en Crisis*, Buenos Aires: Siglo XXI.

Rodríguez Moyano, I. (2012) 'Capital cultural y estrategias educativas de las clases altas de la Ciudad de Buenos Aires', in Ziegler, S. and Gessaghi, V. (eds), *Formación de las Elites. Investigaciones y Debates en Argentina*, Buenos Aires: Manantial-Flacso.

Sábato, J.F. (1988) *La Clase Dominante en la Argentina Moderna. Formación y características*, Buenos Aires: CISEA-Gel.

Servetto, S. (2010) 'Procesos de socialización en las escuelas católicas de Córdoba', paper presented at Primer Seminario Taller de Antropología y Educación, La Antropología de la Educación en Argentina. Problemas, Prácticas y Regulaciones Políticas, Córdoba, April.

Sigal, S. and Gallo, E. (1971) 'La formación de los partidos políticos contemporáneos: la UCR (1890–1916)', in Di Tella, T.S., Germani, G., Graciarena, J. *et al.*, *Argentina Sociedad de Masas*, Buenos Aires: EUdeBA.

Southwell, M. (2011) 'La educación secundaria en Argentina. Notas sobre la historia de un formato', in Tiramonti, G. (ed.), *Variaciones sobre la Forma Escolar. Límites y Posibilidades de la Escuela Media*, Rosario: Homo Sapiens Ediciones.

Svampa, M. (2001) *Los que ganaron. La Vida en los Countries y Barrios Privados*, Buenos Aires: Biblos.

Tiramonti, G. (2004a) 'La configuración fragmentada del Sistema Educativo Argentino', *Cuadernos de Pedagogía*, Rosario, 12: 33–46.

Tiramonti, G. (2004b) *La Trama de la Desigualdad Educativa. Mutaciones Recientes en la Escuela Media*, Buenos Aires: Manantial.

Tiramonti, G. (2007) 'Subjetividad, pertenencias e intereses en el juego de la elección escolar', in Narodowski, M. and Gómez Shettinni, M. (eds), *Familias y Escuelas. Problemas de Diversidad y Justicia Social*, Buenos Aires: Prometeo.

Tiramonti, G. and Ziegler, S. (2008) *La Educación de las Elites. Aspiraciones, Estrategias y Oportunidades*, Buenos Aires: Paidós.

van Zanten, A. (2009) 'The sociology of elite education', in Apple, M., Ball, S. and Gandin, L. A. (eds) *International Handbook of the Sociology of Education*, London: Routledge.

Villa, A. (2005) 'Estrategias de reproducción en las familias de los sectores sociales altos y medios altos: un estudio sobre las biografías socioeducativas de las familias tradicionales de la ciudad de La Plata', unpublished thesis, FLACSO.

Ziegler, S. (2007) 'Los de excepción: un retrato de las elecciones escolares de las familias de sectores favorecidos en la Ciudad de Buenos Aires y el Conurbano Bonaerense', in Narodowski, M. and Gomez Shettinni, M. (eds), *Familias y Escuelas. Problemas de Diversidad y Justicia Social*, Buenos Aires: Prometeo.

Ziegler, S. (2004) 'La escolarización de las elites: un acercamiento a la socialización de los jóvenes de sectores favorecidos en la Argentina actual', in Tiramonti, G. (ed.), *La Trama de la Desigualdad Educativa. Mutaciones Recientes de la Escuela Media*, Buenos Aires, Manantiales.

Part II
Elite Institutions in National and Local Contexts

Combining a social and institutional approach to the study of elite education is essential to understanding the creation and reproduction of educational advantage. As discussed in the previous part, families and educational institutions, within a broader supportive policy context, drive processes of elite reproduction. This part focuses specifically on the elite education institution itself, and considers how the local and national context within which it is embedded shapes what is 'elite' about these institutions.

Shamus Rahman Khan examines how elite institutions are central to the processes that produce elite groups today. He illustrates the close links that exist between elite families and elite schools, largely due to the residential segregation that exists across many parts of America, but also because most American elite schools are private. Khan defines elite schools as having control over, or access to, resources (economic resources, academic capital, social ties to elite families and other elite institutions, cultural capital) but also as promoting values of liberalism and individualism. Khan emphasizes, as van Zanten did, that these elite institutions rely on the principle of meritocracy to justify the advantages such an education accrues for their students.

The importance of attending to national histories and current socio-political-economic contexts to understand elite education is also illustrated by the Brazilian case. Ana Maria Almeida demonstrates how the reproduction of elite groups in Brazil has, for several years, been made possible through processes of social closure and economic segregation: expensive private primary and secondary schools educate the children of the elite, who then go on to study at the most prestigious public universities. She also considers how the traditional elites and aspiring middle classes look outside the national context to secure further educational advantages, especially in light of policies of widening participation in higher education.

The next chapter focuses on Germany. Germany's educational system was based on both strong differentiation (and social segregation) between three types of secondary schools – the *Volksschule*, the *Realschule* and the *Gymnasium* (with only the latter delivering the *Abitur* necessary to attend university) – and the absence of significant differences in prestige among different types of higher education institutions. However, as Ulrike Deppe and her colleagues show, new international pressure to perform well in the international league tables means there have been policy developments aimed at introducing further stratification at both secondary and tertiary levels conducive to the emergence of a specifically German type of elite education trajectory.

Rachel Brooks and Johanna Waters focus on the geographic positioning of elite schools in England. They show that although these schools are frequently perceived as having a strong international orientation and although they emphasize on their websites elevation and 'apartness' through representations of their buildings and grounds, in fact they engage in many ways with their local community and especially with local schools. Through a focus on volunteering in local neighbourhoods, these schools seek to emphasize the public benefits private schooling can offer, while also recouping these actions in ways that reinforce their students' privilege.

4 Changes in Elite Education in the United States

Shamus Rahman Khan

To speak of "changes in elite education" in America is a difficult task. The first challenge is to define "elite" (cf. Khan 2012a). Does it refer to the status of the institution or the families who populate it? Quite obviously, these two are related, but they are not the same. For example, Stuyvesant High School in the city of New York has one of the most competitive systems of admission of any school in the world. And it provides students with one of the world's best educations. Families from around the city prepare their children to take an entrance exam, and only 3 percent of those students who take the exam are accepted (making it twice as hard to get into as Harvard). But elite families do not overwhelmingly attend Stuyvesant – no doubt in part because the strict admissions competition means they're not that likely to get it. For this "pure meritocracy" does not favor their status and as an "open" institution it does not quite service their needs. For much of the twentieth century Stuyvesant was a heavily Jewish institution, and it has steadily shifted to being predominantly Asian. In 2014 almost 75 percent of the students from Stuyvesant are from Asian families. So, is Stuyvesant an elite high school? If we were to look at selectivity and academic excellence, the answer is unquestionably yes. And such excellence results in a high degree of social influence. Yet prominent and wealthy families rarely send their children to Stuyvesant. And as such, other aspects that mark elite institutions – their social, cultural, and symbolic transference to children – are less pronounced at Stuyvesant than at other far less competitive schools. By such criteria, Stuyvesant is not an elite school.

The reader might rightly object that this high school is hardly representative of elite education more generally. I have chosen a rather unique case here to make a point. For the simple fact of the matter is that almost overwhelmingly elite families and elite schools are tightly coupled. There are two reasons for this. First, residential segregation in America means that wealthy families rarely live anywhere but near other wealthy families (Massey and Denton 1993). And so their local schools are both well funded, and relatively economically homogeneous. The second is that most elite schools are private. While many offer financial aid, in general such private schools have a considerable financial barrier to entry, servicing the families of wealthier Americans. About half the families who send their children to Harvard, for example, have incomes above $200,000 (well within the top 5 percent of American families, to say nothing of the global population the school draws upon). And yet, while many schools are overwhelmingly populated with wealthy families, this does not necessarily make such schools elite, like

Harvard. Often these second- or third-tier wealthy schools lack academic, cultural, or historic prestige. It is neither enough to be highly selective, nor extremely rich to be an elite school. Instead, the definition of our object lies elsewhere.

What defines elite schools is that they have vastly disproportionate control over or access to a wide range of relevant resources. Those resources include academic capital, social ties to elite families and other institutions of power, the capacity to guide and transfer culture, and considerable economic capacity. Yet the value of each of these resources to being elite is a shifting target. As we shall see, ties to what we might think of as prominent families is less central to elite educational status today than it was just a generation ago. In this sense, elite schools are not elite because of their properties or competitiveness, nor are they elite because of who attends. Instead, these institutions exist within a complex web of relations that constantly define and redefine what it means to be elite; elite status is contingent on the varying institutional arrangements within which schools are embedded.

This brings us to the second challenge in thinking through transformations in elite schooling. That is, simply, that it is impossible to talk about transformations in the elite education without talking about broader transformations among the American elite. Thanks to the pioneering work of Thomas Piketty and his co-authors (Atkinson and Piketty 2007, 2010; Piketty 2014; Piketty and Saez 2003, 2006), this story is rather broadly known. But it requires some repeating. In this chapter I will first outline transformations in the American elite. I will then use those transformations to reflect upon this elite's relationship to elite schools more generally. For this second section, I will consider some of the social, cultural, economic, and intellectual aspects of this educational transformation. I will conclude by considering the implications of these two trends – changes in elites and elite schools – for understanding the United States.

Understanding the Transformation of the American Elite

The "problem of elite schooling" is more or less problematic depending upon the social context. The most important aspects of this context is inequality. For when resources are more inequitably distributed, then the rewards to the capital controlled or accessed through time spent at elite institutions is far greater.

When we think of inequality we think, almost reflexively, about poverty. Poverty is often harmful, sometimes deadly. And poverty is often the result of social processes and ascribed conditions, rather than individual level failures. Yet this observation points to an important point: poverty is not an aspect of the poor. It is a relationship between the poor and others in society. The character of that relationship is one of the central questions of social stratification. We can have either more or less inequality, and such inequality can be more or less durable across generations. When we consider these points we realize that inequality is not the study of poor people; it is the study of the relations between all people in society. And this leads us to think not just about the poor, but also the rich. When we study the rich, we see how they have been the engines of increasing inequality over roughly the last forty years. While most Americans have seen their wages stagnate, the rich have seen theirs increase rapidly (for a broad overview, see Khan forthcoming).

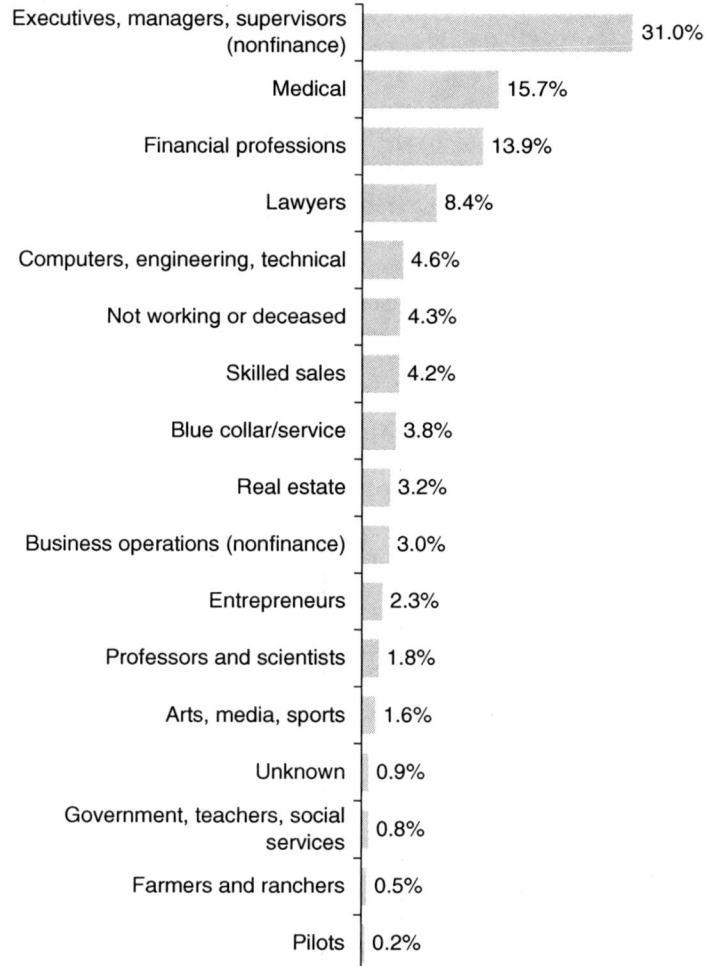

Figure 4.1 Professional composition of the 1 percent.

Source: Graph by Mother Jones (Gilson 2011), using data in Bakija *et al.* (2012).

First, let's get a sense of the trends. Economists Thomas Piketty and Emmanuel Saez have used tax return data to show just how much wealthier the top 1 percent (Figure 4.1) are today than they were 40 (or even 20 or 10) years ago (Piketty and Saez 2003, 2006). For our purposes, there are two basic trends to be gleaned from their work. First, while the top 10–1 percent have experienced some shifts in their incomes over the period, overall their percentage claim of the national income is roughly flat. By contrast, the experience of the 1 percent has been incredibly variable; they have earned between 9 and 24 percent of the total national income. Today the 1 percent are at near-historic highs in the amount of income they control: almost 25 percent (and if we were to look at wealth the story would be even more dramatic – they control some 40 percent of the national wealth).

Second, the 1 percent are where much of the action is; variables must vary to serve as the basis of an explanation. The 1 percent are where most of the historic variation lies, and as such they explain most of the changes in inequality in America. From 1913 to 1944 we have what Paul Krugman has called, "The Long Gilded Age" – a period of relatively high inequality where the rich seized a disproportionate amount of the national income. In the immediate post-war period, as social policies worked to provide broader educational opportunities and redistribute incomes through tax policy, the national income experienced a "great compression." We can think of this period (1945–1978) as "middle-class America" – a period where there were relatively low levels of inequality. Finally, starting in the late 1970s we see a dramatic change, "the great divergence," with the 1 percent beginning to pull away from the rest. The social contract of redistribution that emerged after World War II was broken and the 1 percent began to earn more and more (paying less and less in taxes). Today they have returned to their gilded-age levels, and America has become steadily more unequal. This is a major part of the shifting context of elite education: one where the wealthy have become wealthier, and the rest have been locked in place.

When looking at these wages, it's important for us to remember that the further up the wage distribution you go, the faster your wages grow. Catherine Rampell, writing for the Economix section of the *New York Times*, illustrated this point using 2011 data from the Tax Policy Center. She shows how the difference between wages of the 50th and 51st percentile of American households is rather small: $1,237 (those families make $42,327 and $43,564 a year, respectively). But the income differences between the 98th and 99th percentile is more than 100 times greater: $146,118 (those families make $369,435 and $506,553, respectively). The further up we go, the more and more dramatic this story becomes. So to be in the 99.5th percentile you must make $815,868; to be in the 99.9th percentile you need to make more than $1.25 million more, or, $2,075,574.

This has important implications for understanding the experiences of the rich and the rest in America. And yet again, this will be of consequence when we think about elite education. Try, for a moment, to put yourself in the position of the American elite. Let's say you're fortunate enough to be in the top 0.1 percent. If you look at someone slightly beneath you economically you find that your wages are growing much faster than theirs are. That is because wage growth is considerable among the elite, and the growth function is almost exponential. But that also has an important implication. The satisfaction of looking down is only met with the anxiety of looking up. That's because if you look at those above you, you see that those who make more money than you do are outpacing your wage gains at an even greater rate than you are outpacing the person beneath you. In short, for the elite the recent experience is one of more mobility and more wage growth than in the past. And this material experience is bound to a lived one of seeing movement all around you: growing wages, more new members who join your ranks because of wage work not capital rewards,[1] with distances between people growing every day. This is an experience of growth and movement – a vital economy. But if you're in the middle of the American wage distribution, you don't see this at all. What you see is a relative stagnation, all around. Your wages aren't growing, and overall, mobility is rather constrained.

Between 1993 and 2010, American incomes grew, on average, 13.8 percent. But yet again, this number is inflated by trends among the top 1 percent. During this period the 1 percent's incomes grew by 58 percent; the bottom 99 percent saw only 6.4 percent income growth. In short, the top 1 percent captured 52 percent of all national growth in this period. Yes, recessions have greater shocks upon the 1 percent, so losses tend to be concentrated within the group. But the speed of income growth seems to be accelerating. During the 2000–2002 recession, the rich experienced 57 percent of the total loss of income; in the recession of 2007–2009, they experienced considerably less of the shock: 49 percent. And during the recovery periods, the 1 percent have captured more and more of the growth. So in the Clinton expansion (1993–2000) they captured 45 percent of the growth; in the Bush expansion (2002–2007) this increased to 65 percent; most recently in the recovery of 2009–2010, the 1 percent has captured a staggering 93 percent of the income gains. This suggests that the challenges of the 1 percent – their capture of the national income – may be increasing.

How have the 1 percent been able to seize such a large share of the national income? Many (particularly economists) have argued that skill-biased technological change (SBTC) explains the wage growth of the rich (Berman *et al.* 1997; Card and DiNardo 2002); this is an explanation that weights educational differences heavily. Scholars suggest that technological innovations have created a new economy where (1) production has become more efficient, requiring fewer workers and (2) the returns to skill of those workers who have the relatively rare skills to take advantage of such technical change has thereby increased. The rich, therefore, will get richer while others are locked in place. However, considerable research has challenged this argument (DiPrete 2007; Fernandez 2001; Kristal and Cohen 2013). First, much of the decline in wages for workers is explained by de-unionization, and not SBTC. The loss of union jobs explains about one third of the increase in inequality over the last three decades (Western and Rosenfeld 2011).

Second, if SBTC were such an important force, why, in a global economy, would the returns to skill be so disproportionate in the United States? Other western nations have also experienced a relative growth of the fortunes of the rich, but in far less dramatic ways. Such cross national comparisons (Atkinson and Piketty 2010) show that such unbridled growth of the rich's wages is not an aspect of twenty-first century capitalism. For if it were, why is that the 1 percent in other capitalist nations haven't experienced the same dramatic degree of growth? Rather than a "natural effect of the market" such trends appear to be the result of both market and extra-market social relations.

For data reasons I tended to emphasize income in this piece. But it is important to remember that if we look at wealth the story is even more dramatic. As Ed Wolff has shown in his work,

> The top 1 percent of households classified by wealth owned 38 percent of all stocks in 2007, the top 10 percent owned 81 percent, and the top quintile held 91 percent. Moreover, 84 percent of all stocks were owned by households earning $75,000 or more and 92 percent by households with incomes of $50,000 or more.
>
> (1998: 36; see also 2002)

Perhaps the most dramatic way to see this is to look at the Gini coefficient. This value ranges from 0 to 1, with 0 meaning perfect equality and 1 meaning perfect inequality.

In 2009, the Gini coefficient in the United States was estimated at around 0.47; this makes the United States much less equal than nations like Sweden (0.23) or Canada (0.32), more equal than nations like Boswana (0.63) or Haiti (0.59), and about the same as nations like Uruguay and Cameroon. But if we were to look at the Gini coefficient by wealth instead of income, we would see something far more dramatic. In 2009, after the real-estate bubble burst and most Americans were left with declining home values – where most of their wealth was located – the wealth Gini coefficient was a staggering 0.865. In other words, the inequality described above is even more dramatic if we look at wealth rather than income; those who are already advantaged, the 1 percent, are perhaps even better off than the Piketty and Saez data show.

It seems incontrovertible that the rich today are far richer than those a generation ago. But we might ask, are they the children of the rich, or do they represent a new rich?[2] And as a "new group" are they constituting elite educational institutions anew? While the vast majority of Americans who go to college attend institutions that are not selective (meaning they accept almost everyone who applies), the elite, as I have tried to show again and again, inhabit a different world. But that world is not unified; the 1 percent are enormously varied. It's important to remember that there are large geographic differences in income distribution in the United States. So if you made $180,000 last year you would be in roughly the top 6 percent of American earners. But you would only be in the top 12 percent of those in Boston, whereas you'd be in the top 1 percent of those in Flint, Michigan. By contrast, to be in the 1 percent in Manhattan you'd need to make about $800,000 each year.

We should remember that the 1 percent is not an analytic category, but a political one. There is an enormous amount of variation within the 1 percent – in fact, there are far greater income differences *within* the 1 percent than there are between the 1 percent and the rest of the income distribution. Graph 1 gives us a sense of the professions that made up the 1 percent in 2010.[3] We see that they are a group that includes mostly executives and managers, but also doctors, lawyers, entrepreneurs, professors, scientists, farmers, arts and media professionals, and even pilots. One in five physicians in America is in the 1 percent. But this is deceptive. Because the further and further we move up the income distribution the scarcer and scarcer doctors become, and the more and more people we see working in finance and managerial positions. Scholars have estimated that since 1980 between 5.8 and 6.6 trillion dollars have been transferred to the finance sector from other sectors of the economy (Tomaskovic-Devey and Lin 2011). This tremendous wealth transfer has allowed for the growth of finance within the 1 percent, particularly as we move into the 0.1 and 0.01 percent.

As I have argued in previous work (Khan 2012a), while many scholars have pointed to a "new gilded age" our elites are also quite different than those in the past. Demographic data on this group is incredibly difficult to acquire (and perhaps unreliable). And so I am somewhat limited in revealing who the elite are. There are, however, a few things I can say. First, as noted earlier, today's elite are much wealthier than the elite of the last 65 years – present economic shocks not withstanding today's elite are wealthier than any elite we've seen since before the second world war (Atkinson and Piketty 2007). Second, elites seem to increasingly be engaged in the finance sector. Looking at the Forbes 400, we see that in 1982 oil and gas were the primary source of wealth of the richest 400 people in the world (making up 23 percent of the Forbes list). Finance was the primary source of wealth of only 9 percent of the world's richest. In contrast by 2007, those working in finance made up 27.3 percent of the Forbes list; oil and gas (along with 1982's other three top categories of manufacturing, real estate, and media/communications) dropped considerably to about 7 percent. This super-elite is also more international than 30 years ago and increasingly likely that such super-elites are "self-made" (Bernstein and Swan 2008). Such trends from a rather tiny sample have evidence in the broader literature as well, where there is evidence for the decline of dynastic wealth since the 1970s and the rise of the "self-made" elites (Edlund and Kopczuk 2009), and where elites are less likely to own capital and increasingly likely to rely upon earnings for their incomes (Piketty and Saez 2003). In brief we can say this about today's elite: they are less likely to have inherited their wealth than those a generation ago, more likely to work in finance, more likely to rely upon earnings than ownership of capital, more global, and more diverse geographically and racially (Domhoff and Zweigenhaft 1999). As we shall see, all of these observations influence (and are influenced by) elite educational institutions.

The cultural understandings of the rich has been a focus of my own work (Khan 2011). Of particular interest to me are the cultural rhetorics that have facilitated and accompanied the changing economic position of the elite: the rise of the tal-ented, deserving, meritorious individual. The culturally important shift in elite identity has been from being a "class" to a collection of individuals – the best and the brightest (Khan 2012b). That is, rather than identifying as a group which is constituted through a set of institutions (families, schools, clubs, a shared cultural-historical legacy), today's elites consider themselves as constituted by their individual talents. What groups them (in their minds) is the fact that they have worked hard and gotten ahead. And in embracing this rather than a class narra-tive, elites think of themselves as meritocrats. This too is enormously consequential for elite education, which I finally turn to now.

Changes in Elite Schools

More often than not, we imagine the past relative to the present. Take the Ivy League. These institutions seem like enduring pillars of elite life. To a degree they are; but such a view clouds as much as it reveals. While today these institutions are global powerhouses that are tremendously competitive, their recent past reveals something quite different. Not long ago these were mostly regional institutions, serving more locally constituted elites. And they were far from competitive. One needs only go back to 1990 to see a time when admissions rates to the University of Pennsylvania were almost 50 percent (in 2014 it is just under 10 percent). In the 1950s, Harvard University admitted 95 percent of applicants from the most elite boarding schools; today these boarding schools would be lucky if 20 percent of those who applied were admitted. The history of certain families and the history of certain elite institutions could not be told without one another. Indeed, elite institutions were the sinews of upper-class families, and vice versa. The rest were mostly absent, or if fortunate enough to attend, "just visiting."

Yet today, such schools have become distinctly more diverse. In 1951 blacks made up approximately 0.8 percent of the students at elite colleges. Today blacks make up about 8 percent of Ivy League students; the Columbia class of 2014 was 13 percent black – representative of the black population in the United States as a whole. Columbia University is now a "majority minority" institution, meaning half its students are non-white. Women today are outperforming men, creating a gender gap in college attendance in favor of women. Without question our elite educational institutions have become far more open racially and to women. This is a tremendous transformation, nothing short of a revolution.

This represents the ways in which elite schools have shifted from being a somewhat closed social clique to "something else." Part of this was initiated by elite schools themselves. Drawing on the work of Nicholas Lemann (2000), and as I've argued in my previous work, starting in the 1950s, schools designed new admissions systems to broaden their base, and participate in the diverse democracy that American was being. The SAT (an admissions test) is a prime example of this transformative impulse.[4]

Rather than accept students because they manifest a character that revealed good heritage, this new system would look beyond the trappings of society and reward people's inherent individual talents. When meritocracy began to make its way into college admissions, then dean of Harvard admissions, Wilbur Bender, worried, "Are there any good ways of identifying and measuring goodness, humanity, character, warmth, enthusiasm, responsibility, vitality, creativity, independence, heterosexuality, etc., etc., or should we care about these anyhow?" As Jerome Karabel has shown, many of these traits were used as proxies for elite status (2005).

Bender, the child of Mennonite parents from Goshen, Indiana, was no elite WASP. But he expressed concerns that echoed throughout the world of elite education in the 1950s and 1960s: what might happen to the elements of character that so marked the old American elite? Would the rise of the meritocracy mean the death of the old elite? With merit we seem to have stripped individuals of the old baggage of social ties and status and replaced it with personal attributes – hard work, discipline, native intelligence, and other forms of human capital that can be evaluated separate from the conditions of social life.

The impact of the adoption of this approach has led to rather contradictory outcomes. It has undercut nepotism. It has been used to promote the opening of schools to talented members of society who previously were excluded. But it has also been used to question policies like affirmative action that take into account factors other than performance on select technocratic instruments. It has been used to justify the increased wages of the already wealthy (as their skills are so valuable and irreplaceable). And it has obscured how outcomes are not simply a product of individual traits. This meritocracy of hard work and achievement has naturalized socially constituted distinctions, making differences in outcomes appear a product of who people are rather than a product of the conditions of their making. Though rich students overwhelmingly populate elite schools, today the explanation is not that they are the "right kind of kids" whose family ties are sufficient for them to belong. Instead, it is because they are more meritorious; it is certainly not because they are richer. Through looking at the rise of the meritocracy we can better understand the transformation of elite and thereby some of the workings of our contemporary inequality.

While elite private colleges send out press release after press release proclaiming how they are helping make college affordable to the average American, the reality of college is that it is a place dominated by the rich. Harvard's "middle income" is the richest 5 percent of our nation. This alone should tell us a lot about our elite educational institutions. While they look more open to us, this is in no small part because to us openness means diversity, and diversity means race. But class matters.

Though poor students experience a host of disadvantages – from lower-quality schools to difficult access to out-of-school enrichment programs to the absence of support when they falter – colleges are largely blind to such struggles, treating poorer students as if they were the same as rich ones. This is in stark contrast to students who are legacies (whose past family members attended the college), athletes, or members of a minority group (Espenshade and Radford 2009). Though students from these three groups are provided special consideration by colleges, increasing their chances of admission, poorer students are afforded no such luxury. They may claim otherwise, but colleges are truly "need blind" in the worst possible way. They are ambivalent to the disadvantages of poverty. The result is a clear class bias in college enrollments. College professors, looking at our classrooms, know this sad truth quite well. Put simply, lots of rich kids go to college. Few poor ones do. At the same time as elite institutions are looking different, the elite are moving further and further away from the rest.

Further, the economic differences between elite institutions and others are staggering. In the last seven years my own institution of Columbia raised over six billion dollars in endowment funds. Harvard expects to raise at least as much in the next five years. To put this in perspective, in a short period of time Harvard will likely raise twice as much as the entire endowment of the University of California at Berkeley. And so while we have seen shifts in populations drawn into elite schools, we also find that their fortunes have also been tied to those they are enmeshed with: the rich. As the rich have gotten fabulously richer, so too have the schools that service them.

The transformation of elite schools is both inspiring in terms of its opening, and yet disturbing in terms of the crippling cultural logics it seems to embrace. In effect, the state transfers billions of dollars per year to elite private schools. At the same time, public school budgets have been cut considerably, and the costs of school are being steadily transferred from the state to students and their families. While elite institutions have been able to continually draw upon the state for support, schools that were once supported by the state are finding their budgets eviscerated. Yet again, we see how the dynamics experienced by the elite are considerably different than those experienced by the rest.

Yet the cultural logic of professor salaries, state funding, or admissions processes fall into a broader conceptualizing within elite schools of "deservingness." This is a kind of market logic that goes something like this: the best students are admitted now, not just the children of a small, stagnant regional elite. The best faculty are recruited, retained, rewarded, and extolled. Competing for funding, the strongest proposals win, and elite institutions are rewarded for their academic quality. The logic is not tradition, history, and social and cultural connectedness. Instead, it is competition, openness, and excellence. As Elizabeth Berman (2012) has argued in her recent book, universities (especially their research arms) have moved from holding themselves apart from commerce and markets, to fully embracing it (particularly in the sciences). This is especially pronounced in elite educational institutions, who have moved further away from the arms of elite families and closer to those of the market.

Implications for Understanding America

The implications of my argument are that elite educational institutions have not been bastions of independent thought, helping them confront economic and cultural logics of the marketplace. Instead, they have been part of a broad cultural transformation in America. Many of us within these institutions may have attempted to swim against this tide, but its power to carry is tremendous. Perhaps the most important part of the transformation in elites in America has been just how wealthy the wealthy have become. The rich are much richer today than they were a generation ago. So too is Harvard. In 1990 its endowment was $4.7 billion; 25 years later and it hovers around $35 billion.

Elite schools have made considerable strides in helping unravel the socially closed and culturally narrow elite. They have done so by, in part, no longer serving as the training ground of regional upper classes. The groups served are now meant to reflect a new world order; the elite are no longer local, but global. And their encounters with "others" within our democratic world are reflected. So too is the sense that the represent not a class, but excellence. But the consequences have not been equality, nor has it meant that these institutions serve as model social communities. Instead, such schools are better understood as social mirrors of our broader dynamics. And those are ones wherein liberal principles are increasingly dominant. The kind of liberalism we see is one tied more closely to the importance of the individual rather than the social connections of the group. While the rise of the concept of the individual was, within our intellectual history, tied to that of the social contract, today it seems we have managed to divorce these notions.

Elites and the educational institutions that serve them have gone from seeing themselves as part of a coherent group, a kind class with particular histories and tastes, to a collection of the most talented and hardest working of our nation. They look more diverse, by which I mean that they now include members they formerly excluded. And such a transformation is far more than window dressing. Yet to act as if the world is flat, when in fact there are huge differentials in investments in children is to be dishonest. Many elite children have at least a million dollars spent on their development – done through parental investments via markets. Most other children have one-tenth that investment. And yet elite institutions pretend as if these students are the same.

If I were to talk about a culture of the elite and elite educational institutions, I would talk about a culture of "individual self-cultivation."[5] Society has recessed in the minds of the elite and the institutions that serve them; if anything, "society" is a producer social problems. What society did was create the biases of old institutions – racism, sexism, exclusion. The resulting view is one where society must be as benign as possible, sitting in the background as we play out our lives in a flat world. And the result of such a stance is a new efficiency, the market. And so we have a seemingly ingenious move. We can blame social problems on the processes whereby we thought in terms of collectivities. With such barriers removed, market equality can take over. We live the results of this triumph today, and it has been a world with less equality, less mobility, and a more empowered 1 percent.

Meritocracy is a social arrangement like any other: it is a loose set of rules that can be adapted in order to obscure advantages, all the while justifying them on the basis of shared values. Markets allow the 1 percent to limit investments in all by undermining public goods and shared, socialized resource allocations. This allows them to increase their own advantage by deploying their economic spoils in markets; they receive returns to these investments, and those without resources to invest are left behind. The result is less equality and more immobility. The 1 percent's story about the triumph of the individual with diverse talents is a myth. In suggesting that it is their work and not their wealth, that it is their talents and not their lineage, elites effectively blame inequality on those whom our democratic promise has failed. Rather than stem the tide of such a transformation, elite educational institutions seem to be a part of it.

Notes

1 There has been more mobility into the elite than among other groups; indeed, today there is more elite mobility than there was in the 1960s. This means that there are more "new elite" among the elite than there once were. This point comes from and is more fully developed in Khan (forthcoming).
2 By this I mean both that the conditions of the rich today are different than those of the past, and they are thereby "new," but also that there are more new members among the rich than there were a generation ago.
3 Another valuable interactive graphic based upon the same data can be found online at: http://www.nytimes.com/packages/html/newsgraphics/2012/0115-one-percent-occupations/index.html
4 The following three paragraphs draw extensively on my previous work (Khan 2011).
5 The next paragraphs draw extensively on Khan (2012b).

References

Atkinson, A.B. and Piketty, T. (2007) *Top Incomes over the 20th Century*. Oxford: Oxford University Press.

Atkinson, A.B. and Piketty, T. (2010) *Top Incomes in Global Perspective*. Oxford: Oxford University Press.

Bakija, J., Cole, A., and Heim, B.T. (2012) *Jobs and Income Growth of Top Earners and the Causes of Changing Income Inequality: Evidence from US Tax Return Data*. Available at: http://web.williams.edu/Economics/wp/BakijaColeHeimJobsIncomeGrowthTopEarners.pdf

Berman, E.P. (2012) *Creating the Market University: How Academic Science Became an Economic Engine*. Princeton, NJ: Princeton University Press.

Berman, E., Bound, J., and Machin, S. (1997) *Implications of Skill-Biased Technological Change: International Evidence.* No. w6166. National Bureau of Economic Research.

Bernstein, P.W. and Swan, A. (eds) (2008) *All the Money in the World: How the Forbes 400 Make – and Spend – Their Fortunes.* New York: Random House.

Card, D. and DiNardo, J.E. (2002) *Skill Biased Technological Change and Rising Wage Inequality: Some Problems and Puzzles.* No. w8769. National Bureau of Economic Research.

DiPrete, T.A. (2007) "What has sociology to contribute to the study of inequality trends? A historical and comparative perspective," *American Behavioral Scientist,* 50(5), 603–618.

Domhoff, G.W. and Zweigenhaft, R. (1999) *Diversity in the Power Elite.* New Haven, CT: Yale University Press.

Edlund, L. and Kopczuk, W. (2009) "Women, wealth, and mobility," *American Economic Review,* 99(1), 146–178.

Espenshade, T. and Randford, A. (2009) *No Longer Separate, not yet Equal.* Princeton, NJ: Princeton University Press.

Fernandez, R.M. (2001) "Skill-biased technological change and wage inequality: Evidence from a plant retooling 1," *American Journal of Sociology,* 107(2), 273–320.

Gilson, D. (2011) "Charts: Who are the 1 percent?" *Mother Jones,* Oct 10, available at http://www.motherjones.com/mojo/2011/10/one-percent-income-inequality-OWS

Karabel, J. (2005) *The Chosen: The Hidden History of Admission and Exclusion at Harvard, Yale, and Princeton.* Boston, MA: Houghton Mifflin.

Khan, S.R. (2011) *Privilege: The Making of an Adolescent Elite at St. Paul's School,* Princeton, NJ: Princeton University Press.

Khan, S.R. (2012a) "The sociology of elites," *Annual Review of Sociology,* 38, 361–377.

Khan, S.R. (2012b) "Elite identities," *Identities,* 19(4), 477–484.

Khan, S.R. (Forthcoming) "The counter-cyclical character of the elite," *Research in the Sociology of Organizations,* 38.

Kristal, T. and Cohen, Y. (2013) "The causes of rising wage inequality: What do computerization and fading pay-setting institutions do?," *SSRN,* available at http://papers.ssrn.com/sol3/papers.cfm?abstract_id=2424144

Lemann, N. (2000) *The Big Test: The Secret History of the American Meritocracy.* New York: Macmillan.

Massey, D.S. and Denton, N.A. (1993) *American Apartheid: Segregation and the Making of the Underclass.* Cambridge, MA: Harvard University Press.

Piketty, T. (2014) *Capital in the Twenty-first Century.* Trans. Arthur Goldhammer. Cambridge, MA: Harvard University Press.

Piketty, T. and Saez, E. (2003) "Income inequality in the United States, 1913–1998," *Quarterly Journal of Economics,* 118, 1–39.

Piketty, T. and Saez, E. (2006) "The evolution of top incomes: A historical and international perspective," *American Economic Review,* 96(2), 200–205.

Tomaskovic-Devey, D. and Lin, K-H. (2011) "Economic rents and the financialization of the US economy," *American Sociological Review,* 76, 538–559.

Western, B. and Rosenfeld, J. (2011) "Unions, norms, and the rise in American earnings inequality," *American Sociological Review,* 76, 513–537.

Wolff, E. (1998) "Recent trends in the size distribution of household wealth," *Journal of Economic Perspectives,* 12(3), 131–150.

Wolff, E. (2002) *Top Heavy: A Study of Increasing Inequality of Wealth in America.* New York: New Press.

5 The Changing Strategies of Social Closure in Elite Education in Brazil[1]

Ana Maria F. Almeida

In any contemporary industrial society, school credentials are powerful indicators of an individual's worth and instruments of access to privileged positions. In Brazil, a country where income inequality is extremely severe, income gains associated to schooling are among the highest in the world, including several of Brazil's Latin American neighbors (OECD 2013). Among all school credentials, college degrees are specially valued. They had already granted a distinctive mark to the agrarian elite that occupied leading positions in the complex state bureaucracy from colonial times through the first decades of the twentieth century. With the intensification of industrialization after World War II and the emergence of a modern labor market, college degrees have become critical to achieving the new upper-level positions.

Processes of social closure existing since colonial times had made it difficult for the middle groups to obtain a college degree, generating highly politicized disputes around the issue of access to higher education in the late 1960s. As demonstrators took to the streets, a reform was introduced that allowed for an expansion of tertiary education, mostly through a newly created *for-profit* sector (Sampaio 2000). This did not substantially change the ways in which the most prestigious slots in the higher education system ended up being reserved to the wealthier families. When the competition for college degrees began to increase again in the mid-1990s, the ensuing dissatisfactions triggered a number of public policies responses.

This chapter examines both the changes brought about by these policy responses and the ways in which Brazilian elite groups have adapted to them, with a focus on the changing strategies of social closure of these elites. The chapter is based on research that examines the transformations in the provision of higher education and in the social origin of its students, as well as the changes in the elite primary and secondary education, during the 2000s. It draws on official statistics, documents, and data produced by the educational institutions, and interviews with parents.

The first section presents the traditional mode of elite education in Brazil, pointing out its strong dependence on the economic resources of the families. The second section shows how this model of elite production and reproduction came to be challenged, in light of two factors: (a) the slower increase in enrollment supply in public universities, in relation to both the total population growth and the larger proportion of students who graduated from high school; and (b) the diffusion of democratic values of equality of opportunities and rights for African descendants and native Brazilians. The third section discusses the effects of these policies on the social composition of the student body of the most prestigious public universities and investigates how elite groups seem to be adapting to those policies and to their expected consequences. It focuses on the case of the metropolitan area of São Paulo, the most populous and richest state in the country.

Segmentation of the Educational System and Social Reproduction

In the history of Brazilian education, the growth of enrollment in higher learning education has been very slow, just as the process of diffusion of basic schooling was very slow. At least until the 1940s, education and, in particular, long-duration education was reserved for the affluent classes.

The fast-paced industrialization and urbanization after World War II did not substantially alter this picture. In 1965, the first year after the military coup, the national participation rate in higher education was 2 percent (World Bank 2000). This situation frustrated the aspirations of the urban middle groups, not least because it prevented them from filling the newly emerging slots in the labor market higher echelons. This led to an unprecedented politicization of the debate about access to college education. In the late 1960s, despite the military dictatorship, mobilized middle-class groups marched on the streets of large cities to demand an increase in enrollment at the public universities. The government repressed the demonstrations, but responded to the demands, both by enlarging the network of public universities and, to a much larger degree, by stimulating the growth of for-profit private higher education through fiscal incentives. The enrollment ratio had reached 11 percent of the standard age group in 1975 (World Bank 2000).

While allowing for some diversification of the elites, due to the gradual incorporation of fractions of the urban middle classes, this expansion of participation instituted a *de facto* social segmentation of the Brazilian higher education system, with students distributed among institutions and majors according to their social origin.[2] Students whose families had more economic and relevant cultural resources were admitted into the most selective majors of the most prestigious institutions, a set comprising the public universities, which are free of charge, and some Catholic universities and professional schools maintained by non-profit foundations, which were in both cases relatively expensive.[3]

The students excluded from this segment of the system enrolled in the least selective majors of the public universities or in another set of institutions, consisting of private, for-profit organizations. The majority of these organizations admitted students through less competitive examinations and offered only less prestigious degrees.

By the early 1980s, this social segmentation of higher education, together with the exclusion of the majority of the population from any higher education whatsoever, was fully in place (and it persists until today, although with some changes, as discussed below). It resulted mainly from another segmentation, created at the lower levels of the educational system, where the fast expansion and diversification of the student body has not been accompanied by the investment needed for the public schools to continue performing well. In the 1970s, these schools dealt with a growing number of students, many of whom had illiterate parents. They also faced a shortage of trained teachers and of adequate facilities. The most privileged groups, traditionally inclined to having their children educated at private elementary and secondary schools, were little affected by this transformation of the public schools. Such was not the case of the middle-class groups. Those families who could afford it, often through great effort and sacrifice (Almeida 2009), opted for traditional Catholic schools or secular private ones – and in the process contributed to making public primary and secondary education even less valued than it was already becoming. This helped consolidate a quite competitive market for private schools, where a group of economically and academically very selective schools distinguished themselves by their capacity to prepare for the demanding entry examinations of the most prestigious – and mostly public, free of charge – institutions of higher learning and the most prestigious majors therein. Other members of the middle groups, with fewer economic resources, but knowledgeable about the educational system, found shelter in a small number of public vocational high schools that offered, together with their vocational training, a general education that was adequate enough to allow a considerable number of their students to enter the public universities (Arco Neto 2011).

This situation would be challenged only in the mid-1990s. In a context of (a) growing mobilization for social rights, (b) substantial increase in the number of high-school graduates, and (c) insufficient supply of places in the higher learning institutions, especially the public ones, the appropriation of the most valued institutions and majors by the elites became one of the symbols of social inequality in Brazil and was denounced as such by social activists, most notably the Black movement, in their interaction with members of the Parliament and journalists.

Reproduction at Risk: Social Inclusion in Higher Learning

The number of college applications increased significantly during the 1990s. The result was a considerable intensification of the competition for places in the public institutions of higher learning, which were not only more prestigious, but also free. The ratio of applicants per freshman place in these institutions grew from 8.9 in 1995 to 9.7 in 2000 (INEP 2002). This reinforced the need for a good preparation for the entry examinations, which could only be found in private primary and secondary schools or in the small segment of public vocational high schools, with the latter, too, becoming the object of increasing demand.

The social selection at the most prestigious universities thus became even more noticeable. In the case of the state of São Paulo, for example, in 2000, 83 percent of all the high-school students in the state were enrolled in public schools, but only 22.2 percent and 30.7 percent respectively of the students at the University of São Paulo and University of Campinas had come from public high schools. This proportion was even smaller in the most selective majors of these two universities, such as Medicine (5.3 percent and 7.3 percent), Mechanical Engineering (6.0 percent and 4.8 percent), and Economics (6.8 percent and 4.3 percent) (FUVEST 2001, COMVEST 2001).

The groups that were hit the hardest by the increasing competition for admission into higher education were the ascending middle-class sectors who lacked the necessary economic resources to pay for expensive private elementary and secondary schools and who faced intense competition for places in the public vocational high schools that would prepare their children sufficiently well for the public universities' exams. It did not take long for these groups to begin to see access to public higher education as a political matter.

Consisting of various organizations, the Black movement was the first organized group to treat the social closure of the most prestigious segment of the educational system as a form of discrimination (Guimarães 2003). It campaigned for affirmative action in the labor market and in public higher education admission policy (Guimarães 2013; Schwartzman and Silva 2012).

During the 2000s, several affirmative action programs were gradually implemented by the government at the federal and state levels and by some public universities. For reasons yet to be properly investigated, the majority of them had the quota format (Feres Jr. *et al.* 2011), reserving freshman places for students from public high schools, African descendents, Native Brazilians, and, more recently, students with physical disabilities. The most important exception has been the state of São Paulo. Instead of quotas, other affirmative actions have been adopted by its three state universities, which include the above-mentioned University of São Paulo and University of Campinas, the two most prestigious universities in the country.

A crucial policy development was a law approved by the Federal Senate in 2012, soon after the Supreme Court of Justice decided, by unanimous vote, that the already-implemented quota programs were constitutional. This law reserves 50 percent of the freshman places in each major at each federal institution for students who come from public high schools. Half of these reserved seats are designated for students whose families have a per capita income no greater than 1.5 times the minimum wage (US$490.00 in May 2014). In addition, the reserved seats must be assigned to self-declared Blacks and Native Brazilians in a proportion no less than the proportion that these groups represent in the total population of the state where the federal university is located. There is a minimum speed at which these rules must be introduced, and by 2016 they must be fully implemented.

In addition to quotas, the federal government has taken at least three other sets of measures to facilitate access to higher education by less advantaged students and/or to prevent student drop out. First, there have been investments to increase enrollment in federal universities: new universities were created; in addition, the existing ones received funds to expand, on the proviso that they introduce "mechanisms of social inclusion in order to ensure the equality of opportunities of access to, and permanence in, the public university to all citizens" (Brasil 2007). This program was instrumental in expanding the quota program at the federal universities in the second half of that decade.

The second set of measures was aimed at the less advantaged students already enrolled at the public universities. In order to reduce their high drop-out rate, the federal government has expanded student aid. In addition, the increase in under-graduate research scholarships has also contributed to this end, although this program is not restricted to poor students (Villas Boas 2003).

The third set of measures is intended to make it easier for the poorer groups to enter the (predominantly for-profit) private higher education institutions. The fed-eral government has created a large program of fiscal benefits for these private organizations in exchange for full or partial tuition waivers for low-income students from public high schools, with places reserved for Blacks and native Brazilians. In 2013, 84 percent of the total beneficiaries identified themselves as Blacks (*pretos* or *pardos*), while 74 percent attended evening classes (Brasil 2012).[4] Students benefited by this program can also apply for student aid in order to cover for other educational expenses – books, lab materials, etc. Moreover, the government has altered the fed-eral program of student loans, targeting lower income students and reducing interest rates, while, at the same time, extending the payback period. Other types of student loans have been created by municipal and state governments, as well as by some private universities. These measures represented an unprecedented incentive to the expansion of the private higher education sector, which, by 2011, already responded for 73 percent of the total enrollment in higher learning in the country (Brasil 2012).

Enrollment in higher education has increased considerably in the 2000s, in both the public and the private sectors, but in absolute terms, much more in the latter than in the former. Many less advantaged candidates focus on the private sector and do not even apply for admission to the public universities, which have more restrictive entry examinations. Even without this additional pressure and despite the recent expansion of the public sector, the ratio of applicants per place in the freshman classes of this sector continues to rise – it was 14, in 2011 (INEP 2012).

In conclusion, some important changes are in place. University degrees are becoming less rare. In addition, because of the gradual implementation of the quota policies, the public universities – which include the vast majority of the top universities in the country – and the most valued majors therein are becoming less accessible to the elites and (amid the growing presence of the quota beneficiaries) tend also to become less attractive to them.

Elite Education: The Persistence of Old Enclaves, and the Creation of New Ones

The new policy landscape sketched in the previous section poses a challenge to the most privileged groups in Brazilian society, if they want to continue enjoying the benefits of an elite education. Focusing on the case of the metropolitan area of São Paulo, this section takes a closer look at the social segmentation of the educational system in the last decade, as well as some of the strategies that the elite groups are adopting in response to their changing situation.

During the 2000s, the expansion of the public university sector in the São Paulo metropolitan area occurred mainly through the creation of the Federal University of the ABC, and of new campuses of two previously existing universities, namely, the Federal University of São Paulo and the state-owned University of São Paulo.

The new campuses created in working-class neighborhoods offer most of the less valued majors, while the new departments providing more prestigious majors are concentrated in the campuses created in non-traditional rising middle-class neighborhoods. At least for now, the elite groups do not seem to have been attracted to these newly created units, and continue to choose, as far as the public-university system is concerned, its old, high-status campus, located in more established neighborhoods of São Paulo city.

In a metropolis with severe problems of urban mobility, the association between the prestige of the neighborhoods and the prestige of the majors in these new campuses has amplified the segmentation within the public sector of higher education, increasing the distance between the students of the most valued majors and the others (Almeida and Ernica, forthcoming).

Among the private institutions, the gap between the ones that cater to students from the most privileged groups and those who do not has also grown, although for different reasons. The enlargement of this sector was generalized, a trend that can also be found in other countries (UNESCO 2009). However, the pattern of expansion varied with the type of institution. On the one hand, there has been, in working-class neighborhoods, a multiplication of institutions that charge strikingly low tuition fees and admit a substantial proportion of students benefiting from the federal government's program of tuition waivers and fiscal incentives. In contrast, other institutions, located in the most affluent neighborhoods of the city, increased their tuition fees or kept them at high levels, and either refrained from joining this program or relegated its students to their least valued majors.[5]

Within the latter group, there are some institutions with a solid academic reputation, particularly two not-for-profit ones that offer degrees in the fields of economics, business and public administration, and, in one case, law. They compete for the most affluent students on an equal footing with the public universities, because their faculty members have degrees from the most prestigious masters' and PhD's programs in Brazil and, not infrequently, abroad.[6] In turn, they have been able to hire these academics not only by offering good salaries, but also by supporting research, which is virtually non-existent in the vast majority of the for-profit, private sector.

Other private institutions have a reputation for social selectivity. Being less selective in academic terms, they have become an alternative for students from wealthy families headed by local professionals and businessmen. They offer both traditional degrees, like economics, engineering, and architecture, and non-traditional ones, such as fashion, cultural production, and graphic design; there are no equivalents in public research universities.

All these (academically and/or socially) elite private institutions of higher learning provide their students with the opportunity of pursuing part of their education in foreign institutions in North America, Europe, Asia or Latin America, under either a joint-degree program or an exchange one. This institutionalized opportunity of international circulation contributes to increasing the prestige of the degrees offered by these institutions (Saint Martin and Gheorghiu 1992).[7]

An increase in *internationalization* has also marked elite education up to the high-school level, not only in São Paulo, but also in some other parts of the country (Aguiar and Nogueira 2012). This deserves a more detailed discussion.

International schools are not a new phenomenon in São Paulo city. Traditionally, they served mainly the families of professionals working for multinational companies and, to a lesser extent, Brazilian families who kept a strong connection with the school's country of origin.

The growing interest of Brazilian families has contributed to their considerable increase in size. As of 2014, there are 13 international schools in São Paulo. In the two schools about which it was possible to obtain this kind of data, both American, the number of students increased approximately 40 percent between 2008 and 2013. The list of colleges and universities where the high-school graduates in those schools enrolled in the last four years shows that a significant proportion of them go abroad, mostly to the United States and a few other developed countries. Others attend the city's most selective private institutions of higher learning, and only a minority goes to public universities in the state of São Paulo.

In addition to the growth of international schools, a second path toward internationalization has been the establishment, in 2008, of an agreement between six traditional high schools in São Paulo and an American university, so that the interested students can, at an extra charge, attend additional classes in their own schools – in English – in order to fulfill the requirements of the American curriculum and thus obtain a double certificate. The number of Brazilian schools participating in this program is now 54, throughout the country.

Third, the participation of schools located in São Paulo in the International Baccalaureate (IB) has also increased in recent years, although the number of high schools that have adopted the IB – eight – is still relatively small. Most of them are international schools trying to improve the curriculum and, at the same time, reinforce their students' chances of being accepted in selective universities abroad. As an admission officer of a North American university explained to a group of students of an international school when discussing admissions criteria, a good performance in IB is highly valued, because the program is standardized and demanding.

The three internationalization strategies mentioned so far – international schools, an agreement with an international high school, and the IB – have in common the partial or complete adoption of the standard curriculum of a foreign country or, in the IB case, of an international organization. Two other alternatives have presented themselves as well.

One takes place in seven out of the ten top-scoring São Paulo high schools at the National Examination of High-School Education (ENEM). In addition to their demanding regular training, these schools have started to offer various types of internationalization opportunities, such as participation in World Model United Nations, advanced summer programs in leading American Universities, specialized language courses in foreign countries, and participation in national and international science Olympiads (in math, physics, astrophysics, etc.). The endeavor is visibly geared toward the accumulation of evidence of academic merit that can be useful in the selection process of North American universities, and is supplemented by the provision of counseling services for students interested in applying to these universities. There are indications that these efforts have been successful. In recent years, the advertising material of at least two of these high schools have highlighted the admittance of some of their students into prestigious North American universities, alongside those who passed the most competitive entry examinations of the public universities in São Paulo.

Lastly, the fifth strategy that privileged families have pursued in search of internationalization is to enroll their children in private bilingual schools. These are schools that follow the Brazilian curriculum, but teach part of it in a foreign language. Most often the second language is English, but in some schools it is Italian, Spanish, German, or Japanese. In many cases, the bilingual program includes very young children, sometimes even babies. The first school of this type was created in the city in 1981. The lack of official statistics makes it difficult to evaluate their growth. According to the data gathered by the (national) Organization of Bilingual Schools, there were 72 schools of this type in the city of São Paulo in 2012.

In light of the adoption of all these internationalization strategies, it is perhaps not surprising that the growth in the number of Brazilians pursuing a full undergraduate degree in the United States was, between 2012 and 2013, approximately 10 percent, the second highest rate in Latin America, after Chile (Open Doors 2013).

This institutional supply of what some authors have termed "international capital" is also segmented along economic lines. The international schools are extremely expensive by Brazilian standards, even more so when it comes to the IB. The Brazilian schools that offer the above-mentioned internationalization experiences are less expensive. With rare exceptions, however, they are not more expensive than the top-scoring elite high schools where internationalization opportunities are not given so much emphasis. This indicates that non-economic cleavages, probably related to differences among various class fractions, also permeate the elite segment of the educational system.

Concluding Remarks

As far as education is concerned, the reproduction of elite groups in Brazil has been, for several decades, based on a threefold process of social closure: the construction of enclaves in relatively expensive private primary and secondary schools, in the departments offering the most selective majors of the public universities, free of charge, and in an extremely small number of private, not-for-profit institutions of higher education, which are very selective in academic or in economic terms. In all these cases, there is a segregation that ultimately has a strong economic character – even in the public universities, from which low-income children, who have attended public schools at the primary and secondary levels (if they did go to any high school at all), are usually barred.

Challenging this situation became more frequent after the fall of the military regime, with the process of redemocratization and the ensuing reorganization and strengthening of social movements. In reaction to popular demand for a more democratic access to tertiary education, several affirmative action programs have been gradually introduced since 2000, especially in the form of quotas. At the same time, the federal government has invested in the expansion of the public-university system and in facilitating the access of poorer students to private colleges and universities, mostly for-profit.

These policies signal important changes in the face of Brazilian higher education. College degrees are becoming more common; more importantly to the elites, many of the spaces that have been in practice reserved for them in the public universities are under threat, especially because of the 2012 federal law of quotas in those universities.

In the case of primary and secondary education, elite families have recently shown a growing interest not merely in internationalization in general, but in the internationalization of the school experiences of their children. How to explain this phenomenon? In a somewhat different context, various studies stress the intensification of international circulation and the lower costs of traveling abroad (Nogueira and Aguiar 2008; Aguiar and Nogueira 2012). The synchrony between the greater commercial openness of the country since the early 1990s and the growth in the supply of international opportunities through schools supports this interpretation. So does the discourse of parents, students, teachers, and human resources officers in interviews, although elite families are not seeking only the acquisition of linguistic competence. As Nogueira and Aguiar (2008) have shown, these families are interested in deepening the exposure of their children to other cultures, in an attempt to ensure the "early incorporation … of intellectual and moral dispositions" required to transform their sons and daughters into "citizens of the world." In turn, the families interviewed for the present research have expressed their interest in providing their children with "the best education" or "the most interesting education." They refer to the local schools and universities as "stuck in time" and "more of the same."

This chapter attempts to contribute to this line of argument by suggesting an additional factor. The movement toward internationalization may also be seen as part of a set of new strategies of social closure deployed by the traditional elites and ascending middle classes, in response, at least since 2000, to the gradual implementation of affirmative actions in the public universities and other measures to democratize access to higher education. Internationalization, especially when accompanied by some form of certification, represents an alternative to university experiences that are increasingly becoming less distinctive and maybe too ordinary in the eyes of the elite.

Notes

1 This research was supported by the National Council for Scientific and Technological Development (CNPq) and the São Paulo State Research Foundation (FAPESP).
2 The notion of segmentation used here is borrowed from the work of Fritz Ringer to designate "the subdivision of educational systems into parallel schools or programs that differ both in their curriculum and in the social origins of their students" (Ringer 1989: 53). As the author shows, this notion is particularly useful when taking into account the social roles associated with the different kinds of education.

3 In Brazil, students have to choose a major by the time they apply to college. They are accepted or rejected in comparison with other candidates for the same major.
4 Public and private universities in Brazil offer full degrees in evening courses. Although developing the same curriculum and, in the case of public universities, being taught by the same faculty of the so-called "integral" courses that take place during the day, these degrees are usually less academically competitive and socially selective.
5 None of the four most prestigious private institutions in the city of São Paulo adhered to this program. Three of them give financial aid to public-school graduates who have passed their entry examination.
6 According to Pohlmann and Valarini (2013), about half of the Brazilian CEOs of the 100 largest industrial firms in Brazil hold a degree from this type of private institutions, while the other half graduated at a public university.
7 A very large program to promote the internationalization of undergraduate students has been recently implemented by the federal government. The public universities owned by the state of São Paulo have taken other iniciatives. In the case of graduate training, the federal government has been sending students to pursue part or all of their degrees abroad since the 1950s (Almeida *et al.* 2004).

References

Aguiar, A. and Nogueira, M.A. (2012) "Internationalisation strategies of Brazilian private schools," *International Studies in Sociology of Education*, 22: 353–368.
Almeida, A.M.F. (2009) *A escola dos dirigentes paulistas*, Belo Horizonte: Argumentum.
Almeida, A.M.F., Canedo, L., Garcia, A., and Bittencourt, A.B. (eds) (2004) *Circulação Internacional e Formação Intelectual das Elites Brasileiras*, Campinas: Editora da Unicamp.
Almeida, A.M.F. and Ernica, M. (forthcoming) "Segmentation in Brazilian higher education," in *Higher Education: Access and Social Inclusion*, Bingley, UK: Emerald.
Arco Neto, N.B. (2011) *Esforço e Vocação*, unpublished dissertation, Universidade de São Paulo.
Brasil, Ministério da Educação (2007) REUNI – Reestruturação e Expansão das Universidades Federais: Diretrizes Gerais. Online. Available at http://portal.mec.gov.br/sesu/arquivos/pdf/diretrizesreuni.pdf (accessed 15 March 2014).
Brasil, Ministério da Educação (2012) ProUni – Representações Gráficas. Online. Available at http://prouniportal.mec.gov.br/index.php?option=com_content&view=article&id=13 6:representas-grcas&catid=26:dados-e-estaticas&Itemid=147 (accessed 20 March 2014).
COMVEST (2001) *Estatísticas do Vestibular*. Online. Available at http://www.comvest. unicamp.br/estatisticas/numeros.html (accessed 23 March 2014).
Feres Júnior, J., Daflon, V., and Campos, L.A. (2011), A ação afirmativa no ensino superior brasileiro – (GEMAA), IESP-UERJ. Online. Available at http://gemaa.iesp.uerj.br/publicacoes/levantamento/levantamento3.html (accessed 25 March 2014).
FUVEST (2001) *Estatísticas do Vestibular*. In: http://www.fuvest.br/vest2000/estat/estat.stm
Guimarães, A.S.A. (2003) "Acesso de Negros às Universidades Públicas," *Cadernos de Pesquisa*, 118: 247–268.
Guimarães, A.S.A. (2013) "Brasil, 1996–2012: anotações para uma sociologia politica da adoção de cotas no ensino superior public," Comunicação apresentada no 546 *AFR Panel: Quotas in Brazilian Universities: History and Current Challenges* – Latin American Studies Association, Washington. Online. Available at http://www.fflch.usp.br/sociologia/asag/Notas%20para%20uma%20sociologia%20politica%20da%20adocao%20de%20cotas%20no%20ensino%20superior.pdf (accessed 10 March 2014).
INEP (2002) Sinopse estatística da educação superior – 2001. Online. Available at http://portal.inep.gov.br/superior-censosuperior-sinopse (accessed 19 March 2014)

INEP (2012) Sinopse estatística da educação superior – 2011. Online. Available at http://portal.inep.gov.br/superior-censosuperior-sinopse (accessed 24 March 2014).

Nogueira, M.A. and Aguiar, A. (2008), "La formation des élites et l'internationalisation des études: peut-on parler d'une "bonne volonté internationale?," *Education et Sociétés*, 1(21): 105–119.

OECD (2013) *Education at a Glance 2013: OECD Indicators*, OECD Publishing. Online. Available at http://dx.doi.org/10.1787/eag-2013-en (accessed 2 April 2014).

Open Doors (2013) *Report on International Educational Exchange*. Online. Institute of International Education. Available at http://www.iie.org/Research-and-Publications/Open-Doors (accessed 29 March 2014).

Pohlmann, M. and Valarini, E. (2013), "Elite econômica no Brasil: discussões acerca da internacionalização da carreira de executivos brasileiros," *Revista de Sociologia e Política*, 21(47): 39–53.

Ringer, F. (1989) "On segmentation in modern European educational systems: the case of French secondary education, 1865–1920," in Muller, D.K., Ringer, F., and Simon, B. *The Rise of the Modern Educational System*, Paris/Cambridge: Maison des Sciences de l'Homme/University of Cambridge Press.

Saint Martin, M. and Gheorghiu, M. (1992) *Les institutions de formation des cadres dirigeants: études comparées*, Paris: Maison des Sciences de l'Homme.

Sampaio, H. (2000) *O Ensino Superior no Brasil – o setor privado*, São Paulo: Hucitec/Fapesp.

Schwartzman, L. and Silva, G.D. (2012) "Unexpected narratives from multicultural policies: translations of affirmative action in Brazil," *Latin American and Caribbean Ethnic Studies*, 7: 31–48.

UNESCO (2009) *Trends in Global Higher Education: Tracking an Academic Revolution*, Paris: UNESCO.

Villas Boas, G. (2003) "Currículo, iniciação científica e evasão de estudantes de ciências sociais," *Tempo Social*, 1: 45–62.

World Bank (2000) *Higher Education in Developing Countries – Peril and Promise*, Washington: The World Bank. Online. Available at http://siteresources.worldbank.org/EDUCATION/Resources/278200-1099079877269/547664-1099079956815/peril_promise_en.pdf (accessed 2 April 2014).

6   Germany's Hesitant Approach to Elite Education

Stratification Processes in German Secondary and Higher Education

Ulrike Deppe, Werner Helsper, Reinhard Kreckel, Heinz-Hermann Krüger and Manfred Stock

Specific elite educational institutions have long been absent from the German educational landscape. In the traditional system of primary, secondary and higher education, qualifications of the same type are deemed equivalent, irrespective of where they were acquired. Until recently, for example, doctorate-granting universities, higher education institutions of applied sciences (*Fachhochschulen*) and traditional secondary schools (*Gymnasien*) showed no discernible difference in rank.

The reason for this 'fiction of equality'[1] lies in the specific historical development of German universities and the German school system. The first modern research universities were established in Germany in the nineteenth century as government-run institutions. Modelled on the University of Berlin, which was founded in 1810, they combined research and teaching, thereby autonomously producing the very knowledge upon which academic education was based. Graduation from one of these research universities opened the door to outstanding career positions, particularly in the state apparatus and the professions, and thus to a 'leadership elite'.

The crucial point of access to this system of academic elite formation did not, however, occur with admission to university, but earlier on in secondary education. Here, after the turn of the twentieth century, a structural distinction was drawn between three fundamental types of schools, the *Volksschule*, the *Realschule* and the *Gymnasium*. Only those in possession of a *Gymnasium* leaving certificate, the '*Abitur*', were entitled to attend university – any university in Germany.

As the decisive link between *Gymnasium* and university, the *Abitur* ensured the absence of hierarchies in universities and *Gymnasiums*, ostensibly at least. The latter saw themselves as prominent educational institutions equipped to train the country's future elite. Initially the gradual expansion of *Gymnasiums* and universities did little to change this situation in structural terms, as they managed to preserve their self-perception of creating an elite. During the post-war years, a growing number of university graduates entered an employment system that absorbed the increase without causing a dramatic deterioration in the social standing of its individual members. Those without an *Abitur* were cut off from the widening avenue of elites, although they did have an alternative in the form of vocational education in the dual education system. This reduced the pressure on *Gymnasiums* and universities but, in comparison with other industrialized western nations, also curbed the expansion of higher education in Germany.

The fiction that educational qualifications and establishments of the same type are fundamentally equal has only recently been called into question. Between 1992 and 2011, the proportion of secondary school leavers from an age cohort qualified to enter higher education rose from 31 per cent to 57 per cent, the proportion of graduates with a first academic degree from 14 per cent to 31 per cent – a demographic quantum leap in fewer than two decades that created considerable financial difficulties. Consequently, cost-saving, 'slim' organization models have become the order of the day, both in secondary and higher education. At the same time, financial concepts for private education – a once somewhat inconsequential notion in Germany – have also gained ground. Furthermore, Germany's schools and higher education institutions are now progressively seen as participants in a globalized performance competition. In particular the comparative PISA tests and global university league tables, where German scholastic performance was found to be modest at best, have led to intense efforts to create high-performance 'elite' educational establishments in Germany and take leave of the prevailing fiction of equality.

The Development of the German *Gymnasium*: Between Loss of Elitism and Vertical, Exclusive Stratification

The history of *Gymnasiums* in Germany since the nineteenth century should be understood as a series of processes of differentiation and subsequent coordination efforts, on the one hand, and as a process of enforcing privileged rights, on the other. During this time the *Gymnasium* established itself as an elitist and exclusive school form, at least as long as *Gymnasium* students made up only a minor percentage of an age cohort. The waves of expansion in upper secondary education that began in the 1950s saw a shift in this exclusive status of the *Gymnasium* (e.g., Müller and Zymek 1987).

The German Gymnasium since the 1950s

The development of *Gymnasiums* in Germany from the 1950s to the present is characterized by six major trends.

1 Differentiation and homogenization: since each of the federal states (*Länder*) in the Federal Republic of Germany is responsible for the structure of its school system, both recurring differentiations and attempts at coordination have been observed (Trautwein and Neumann 2008).

2 The continuing expansion of the *Gymnasium*: more and more pupils of an age group attend a *Gymnasium*, a process driven forward by parents attempting to preserve or raise the social status of their children. This expansion is furthermore fed by a significant growth in the number of girls

attending a *Gymnasium*, coupled with the fact that fewer pupils leave a *Gymnasium* prematurely. Indeed in 2011, the total percentage of pupils in school year five attending a *Gymnasium* in Germany had already reached 41 per cent, while in Eastern Germany this figure was over 45 per cent (Autorengruppe Bildungsberichterstattung 2012). There are indications that at least half of the children in Germany now attend a *Gymnasium*. This means that although *Gymnasiums* have maintained their selective status, they have lost their socially 'exclusive' character.

3   Decoupling of school form and school qualifications: in 2010, almost a quarter of pupils at a 'traditional', general education *Gymnasium* failed to acquire their *Abitur* (Autorengruppe Bildungsberichterstattung 2012: 274). This trend is likely to reinforce the newly emerging duality of the German school system (Zymek 2013). Serious differences in competence were nonetheless found between the *Abitur* awarded by general education *Gymnasiums*, on the one hand, and the lower academic performing 'vocational' *Gymnasiums*, *Gesamtschulen* and neighbourhood schools, on the other (Trautwein *et al.* 2007). This puts the *Gymnasium*'s monopoly on awarding the *Abitur* into greater perspective, while at the same time clearly suggesting evidence of grave inconsistencies in the quality of the *Abitur* itself.

4   Demographic changes: although *Gymnasiums* are in a position to compensate for the general decline in pupil numbers with higher *Gymnasium* attendance, their existence is still threatened. The first-order competition among *Gymnasiums* for pupils is intensifying, as is the second-order competition for selected pupils and high performers (Maroy and van Zanten 2009). In fact, the number of *Gymnasiums* in some urban areas of Eastern Germany has halved since 2000 as a result of the plunge in birth rates since 1990, with overall *Gymnasium* levels in the region down by almost a third (Deppe and Kastner 2014).

5   Changes in school management: as a result of the selective realization of 'educational quasi-markets' (Ball 2006; Bellmann 2008) in Germany, competitive trends have become more widespread. This puts pressure on *Gymnasiums* to create their own profile, in turn encouraging differentiation in upper secondary education (Altrichter *et al.* 2011).

6   Further privatization of upper secondary education: the last two decades have seen a rise in the number of private *Gymnasiums* (Ullrich and Strunck 2012; Deppe and Kastner 2014). The number of publicly owned *Gymnasiums* in Eastern Germany dropped from 724 in 1992 to 510 in 2011. During the same period, the number of private *Gymnasiums* increased from 24 to 114 (Deppe and Kastner 2014). In the states of western Germany, the number of private *Gymnasiums* has also grown (ibid.). Here private *Gymnasiums* are not only spreading but also becoming more distinctive (Helsper 2006; Ullrich 2014).

Of all these developments, it is educational expansion – combined with changes in the management of the school system – and privatization trends that have contributed most to stratification processes in upper secondary education.

Differentiation in the Field of Upper Secondary Education in Germany

When the *Kultusministerkonferenz* (German *Länder* conference of education ministers) harmonized all *Gymnasium* types in the 1960s and allowed each one to provide a general university entrance qualification, existing hierarchies between different gymnasium types in terms of capacity to provide such a qualification were finally removed. Officially speaking, this meant equality of *Gymnasiums* when it came to preparing pupils for university. Beneath this official uniformity, however, there is evidence of differentiation – either new or handed down – in the area of upper secondary education (Helsper 2006).

Ullrich (2014) defines three more or less conventional pathways to academic excellence. First, more than two hundred traditional *Gymnasiums* specialize in classical philology and have maintained or reformed their classical curricular profiles. By simultaneously instructing pupils in two foreign languages as well as in Latin from the start, they appeal to families interested in high culture. A more recent variant is the bilingual gymnasium. In addition to German, certain subjects are taught in English, French or other languages. Bilingualism often involves the awarding of a second, international university entrance qualification in addition to the *Abitur*, such as the *AbiBac* or the International Baccalaureate. These *Gymnasiums* cater to families with high levels of cultural capital and a growing interest in international education. *Gymnasiums* specializing in music, the arts or sports represent a third line. They aim to recruit specific 'functional elites' which are supposed to be top performer in a specific sphere of competence and include 'elite sports schools' (Krüger *et al.* 2014).

More recent developments alongside these traditional lines of differentiation refer in particular to support for the intellectually gifted and can be traced back to the 1980s when *Schnellläuferklassen* (literally 'sprinter classes') and *Begabtenzüge* (special classes for the gifted) were first introduced in *Gymnasiums*, allowing pupils to acquire their *Abitur* more quickly. In eastern Germany, *Gymnasiums* that specialize in mathematics, the natural sciences or languages use additional selection procedures based on academic and cognitive tests that build on the tradition of former East Germany's *Spezialschulen* (literally 'special schools') to promote gifted pupils (Strunck 2008; Ullrich and Strunck 2008; Ullrich 2014). In the last ten years, special 'state *Gymnasiums* for the gifted' have emerged in a number of Germany's federal states, where pupils are selected on the basis of multi-stage assessments, and join these boarding schools between the seventh and ninth school year (Ullrich 2014). In short, the last two decades have seen the establishment of a hitherto non-existent segment of upper secondary education in Germany, one that is based on a second, exclusive selection of top-performing *Gymnasiums* pupils.

The spread of privately owned *Gymnasiums* discussed above has likewise led to substantial change in this area. In addition to the already discernible lines such as boarding schools that focus on progressive education or the more traditional church-run *Gymnasiums* (Gibson 2014), bilingual and English-language *Gymnasiums* with international profiles have mushroomed. This rapid development since the end of the 1990s resulted in the establishment of more than forty international schools in

Germany. Either bilingual or English-speaking, these schools are characterized by internationally oriented and partially homogenized curricula, the acquisition of international study qualifications in addition to the German *Abitur*, and so-called 'pillarization' in the form of a 'holistic education plan' that begins with kindergarten and continues with primary school through to the *Gymnasium*.

Germany's upper secondary landscape is thus marked by traditional as well as new differentiations. As the number of pupils attending gymnasiums has continued to expand and the gymnasium itself become something of a 'mass secondary school', both traditional and new lines of differentiation have begun to act in concert and allow for distinction and exclusion in the upper secondary field.

Plural Differentiation or Vertical Stratification of Gymnasiums?

It remains to be seen, however, whether this produces new hierarchies in the upper secondary field. A number of prominent gymnasiums with a progressive education, for example, charge annual school fees in excess of €30,000 and several international gymnasiums take an annual fee of €20,000. The overall cost of such 'pillarized' international educational trajectories, which begin at the age of two or three, terminate with the acquisition of internationally recognized qualifications and include kindergarten, primary school and gymnasium tuition, can amount to €250,000 per child. This should be understood as a recent development in the German education system, one that appeals to internationally oriented parents with high levels of economic and cultural capital and opens up exclusive, internationally oriented and composite educational opportunities for their children.

A second line of segregation hitherto unseen in the German upper secondary education landscape involves the separation of 'gifted' pupils. This is where, usually at state boarding schools, high performers with high educational aspirations are separated from other pupils of the same age and organized in their own pedagogical peer milieu. This results in new, exclusive institutional performance, where education milieus are not defined by 'money', since these boarding schools cost no more than a few hundred euros per month.

Finally, there is empirical evidence of strong socio-economic differences in the composition of *Gymnasium* pupils (Maaz *et al.* 2009; Helsper 2012). Indeed the social composition differs radically from one *Gymnasium* to another and where it becomes more privileged, pupil competence increases significantly. The highest competence levels are to be found in a small group of gymnasiums (around 10 per cent) with pupils from elitist and socially privileged backgrounds (Maaz *et al.* 2009). This points first of all to a form of secondary selection or 'second creaming' in the upper secondary field, a method used by *Gymnasiums* to fine-tune their choice from a group of pupils already selected. Second, it indicates the location in highly privileged regions or neighbourhoods of *Gymnasiums* that are thus in a position to recruit highly privileged pupils and with them the economic and cultural capital of their families.

Attewell (2001: 267) refers to three 'patterns of parental strategies for enhancing their children's educational prospects' that create school distinctions, namely, region, money and performance. In Germany's upper secondary field there is also evidence of vertical differentiation in all three dimensions. Overall, not only is the existence of a pluralized differentiation of the *Gymnasium* emerging in the upper secondary field along these lines but also vertical segregation. Public discourse suggests evidence of first-, second- and third-order *Abitur* qualifications: now that the education system has undergone a process of opening up, the *Abitur* can, first, be acquired at a variety of schools other than a 'normal' *Gymnasium* – although the former seems somewhat 'devalued' compared with the latter; second, the *Abitur* can be acquired at 'normal' gymnasiums with no pupil selection; third, the *Abitur* can be acquired at an 'exclusive' *Gymnasium*, where it constitutes an international and exclusive university qualification. Thus alongside the 'parentocracy' diagnosed by Zymek (2009; critically on the thesis of 'parentocracy' see Waldow 2014) – the private promotion of children by educationally aspirational parents with high levels of cultural capital – new lines of segregation are appearing in the upper secondary field.

It is unclear, however, to what extent vertical stratification of the upper secondary field will increase dovetailing with excellent universities in the future. This area calls for further observation and empirical research.

Stratificatory Differentiation in Germany's Higher Education System

Severe Overcrowding and the Introduction of Fachhochschulen

Universities in the Federal Republic of Germany were already under pressure after the first wave of educational expansion in the 1950s and 1960s, since teaching and research capacities were unable to cope with the increasing number of people, especially women, who had an *Abitur* and wanted to attend university. The Constitution of the Federal Republic of Germany guaranteed anyone with the *Abitur* a place at university, a basic right that could not be circumvented. This led to two principal changes: first, the introduction of a *numerus clausus* for highly sought-after university courses such as medicine, pharmacy, biology and psychology, and the constitution of a centralized body (ZVS) to allocate course places and distribute applicants as fairly as possible across all universities in Germany. The allocation procedure was based on bureaucratic considerations and took criteria such as *Abitur* grades, waiting periods and social aspects into account.

Second, the beginning of the 1970s saw the creation of a new type of higher education institution of applied sciences, the *Fachhochschule* (FH). FHs had no research budget of their own. Their objective was to teach, to be more cost-effective than traditional universities and to provide practical training. In other words, a second type of higher education institution below university level was introduced to relieve some of the pressure on universities. The success of this venture was to remain limited. Today only around a third of the students in Germany attend FHs, while the other two-thirds study at universities or equivalent institutions (Bundesamt für Statistik 2013: 10). This is partly due to the subjects offered by FHs, which are confined for the most part to engineering and the economic and social sciences. In other words, despite the establishment of *Fachhochschulen* the student population of the research universities continued to expand, pushing their performance to its limits. This was aggravated by the state of university funding, which lagged behind the steadily growing participation rates in higher education. In the late 1990s, *Fachhochschulen* acquired the official English designation of 'universities of applied sciences'. Today there is a trend among Germany's FHs towards alignment with universities. The pan-European introduction of the bachelor and master system in the early 2000s has led to the formal equality of *Fachhochschulen* qualifications and university degrees. More and more *Fachhochschulen* are seeking to establish themselves as research universities and have for some time been fighting for the right to award doctorates.

In the face of a burgeoning education system, the attempt in the 1970s to secure university status for the newly introduced teaching-intensive FH institutions was thus only a partial success, since popular degree studies such as medicine, law or teaching remain the prerogative of universities. A new trend towards levelling out stratification between the traditional doctorate-granting universities and the new universities of applied sciences has emerged, in turn reviving the fiction of equality across the higher education sector.

External Research Funding and Collaborative Research Centres as Distinguishing Features

Today, initiatives aimed at introducing stratificatory differentiations to higher education are visible in quite a different area – the field of research. It is important to bear in mind that the self-image of German universities as the world's leading centres of academic research suffered a considerable setback about a century ago, when publicly funded academic research institutes began to emerge entirely *separately* from universities. There are now almost 250 publicly funded non-university academic research institutes in Germany, including 80 Max Planck Institutes. With no major teaching commitments, they are free to devote themselves to basic scientific research, rather like the CNRS institutes in France (BMBF 2012: 59ff.).

By the end of the 1970s it was evident that the disproportionately large increase in student numbers bore the risk of university research being 'overshadowed by teaching' (Schimank 1995) and migrating more and more to non-university research institutes. To counteract this trend the German Research Foundation (DFG) began financing long-term Collaborative Research Centres (SFBs) at universities, thus providing the opportunity to carry out large-scale research projects detached from regular teaching activities. Awarded in accordance with the strictest quality criteria, applications for these prestigious SFBs could be made by any university. As the years passed this meant that a relatively small number of universities received the lion's share of SFBs and other project-related external funding. DFG calculations between 2002 and 2004 show that just ten of the 108 universities in existence in Germany today received approximately

30 per cent of all third-party research funding for which data is available, while twenty universities obtained around 50 per cent, and forty almost 80 per cent (Hartmann 2010: 372). Thus, most of the remaining universities with a strong focus on teaching have seldom been recipients of research funding if at all.

This substantial de facto inequality of German universities when it comes to external funding has, however, rarely been a topic of public debate. Since all universities without exception can, in principle, attract external funding and apply for an SFB, perceptions have continued to be dominated by the traditional postulate of equality.

Attempts at Hierarchical Differentiation in the University Field Through the Excellence Initiative

A new stratificatory dynamic emerged when in January 2004 the Federal Government announced its intention to promote ten 'elite universities' in Germany. Since public opinion in Germany proved resistant to the concept of 'elite', it ultimately became the 'Excellence Initiative' and was launched by the Federal Government and the federal states in 2005. To apply for a generous, five-year fixed-term funding of *Exzellenzcluster* (clusters of excellence rather like giant SFBs), *Graduiertenschulen* (graduate schools based on the existing format of DFG Research Training Groups) and *Zukunftskonzepte* (institutional development strategies), universities were required to undergo a rigorous assessment process. The winners of the *Zukunftskonzepte* contest are known colloquially as *Elite-Universitäten* or elite universities (Leibfried 2010). Close cooperation with non-university research institutes was very much encouraged as a means of reducing their distance to universities. Three rounds of funding have produced successful applications from forty universities to date, including eleven establishments that will continue to be known unofficially as 'elite universities' until the programme terminates in 2017. Berlin's Humboldt University and *Freie Universität* as well as the *Ludwig-Maximilians-Universität* and TUM in Munich have emerged as strong leaders, closely followed by Heidelberg, Aachen and Dresden; taken together they have secured a third of the clusters of excellence, almost half of the graduate schools and the lion's share of funding (Hartmann 2013: 3ff.). Hence, a three-layered, non-fixed structure has gradually emerged on the German university landscape – at the top are the eleven 'elite universities', followed by the other winners from the Excellence Initiative, and finally the rest, consisting of approximately seventy unsuccessful universities, most of which also perform poorly in DFG funding tables. It remains to be seen whether this will be a permanent structure that continues to exist when the funding period comes to an end as planned in 2017.

The question now arises as to whether this highly meritocratic hierarchical structure in the field of research will likewise lead to social differentiation in student bodies. Initial empirical findings suggest indeed that students from academic families choose to study at one of the 'excellence universities' disproportionately often (Stiftung Neue Verantwortung 2011). This notwithstanding, it is well known that the German school and higher education system as a whole is characterized by high social selectivity (Autorengruppe Bildungsberichterstattung 2012) – a fact that public debates have seen as a breach of the principle of social equality rather than a welcome indicator of successful elite formation. In Germany there is little social acceptance of 'elite' universities as arenas for the socially exclusive recruitment of key scientific, economic and political leaders. Hence, while research clearly dominates as a distinguishing feature and initial signs of institutional stratification following the introduction of the Excellence Initiative have been seen, the principle of equality still applies when it comes to standards of academic teaching and academic qualifications. Nevertheless, even here fresh attempts at 'elite formation' have recently been observed.

Study Programmes for Future 'Elites' at Private and Public Institutions of Higher Education

Efforts are currently being made to introduce stratificatory distinctions so as to single out certain study programmes or higher education institutions. This applies in particular to private universities; unlike state universities these are not bound by fundamental rights that standardize education in the sense of a common civil right. In principle, private universities are free to be highly selective about whom they admit since they are not subject to rules regarding teaching capacities. And, of course, the vast tuition fees occasionally charged by private universities have a more socially selective effect than is the case at public universities with very low tuition fees or none at all. Today, however, only about 5 per cent of students in Germany attend one of the country's ninety private higher education institutions (Stifterverband 2010: 6).

A number of areas with emerging vertical differentiation can be identified in Germany's higher education system. The following are some examples:

1   Public higher education: by funding its 'Elite Network of Bavaria' the federal state of Bavaria programmatically raises claims to elite education. The integral network involved the establishment of twenty-one so-called 'elite graduate programmes' at Bavarian universities, said to be characterized by excellent study conditions. The initiative came from the political sphere.
2   Likewise, in the area of public higher education: the aforementioned graduate schools funded by the Excellence Initiative. They offer structured doctoral programmes and aim to produce a new generation of outstanding scientists. The creation of these graduate schools was also a political decision.
3   Private sector: higher education establishments that seek to secure a prominent position. These are the rare private institutions with university character and their own research ambitions. At the same time, a handful of these establishments claim to instruct students in management and governance for positions of leadership in business and society. They point to excellent study conditions and highly selective admission processes, boast top ranking in league tables and charge tuition fees that are high by German standards.
4   Public sector: some state universities also launch initiatives – most of them the brainchild of professors or individual institutes – to develop 'outstanding' study programmes with specific student–teacher ratios and admission regulations.

While no overt stratificatory distinctions have yet been observed in the above-mentioned areas, initial efforts are under way to institutionalize rank distinctions between universities and study programmes. Be that as it may, it is still unclear which higher education establishments and study programmes will actually succeed in securing relatively stable positions within any such stratified structure. A German higher education 'top level' – one that meets with the corresponding social recognition – is less firmly institutionalized than is the case in the field of research, where a degree of stratification has taken place through the implementation of the Excellence Initiative.

Selection at the Transition Between Exclusive Upper Secondary Education and Higher Education

Apart from the subject-specific national and local *numerus clausus*, pupils leaving exclusive schools have at first glance no immediate advantages when it comes to gaining access to exclusive higher education. Two points should, however, not be ignored. While it is true, on the one hand, that very few universities have so far availed of entrance tests to determine subject-specific aptitude, some of those who do leave selection to external companies and bill the applicants for costs. Lawyers are also enjoying a lucrative new system, whereby prosperous would-be students are offered legal assistance at a fee so they can 'sue their way in' to a subject. Furthermore, private universities are the location for a socially selective alternative to study programmes tied to local *numerus clausus* when they provide comparable study programmes with no admission restrictions – albeit their tuition fees are higher than average.

Several longitudinal studies by the Higher Education Information System (HIS) and others (e.g., Bornkessel and Kuhnen 2011; Lörz 2012; Scheller *et al.* 2013) have demonstrated that selectivity during the transition from the school to the higher education system is undergoing further reinforcement. Children 'from less privileged social classes and women', for instance, who are already underrepresented in *Gymnasiums*, are less inclined to take up studies 'than children from the upper classes and men with similar or worse *Abitur* grades' (Mayer 2003: 624). Children from non-academic families also tend to choose *Fachhochschulen* rather than universities, and are less likely to study disciplines such as law or medicine (ibid. 624f.). Furthermore, it has been observed that status groups with high cultural capital and educational aspirations are more likely to enrol at universities with high positions in (global) university league tables (Lörz and Quast 2011). There is evidence of systematic participation of the privileged population in the choice of leading universities. It seems that the Excellence Initiative may have sent first crucial signals for the expansion of elite education in the sphere of higher education (Winkler 2014).

Conclusion

The developments presented here indicate the emergence of a specifically German path to elite formation. In the last decade, in particular, vertical differentiation in upper secondary and higher education has been more pronounced.

This is most noticeable in the school sector in terms of differences in *Gymnasium* profiles, traditions and reputations, all of which can lead to ample variation in their social composition. In addition to *Gymnasiums* with long traditions of implied exclusive education, the last ten years has seen the expansion of *Gymnasiums* geared towards the gifted or focused on bilingualism, and a rapidly growing international school segment with internationally tailored final qualifications attractive to international, professionally mobile parents as well as to wealthy German families. Even clearer contours of institutional stratification are emerging in the area of research in the German higher education system, with education policy having set the ball rolling in 2004. The Excellence Initiative will continue to be financed until 2017 and has already resulted in particularly high levels of funding for a small, select group of top universities. The global institutionalization of 'policies for excellence' has put pressure on the German higher education system (Rostan and Vaira 2011), with a range of universities making initial attempts in the area of teaching to establish internationally visible degree programmes as a breeding ground for a new generation of excellent scientists and business and social leaders.

However, since an institutional 'pillarization' of the elite education system involving upper secondary schools and universities, as in the case of the UK, the USA or France (see van Zanten 2010), has not yet taken place in Germany, the exact nature of the transitional paths between these exclusive educational settings remains unclear and has been the subject of very few empirical studies. Research is also lacking on the transition between elite secondary schools and renowned national and international universities, as well as on the graduate career paths to the labour market of the students and doctoral candidates of such universities. Neither is there reliable empirical data on the social background of students from these emerging elite schools and universities. Carrying out investigations of this kind poses a key challenge for future educational research, as does the continued observation of processes of vertical differentiation and hierarchization in the German education system (see Krüger *et al.* 2012).

Note

1 All citations from German sources have been translated into English.

References

Altrichter, H., Heinrich, M. and Soukup-Altrichter, K. (2011) 'Governance-Regime der Schulprofilierung', in H. Altrichter, M. Heinrich and K. Soukup-Altrichter (eds) *Schulentwicklung durch Schulprofilierung?*, Wiesbaden: VS Verlag: 215–241.

Attewell, P. (2001) The winner-take-all high school: organizational adaptations to educational stratification, *Sociology of Education*, 74(4): 267–295.

Autorengruppe Bildungsberichterstattung (2012) *Bildung in Deutschland 2012*, Bielefeld: Bertelsmann.

Ball, S.J. (2006) *Education Policy and Social Class*, New York: Routledge.

Bellmann, J. (2008) 'Choice policies – selection, segregation and distinction in Rahmen von Bildungsmärkten', in H. Ullrich and S. Strunck (eds) *Begabtenförderung an Gymnasien*, Wiesbaden: VS-Verlag: 249–271.

Bornkessel, P. and Kuhnen, S.U. (2011) 'Zum Einfluss der sozialen Herkunft auf Schulleistung, Studienzuversicht und Studienintention am Ende der Sekundarstufe II', in P. Bornkessel and J. Asdonk (eds) *Der Übergang Schule – Hochschule*, Wiesbaden: VS Verlag: 47–104.

Bundesamt für Statistik (2013) *Studierende an Hochschulen – Fachserie 11 Reihe 4.1 – endgültige Ergebnisse – Wintersemester 2012/2013*, Wiesbaden.

Bundesministerium für Bildung und Forschung (BMBF) (2012) *Bundesbericht Forschung und Innovation 2012*, Berlin: BMBF.

Deppe, U. and Kastner, H. (2014) 'Exklusive Bildungseinrichtungen in Deutschland', in H.-H. Krüger and W. Helper (eds) *Elite und Exzellenz im Bildungssystem – Nationale und internationale Perspektiven*, Zeitschrift für Erziehungswissenschaft, special issue 19, Wiesbaden: Springer VS: 263–283.

Gibson, A. (2014) 'Exzellente Persönlichkeiten und verantwortungsbewusste Potenzialträger im Fokus – Konstruktionen des Schülerhabitus in exklusiven Internatsgymnasien', in W. Helper, R.T. Kramer and S. Thiersch (eds) *Schülerhabitus*, Wiesbaden: VS-Verlag: 374–394.

Hartmann, M. (2010) Die Exzellenzinitiative und ihre Folgen, *Leviathan*, 38: 269–287.

Hartmann, M. (2013) Die Exzellenzinitiative und die Hierarchisierung des deutschen Hochschulsystems. Available http://www.nachdenkseiten.de/?p=16967 (accessed November 2013).

Helper, W. (2006) 'Elite und Bildung im Schulsystem – Schulen als Institutionen-Milieu-Komplexe in der höheren Bildungslandschaft', in J. Ecarius and L. Wigger (eds) *Elitebildung – Bildungselite*, Opladen: Barbara Budrich: 162–188.

Helper, W. (2012) 'Distinktion in der gymnasialen Schullandschaft: Vom Gymnasium als Unterschied zu Unterscheidungen im Gymnasialen?', in S. Lin-Klitzing, D. Di Fuccia and G. Müller-Frerich (eds) *Aspekte gymnasialer Bildung*, Bad Heilbrunn: Klinkhardt: 116–135.

Krüger, H.-H., Helper, W., Sackmann, R., Breidenstein, G., Bröckling, U., Kreckel, R., Mierendorff, J., and Stock, M. (2012) Mechanismen der Elitebildung im deutschen Bildungssystem. *Zeitschrift für Erziehungswissenschaft*, 15(2): 327–343.

Krüger, H.-H., Keßler, C., Otto, A. and Schippling, A. (2014) 'Elite und Exzellenz aus der Perspektive von Jugendlichen und ihren Peers an exklusiven Schulen', in H.-H. Krüger and W. Helper (eds) *Elite und Exzellenz im Bildungssystem – Nationale und internationale Perspektiven*, Zeitschrift für Erziehungswissenschaft, special issue 19, Wiesbaden: Springer VS: 221–241.

Leibfried, S. (ed.) (2010) *Die Exzellenzinitiative. Zwischenbilanz und Perspektiven*, Frankfurt, New York: Campus.

Lörz, M. (2012) 'Mechanismen sozialer Ungleichheit beim Übergang ins Studium: Prozesse der Status- und Kulturreproduktion', in R. Becker and H. Solga (eds) *Soziologische Bildungsforschung*, Kölner Zeitschrift für Soziologie und Sozialpsychologie, special issue 52, Wiesbaden: Springer VS: 302–324.

Lörz, M. and Quast, H. (2011) Soziale Ungleichheit bei der Wahl der Hochschule? *HIS:Magazin*, 4, 2–4.

Maaz, K., Nagy, G., Jonkmann, K. and Baumert, J. (2009) Eliteschulen in Deutschland?, *Zeitschrift für Pädagogik*, 55(2): 211–228.

Maroy, C. and van Zanten, A. (2009) Regulation and competition among schools in six European localities, *Sociologie du travail*, 51(1): 67–79.

Mayer, K.U. (2003) 'Das Hochschulwesen', in K.S. Cortina *et al.* (eds) *Das Bildungswesen in der Bundesrepublik Deutschland*, Reinbek: Rowohlt: 581–624.

Müller, D.K.and Zymek, B. (1987) *Datenhandbuch zur deutschen Bildungsgeschichte, Vol. 2, Part 1*, Göttingen: Vandenhoeck & Ruprecht.

Rostan, M. and Vaira, M. (2011) 'Structuring the field of excellence', in M. Rostan and M. Vaira (eds) *Questioning Excellence in Higher Education*, Rotterdam: Sense Publishers: 57–74.

Scheller, P., Isleib, S. and Sommer, D. (2013) Studienanfängerinnen und Studienanfänger im Wintersemester 2011/12. Tabellenband. *HIS: Forum Hochschule*, Hannover: HIS.

Schimank, U. (1995) *Hochschulforschung im Schatten der Lehre*, Frankfurt: Campus.

Stifterverband für die Deutsche Wissenschaft (2010) *Rolle und Zukunft privater Hochschulen in Deutschland. Eine Studie in Kooperation mit McKinsey & Company*, Essen: Edition Stifterverband.

Stiftung Neue Verantwortung (2011) *Wege aus der Exzellenzfalle*, Policy Brief 4/2011.

Strunck, S. (2008) 'Kontinuitäten im Wandel. Spezialschulen und Spezialklassen in den neuen Bundesländern', in H. Ullrich and S. Strunck (eds) *Begabtenförderung an Gymnasien*, Wiesbaden: VS Verlag: 101–121.

Trautwein, U. and Neumann, M. (2008) 'Das Gymnasium', in K.S. Cortina, J. Baumert, A. Leschinsky, K.U. Mayer and L. Trommer (eds) *Das Bildungswesen in der Bundesrepublik Deutschland*, Reinbek: Rowohlt: 467–502.

Trautwein, U., Köller, O., Lehmann, R. and Lüdtke, O. (eds) (2007) *Schulleistungen von Abiturienten*, Münster: Waxmann.

Ullrich, H. (2014) 'Exzellenz und Elitebildung in Gymnasien. Traditionen und Innovationen', in H.-H. Krüger and W. Helsper (eds) *Elite und Exzellenz im Bildungssystem – Nationale und internationale Perspektiven*. Zeitschrift für Erziehungswissenschaft, special issue 19, Wiesbaden: Springer VS: 181–201.

Ullrich, H. and Strunck, S. (eds) (2008) *Begabtenförderung an Gymnasien*, Wiesbaden: VS Verlag.

Ullrich, H. and Strunck, S. (eds) (2012) *Private Schulen in Deutschland*, Wiesbaden: VS Verlag.

van Zanten, A. (2010) 'The sociology of elite education', in W. Apple, S.J. Ball and L.A. Gandin (eds) *The Routledge International Handbook of the Sociology of Education*, New York: Routledge: 329–337.

Waldow, F. (2014) 'Von der Meritokratie zur Parentokratie? Elitenreproduktion und die Legitimierung der Zuweisung von Lebenschancen im englischen Bildungssystem', in H.-H. Krüger and W. Helsper (eds) *Elite und Exzellenz im Bildungssystem – Nationale und internationale Perspektiven*, Zeitschrift für Erziehungswissenschaft, special issue 19, Wiesbaden: Springer VS: 43–58.

Winkler, O. (2014) Exzellente Wahl. Soziale Selektivität und Handlungsorientierungen bei der Wahl von Spitzenbildung im Hochschulbereich, *Zeitschrift für Soziologie der Erziehung und Sozialisation*, 34(3): 1–17.

Zymek, B. (2009) Prozesse der Internationalisierung und Hierarchisierung im Bildungssystem, *Zeitschrift für Pädagogik*, 55(2): 175–194.

Zymek, B. (2013) Die Zukunft des zweigliedrigen Schulsystems in Deutschland, *Zeitschrift für Pädagogik*, 59(4): 469–482.

7   The Boundaries of Privilege

Elite English Schools' Geographies and Depictions of a Local Community

Rachel Brooks and Johanna Waters

Elite schools are often perceived as having a strong international orientation. In part, this is related to the relatively large number of international pupils who attend them, their history of educating global elites, and their adoption of international curricula (Hayden, 2011; Rizvi and Lingard, 2010). Nevertheless, in this chapter, we draw on an analysis of the websites, prospectuses and other publicly available material from 30 elite schools in England, to argue that the geographical positioning of such schools is more complex. There is, for example, a clear tension between their need to depict a sense of elevation and 'apartness', on the one hand, and a desire to be involved (or to be seen to be involved) with activities outside their physical boundaries, on the other. In the chapter, we consider what an engagement with the 'local community' actually means for elite schools – the extent to which they can be described as locally 'embedded', and whether the spaces and boundaries of the school (and thereby 'eliteness') are actually extended, albeit temporarily. The chapter speaks to debates in the sociology of education on the reproduction of privilege and in geography on understanding the spatalities of schooling.

The first part of the chapter draws on extant literature to discuss the spatial practices of schools. We argue here that we know relatively little about such practices in relation to elite institutions. We then move on to describing the research methods that underpinned the study, and outline our key findings. In particular, we contend that representations of the local community are often foregrounded on elite schools' websites – through links to local state schools, voluntary activity, community partnerships and the ways in which pupils move through specific 'local landscapes'. The final part of the chapter argues that while this emphasis on the local may seem at odds with assumptions about the increasing international orientation of elite schools, it articulates closely with the historical emphasis on the 'beneficence' of elite schools and also more recent political imperatives – including the need of private schools, in particular, to demonstrate 'public benefit' to legitimate their status as charitable institutions.

Spatialities of Schooling: Elite Schools' Spatial Practices

> The social geographical importance of schools extends well beyond their physical boundaries.
>
> (Collins and Coleman, 2008: 291)

Recent work on the 'geographies of education' has made a powerful case for examining the 'spatialities' of schooling. Holloway and Jons (2012: 482), for example, assert: 'the importance of spatiality in the production, consumption and implications of formal education systems from pre-school to tertiary education and of informal learning environments in homes, neighbourhoods, community organisations and workspaces' (see also Reh *et al.*, 2011; Kraftl, 2013). 'Spatiality' involves the assumption that spatial practices and social processes are inextricably linked and co-constitutive. In other words (and here we draw upon Kraftl's (2012) use of Pile and Keith's (1993) definition), the term 'spatiality' aims to 'capture the ways in which the social and spatial are inextricably realized in one another; to conjure up the circumstances in which social and space are simultaneously realized by thinking, feeling, doing individuals' (Pile and Keith, 1993: 6).

The intention of much of this work on education and spatialities has been explicitly to foreground and shed light upon the wider processes (political, economic, social) underpinning the functioning of societies (Hanson-Thiem, 2009). It makes little sense, we concur, to examine schooling 'in isolation', without attending to its far-reaching impacts and implications. Schools are not just 'in society' but help to *create* society, and this is as true for elite and exclusive schools, as it is for state-funded comprehensives. It is striking to note, then, that to date 'elite schooling' has largely evaded academic scrutiny. Elite (and particularly high-fee-paying independent) schools are far less likely than their state-funded counterparts to be involved in, and the subject of, critical social science research. This situation is a difficult one to redress, not least because much research on schools requires schools' participation and co-operation, and this is far harder to achieve when dealing with the relatively small number of schools at the 'top'. One possible solution, and one that we have applied in this chapter, is to utilise the extensive web materials on elite schools available for public viewing. More details of our methodology are given in the next section.

This chapter is concerned with schools' quotidian 'spatial practices' and the implications of these practices. There are two broad ways in which the spatialities of schooling have been and continue to be studied, and this is represented by 'inward looking' and 'outward looking' research. In the first instance, researchers have been interested in the ways in which space is organised and utilised within school grounds – in playgrounds, class rooms, lunch halls, and so on (e.g. Kraftl, 2006). The social geography of schooling has examined schools as 'containers' of social processes. In the second instance, and this is what interests us primarily in this chapter, work has considered if and how a school engages with the 'outside' – its place, as Collins and Coleman (2008: 283) write, 'within broader social landscapes.'

In their discussion and detailed review of work on the social geographies of education, Collins and Coleman (2008: 281) purposively seek to look 'within, and beyond, school boundaries'. They are highly attentive to the ways in which schools' geographies turn both inwards and outwards. In this chapter, we are particularly interested in what they have to say on how school spaces extend 'beyond their physical boundaries' (ibid.: 291). They write:

As (typically) long-term institutions, they [schools] are sites of common experience within neighbourhoods, which link different generations and provide a physical site for the maintenance of local social contacts. Thus, schools may not only reflect the characteristics of the neighbourhood (e.g. in terms of socio-economic status), but also contribute to building place-based histories and characteristics, and social cohesion. That said, the connection between school and place is not always a positive one – and is, in any case, challenged by neoliberal notions of educational markets and school choice.

(Collins and Coleman, 2008: 291)

The link between schools and their wider community is seen to be particularly strong at primary level, where individuals are far more likely to attend a local school, and less likely to travel significant distances. However, overall, their discussion pre-supposes a certain model of state provision and does not reflect the elite/selective/private school sector in England. Very few pupils are likely to have grown up in the area immediately surrounding their school grounds, so we need a different concept for describing social and community interaction within the elite school sector. Collins and Coleman's (2008: 292) discussion moves closer to theorising this spatial relationship when discussing the notion of 'school choice' and 'neoliberal education frameworks': 'In such scenarios, the spatial contract linking schools and their imme-diate neighbourhoods has been discarded'. This notion of a 'spatial contract' is an interesting one, and we will explore this in more detail in relation to our empirical material later on in the chapter. As we will show, a spatial contract, as such, *does* seem to exist for the most elite schools in that they all actively pursue social interac-tion and relationships with their surrounding communities. The extent to which 'moral' or 'strategic' motives underpin these interactions, however, is a moot point, and something we will return to later in the chapter when we attempt to analyse elite schools' interactions with local communities.

Research Methods

This chapter explores elite schools' spatial practices by drawing on a detailed analysis of the websites and prospectuses of 30 'elite' schools (with sixth-forms) in England. Our sample comprised three main groups of schools: 'influential' private schools – the ten schools identified by as having educated around 12 per cent of the 'leading high flyers' in the UK (Sutton Trust, 2012); 'high-performing' private schools – we identified ten such schools using the Department for Education's league table of A/AS Level point scores per pupil for 2012; and 'high-performing' state schools – again, we identified ten such schools using the Department for Education's A/AS Level league table. Including all three types of schools enabled us to explore some of the diversity across a range of elite schools. Our sample was also geographically diverse, including institutions across England.

For all 30 schools, we conducted a detailed analysis of their webpages, prospectuses and any additional documents that were publicly available on the website, such as newsletters. As we have argued elsewhere (Brooks and Waters, 2014), these materials represent a crucial means of communication for all schools; indeed, websites and prospectuses have become important parts of what Wardman *et al.* (2010) call the 'symbolic architecture' of educational institutions. The high quality of the majority of the websites we analysed suggests strongly that the schools had invested significant amounts of money in their design and upkeep, and are thus likely to be perceived by them as a key means of communication. Although such materials provide no concrete evidence of the actual practices within schools, they offer an important insight into how the institutions wish to present themselves to the outside world and the messages they hope to convey to current and prospective pupils and their parents, the local community, competitor schools and other interested parties.

Our analysis of the websites and other materials focused on both words and images. We were interested in not only what was said but in how content was presented, and the deployment of photographs and other types of image. However, in this chapter, for the reasons explained below, we draw largely on the textual information. We used both content and discourse analysis. The former was used to investigate the extent to which certain themes were mentioned and/or represented, and we used a detailed grid to record this information. Discourse analysis was then used, in a second stage of analysis, to explore the way in which the various themes we had identified across the data set as a whole were constructed. In both parts of the analysis, we sought to explore any differences between the three categories of school in our stratified sample – but also differences within particular categories (e.g. between boarding and day schools within the private sector) and across categories (e.g. by geographical location) (Waters and Brooks, 2014). In this chapter, however, we focus on one theme that emerged strongly across the data set as a whole, namely the way in which the *local* was foregrounded in the materials of a majority of the schools.

Schools' Depictions of 'Local Engagement'

Compared with the limited ways in which international/global scenes are depicted on elite schools' websites, images and descriptions of 'local' engagement are surprisingly prolific, with a few prominent exceptions. Many schools have involvement in and with 'the local' built into their 'mission statements', suggesting the importance of this aspect to schools' outlooks and objectives. It is notable, however, that whereas textual representations of 'the local' are abundant on web pages, images tend to be of the school grounds and buildings only – often emphasising imposing architecture and extensive playing fields. Therefore, the following discussion focuses largely on what is written within websites, although we return to the contrast with what is represented through pictures and photographs in the concluding part of the chapter. In what follows, we provide a description of three 'exemplar' schools from our sample, before drawing upon the whole sample to consider the main features of elite schools' engagement with the 'local'.

School 1: 'All of our community activities are an important part of our pupils' development and wider education'. The first example – an elite, high-fee, independent boys' school – is vis-à-vis other comparator schools in our sample relatively modest when it comes to claims about local engagement and involvement. Nevertheless, it serves as a useful example of the kinds of activities and engagements elite schools in England are interested in pursuing. Like most elite schools in our sample, as discussed in detail below, the school is particularly keen to stress its 'close relationship' with local state schools. The local council is heavily involved in this arrangement. School 1 participates in a schools' 'Learning Partnership,' which includes eight state-funded secondary schools, and supports activities such as 'paired reading'. Saturday school allows primary pupils from the surrounding area to come to School 1 to participate in 'an enhanced learning programme' – again organised by the local council but hosted by the school. School 1 is also lead sponsor of a local Academy[1] and is involved in the Academy's governance as well as encouraging staff exchanges and offering 'support'. The Principal of School 1 is chair of the Academy's academic committee. In addition to involvement in local schools, School 1 offers lunch-time concerts during term time. These concerts enable pupils 'to give free public performances which have been widely celebrated'.

School 2: 'Our staff and pupils engage with the wider community in a number of different ways, but particularly as mentors (boys) or school governors (staff) of local maintained schools and academies. Community service is provided by boys taking food and clothing to homeless people in [the local area], by visiting the elderly and by playing the organ in four local churches.' This school is a high-fee, independent boys' school. The school has a section on its website entitled 'Access, engagement and outreach', and the gist of this is summed up in the following statement:

> [The school's] governing body ... attaches great importance to good relations with the people and organisations in the local area and seeks actively to extend [the school's] educational reach as far as possible by awarding scholarships and bursaries and by making [the school's] expertise and facilities available to students who are not its pupils ...

Like School 1, local engagement is framed in part through 'educational links' – an attempt to share some of the school's academic success with less fortunate and well-equipped schools. The school undertakes a very wide range of activities involving local state schools, including: (i) academy sponsorship; (ii) school partnership with six neighbouring schools; (iii) participation in a local business partnership; (iv) running educational summer schools for 130 state schools; (v) offering an annual summer school for gifted and talented students from the local area; (vi) providing rowing and choral courses; and (vii) giving mock Oxbridge interviews to pupils at local state schools. Wider 'benefits to our local community' include providing local clubs and societies with access to the school chapel, sports fields, golf course, sports facilities, school hall and school theatre. A local primary school also uses some school facilities to 'enhance its curriculum'. School 2's pupils 'go out into the community' and work in charity shops, visit elderly people in their homes 'for a cup of tea and a chat' or to help with the garden. They help with horse-riding classes for disabled people and tend the graves of local soldiers killed in action during World War Two. These 'local' activities fit squarely into the school's broader aims; School 2's 'commitments' refer to pupils making a contribution 'to the life of the school and the community'.

School 3: '[the school aims] to have a strong relationship with the local community'. School 3 is also a high-fee, independent boys' school, and has a prominent section on its website titled: 'Helping the community'. Some of the ways in which it claims to do so include: managing a local charity; opening school facilities up to 'local schools and the community'; and allowing local schools to use sports facilities in the mornings. A 'specific organisation' – the 'Friends of [School]' – was set up with the aim of facilitating local involvement in the school. Members are invited to school functions and the school also lays on activities for them such as dances and concerts. In addition, school facilities are used by the local Territorial Army regiment and police force. 'Community service' also features strongly in this school's promotional materials, which includes: visits to elderly in their homes and in residential homes; helping at an elderly day care centre; visiting disabled people in their homes; hosting a tea party for elderly; local (and, unusually for this sample, *national*) fundraising; and working for the local YMCA. The school even 'pays for a street cleaner to clean public streets in [local area]'. In addition, pupils go out to read with younger children at a range of local schools. As noted, significantly, on the website, one school is a 20-minute bike-ride away. Here, pupils run classroom and sports activities with disabled children and children with learning difficulties.

The spatialities of these activities are fascinating, and clearly depict both 'inward' and 'outward'-looking conceptions of community engagement. Perhaps the majority of a school's engagement with the local involves *letting the local 'in'* – opening up its facilities and grounds to the community. The boundaries of the school (and thus of the privileges it imparts) are transgressed, albeit for limited and controlled periods of time. However, also important is the need to send pupils 'out into the community'. We will elaborate on this in the section below.

Engagements With a 'Wider Community': Themes From the Data

The local community is represented in a number of ways on elite schools' websites, but we have identified four common themes, which we will describe, briefly, in turn: links to local state schools; volunteering; community partnerships; and moving through 'local landscapes' (embodied, localised mobilities beyond the school grounds).

From our reading of elite schools' websites, schools prize and value their links to local state schools above all other forms of local engagement. As described above, these links can take a number of different forms, but most commonly involve: sponsoring an Academy; allowing local schools use of elite school facilities (usually sports facilities); providing enhanced learning through summer schools or weekend schools (including Oxbridge entrance support); elite school pupils entering local schools and providing 'mentoring' or reading support; and school staff at the elite school sitting on the governing body of local state schools and thereby giving of their expertise.

All of the elite schools we studied place some emphasis on the notion of pupil volunteering. Most commonly, this involves supporting local elderly people through home visits and local disabled charities through visits and fundraising.

Community partnerships are far more complicated to depict as they take on a wide and varied number of forms, differing from school to school. Community partnerships can include being part of a wider consortium of local schools, with the notion that all schools, including less elite state schools, will benefit from this arrangement. They usually involve the school 'opening up' its facilities for use by community 'partners': police, territorial army, charities, local council, and so on.

Finally, as observed above, it is notable that community engagement involves not just the outside 'coming in' (the opening up of school facilities to external parties) but also places stress upon the necessity of pupils 'going out into the community' – on foot or by bike, and getting their hands dirty. All schools encourage pupils to leave the school grounds on at least a weekly basis and to engage with people unconnected with the school. These interactions are clearly highly controlled and monitored. Interestingly, however, oftentimes this involves pupils entering vulnerable others' residential space (homes or care homes). These encounters in intimate, personal settings require some examination in relation to the spatialities of schooling. What is the impact on pupils and on 'visitees' of regular visitations in residential settings? Answering this is beyond the scope of this chapter and would require further, qualitative research. However, it is useful to point out that the spatialities of schooling are being stretched and contorted through elite schools' engagements with and in 'the local'.

Explaining 'Local Engagement'

The emphasis on the local would perhaps seem at odds with arguments that elite schools are now operating within 'global circuits' of education – competing with elite schools in other countries, rather than only those in the UK, and that education is becoming increasingly internationalised at all levels (Hayden, 2011). Nevertheless, the local focus, documented above, is in line with both the history of English elite schools, and the political imperatives that have come into play more recently. Below, we explore the ways in which a focus on the local community has been underpinned by: the historical commitment of elite schools to community service, volunteering and character education; more recent invocations to forge closer partnerships with state schools; and incentives to engage in voluntary work and local engagement projects as part of 'Big Society' initiatives.

The Historical 'Beneficence' of Elite Schools

The ideal of service has long been an important component of elite schools in England – and particularly those in the private sector. Writing in the 1920s, the influential educationalist and private school head teacher, Cyril Norwood, defined an 'English tradition' of education largely in relation to an ideal of service (McCulloch,

2004). Indeed, he argued that the commitment to community service, evident in English private schools, should be taken up by all schools across the country:

> I put forward the ideal of the highest English tradition, of that education which trains a generation through religion and discipline, through culture of the mind and perfection of the body, to a conscious end of service to the community, as an ideal which shall inspire the whole of our education in every type of school, and create the democracy of the future.
>
> (Norwood, 1929: 244)

This ideal has endured, and is still seen as an important characteristic of elite schools (Seldon, 2014). Indeed, private schools typically offer 'community service' options to their students to be pursued in afternoons, evenings and/or weekends. This emphasis on service to the local community has been theorised in various ways. First, it has been seen as a significant part of the 'character education' of those attending such schools – with interaction with local populations considered a key means of developing traits such as kindness, commitment, loyalty and determination (Holt, 2008). Although character education has a long history – and can be traced back to Thomas Arnold's emphasis on inculcating 'muscular Christianity' through a private school education, it remains significant today. Indeed, studies of elite schooling in contemporary society have suggested that voluntary service (locally and further afield) is often an important means of 'resourcing the self' – developing characteristics of value in the labour market and society more widely (Allan and Charles, 2013). Second, it has been understood as a means of expiating the guilt that may be associated with privilege (Kenway, 2013). Research with young people from privileged backgrounds has suggested that involvement in activities intended to promote social justice – often located within local communities – can, in many cases, be understood as means of assuaging negative feelings associated with privilege. Indeed, Howard (2013) argues that service to the local community can have significant ideological value for students from privileged backgrounds, by making clear to others that they are using their advantage, not just for themselves, but for the benefit of others. Finally, such local involvement has also been understood as a means of affirming the legitimacy of elite schooling, and the position of elites within society more generally (McDonald *et al.*, 2012; Kenway, 2013). As Howard (2013: 198) writes:

> Benevolent acts … have considerable ideological value not only in diverting attention away from the power of dominant groups but also in convincing subordinates that they are concerned for others and are compassionate, kind and giving. Such ideological messages that place the wealthy in a positive light protect their class interests and power.

In this way, service to the local community can be conceptualised as part of a long-standing and largely conservative agenda, intended to deflect criticism of elite schooling, and legitimate its place in society.

Contemporary Political Imperatives

While an emphasis on the local community may be viewed as part of the historical orientation of many elite schools, it can also be seen as inextricably linked to more recent, and explicitly political, imperatives. Within England, over the past decade, private schools have come under considerable pressure to demonstrate that they are worthy of the charitable status that they have traditionally enjoyed (which exempts them from various taxes). Legislation introduced by the Labour government in 2006 removed the presumption that the provision of education, in itself, was an automatic public benefit. Instead, private schools are now required to demonstrate the specific ways in which they are engaging with communities beyond the school walls. Some of this work has been done on a collective basis. For example, the Independent Schools Council, the body that represents private schools in England, published a report entitled *Good Neighbours* (ISC, 2003a), which attempted to show the close links already in place between private schools and local state schools and community groups. The report stated that there was a 'strong and enduring desire on the part of the enormous majority of independent schools to fulfil their charitable purpose and obligations and to contribute positively to their community' (ISC, 2003b, n.p.). It is obviously in the interests of individual schools, as well, to develop and/or sustain links to the local community, to ensure that their charitable status is not jeopardised, and to publicise these clearly on websites, prospectuses and other publicly available documents (see also McDonald *et al.* (2012) who make a similar argument with respect to Australian private schools). Thus, the legitimating function of local representations within marketing materials is again underlined.

Furthermore, under both the current Conservative–Liberal Democrat coalition government and the previous Labour administration, private schools have been strongly encouraged to work closely with state schools – and particularly those in close geographical proximity. Labour's manifesto for the 1997 general election stated that the party wished 'to build bridges wherever we can across education divides. The educational apartheid created by the public/private divide diminishes the whole education system' (Labour Party, 1996, n.p.). On assuming power, it quickly introduced funding to incentivise collaboration through the Independent–State School Partnership scheme. Although the scheme was ended by the current Coalition government, similar expectations of partnership remain. Indeed, the Chief Inspector of Schools recently argued that private schools need to do much more in this area, and described the current level of activity as 'crumbs off your tables, leading more to famine than feast' (Wilshaw, 2013). A more proactive approach has also been called for by the Secretary of State for Education who has urged more private schools to sponsor state-funded Academies, and become Teaching Schools[2] (Department for Education, 2013). In part, such initiatives have been informed, at least officially, by the desire to reduce what Labour referred to as the 'educational apartheid' of the two systems. However, they are also underpinned by an implicit (and sometimes explicit) assumption that the quality of education in the state sector can be enhanced if schools adopt many of the practices and values of the private sector, while private schools can benefit from the security and respectability that state support can bring (Tapper, 2003; Seldon, 2014).

Within this climate, the school website may offer an important opportunity for demonstrating alignment with this particular political agenda, to ensure that the 'public benefit' of the school is clear, and the legitimacy of its charitable status does not come under question.

Volunteering, Community Engagement and the 'Big Society'

The emphasis on representing local engagement within schools' websites can also been seen as articulating with broader policy agendas – beyond the education-specific imperatives discussed above. In particular, under the current and previous administration there has been a strong emphasis on volunteering and civic engagement. Holdsworth and Brewis (2014: 204) argue that in recent years in the UK, 'the figure of the selfless volunteer has been reinterpreted as a key social actor who can bridge community needs with individual reward and recognition'. Indeed, various scholars have contended that, as the boundaries of the welfare state have been redrawn, increasing emphasis has been placed on both groups and individuals for the delivery of community services. In this way, the 'Big Society' agenda advanced by the current Coalition government in the UK is seen as a means of transferring the responsibility and cost of delivery of some community services from the state to civil society (Kisby, 2010).

This increasing emphasis on the importance of volunteering has also been articulated from within the educational system. Active learning within community settings was an important part of the citizenship curriculum introduced into schools in 2002 (Brooks and Holford, 2009). Moreover, analyses of the higher education system have shown how the reframing of 'extra-curricular' activities as 'co-curricular' activities has been associated with an expectation that students develop synergies across their various university experiences and activities to help increase their employability on graduation (Holdsworth and Brewis, 2014). While those leaving elite schools are perhaps less in need of help in securing good labour market outcomes than their peers from less prestigious schools (Macmillan *et al.*, 2013), it was notable from our analysis that 'co-curricular activities' were emphasised clearly in many of the schools' websites. The foregrounding of local, voluntary activity within the websites and other materials tends to support Holdsworth's (2010: 422) contention that student volunteering has come to be endorsed as a panacea for a wide range of problems. She writes:

> Volunteering is assumed to assuage disputes between [educational institutions] and local communities; promote a positive image of the [institution] locally; enhance students' employability; provide students with fun and stimulating experiences and opportunities to make friends – as well as developing students' sense of civic duty and responsibility.

Conclusion

In this chapter, we have argued that 'local engagement' is an important theme in elite schools' representations of themselves to the outside world. Despite many of the schools having an international reputation and a considerable number of international pupils (Brooks and Waters, 2014), it was links with *local*, rather than international, communities that were emphasised on prominent webpages and in other publicly available materials. Although Collins and Coleman (2008) have suggested that, under the neo-liberal state, the 'spatial contract' linking schools and their immediate neighbourhoods has been lost (through the operation of a marketplace, in which families are encouraged to consider schools further afield), our textual data suggest that, for elite schools at least, local links remain important.

This foregrounding of the local may appear in tension with the images used on the majority of the schools' websites which, as we noted earlier, focus on their own grounds and buildings and tend to reinforce notions of elevation and 'apartness' (Waters and Brooks, 2014) through representations of grand architecture and extensive playing fields. However, we suggest that the two are not necessarily contradictory. Indeed, we have argued that an emphasis on local engagement, particularly through volunteering, has been part of the historical orientation of elite schools, and has been theorised as a means of ensuring the survival of such institutions – through demonstrating public benefit. The need to demonstrate such benefit has become more acute in recent years, as a result of changes to charity law, expectations of partnerships between state and private schools, and a redrawing of the boundaries of the welfare state. In this way, schools' decisions to foreground representations of the local within their 'public face' can be seen as an attempt to legitimate their social function, and thus – ultimately – a means of protecting their elevation and 'apartness'.

The examples given in this chapter have something significant to say, we contend, about the contemporary spatialities of (elite) schooling. As we have argued, schools would seem to take either an 'inward' or 'outward' approach to local engagement, generally preferring a mixture of the two. On balance, schools are far more keen to 'let the outside' into the school, as it were – drawing the local community into the space of the school. At the same time, it has been shown that school pupils are encouraged to leave the confines of the school and to 'get their hands dirty' within the neighbourhoods immediately surrounding the school. This often involves pupils undertaking activities in outside domestic spaces, thus extending the spaces of the school far beyond the traditional school setting. Far more research is still needed, however, on understanding the spatialities of elite schooling and how these spatialities help create – or reinforce – the boundaries of their privilege.

Notes

1 Academies are state-funded independent schools.
2 Teaching Schools play a leading role in the training and professional development of teachers, often working in partnership with a university department of education.

References

Allan, A. and Charles, C. (2013) 'Cosmo girls: Configurations of class and femininity in elite educational settings', *British Journal of Sociology of Education* (online advance publication).

Brooks, R. and Holford, J. (2009) 'Citizenship, learning and education: Themes and issues', *Citizenship Studies*, 13(2): 85–103.

Brooks, R. and Waters, J. (2014) 'The hidden internationalism of elite English schools', *Sociology* (advance online access).

Collins, D. and Coleman, T. (2008) 'Social geography of education: Looking within, and beyond, school boundaries', *Geography Compass*, 2(1): 281–299.

Department for Education (2013) Press release: 'Michael Gove calls on independent schools to help drive improvements to state education'. Available online at: https://www.gov.uk/government/news/michael-gove-calls-on-independent-schools-to-help-drive-improvements-to-state-education (accessed 24/01/14)

Hanson Thiem, C. (2009) 'Thinking through education: The geographies of contemporary educational restructuring', *Progress in Human Geography*, 33(2): 154–173.

Hayden, M. (2011) 'Transnational spaces of education: The growth of the international schools sector', *Globalisation, Societies and Education*, 9(2): 211–224.

Holdsworth, C. (2010) 'Why volunteer? Understanding motivations for student volunteering', *British Journal of Educational Studies*, 58(4): 421–437.

Holdsworth, C. and Brewis, G. (2014) 'Volunteering, choice and control: A case study of higher education volunteering', *Journal of Youth Studies*, 17(2): 204–219.

Holloway, S. and Jöns, H. (2012) 'Geographies of education and learning', *Transactions of the Institute of British Geographers*, 37(4): 482–488.

Holt, J. (2008) *Public School Literature, Civic Education and the Politics of Male Adolescence*, Aldershot: Ashgate.

Howard, A. (2013) 'Negotiating privilege through social justice efforts', in C. Maxwell and P. Aggelton (eds) *Privilege, Agency and Affect: Understanding the Production and Effects of Action*, Basingstoke: Palgrave.

Independent Schools Council (2003a) *Good Neighbours: ISC Schools and Their Local Communities*, London: ISC.

Independent Schools Council (2003b) *Schools become even better neighbours*, ISC press release. Available online at: http://www.isc.co.uk/press/press-releases/older/2003-06-17 (accessed 24/01/14)

Kenway, J. (2013) 'The gift economy of elite schooling', paper presented to the International Studies in the Sociology of Education Conference, London, 19 November.

Kisby, B. (2010) 'The Big Society: Power to the people?', *The Political Quarterly*, 81(4): 484–491.

Kraftl, P. (2006) 'Ecological architecture as performed art: Nant-y-Cwm Steiner School, Pembrokeshire', *Social and Cultural Geography*, 7(6): 927–948.

Kraftl, P. (2012) *Geographies of Alternative Education: Diverse Learning Spaces for Children and Young People*, Bristol: Policy Press.

Kraftl, P. (2013) 'Towards geographies of "alternative" education: A case study of UK home schooling families', *Transactions of the Institute of British Geographers*, 38: 436–450.

Labour Party (1996) *New Labour Because Britain Deserves Better*, London: The Labour Party. Available online at: http://www.politicsresources.net/area/uk/man/lab97.htm (accessed 24/01/14)

McCulloch, G. (2004) 'From incorporation to privatisation: Public and private secondary education in twentieth century England', in R. Aldrich (ed.) *Public or Private Education? Lessons from History*, London: Woburn Press.

McDonald, P., Pini, B. and Mayes, R. (2012) 'Organizational rhetoric in the prospectuses of elite private schools: Unpacking strategies of persuasion', *British Journal of Sociology of Education*, 33(1): 1–20.

Macmillan, L., Tyler, C. and Vignoles, A. (2013) *Who Gets the Top Jobs? The Role of Family Background and Networks in Recent Graduates' Access to High Status Professions*, London: Institute of Education Working Paper.

Norwood, C. (1929) *The English Tradition of Education*, London: John Murray.

Pile, S. and Keith, M. (eds) (1993) *Place and the Politics of Identity*, London: Routledge.

Reh, S., Rabenstein, K. and Fritzsche, B. (2011) 'Learning spaces without boundaries? Territories, power and how schools regulate learning', *Social and Cultural Geography*, 12(1): 83–98.

Rizvi, F. and Lingard, B. (2010) *Globalizing Educational Policy*, London: Routledge.

Seldon, A. (2014) *Schools United: Ending the Divide Between Independent and State*, London: Social Market Foundation.

Sutton Trust (2012) *The Educational Backgrounds of the Nation's Leading People*, London: The Sutton Trust.

Tapper, T. (2003) 'From Labour to New Labour: Bridging the divide between state and private schooling', in G. Walford (ed.) *British Private Schools: Research on Policy and Practice*, London: Woburn Press, pp. 11–30.

Wardman, N., Hutchesson, R., Gottschall, K., Drew, C. and Saltmarsh, S. (2010) 'Starry eyes and subservient selves: Portraits of "well-rounded" girlhood in the prospectuses of all-girl elite private schools', *Australian Journal of Education*, 54(3): 249–261.

Waters, J. and Brooks, R. (2014) '"The magical operations of separation": English elite schools' on-line geographies and functional isolation', *Geoforum* (advance online access).

Wilshaw, M. (2013) Michael Wilshaw's speech to HMC conference, *The Guardian Teacher Network*, October 2013. Available online at: http://www.theguardian.com/teacher-network/teacher-blog/2013/oct/02/ofsted-michael-wilshaw-independent-schools (accessed 24/01/14).

Part III

The Impact of Globalization on Institutional and Student Identities

The third part of this volume examines the internationalization of higher education institutions, the international circulation of elite higher education students, and the various ways in which these processes contribute to the development of global elite identities.

The chapter by Chiang, Meng and Tian looks at the effects of globalisation on the Chinese higher education system. It analyses diverse policies launched by the Chinese government to address the challenges of developing a 'knowledge economy' and to ensure China's elite universities become global players in the higher education market. The authors show that these policies have succeeded in creating a new elite sector in higher education and propelled a small group of higher education establishments to the top tier of world-class universities. One of the consequences of this has been that cultural resources and geographical location have become critical in driving the reproduction of national social inequalities.

Fazal Rizvi's chapter considers how Indian elite schools have embraced the discourse of 'Asia Rising'. He examines how elite schools modelled initially on the British nineteenth-century public schools have reconstituted themselves as having an international outlook in order to distinguish themselves and offer educational advantages to their students and those parents with 'new' money to invest in education. Nevertheless, Rizvi also illustrates that in this process, schools have to engage in a complicated exercise of trying to combine both a sense of identity forged out of their colonial history, postcolonial determination and global orientations.

The third chapter in this part, by Darchy-Koechlin, Draelants and Tenret, examines the effect of internationalization on the French *grandes écoles*. Due to a rigorous entrance examination, which has strong public support as legitimating the selection of elite French students, it is difficult for these institutions to recruit students from outside the French education system. The authors discuss how strong support for the *concours* ensures that international students who must gain entry through a different selection process are positioned as not having secured their place in these elite institutions on meritocratic grounds by their fellow students. In this way, French elites reinstate their particular distinction.

Finally, Kenway, Langmead and Epstein examine girls' elite schooling in the context of globalization and the need to prepare elite subjects to make their mark in this much larger space. The authors argue that increasingly, the demand that girls be prepared for success on the global stages is incongruent with being educated in a cocoon of a single-sex school. How can girls be adequately prepared to rise to the top of the corporate world? The chapter examines closely how single-sex elite girls' schools have developed (rhetorical) strategies for dealing with this concern expressed by girls and their families through positioning themselves as inculcating a progressive feminism among their students.

8 Globalization and Elite Universities in China

Tien-Hui Chiang, Fan-Hua Meng
and Xiao-Ming Tian

Introduction

Through an interplay of political, cultural and economic processes, the United States and Western economies have exported the philosophy of neoliberalism around the globe. This has fused many countries into an interlocking body of social and economic relations (Harvey 2005; Wallerstein 2004). This export process has transformed local value systems and has established a single value system as a new world order. The OECD has further created and disseminated a discourse that has established a set of linear and mutually reinforcing relationships within the framework of globalization, international competitiveness, human capital and higher education (Stromquist 2002). As argued by Foucault (1990, 2003), such a discourse can transform social actors into docile and productive bodies, who willingly subject themselves to the commands of the dominant group. People's souls are successfully being remoulded (Popkewitz 2000) via this new form of governing technology (Ball 2006). Consequently, many countries have redefined their political rationalities and are abandoning the goal of achieving social justice in order to adopt international competitiveness as their new mission. This is evident, for example, in the almost universal commitment of nation states to making the expansion of higher education a top priority in their political agendas (Chiang 2011, 2013).

As neo-liberalists have promoted the value of free-market logic, arguing that it is able concomitantly to improve efficiency and ensure service quality, the tenets of managerialism have also been applied to higher education. All higher education institutions are required to demonstrate their performance in outcomes which are measured, compared and ranked (Ball 2006; Torres 2006). Resources and symbolic value are accumulated by those institutions that achieve the highest rankings. At the same time, the uneven distribution of wealth and income inequality reinforce economic and cultural reproduction, with unprivileged rural students in China unable to access the top universities. This essay sets out to shed some light on this issue by exploring the situation in China, which has become a key member of the global higher education market. We focus on the macro issues, by examining the student composition of the top Chinese universities. We further analyse associated factors, such as economic policies and higher education policies. We argue that the pressures of globalization have given the Chinese government no choice but to undertake the development of international competitiveness through the channel of top universities if it wants to flourish in the global market. As Luhmann (1995) argues, in order to maintain an independent operation, a system has to engage in a process of functional evolution that makes its functions unique; otherwise, this system will be subsumed by other systems. This evolution involves the strategy of 'reference', allowing the system to develop the best action plan/project to meet the requirements of a new social context. A core referential action in the context of globalization is that of maximizing international competitiveness. Success in the global market both serves to maintain political authority and brings benefits to citizens by raising standards of living. Globalization then becomes not simply a capitalist game but also a synthesis of economic and political action (Chiang 2013).

However, one cost which results from the rationality of international competition is increased social and economic inequality, as can be seen in the student composition of top universities. According to Offe (1996), internal rationality guarantees that the state implements its legitimate obligations. Therefore, this cost must be viewed as a side-effect of a policy that aims to enlarge the scope of economic activities, creating more jobs for its citizens. This relationship suggests that joining the global market has become a vital way of implementing this obligation for the Chinese government. However, as Offe argues, the state must win people's trust, in order to sustain its legitimate sovereignty. Therefore, opening a gateway for rural students to access top universities can improve social equity and cohesion. The Education Action Project, an initiative that Premier Keqiang Li announced in March 2014, is an attempt to increase by at least 10 per cent the number of rural students at top universities (Yuan and Zhang 2014). This is a political policy as much as an educational one.

Globalization, International Competitiveness and Higher Education

It is argued that the emergence of globalization has involved an interplay between American imperialism, international markets and a great change in politics. Regarding American imperialism, the United States has employed the strategy of liberalization in international trade, as evidenced by the United Nations Monetary and Financial Conference at Bretton Woods in 1944, the agreements which led to the establishment of international trade and financial arrangements, such as the General Agreement on Tariffs and Trade (GATT, a former incarnation of WTO), the IMF and the WB (Hytrek and Zentgraf 2008). The United States also took the decline of the British Empire in the 1960s as a great opportunity to practice American imperialism, by adopting the policy of liberalization in international trade. This was evidenced in attempts during the GATT Kennedy Round Negotiations to lower tariffs in the European Community. This action further generated the phenomenon of 'the Eurocurrency Market', instigated by a large volume of overseas investments by American companies that led to the development of transnational enterprises (Miyoshi 1996). This increasingly global fusion of the economy had a profound influence on the shaping of a new global context from 1979 to 1985, when industrialized societies devoted themselves to exporting, which resulted in an expanded global market. The entry of former socialist countries into the global market starting in 1990 has further reinforced the influence of globalization (Frieden 2006).

Along with the expansion of international trade, there has been a shift from great government to neoliberalism in politics. The idea of great government assumes that a free-market mechanism cannot replace the government's obligation, because even a booming economic situation cannot benefit all citizens (Keynes 1935). However, the theory of great government lost its legitimacy in the late 1960s due to the fact that welfare socialism had accumulated a considerable amount of national debt, which was viewed as a key element in eroding national competitiveness (Harvey 2005). The economic recession of the 1970s, caused by the oil crisis, further intensified the voices questioning welfare socialism and led most politicians to attempt to distance themselves from Keynesianism (Hytrek and Zentgraf 2008). This new social and political context offered neoliberalism a huge space to develop its influence, and it eventually became a legitimate ideology in the 1980s, when Ronald Reagan and Margaret Thatcher were in power and had committed themselves to promoting the logic of a free market (Frieden 2006; Glyn 2006).

Under American leadership, neoliberalism has been transformed into a new world value and thus is spreading globalization around the world (Heywood 2003; Stiglitz 2002). As the size of the global market has significantly expanded, the arena of competition has changed, moving from the domestic level to the international stage. Furthermore, globalization addresses the application of knowledge and pushes many countries into a competitive arena that requires skills. International competitiveness thus becomes a crucial ingredient for these countries' survival in the global market. This component helps them improve their national strength and, thus, benefits their citizens through better living conditions.

It is argued that this objective can be achieved by expanding higher education (Chiang 2011; Stromquist 2002). Under the control of the United States, which has been acting as a transnational neoliberalism export corporation (Berberoglu 2003; Wallerstein 2004), the OECD legitimizes the linkage between international competitiveness and human capital when it assumes that higher education institutions are the main sites for improving the quality of human capital, which, in turn, is the main force driving the economic development of a country (Chiang 2011). Consequently, as many countries have accepted the assumption of linear relationships between globalization, international competitiveness, human capital and higher education, the expansion of higher education has become a top priority on their political agenda (Stromquist 2002). Free-market logic further urges institutions of higher education to demonstrate their abilities in performativity (Ball 2006). This competition-based approach reinforces the idea of evaluation, compelling them to conform to the principles of public managerialism (Torres 2006). Therefore, university ranking is a crucial yardstick of their performance (Chiang 2014). This further serves to legitimize the value of the top universities, which then have the right to exclusively dominate educational resources.

Globalization, Equity and Cultural Reproduction

Relevant studies show that globalization has caused social equity to deteriorate, because the gap in incomes between rich and poor has increased. This is manifest in the fact that between 1979 and 2006, the average after-tax income of the richest 1 per cent of American households rose from $337,100 to $1.2 million, compared with an average national growth in income from $47,900 to $71,900 (Hacker and Pierson 2010). Similarly, CEOs collected an average weekly income of $155,769 in 2003, which was over 300 times the weekly salary of labourers ($517). In comparison, the ratio in 1982 was 42:1 (Hytrek and Zentgraf 2008). Rapley (2004) further pointed out that this increase in inequality from the 1980s to the 1990s occurred across both developed and developing countries. In terms of obtaining profit, professionals and those in high-ranking positions, such as CEOs, were winners and the rest were losers.

This economic inequality may further intensify the phenomenon of cultural reproduction, specifically in situations in which class reproduction is not rooted in the production process but the cultural field. This occurs because social value determines legitimate knowledge, which is the main source for constructing curriculum knowledge (Bernstein 1990, 1996; Bourdieu 1993; Bourdieu and Passeron 1977). As argued by Gramsci (1971), power has the ability to construct mainstream social cultures, meaning that which is normally viewed as legitimate. Therefore, with the influence of the middle class being predominant in modern society, their cultures tend be to be viewed as the orthodox source for developing curriculum content, resulting in a curriculum that values abstract concepts and logical relationships. Such an academic curriculum largely projects the thoughts and lifestyles of middle-/upper-class cultures and disconnects that of working-class cultures. Tunstall's (1973) findings show that physical labour does not draw heavily on mental abilities, but rather physical strength. Willis (1977) also found that the working class explicitly displays masculinity and practical-oriented culture rather than reasoning behaviour. Those findings indicate that the cultural competences of working-class students are insufficient in bridging the gap between the academic curriculum and their practical-oriented life. They are forced to learn another group's culture and thus face learning difficulties. Consequently, most working-class students do not have excellent academic performances and thus tend to fail in meritorious society (Bernstein 1996).

This relationship shows that their failures are not derived from their mental conditions but their reasoning ability, which is largely moulded by the context in which they are positioned. Bourdieu (1990, 2000) argues that although the actor behaves like an autonomous agent, a disposition directs his reactions towards the outside world. Inner mechanisms, which is conceptualized as *habitus* and refers to a system of perception, reasoning and reaction, is not innate but rather moulded within a specific type of context, conceptualized as 'social space', in which a certain type of cultural capital is provided by parents. For Bernstein (1990, 1996), an academic curriculum embodies a strong classification, referring to a knowledge structure inclining to a vertical model, so that acquiring its contents requires a logical reasoning ability that is reliant upon appropriate linguistic ability being moulded in the family, termed as 'initial recontextualization'. In terms of interaction, a democratic mode, which middle-class parents employ, creates an open and interactive context for dialogue, allowing their children to have more time and space for exploring the meanings of issues that they are engaged in. Consequently, middle-class children are able to develop an elaborate code of abstract terms that help them use logical reasoning, conceptualized as 'un-context bound' competence, which is the key skill required to decode an academic curriculum. In contrast, working-class parents generally employ an authoritarian style in raising their children and thus depress them into a didactic mode that tends to result in them developing a restricted code. This does not facilitate their use of logical reasoning, termed context-bound competence.

Both Bourdieu and Bernstein provide outstanding insights in decoding the phenomenon of cultural reproduction. Related studies have verified their arguments and have identified big differences in educational values and strategies between different social classes. Middle-class parents tend to recognize the value of higher educational certificates on the job market, so that they develop long-term expectations, viewing educational achievement as a legitimate ticket for accessing the white-collar club (Ball *et al.* 1997). Furthermore, they are anxious about their children's future careers because social development is dynamic and unpredictable (Ball 2006). Such anxiety triggers their 'rational capital', or their ability to employ their rational ability to initiate systematic actions, including vision, organization, action, monitoring and revision (Chiang 2010). Such rational capital is manifest in a series of educational studies, such as school selection (Ball 1994) and participation in the child's learning (Reay 1998). Consequently, middle-class parents invest a lot of cultural capital (Bourdieu 1993) in constructing an academic context for cultivating their children's logical reasoning abilities.

In contrast, blue-collar jobs require a limited level of training and in turn diminish working-class parents' recognition of educational functions that can be actualized in the long term. Consequently, they tend to possess only short-term expectations, hoping their children will be able to join the work force as soon as possible (Ball et al.1997). Furthermore, shop floor culture reveals that vigour and strength are the key elements needed for them to finish their jobs (Willis 1977). Such characteristics tend to deprive the rational capital and educational recognition of working-class parents. Their children are positioned within a practical-oriented context that tends to block insiders from developing an appropriate habitus for learning logical relationships. Consequently, it is very hard for them to overcome this cultural constraint embedded in an academic curriculum.

Who Can Access the Top Universities in China?

As the previous analysis has shown, globalization has exacerbated the inequality in wealth distribution. If this situation were to occur in China, students from better economic regions would have greater chances of accessing top universities than others. In fact, the findings of relevant studies show that globalization has intensified the phenomenon of cultural reproduction in higher education. As the Open Door Policy has financially benefited many people in agricultural regions, these improved financial conditions have motivated young people from agricultural regions to acquire university degrees. This can be seen in the fact that the total percentage of this group who attended the university entrance examination jumped from 55.95 per cent (1,570,499 out of 2,806,868) in 1997 to 60.99 per cent (5,692,193 out of 9,333,221) in 2010 (DDP 2011). Although, in terms of numbers, this group seems to be predominant, they are positioned in a much less privileged status than their counterparts from urban regions. Relevant studies have consistently documented this inequality, finding that the number of rural students registered at top universities has declined. For example, the percentage of students from agricultural regions at Tsinghua University dropped from 21.7 per cent in 1990 to 17.6 per cent in 2000. A similar picture can be seen at Beijing University, with the percentage of rural students declining from 18.8 per cent in 1991 to 16.3 per cent in 1999, and at Beijing Normal University, where it fell from 28.0 per cent in 1990 to 22.3 per cent in 2002 (Xinhuanet 2005). Liu and her associates (2009) uncovered a similar situation, finding that this group at Beijing University had shrunk from between 20 per cent and 40 per cent from 1978 to 1998 to around 15 per cent between 2000 and 2005. Another study provided a more striking profile by discovering a huge gap between the proportion of urban and rural contenders at the entrance examination of Tsinghua University, and the proportion of successful applicants. Rural students represented 62 per cent of contenders and only 17 per cent of successful applicants in 2010 (*Southern Weekly* 2011).

The above studies also show that urban regions have become the main suppliers of students to high-ranking universities. This restricted context tends to leave local – as opposed to national – universities as the main option for rural students, as is evidenced by the great proportion of students from agricultural areas attending institutions such as Tangshan College, North China Coal Medical University and Hebei Polytechnic College and rose to 63.3 per cent on average in 2003 (Xinhuanet 2005). Dong-Ping Yang's evidence shows that this inequality between the local and the national has become worse over time. For example, the number of students from agricultural areas in Hubei province who enrolled at junior colleges swelled from 39 per cent to 62 per cent in the period from 2002 to 2007 (Southern Weekly 2011). All the studies above have consistently reported the phenomenon of student stratification at higher education institutions, which blocks rural students' access to top universities and at the same time ensures the cultural reproduction of more privileged social groups. As social context and education policies profoundly shape educational trends and results, globalization and its relevant policies in education contribute greatly to the production of this inequality.

Globalization in China

After he became the 'paramount leader' in 1978, Deng Xiaoping was determined to transform China into a modernized country able to participate in international trade. This was part of a programme called *Gaige Kaifang* (literally 'Reforms and Openness'), often summed up as the *Four Modernizations*. Large-scale economic reform commenced in 1979, as evidenced by the establishment of Special Economic Zones in Shenzhen, Zhuhai, Xiamen and Shantou. The influence of this approach was further expanded by the introduction of the Open Door policy in 14 harbour cities in 1984, starting with Tianjin, Shanghai and Guangzhou, and extending to specific regions in 1985, such as the Yangtze River Delta and the Pearl River Delta (Deng 2001), and the creation of the Financial Zone in Pudong, Shanghai in 1990 (SCPRC 1990). This Open Door policy triggered major economic growth, which grew by an average of 9.97 per cent annually from 2000 to 2013. The GNP increased from RMB 10,965 billion in 2001 to RMB 51,947 billion in 2012, and the GDP per capita grew from RMB 8,621 to RMB 38,459 (NBS 2013a). The official statistical data shows that unlike the globalization occurring in other countries, wealth distribution was much more even in China, as demonstrated by the fact that differences in incomes per capita between urban and rural regions were much more stable, remaining at a ratio of about 3:1 For example, it was 2.79:1 in 2000 (RMB 6,280 versus RMB 2,253), 3.22:1 in 2005 (RMB 10,493 versus RMB 3,254) and 3.10:1 in 2012 (RMB 24,564 versus RMB 7,916) (NBS 2006, 2013a). Furthermore, the gap in household incomes between wealthy coastal cities and other regions significantly decreased, as evidenced by the ratio of the GDP per capita between Shanghai and Gansu province, which was reduced from 7.28:1 in 2000 (RMB 30,047 versus RMB 4,129) to 3.88:1 in 2012 (RMB 85,373 versus RMB 21,978) (NBS 2013a).

However, the distribution of wealth from this economic growth has been uneven. In terms of economic development, China can be classified into three regions. Figure 8.1 shows these geographic segments. As the Open Door policy was first and most intensively implemented in coastal areas, followed by a more modest promotion in the central region and an unsystematic and insufficient implementation in the western region, wealth generation has significantly increased and been concentrated to the big cities in the coastal zone, and decreased when going from east to west. In other words, the gap in wealth distribution among those three regions is huge. For example, most of the top wealthy cities and provinces, such as Beijing, Shanghai, Jiangsu, Zhejiang and Guangdong, are all located in the coastal region. In contrast, the economic conditions of most of the western region are underdeveloped and even poor, so that people's incomes are much lower than those in the other two regions. One of the crucial indicators of these differences is the price of housing. The average cost per square metre in Beijing is RMB 23,600 (The Beijing News 2014), which is far beyond the incomes of most people in other regions. In fact, the real market prices are much higher than this figure. According to our observations, in 2014, it is around RMB 50,000 per square metre for previously owned houses and RMB 80,000 per square metre for new houses in the third zone in Beijing. It is even higher in the second zone. The annual expenditure on education and cultural consumption per household can be viewed as another core indicator to

Figure 8.1 The distribution of economic development in China.

further test our assumption. Its nation-wide level was RMB 446 in 2012, against RMB 1,153 in Beijing and RMB 952 in Shanghai (NBS 2013a). These gaps reveal that while the Open Door policy created a considerable amount of wealth for the coastal cities, most people in other regions did not benefit to a great extent from economic growth.

Influencing the Elite Universities Through Policy

From the perspective of cultural reproduction, we would predict that the better economic conditions in the coastal region would enable parents to invest greater volumes of economic capital in their children in order for them to have better academic performances, thus sustaining both economic and cultural reproduction. The outcomes of recent higher education policies, notably the 211 Project and the 985 Project, appear to confirm our prediction.

The 211 Project

Although the number of higher education institutions in China significantly expanded to over 1,000 by the 1990s, neither of the top two institutions, Beijing University and Tsinghua University, were recognized as world-class universities by the international community. Premier Peng Li (1988–1998) dedicated himself to transforming some selected universities into institutions of international standard by announcing the 211 Project in 1991. This idea became official policy in February 1993 – the Chinese Education Reform and Development Outline – and was aimed at raising 100 universities to world-class level by the twenty-first century (MOE 1993). It only covered 15 universities originally but greatly enlarged its scope to 116 (BIT 2008).

These selected top universities received considerable extra capital from the central government between 1995 and 2005, to the tune of RMB 36,826,000,000. Such extra financial resources assisted the 211 Project universities to develop their measurable academic performance and improve their international reputation (The 211 Project Working Group 2007). Consequently, the 211 Project certified those selected higher education institutions as 'top universities' with official recognition and exclusive privileges, notably huge additional funding. This policy created incentives for those top universities to recruit excellent academic researchers. According to the 2014 Chinese University Evaluation Report, 77 out of the top 80 universities were involved in the 211 Project (Cuaa net 2014). Therefore, the 211 Project universities can be characterized as the 'Elite Universities Group'. This also enabled them to achieve academic awards and prizes more easily than non-participating competitors, as evidenced by the fact that 56 per cent ($N = 764$) of distinguished young scholars of the National Science Council were from 211 Project universities (The 211 Project Working Group 2007).

The 985 Project

In order for China to obtain a privileged position in the knowledge-based society era, President Zemin Jiang (1993–2003) emphasized the value of top universities in a speech given at the ceremony for the 100th anniversary of Beijing University, on 4 May 1998. He argued that top, world-class universities were the main sites for improving the quality of human capital and, in turn, enhancing China's international competitiveness. This talk prompted the Ministry of Education (MOE) to launch the 985 Project, aiming to establish world-class universities whose mission would be to achieve international competitiveness. Initially, only Beijing University and Tsinghua University were on the list because of their well-established reputations. However, in order to create more world-class universities and reduce the gap between Beijing city and other regions, the 985 Project expanded its pool from two to nine in 1999 and provided extra funding of RMB 7,800,000,000 in total. Eventually, by 2011, the 985 Project included 39 higher education institutions that were also on the list of the 211 Project. This programme in effect bestowed the symbol of exclusive academic excellence upon those 39 universities and allowed them to legitimately claim the title of elite university. This distinguished reputation was further confirmed by independent ranking systems, as noted in the 2014 Chinese University Evaluation Report, which reported that the top 30 universities in China were all the 985 Project universities (Cuaa net 2014).

Figure 8.2 The geographic locations of the 211 Project universities.

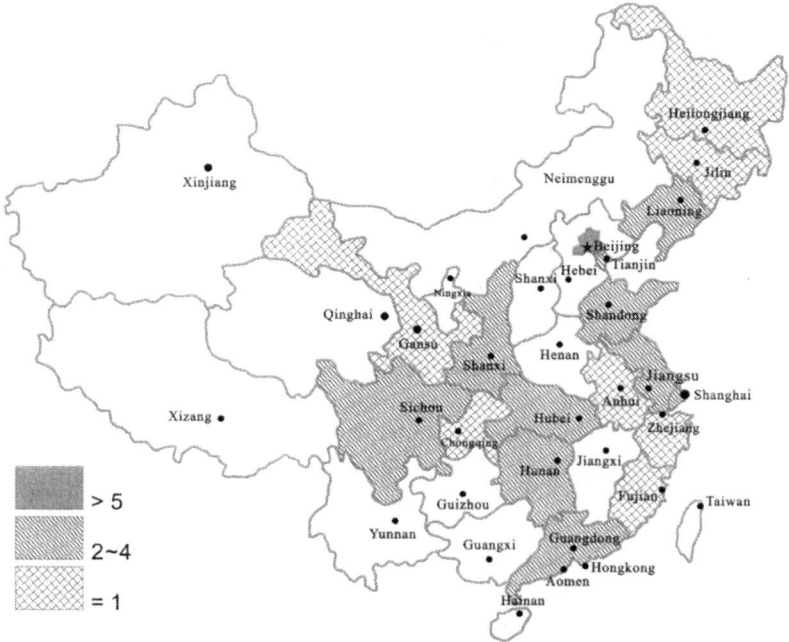

Figure 8.3 The geographic locations of the 985 Project universities.

The Correspondence Principle Between Top Universities and Economic Regions

Figure 8.2 indicates that the 211 Project universities were concentrated in the coastal zone, with 57.8 per cent (67 out of 116) being located in that region. The western region only included 19.8 per cent (23). This unbalanced picture reappears in Figure 8.3, which shows that the coastal zone was home to 61.5 per cent of the 985 Project universities (24 out of 39), as opposed to 18.0 per cent in the western region. If we compare Figures 8.1–8.3, it is clear that the uneven distribution of top universities corresponds to the three economic regions. In other words, the coastal region possesses both economic and education privileges, which can be viewed as key factors contributing to the constitution of cultural reproduction at top universities.

The Unequal Allocation of Financial Resources for Education

The unequal allocation of financial resources further cements the segmentation between top universities and lower universities. Basically, higher education institutions in China are officially classified into two categories: national and local. The MOE is in charge of national universities and local authorities are responsible for local universities. Most national universities belong to either the 211 Project or the 985 Project. In contrast, local universities are largely excluded from these two projects. According to official data from the National Bureau of Statistics (NBS), the financial gap between national and local universities has substantially increased, as indicated in Figure 8.4 (NBS 2013b), which shows that this gap has continued to widen since 1998, when the 985 Project was launched. In 1996, education spending per student at national universities was slightly higher than that at local universities, with a ratio of 1.3:1 (RMB 9,319 versus RMB 7,322).

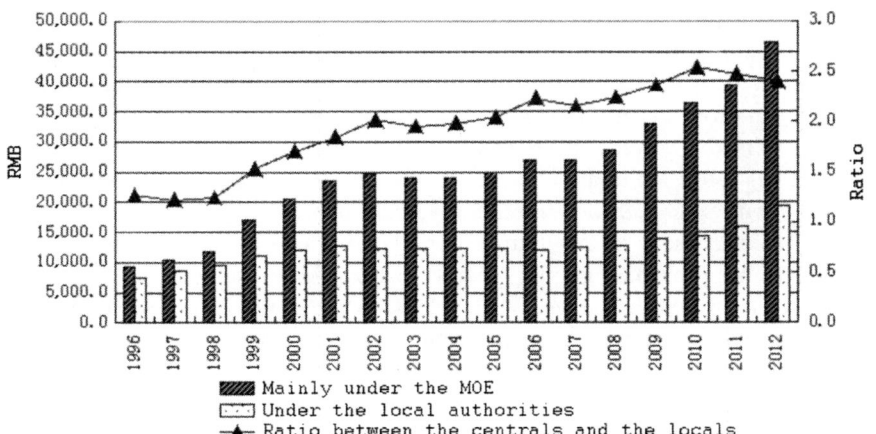

Figure 8.4 Average expenditure of students on education.

However, this discrepancy increased to 1.7:1 in 2000 (RMB 20,590 versus RMB 12,078), 2.0:1 in 2005 (RMB 24,847 versus RMB 12,163) and 2.5:1 in 2010 (RMB 36,449 versus RMB 14,374). Although this trend has since declined slightly, the imbalance remained rather high in 2012, at 2.4:1 (RMB 46,575 versus RMB 19,420).

The allocation of financial resources to rural and urban high schools is also extremely uneven, with an expenditure per student at urban high schools of RMB 9,978, compared with RMB 7,878 at rural high schools (NBS 2013b). Furthermore, urban high schools are equipped with better facilities than rural high schools. Students at urban high schools enjoy an average of 7.6 square metres of building space each, while students at rural high schools have only 5.6 square metres (NBS 2011). This inequality in resource allocation further reinforces the reputation and effectiveness of urban high schools, allowing them to recruit most academically excellent junior high-school graduates.

Conclusion

While the Open Door policy has produced much wealth in China, a gap in incomes has become visible, as evidenced by the fact that this wealth is concentrated in coastal zones and is significantly less the further west you travel. This uneven distribution reinforces both economic and cultural reproduction and affects access to the national and international labour market. Our evidence further shows that this inequality can also be partly attributed to higher education policies. While the 211 Project and the 985 Project successfully constructed top universities, these elite universities acquired exclusive privileges, such as extra funding and official recognition. Another side-effect of these projects was that of limiting the access of rural students to these elite universities, given their uneven geographic distribution. All these factors indicate that the Open Door policy and the approach to creating elite universities together have created an unequal context in favour of urban students. A project attempting to open a gateway for rural students to access top universities has addressed this problem. This project further demonstrates the role of the state as both an economic and political agent, seeking economic growth and social equity. When inequality becomes a social phenomenon, the state needs to redress this inequality in order to sustain its neutrality and win people's trust. If it fails in this mission, social discourses come to justify its inclination to capitalists.

China has sought to address the challenges of knowledge production, international economic competitiveness and the development of a high-skills labour force by intervening directly in the status order of higher education to create an 'elite' sector. This has promoted a small group of national universities to the top tier of world-class universities. All these relationships further suggest that while globalization has exerted a profound influence on participating countries, individual nations, including China, may develop different strategies to obtain the best advantages. However, this economy-led approach to higher education planning has had the unintended consequence of eroding social justice and equity. Rural students are massively over-represented at 'local' universities that are less well funded, award degrees of lower status and exchange value, and offer limited access to high-income jobs. Achieving a balance between economic interests and social justice is a major challenge for the state, and functions as a key element in regulating its direction.

References

Ball, S. (1994). *Education Reform: A Critical and Post-Structural Approach*. Buckingham: Open University Press.

Ball, S. (2006). Performativities and fabrications in the education economy: Towards the performative society. In H. Lauder, P. Brown, J. Dillabough and A.H. Halsey (eds) *Education, Globalization & Social Change* (pp. 692–701). Oxford: Oxford University Press.

Ball, S.J., Bowe, R. and Gewirtz, S. (1997). Circuits of schooling: A sociological exploration of parental choice of school in social-class context. In A.H. Halsey, H. Lauder, P. Brown and A.S. Wells (eds) *Education, Culture, Economy, and Society*. Oxford: Oxford University Press.

Berberoglu, B. (2003). *Globalization of Capital and the Nation-State: Imperialism, Class Struggle, and the State in the Age of Global Capitalism*. Oxford: Rowman & Littlefield.

Bernstein, B. (1990). *The Structuring of Pedagogic Discourse*. London: Routledge.

Bernstein, B. (1996). *Pedagogy, Symbolic Control and Identity*. London: Taylor & Francis.

BIT (Beijing Institute of Technology) (2008). *One of the First Batch of the 211 Project Universities*. Data retrieved 28 April 2014 from http://www.bit.edu.cn/xxgk/tjzl/67816.htm

Bourdieu, P. (1990). *In Other Words: Essays Towards a Reflective Sociology*. Stanford, CA: Stanford University Press.

Bourdieu, P. (1993). *The Field of Cultural Production: Essays on Art and Literature*. Cambridge: Polity.

Bourdieu, P. (2000). *Pascalian Meditations*. Cambridge: Polity.

Bourdieu, P. and Passeron, C. (1977). *Reproduction in Education, Society and Culture*. London: Sage.

Chiang, T.H. (2010). A sociological analysis in curriculum policies and social inequality: Rational capital and educational actions of different social class parents. *Beijing Tsinghua Journal of Education*, 6, 19–26.

Chiang T.H. (2011). How globalization drives the higher education policy of the state. *Journal of Education Sciences*, 1, 7–20.

Chiang, T.H. (2013). Pursuing ideology or conforming reality: Why does education shift its function from equity to competitiveness in the era of globalization? *Journal of Global Economy*, 9(4), 249–262.

Chiang, T.H. (2014). Globalization, market logic, the state and the resettlement of higher education. *Global Business & International Management Conference Journal*, 7(1), 2–10.

Cuaa net (2014). *The 2014 Chinese University Evaluation Report*. Data retrieved 11 April 2014 from http://www.cuaa.net/cur/2014/2014zgdxpjyjbg.pdf

DDP (Department of Development & Planning) (2011). *Educational Statistics Yearbook of China*. Beijing: People's Education.

Deng, X. (2001). *The Selections of Deng Xiaoping*, Vol. 3. Beijing: People's Press.

Foucault, M. (1990). *The History of Sexuality*. London: Penguin.

Foucault, M. (2003). *Society Must be Defended*. New York: Picador.

Frieden. J. (2006). *Global Capitalism: Its Fall and Rise in the Twentieth Century*. New York: Norton.

Glyn, A. (2006). *Capitalism Unleashed*. Oxford: Oxford University Press.

Gramsci, A. (1971). *Selections from the Prison Notebooks of Antonio Gramsci.* New York: International Publishers.

Hacker, J.S. and Pierson, P. (2010). *Winner-Take-All Politics: How Washington Made the Rich Richer and Turned Its back on the Middle Class.* New York: Simon & Schuster.

Harvey, D. (2005). *A Brief History of Neoliberalism.* Oxford: Oxford University Press.

Heywood, A. (2003). *Political Ideologies* (3rd edition). Basingstoke: Palgrave Macmillan.

Hytrek, G. and Zentgraf, K.M. (2008). *America Transformed: Globalization, Inequality, and Power.* New York: Oxford University Press.

Keynes, J.M. (1935). *The General Theory of Employment, Interest, and Money.* Publisher unknown.

Liu, Y.S., Wang, Z.M. and Yang, X.F. (2009). Selection of elites: Views from social status, geographical variation and capital gaining. *Tsinghua Journal of Education*, 30(5), 42–59.

Luhmann, N. (1995). *Social Systems.* Stanford, CA: Stanford University Press.

Miyoshi, M. (1996). A borderless world? From colonialism to transnationalism and the decline of the nation-state. In R. Wilson and W. Dissanayake (eds) *Cultural Production and the Transnational Imaginary* (pp. 78–106). London: Duke University Press.

MOE (The Ministry of Education) (1993). *China's Education Reform and Development Outline.* Data retrieved 10 April 2014 from http:// www.moe.gov.cn/publicfiles/business/ htmlfiles/moe/s6986/200407/2484.html

Offe, C. (1996). *Modernity and the State.* Cambridge, MA: MIT Press.

NBS (The National Bureau of Statistics) (2006). *China Statistical Year Book.* Beijing: Statistic Press.

NBS (The National Bureau of Statistics) (2011). *China Education Finance Statistical Yearbook.* Beijing: China Statistic Press.

NBS (The National Bureau of Statistics) (2013a). *China Statistical Year Book.* Beijing: Statistical Press.

NBS (The National Bureau of Statistics) (2013b). *China Education Finance Statistical Yearbook.* Beijing: China Statistic Press.

Popkewitz, T. (2000). Reform as the social administration of the child: Globalization of knowledge and power. In N.C. Burbules and C.A. Torres (eds) *Globalization and Education: Critical Perspectives* (pp. 157–186). New York: Routledge.

Rapley, J. (2004). *Globalization and Inequality.* London: Lynne Rienner.

Reay, D. (1998). Cultural reproduction: Mothers' involvement in their children's primary schooling. In M. Grenfell and D. James (eds) *Bourdieu and Education: Acts of Practical Theory.* London: Falmer.

SCPRC (The State Council of the People's Republic of China) (1990). An official reply on the issue of development and opening of Pudong. Beijing: SCPRC's Official Laws and Regulations Documents, 2 June.

Southern Weekly (2011). *Poor Children Have no Spring? Why the Key Universities are More and More Far Away from Poor Children.* Data retrieved 10 April 2014 from http://www. infzm.com/content/61888.

Stiglitz, J.E. (2002). *Globalization and Its Discontents.* London: W.W. Norton.

Stromquist, N.P. (2002). *Education in a Globalized World.* Oxford: Rowman & Littlefield.

The 211 Project Working Group (2007). *The Report of the 211 Project Developments from 1995 to 2005.* Beijing: Higher Education.

The Beijing News (2014). *The Prices of House Have Increased 13%.* Data retrieved 2 May 2014 from http://estate.caijing.com.cn/2014-01-10/113798489.html

The Xinhuanet (2005). *Proportion of Rural Students in Key University is on the Decline.* Data retrieved 10 April 2014 from http://news.xinhuanet.com/edu/2005-02/16/content_2581541.htm.

Torres, C.A. (2006). Globalization and higher education in the Americas. In R. Rhoads and C.A. Torres (eds) *The University, State, and Market* (pp. 3–38). Stanford, CA: Stanford University Press.

Tunstall, J. (1973). Work and the social life of fishermen. In P. Worsley (ed.) *Modern Sociology.* London: Penguin.

Wallerstein, I. (2004). *World-Systems Analysis.* London: Duke University Press.

Willis, P. (1977). *Learning to Labor: How Working Class Kids Get Working Class Jobs.* New York: Columbia University.

Yuan, C.L. and Zhang, G. (2014). An increase of 28000 rural children in the key universities this year. *China Youth Daily*, 2014–03–08(02).

9   The Discourse of "Asia Rising" in an Elite Indian School

Fazal Rizvi

In recent years, much has been written about the rise of Asia as an economic and political power. Both academic and popular books have sought to describe and explain the strong economic performance of many Asian countries, not only China and Korea but also India and the ASEAN countries. Impressed by this success, journalists and scholars in Europe and the United States have been competing with each other to find appropriate metaphors to capture the changing economic and political architecture of the world. Fareed Zakaria (2006) has, for example, used the term "Post-American World" to describe the rise of Asia and by implication the decline of America. The title of Martin Jacques's (2009) recent book is *When China Rules the World*; and a part of the title of Tom Friedman's new book, written jointly with Mandelbaum (2012), is *That Used to be Us*. This book not only attempts to explain how and why America has fallen behind but also assumes the inevitable and continuing rise of Asia.

Such hyperbole is of course not confined to American and British journalists. Scholars of Asian backgrounds too have celebrated the economic and political rise of Asia, even if they are also more inclined to express its darker side. Xu Youyu and Hua Ze (2013), for example, have written about the "rising dragon" to describe China's journey to global prominence, but have also told the stories of repression. Amitav Acharya (2008) has argued that the continuing success of Asia will depend on the quality of leadership provided by the major nations of Asia, and their ability to overcome persistent rivalries and respond to new transnational challenges. Pankaj Misra (2012) claims that, despite many setbacks, the region is witnessing an Asian renaissance, recovering some of its lost glory. Mohsin Hamid (2013) has written a best-selling novel entitled *How to Get Filthy Rich in Rising Asia*.

What the title of Hamid's whimsical novel suggests is that the idea of "Asia Rising" is now embedded within a globally circulating popular imagination. It reflects a popular discourse, structured around a set of ideas and assumptions that are now implicitly and widely accepted. In Asia, this discourse expresses a postcolonial confidence that suggests that the legacies of colonialism have finally been washed out, and that, in an era of globalization, Asian societies will continue to grow in stature. This confidence is also widely, though not uniformly, found among the Asian upper middle class – residing in metropolitan areas, in particular. They assume that the rise of Asia represents the birth of a new global order, not only in economic and political terms but also culturally. This suggests the capacity of Asians to participate confidently in the making of the global cultural economy, with Asian youth taking the lead.

This chapter is based on the assumption that the elite schools of Asia are one place in which the popular discourse of "Asia Rising" is likely to be found. Asia of course describes a vast area of great cultural diversity. If this is so then the various expressions of the discourse of "Asia Rising" are likely to be context-specific, inflected by the particular traditions that apply to various countries. In this chapter, I want to use data collected as part of a large international project,[1] which examines the dynamics of new class formations in elite schools established during the nineteenth century in the image of British public schools, to explore some of the ways in which an elite school in India relates to the discourses of "Asia Rising." In particular, I want to discuss how this discourse constitutes a class imaginary through which elite schools in Asia are now negotiating the forces of globalization, making global connections in order to position themselves within the emerging transnational space of privilege.

The Rise of Asia

In empirical terms, the rise of Asia is easily demonstrated. A recent Australian Government White Paper (2012) reports how, over the past three decades, Asian economies have grown at an unprecedented pace and scale. It has noted that while the growth rates across Asian countries have been uneven, they have, over the past two decades, averaged between 8 and 10 percent. The fast-growing population in Asia, the White Paper suggests, is no longer an economic problem, but is viewed instead as a "demographic dividend." The growing youth population of Asia is regarded as a major driver of the global economy. The White Paper claims that the impact of Asia on global markets has been profound: it has transformed the way the world produces goods and services. Asia does not only account for almost one-third of world trade in manufacturing, it has also become a major center of service industries. It is now a major net exporter of capital to the rest of the world, with its foreign exchange reserves soaring over the past decade in particular.

This, and much more, has transformed the way people now live in Asia. Since the early 1990s, incomes have greatly increased, with more than 400 million lifted out of extreme poverty, even as income disparities have also grown. The rates of literacy and educational participation have increased markedly. With the benefits of better education and investment, both public and private, many young people are now productively employed. Average life expectancy has increased in most Asian countries, as governments have been able to substantially increase their health expenditure. Economic growth has led to the urbanization of many Asian societies. According to the White Paper (2012: 23), around 44 million people in Asia leave rural areas every year in search of better opportunities in the cities, although this creates its own problems. Many of the new jobs are now in the information sector, making Asia a world center of innovation and technological development. As incomes in the region have grown, an increasingly wealthy and mobile class has emerged, with shifting patterns of consumption.

According to the White Paper (2012: 62), "the Asian region is expected to become home to the world's fastest growing middle class, whose pursuit of an improved quality of life will see Asian economies emerge as the world's dominant consumer markets." In Asia, this is not only changing spending patterns but is also transforming social preferences, cultural tastes and personal aspirations. This is evident in the large malls that now exist in many Asian cities, where young people "hang out", looking for the latest in technology and other consumer goods. They also desire new cultural practices, such as those provided by the global chains of cafes and cinemas. According to McKinsey and Company (2010), in urban China, within the next decade, the discretionary spending for such goods and services is expected to be 45 percent of the household's total expenditure. Not surprisingly, therefore the consumer tastes across Asia are "becoming aspirational and more discerning" (White Paper 2012: 61), with a diversified range of choices, together with a desire for higher quality brand products.

The White Paper uses the term the "Asian Century" and makes the confident prediction that Asia will continue to grow and will become pivotal in shaping the global economy and political architecture. It is not only Australia, however, where the term "Asian Century" has been used to describe the rise of Asia. While the exact origin of "Asian Century" is unclear, it is widely believed to have been first used by the Chinese and Indian premiers, Den Xioping and Rajiv Gandhi, at their meeting in 1988. It has subsequently been used not only by Asian political leaders but also by Asian media more generally. In recent years, Asia's robust and consistent economic performance has perhaps reinforced the possibility that, despite some setbacks, Asian economic power will continue to grow, and con-comitantly some Asian countries will assume global leadership roles in significant areas, including international relations, technology development and soft power (Nye 2005). This both reflects and feeds a growing political and cultural confi-dence throughout Asia, especially among its wealthier and globally mobile populations (Ong 2006).

Claims surrounding the rise of Asia do not of course apply equally to all of Asia's diverse nations and communities. As noted, Asia is a region of great diver-sity, across ethnic groups, languages, histories, political systems, and natural resources. The economic performance of its various communities has been var-ied, as indeed have been the shifts in their cultural tastes and aspirations (MacDonald and Lemco 2011). Rural and urban differentiations and differences across class and gender have been significant. Some communities relate more easily to the discourse of "Asia Rising" than others. For many living on the mar-gins of economic development, the rise of Asia is simply a fiction. Indeed their lives and traditions have been severely damaged by recent economic, political and cultural changes. On the other hand, in countries such as Singapore and Korea, the discourse of "Asia Rising" is widely embraced as it describes major improvements in people's lives. In contrast, in other parts of Asia, this discourse applies only to a small section of their community, and is arguably used as an ideological tool with which to mask growing social inequalities, and to subdue subaltern voices.

This was certainly the case with the campaign by the Indian government in 2004 to promote its own version of the discourse of "Asia Rising." The campaign called "India Shining" was developed by the *Bharatiya Janata Party* (BJP) as part of its efforts to promote India internationally and also engender a sense of pride among Indians about its rapidly growing economy. An advertising firm developed the slogan "India Shining," which was then promoted through national television and newspaper advertisements. The campaign generated a great deal of enthusiasm among India's growing middle class, but backfired with the nation's poor, drawing ridicule from various columnists and political parties opposed to the BJP criticizing the government for glossing over a variety of India's social problems, including poverty and social inequality. The campaign was subsequently modified, with a new campaign in which the nation was portrayed as "India Poised," rather than already "shining." However, even today, many in the Indian media and middle class continue to use the phrase "India Shining" to express a high degree of confidence in the nation's future.

This simple example indicates how the discourse of "Asia Rising" can generate a diversity of conflicting responses within the same country. This is hardy surprising since popular discourses often reveal some underlying truths, but can also operate hegemonically. Like other discourses, the idea of "Asia Rising" has been popularized in a range of different ways by various institutions. Important among these institutions are schools, where such discourses can often be embedded within the structures of curriculum and pedagogy, as well as practices of governance, both formal and informal. In what follows, I discuss some of ways in which an elite school in India – Ripon College[2] – relates to the discourse of the rise of India as an economic and political power, and how it prepares its students for a world in which their sense of identity is tied to various hegemonic perceptions about India's locatedness in rapidly changing global circumstances. More broadly, I want to discuss how the discourse of "Asia Rising" is associated with a class imaginary through which elite schools in Asia are now negotiating the forces of globalization, making global connections in order to position themselves in a transnational space of privilege.

Reimagining India

Ripon College was established in 1882 for the sons of the royal aristocracy in Central India. The destiny of the princes who attended Ripon was already known: they were to become the rulers of the provinces their families had owned and governed for generations. Under the British Raj, however, they needed a particular kind of education, enabling them to negotiate the terms under which they were permitted to continue to rule over their territories under the protection of the colonial authorities. From the perspective of the Indian aristocracy, Ripon College provided an education that enhanced its political and cultural standing with the British. The British regarded the College as part of its efforts to modernize the Indian states through the agency of "indirect rule" (Copland 1982: 123). Ripon College thus represented a compromise of a sort, through which the interests of both the colonizers and the elite amongst the colonized were realized.

This strategic alliance led the local aristocracy to fund the College, while the British authorities managed it. They developed the curriculum around a set of beliefs about the inherent superiority of British cultural traditions. It was assumed that for India to modernize, students needed access to the study of western mathematics, sciences and, of course, the English language. Through the teaching of English literature, the students were expected to develop British sensibilities – their habits of thought. Yet, while the goals of colonial education seemed clear enough, its practice was much more nuanced. As Homi Bhabha (1994) has shown, the relationship between the colonizers and colonized is always ambivalent. While the colonizer encourages the colonized to "mimic" the colonial habits, assumptions, values, and institutions, the outcome is never a simple reproduction of the dominant practices, but the production of practices that are "hybridized."

For most of the twentieth century, Ripon College was focused on producing graduates who could provide leadership to their communities. During the colonial period, this involved learning about the administrative requirements of British rule in India, and managing, through indirect rule, the affairs of their own territories. Over time, Ripon College educated Indian princes who were politically compliant and culturally harmonized with British interests. Even before independence, however, Ripon College had begun to enroll students from other elite parts of the Indian community, including sons of Indian civil servants and leading merchants. After independence, the College became even more focused on educating for national leadership. As the new nation required people with scientific, administrative and political skills for its economic development, the College prided itself in providing its students an education that was aligned to India's national interests. It became co-educational, and opened its doors to wider sections of the community.

Over the past decade, however, like most other elite schools in India, Ripon College has become deeply conscious of the ways in which the Indian state has embraced the forces of globalization. Until 1991, the Indian economy was largely nationally focused, with rigidly controlled rules for engaging in economic activity and foreign trade. Tariffs were high and financial flows in and out of the country were not encouraged. The Indian bureaucracy had become a major barrier to entrepreneurial activity. This changed in 1991, with the Indian Government deregulating its financial sector, permitting foreign capital to flow into the country; lowering tariffs which enabled industrialists to import machinery and export the goods produced; and more generally opening its economy to global markets. In short, the Indian Government now accepts the neo-liberal mantras of a minimalist state, liberal individualism and the market as a solution to most of India's entrenched social and economic problems.

The extent to which these neoliberal reforms account for India's growth rates of 9 percent per year over the past two decades is a question that is widely debated among scholars and politicians alike. McKinsey and Company (2013) edited a collection of short papers by some of India's leading industrialists and commentators who were in doubt that it was indeed these reforms that had "unlocked India's potential as Asia's next superpower." Jagdish Bhagwati (2004) insists that India's decision to open its economy to global markets has been good for both its elite and its poor. While arguing that globalization of economy has added to India's problems of poverty, inequality and infrastructure, Appadurai (2012: 4) nonetheless acknowledges that Indian corporations have benefitted greatly from neoliberal reforms, especially as they build on the nation's "long acquaintance with English, the energy of free enterprise, a highly skilled and innovative software industry, and some of the finest scientists and technologists in the world."

What is abundantly clear then is that the neoliberal reforms have expanded the Indian middle class. Those who were already in business have been able to extend their enterprises into the global arena, while the Indian elite, both old and new, has been able to enjoy consumer goods and services that were previously unavailable in India. The popular media has hyped up the possibilities, imagining an India that is not only dominant in Asia but also in the world. The Indian diaspora has been able to connect back to India, and bring in large quantities of new foreign direct investment. At an old colonial school such as Ripon College, where "old money" ran the show, "new money" has made an entrance, and now jostles for influence and prestige. Around the turn of the century, according to Gurcharan Das (2002: 245), there was already ample evidence to suggest that "the old industrial empires will sell out gradually to new, more able entrepreneurs." Das insisted that India needed to re-imagine itself around the aspirations of its entrepreneurs; and that the institutions that did not respond effectively to these aspirations would simply wither away.

Local Lives and Global Aspirations

To what extent then do the parents and students at Ripon College share the perceptions of a globally aspirational India that Das describes? In what ways is Ripon College responding to the demands of a globally oriented India? How is it engaging with the contemporary processes of globalization, seeking to transform its outlook and produce graduates who are able to meet the challenges of the global circumstances? And to what extent have these changes transformed class relations at the College and more broadly in India?

Very few of the students at Ripon College are now from the Indian aristocracy – the descendants of the original donors who founded the College. Most are from commercial families who have benefited greatly from neoliberal reforms in India. They have been able to expand their businesses, and aspire to access global markets. In their minds, there is little doubt that India is at the cusp of greatness. They worry, however, that India could throw away its advantages if it does not invest heavily in rebuilding its crumbling infrastructure. They view schools as part of this infrastructure, and are happy to invest in the education of their children.

The families of the students at Ripon College are thus highly supportive of the reforms initiated by the current Principal. These reforms are largely focused on the College's attempts to internationalize its work by forging links with similar schools around the world, establishing programs of student and faculty exchange, globalizing its curriculum options, and promoting the importance of global citizenship. According to a parent: "Ripon College was faltering badly in the 1990s. Now, with the new Head, there is great energy in the school, especially with his international program." Other parents also regard the College's international program as essential for meeting the needs of the Indian economy, which is now inextricably tied to global markets, and hence their economic interests. Another parent insisted that India's potential as an economic power will not be realized if schools like Ripon College do not produce graduates who are entrepreneurial, and thus able to benefit from the opening up of the Indian economy to global markets.

Another parent, Mr. Nath, sees a direct link between his business interests and the education he would like his son to get at Ripon College. Mr. Nath runs a national company dealing with food products, and would like to expand his business globally. He is convinced that there is a market for this, but his company lacks international networks. He would like his son to develop these networks by going to the United States for tertiary studies, becoming a Vice President of the company upon his return. Mr. Nath believes that there are many other such family companies throughout India, who insist that elite schools such as Ripon College have an important role to play in "globalizing Indian businesses." This role includes not only the formation of globally integrated networks but also competences and sensibilities that are necessary for commercial success at the global level. Mr. Nath was therefore happy to send his son on an educational exchange to Europe.

While recognizing that much more still needs to be done, Mr. Nath has no doubt that India is already "shining." In a focus group, he insisted that: "We have come a long way in a very short time. Just twenty years ago, the Indian economy was near collapse. Economic reforms changed all that. Now we are convinced that anything is possible." Others in the focus group agreed, and a voice that doubted the hype was quickly howled down. But even this voice of exception agreed on the importance of an elite education to India's future. Another member of the focus group argued that: "It is the elite schools that can provide students the kind of international experiences that Ripon offers. Most schools in India do not have the resources." He went on to insist that "we are no longer embarrassed about wanting to be rich … I want my girls to aspire to the best that the world has to offer."

In focus groups, conducted as part of the research project, mothers were noticeably more vociferous and forceful in their global aspirations for their children. They appear to play a more active role in ensuring that their children are focused on their studies, work hard, and keep "an eye on the prize" in what they consider to be a highly competitive educational market. For them, the "prize" is a place in one of the leading universities in the United States or United Kingdom. Many of these mothers choose not to go out to work in order to devote more of their time to the education of their children. This impression is consistent with the findings of Donner (2008), which show how middle-class women in India understand and experience economic change through transformations of family life, devoting much of their life to the education of their children. They compete with other mothers to get their children into the best universities abroad, often making huge financial and personal sacrifices.

The students at Ripon College have little choice but to follow the wishes of their parents, often embracing the parents' aspirations for them as their own. Many students report feeling intense pressure to succeed academically to justify the sacrifices their mothers have allegedly made for them. Teachers at Ripon College estimate that a little over 50 percent of their students aspire to go abroad for education, a little over 25 percent make a concerted effort to apply for a place, but less than 10 percent succeed in eventually studying at a university overseas. According to the teachers, these numbers have trended upwards over the past decade, as an increasing number of families find the financial means in a growing economy. These families often anticipate high returns, either in terms of permanent settlement abroad or higher levels of income upon their return. More importantly, they expect enhanced social status within the local communities in which they reside. In this sense, their local lives are shaped by global aspirations (Kennedy 2010).

What is sad about this shift in attitudes at Ripon College are the perceptions of the students who have no financial means to even remotely entertain the possibility of their families funding an education abroad. These students go to elaborate lengths to hide the fact of this impossibility from their wealthier friends. A scholarship student at Ripon College, for example, tried to hide from his friends the fact that he would not be able to study abroad by talking incessantly about leading Ivy League schools in the United States, and their global rankings. This enabled him to participate in the conversations among Year 11 students about how they might go abroad after graduating from Ripon. In this way, he sought to position himself in the dominant relations of social class within the College, minimizing the effects of social differentiations around the global aspirations of most of his friends.

This is not to suggest that the students at Ripon uniformly embrace the hype about "India Shining." Many point to the serious inequalities that are evident throughout their own cities. They recognize the contradictions of the policies of economic liberalization that have rendered many in India without a realistic chance of participating effectively within the local economy, let alone the global markets that are now widely celebrated in India. The teachers at the College are conscious of the need to foster in their students a sense of morality through programs such as Service Learning, and through conversations in which the plight of the poor and injustices associated with economic liberalization are widely examined, even as they help reproduce the elite social status of the students in a range of other ways.

Global Networks and Educational Responses

As early as 2000, the Board of Governors had recognized that if Ripon College were to hold its status as one of the leading public schools in India, it had to respond effectively to the growing global aspirations of its parents and students. As commerce in the city in which Ripon College is located became more globally focused, in line with the Indian Government's decision to open its economy to global markets, the Board could not ignore the role it assumed education needed to play to prepare the students to engage with the global transformations. When the position of the Principal at Ripon College became vacant, the Board searched widely for an educational leader who had international experience and cosmopolitan sensibilities, and who had the capacity to "internationalize" the College. After a long search, it appointed a distinguished educator who had taught at prestigious schools in Britain and India, and whose own family had aristocratic links. The new Principal was given unprecedented level of authority to transform the College.

One of the new Principal's first actions for reform was to apply to join Round Square (RS), an international network of schools, with "a strong commitment, beyond academic excellence, to personal development and responsibility."[3] The Round Square seeks to realize this commitment through the promotion of six IDEALS of learning: Internationalism, Democracy, Environment, Adventure, Leadership, and Service. The RS schools are expected to incorporate these ideals into all aspects of the curriculum, both formal and informal. The College failed in its first application for membership, presumably because it could not demonstrate a commitment to the RS's six ideals. This failure gave the Principal an opportunity and a stronger rationale to undertake reforms at the College, particularly with respect to pedagogy, moving away from didactic ways of teaching, and student participation in decisions that affected them. The College also initiated a range of new Service Learning activities, especially around environment and leadership.

In 2005, Ripon College was finally admitted to the RS network of schools. Being a member of a network of elite schools around the world has transformed the College's perception of itself. The College now views itself as a global school, internationally connected to most parts of the world through its programs of staff and students exchange. Ripon students now have an opportunity to spend extended periods of time abroad, as well as attend debating contests and United Nations youth conferences. The competition for participation in these opportunities is intense, with financial support from parents readily forthcoming. International students from North America and Europe in turn come and study at Ripon for periods as long as a whole academic year, engaging with local students in both formal and informal settings. This exchange has steadily transformed students' sense of their identity, their relationships to each other, the image they have of their College's links to the broader community, their educational and career aspirations, and more broadly the perceptions they have of the discourse of "India Rising."

With their aspirations increasingly directed towards global futures, many parents and teachers at Ripon College felt that the local curriculum offered by the Central Board of Secondary Education (CBSE) did not provide them with the kind of preparation they felt useful for tertiary studies abroad. In 2009, the College therefore decided to offer an international qualification – the International General Certificate of Secondary Education (IGCSE) offered by the Cambridge Examination System – as one of its six steams in senior years. The College expected adequate demand but was overwhelmed with interest in this option, and had to be highly selective with the students it considered "appropriate" for IGCSE. Multiple criteria were used to select these students, including their commitment to internationalization and their plans for future studies. The College now offers both the local CBSE and international IGCSE, and insists that each of these two options is equally valued. However, our interviews revealed this not to be case, with parents and students alike believing that IGCSE is better resourced and by and large accepts students from wealthier families with cosmopolitan sensibilities. Indeed, this contrast appears to have created a new form of social differentiation within the College.

Ten years after the appointment of the current internationally minded Principal, Ripon College's international initiatives and networks have become major defining characteristics of its identity. Within the College, social relations are increasingly delineated by the extent to which students participate in international activities and are able to take advantage of the opportunities of global travel and learning. Within India, the College is now able to differentiate itself within an educational market in which old elite schools compete with the new corporate international schools, offering International Baccalaureate programs. Ripon College offers not only international programs but also a long history of social distinction. Furthermore, Ripon College can also boast a close association with leading elite schools around the world. For example, in 2013, it hosted a major conference of the principals of what are called G20 schools, some of the leading elite schools from around the world, such as Eton College, Geelong Grammar, and Raffles Institution. The conference was a grand affair at which some of India's major power brokers spoke. Its proceedings were widely reported in Indian media, reinforcing the perceptions in India of Ripon College as not only a heritage school but also a school that is located in a transnational space of privilege.

New Class Formations

Ripon College's class position within India has, of course, always been clear: it was set up self-consciously as an elite school. However, the strategies it has pursued to internationalize its work in recent years suggest a new class politics. The College is now seeking to perform its class relations differently, locating itself in a wider transnational space. While retaining some key traces of its colonial history, and also some of its postcolonial sensibilities, the College is now attempting to align itself to new discourses of global conditions, opportunities, and aspirations. Theoretically, then, how does the case of Ripon College help us to think about contemporary processes of class formation, not only in national but also in transnational terms? To what extent is the College no longer attempting to produce national leaders but a "transnational capitalist class"?

The idea of transnational capitalist class was first proposed by Leslie Sklair (2001) to explain how globalization has transformed the ways in which class now works, through transnational corporations, media, and other institutions of consumption. Sklair (2001: 4) attempts to show how "a new class is emerging and how it pursues people and resources all over the world in its insatiable desire for private profit and external accumulation." He suggests that the transnational capitalist class is composed of "corporate executives, globalizing bureaucrats and politicians, globalizing professionals and consumerist elites." Robinson (2004) has similarly argued that the rise of the new capitalist class not only works through global circuits of investment and production but also through institutions that are comfortable ideologically with relations of class that they represent. Building on Robinson's work and using social network analysis, Carroll (2010) has mapped the changing field of power generated by elite relations in the interests of world's largest corporations and the related political organizations.

It might be argued that the ideological work of Ripon College is located within this field of power. In so far as Ripon College is increasingly catering to the needs of parents and students with global aspirations, embedded in the "culture-ideology of consumerism" (Sklair 2001: 4), it is contributing to new class formations, no longer tied to national interests but to a global system of accumulation. The College is working with new borders and practices of class, encouraging cultures, classed behaviors and identities that are located in a transnational space. It is attempting to develop in students a sense of themselves and others as cosmopolitan consumers, linked to social and business networks that span the globe.

As plausible as this thesis might appear, it is arguably mistaken in its characterization of the relationship between globalization and new class formations in India. In recent years, the complex relationship between globalization and economic liberalization and India's emerging class politics has been examined by a number of scholars. In most cases, this examination has been supported by rich ethnographic research. In their book, Ganguly-Scrase and Scrase (2009), for example, challenge the notion of a homogenous class analysis, such as that proposed by Sklair, Robinson, and Carroll. They show that while many in India have clearly benefited greatly from the country's drift towards neoliberal economic policies, many others among the Indian elite itself are skeptical of the advantages secured from these reforms. They are deeply conscious of the contradictions associated with India's liberalization program, as Dreze and Sen (2013) observe.

Chowdhury (2011) has argued that the globalization of Indian economy and cultural life has generated a range of complex and social tensions, transforming the construction of the Indian citizen, as well as the complex interactions between culture and political economy. Fernandes (2006) has explored the changing dynamics of sociality, which she insists has shifted the nature of Indian politics and class formation, but in ways that are distinctively Indian, linked to its cultural tradition, colonial history, and democratic politics. According to Brosius (2014), the upwardly mobile middle classes in India are increasingly looking to the transnational space in which to locate their identity, giving expression to new social formations and aspirations, modes of consumption and ways of being in contemporary urban India. But, equally, this global aspiration is filtered through a deep commitment to India's religious, linguistic, and cultural traditions.

Traditionally, descriptions of social class have either been located within the framework of the nation-state specified in terms of social stratification or presented in terms of the global relations of power, as is the case with Sklair's analysis of transnational capitalist class. The case of Ripon College shows this binary to be misleading. For the global aspirations at the College are clearly affected by global forces. So while the global connections that the College has made with elite schools around the world are helping to reshape the class imagination of its students and staff, these shifts are not entirely disconnected from the College's colonial history and its relationship to its broader community. It is clear that Indian national traditions continue to matter to the College, as its students are encouraged to interpret and imagine the possibilities of globalization through the prism of a national imaginary.

The local is clearly resilient. The power of global capitalism is not as hegemonic as Sklair and others assume. It is a mistake therefore to essentialize the global as somehow separate, external, and hegemonic in the shaping of the local's destiny and character. But nor is it irrelevant in the new formations of class relations at elite schools such as Ripon College. As Doreen Massey (1994) argued more than twenty years ago, we need a progressive sense of the local where boundaries are open and social actors are continuously engaged in constructing their sense of the place, out of both internal factors and influences that are produced in their entanglement with places elsewhere. The local and global processes are meshed together in producing shifting class relations through the continuing particularity of place despite global influences.

Conclusion

The seemingly global discourse of "Asia Rising" is clearly embraced at Ripon College, but in ways that are filtered through its national meaning. In India, attempts have been made to promote a discourse in which the notion of "Asia Rising" has been translated into "India Shining" and "India Poised." But given India's critical and democratic traditions, these attempts have been treated by some with considerable suspicion, even cynicism. In line with this national disposition, there is considerable confidence at Ripon College in its engagement with the global. This engagement, however, is accompanied by a high degree of criticality, with efforts to retain the College's sense of identity, forged out of its colonial history, postcolonial determination, and now global aspirations. In this way, Ripon College's self-perception involves imagining itself as an elite school that is committed to its community, even as it attempts to use its global resources and connections in a highly strategic and contingent fashion. It retains many aspects of its classed privileges from the past but it also uses its increasingly global orientation as an additional component to new class formations.

Notes

1 Funded, over 2010–2014, by the Australian Research Council, this project, "Elite Schools in Globalizing Circumstances" aims to determine the ways in which elite schools in the British public schools tradition are interpreting and negotiating the pressures and opportunities associated with globalization. Members of the research team, which includes Jane Kenway, Fazal Rizvi, Debbie Epstein, Cameron McCarthy, Aaron Koh, and Johannah Fahey, have conducted six case studies of schools in the UK, Australia, Hong Kong, South Africa, India, and Cyprus.

2 As is required by the research ethics committee of the administering organization of this project – Monash University in Australia – the names of the school and the interviewees who have been cited in this chapter have been kept confidential, and are replaced with aliases.
3 http://www.roundsquare.org/

References

Acharya, A. (2008) *Asia Rising: Who is Leading?* Singapore: World Scientific.
Appadurai, A. (2012) "Introduction," in A. Appadurai and A. Mack (eds) *India's World: The Politics of Creativity in a Globalizing Society*, New Delhi: Rain Tree Publishers.
Australian Government (2012) *Australia in the Asian Century* (White Paper), Canberra: Commonwealth Government of Australia.
Bhabha, H.K. (1994) *The Location of Culture*, London: Routledge.
Bhagwati, J. (2004) *In Defense of Globalization*, London: Oxford University Press.
Brosius, C. (2104) *India's Middle Class: New Forms of Urban Leisure, Consumption and Prosperity*, New Delhi: Routledge.
Carroll, W. K. (2010) *The Making of a Transnational Capitalist Class: Corporate Power in the 21st Century*, London: Zed Books.
Chowdhury, K. (2011) *The New India: Citizenship, Subjectivity and Economic Liberalization*, London: Palgrave Macmillan.
Copland, I. (1982) *The British Raj and the Indian Princes*, New Delhi: Orient Longman.
Das, G. (2002) *India Unbound: The Social and Economic Revolution from Independence to the Global Information Age*, New York: Anchor Books.
Donner, H. (2008) *Domestic Goddess: Maternity, Globalization and the Middle Class Identity in India*, Aldershot, UK: Ashgate Publishing.
Dreze, J. and Sen, A. (2013) *An Uncertain Glory: India and its Contradictions*, Princeton NJ: Princeton University Press.
Fernandes, L. (2006) *India's New Middle Class: Democratic Politics in an Era of Economic Reform*, Minneapolis: University of Minnesota Press.
Friedman T. and Mandelbaum, M. (2012) *That Used to be Us: How America Fell Behind in the World It Invented and How We can Come Back*, New York: Picador.
Ganguly-Scrase, R. and Scrase, T. (2009) *Globalization and the Middle Classes in India: The Social and Cultural Impact of Neoliberal Reforms*, London: Routledge.
Hamid, M. (2013) *How to Get Filthy Rich in Rising Asia*, New York: Riverhead Books.
Jacques, M. (2009) *When China Rules the World: The End of the Western World and the Birth of a New World Order*, New York: Penguin.
Kennedy, P. (2010) *Local Lives and Global Transformations: Towards World Society*, London: Palgrave Macmillan.
MacDonald, S. and Lemco, J. (2011) *Asia's Rise in the 21st Century*, New York: Praeger.
McKinsey and Company (2010) *Annual Chinese Consumer Study 2010: Trading Up or Trading Off?*, *Insights China*, http://solutions.mckinsey.com (accessed 4 April 2014).
McKinsey and Company (2013) *Reimagining India: Unlocking the Potential of Asia's Next Superpower*, New York: Simon & Schuster.
Massey, D. (1994) *Space, Place, and Gender*, Cambridge: Polity Press.
Misra, P. (2012) *From the Ruins of Empire: The Revolt Against the West and the Remaking of Asia*, London: Penguin.
Nye, J. S. (2005) *Soft Power: The Means of Success in World Politics*, New York: Perseus Books.

Ong, A. (2006) *Neoliberalism as Exception: Mutations in Citizenship and Sovereignty*, London: Routledge.

Robinson, B. (2004) *A Theory of Global Capitalism: Production, Class and State in a Transnational World*, Baltimore MD: Johns Hopkins University Press.

Sklair, L. (2001) *The Transnational Capitalist Class*, Oxford: Blackwell.

Yougu, X. and Ze, H. (2013) *In the Shadow of the Rising Dragon*, London: Palgrave Macmillan.

Zakaria, F. (2006) *The Post-American World*, New York: Penguin.

10 National and International Students' Definitions of Merit in French *Grandes Écoles*

Brigitte Darchy-Koechlin, Hugues Draelants and Elise Tenret

Introduction

In order to maintain their position and power, elites usually have to face the question of their legitimacy (Weber 1922). One of the main means of legitimacy in modern democracies is found in the creation of meritocratic selection devices (Parsons 1951; Young 1958). In the education-based meritocratic model (Tenret 2011), school achievement is crucial in justifying high-status/high reward positions, as purporting to provide and certify the distinctive skills and competencies which are associated with such positions. In the case of France (Duru-Bellat 2006; Iribarne 2006) elites are selected and trained through a distinctive and integrated track following from the *baccalauréat* (secondary school certificate). From among the highest school achievers a small number among those who apply are selected to enrol in a special programme called *classes préparatoires* where they are 'prepared' over two to three years for the *concours*, the highly competitive entrance exams to the *Grandes Écoles*.[1]

However, this meritocratic model relying on a dual higher education system has been criticized in two directions. On one hand, the work of Bourdieu and Passeron from the 1960s, showed the importance of particular forms and volumes of cultural capital in academic success leading to elite reproduction. This consequently questioned the ability of schools to guarantee a fair and equitable selection (Bourdieu and Passeron 1964, 1970; Bourdieu 1989). More recent research on social closure of elite formations (Euriat and Thélot 1995) has renewed criticisms of the legitimacy of such a socially biased selection. On the other hand, since the early 2000s and in a context of increasing globalization, the low ranking of the *Grandes Écoles* in international league tables (such as the *Academic Ranking of World Universities* also known as the Shanghai ranking and the *Times Higher Education World University Ranking*)[2] has raised the question of the efficiency of the French model[3] (Harfi and Mathieu 2006).

These internal and external criticisms of the French elite education system have had both political and institutional implications. They have led institutions to open new entrance pathways in the *Grandes Écoles* for students from disadvantaged backgrounds and for international students. In selecting these new students, various procedures – ranging from *main competitive exam, specific competitive exam, no competitive exam* – have been implemented by these institutions, depending on their status (public/private) and their core curriculum (academic/vocational) as well as on path dependency pathways related to their institutional history (Darchy-Koechlin 2013).

Such measures directly question the legitimacy of French meritocracy and of the elite education system, which was built around the uniqueness of the entrance competitve exam, the cornerstone of this system, and of the *Grandes Écoles'* Malthusian elitism. How do *Grandes Écoles* and their students react to these measures? What are their perceptions of the legitimacy of their position? To answer this question, we conducted 150 semi-structured interviews with first- and last-year students from four of the most prestigious French *Grandes Écoles* (École Normale Supérieure, École Polytechnique, HEC, Sciences Po).[4] We interviewed both national and international students (about a third of the respondent pool) in each of the four *Grandes Écoles*.

The Definition of Merit and its Perception by Students

By its very solemn and codified nature, the competitive exam offers both institutional and social recognition of the GE students' merit, and has been an essential ingredient for future elites' self-perception and perception by others as deserving. That is why the first definition or, what we have called the 'zero definition' that students give of their own merit, most frequently mentions the sanction of the competitive exam: if the institution has 'elected' them, they certainly deserve it. By using this expression we mean that merit is a question that, in principle, no longer arises. It is obvious for the interviewed students, as for their institutions, that they deserve their place. This 'zero definition' of merit is simultaneously the most spontaneous and most basic; the zero is used to denote the lack of conceptual content that characterizes this circular or tautological definition of merit ('I merit because I deserved entering here'):

> The question (do you feel that you deserve being in this school?) is weird. Because for me, the system of competitive exam implies that merit depends solely on the success in the entrance examination. It seems that it is truely hypothesis. Having passed the ENS means we passed the competitive exam. So we cannot have stolen our place.
>
> (Antonin, École Normale Supérieure)
>
> I think anyone who has passed the competitive exam deserves his place. That is logical. It is as if you said to me: 'Do I deserve to have the Bac [*Bacccalauréat*]?' He had his Bac, he got it.
>
> (Julien, HEC)

These reactions show how the competitive exam is considered or presented as the ultimate proof or, in a number of cases, as the unique evidence of merit, thereby providing a restrictive definition of the concept.

The statements of these students echo Bourdieu's analysis of the entrance exam as a true 'rite of consecration' (Bourdieu 1989), considered fair, insofar as it appears to meet two requirements: through anonymity and standard tests of selection procedures, it is supposed to ensure equal treatment of applicants; given the purely academic nature of the subjects tested, any enrolled and deserving student has in theory the opportunity to pass the examination.

Success in the competitive exam is a key element for the *Grande École* in legitimizing the merit of the 'chosen' (Karabel 2005), they have every incentive to maintain the meritocratic fiction on which their reputation for excellence and prestige rests. In fact, the welcoming and integration rites put in place by the institutions serve to confirm and provide a second consecration to confirm and celebrate success in the entrance examination, through the use of performative speech that decisively ushers the candidates into their new role as elite:

> If there is one message that we can deliver to you today at the start of your career here at this school, it is this: you may rest assured and maintain an unwavering confidence in the quality of the intellectual and scientific training you are about to receive at our institution. Trust in what you are about to learn; make no mistake, the education being offered to you is without a doubt among the best in France if not the world. [...] All roads will be opened to you. But for this to be true, it is important for you to believe in the intellectual value of what you possess. Your future is bright.
>
> (Director's commencement speech to the
> entering students of the École Normale Supérieure)

As we have shown elsewhere (Darchy-Koechlin *et al.* 2015), the preparatory class[5] plays also a role of '*propaedeutics* of meritocracy'. In the course of time spent in prep school and as students invest in their education, their sense of legitimacy, their feeling of deserving their status as member of a chosen and future academic and social elite increases, even among those who harboured doubts initially. The intense pace of work imposed throughout the preparatory class works to 'convert' them. The preparatory class thus ensures that students are gradually accepting of the verdict of the competitive exam and the resulting hierarchies and distinctions. Indeed, more than the legitimacy of their present position, it is the legitimacy of their future place in the highly selective entrance exam that the preparatory class intends to ensure that it will be accepted by the students themselves. This is why we can see the prep schools as an 'antechamber of meritocracy', as they help convince those who attend them that it is only success at the competitive exam that will grant them access to an elite position.

Changes and Limits to Changes in the Definition of Merit Within the *Grandes Écoles*

There is a significant change in the operational definition of merit within *Grandes Écoles* themselves which can be characterized as a process of 'cooling out' (Clark 1960). Whereas the entrance rituals which welcome new students are intended to acknowledge and confirm their academic success to themselves and to the institution, their family members and the entire nation at large, they also signal that this *Grande École* track itself will be critical into transforming them into 'elites'.

In fact, the commencement ceremonies in the four case study *Grandes Écoles*, through a performative speech, serve both to recognize past achievements and to signal the future work to be done if they are to translate their promise into the possibility of entry into elite positions. In this way, Sciences Po's director remarked to the students during his commencement speech in 2009, the terms in which the former president of the National Foundation of Political Sciences, addressed the chosen ones:

> He enjoined them to assume the responsibilities their admission had granted them by the very fact of it, to show themselves forever grateful that chance, hazard or Providence had got their foot on the ladder. And to know that they were not the elite of the nation.

The Director of Sciences Po added:

> They still have not said anything, done anything, seen anything [...] Being admitted to Sciences Po does not confer status, entering at Sciences Po is a starting point, not a point of arrival. [...] Belonging to elite is not decided. One is not self-proclaimed member of elite ...

The reasons for this process are diverse. The discourses first of all aim to help the successful candidates understand that, however deserving they may be, they still have to demonstrate, by their accomplishments within the *Grande École*, that the institution made a winning bet on the educational and human capital they represent. Clearly, the institution expects a real 'return on investment' for individuals whose training cost is very high. This institutional strategy also aims to raise awareness among the new students that the rules of the game will no longer be the same, regardless of their success and ranking in the competitive exam, as preparation for social functions and professional elite positions require the acquisition and sanction of skills other than the purely academic. Indirectly, this strategy serves to legitimize the very existence of the *Grandes Écoles*, which are claiming more than a simple role of 'empty shells' welcoming the successful candidates at the entrance exam.

This commencement strategy also erases the systems of school hierarchy that emerge through recruitment channels and standing in the competitive exam. Furthermore, it increases the schools' internal social cohesion and encourages a sense of commonality among students rather than emphasizing the principle of inter-individual competition which tends to prevail during the process of the application. Competition could be an obstacle in building strong solidarities between students (Cuche 1988; Bourdieu 1989; Faguer 1991). The effectiveness and excellence of the *Grandes Écoles* are indeed largely based on their ability to integrate individuals and to foster a sense of belonging to an elite corps and to projects of 'common good'. In other words, the *Grandes Écoles* thus operate, at face value at least, as a 'levelling out machine': the only important thing is to have been accepted and to be among the chosen. If the competitive exam is based on a process of selection and distinction of individuals on the basis of merit, the schooling in the *Grandes Écoles* is about something else, it relies on a process of aggregating these individuals.

The academic excellence of the newly admitted students is then relativized and presented as a means rather than an end in itself. They have yet to join the ranks of the 'true elite' which is presented as 'total', polymorphic and versatile, rather than simply endowed with academic virtues. This strategy of 'cooling out', more generally, has an ethical dimension in as much that it ensures that new entrants adopt the moral posture deemed most appropriate, that is to say the discretion, humility and sense of responsibility appropriate to a state elite (Draelants and Darchy-Koechlin 2011) and, at the same time, this is set over and against the charge of arrogance that regularly arises in French public debate about the state elites, an accusation based on a mix of reality and stereotype.

The fact that the *Grandes Écoles* develop and recognize another form of merit that could be termed 'collective merit' which, although it occupies a limited place in the French education system, breaks with the tradition and practices of working alone and inter-individual competition promoted by secondary education and elite prep schools. This different form of pedagogical relation is evident in some of the *Grandes Écoles*, where we observed that students were encouraged in some pro-grammes to design and implement a business project or to conduct an investigation and then to present their result in small teams. The evaluation by a jury of such projects is not individual but examines the teamwork and cooperation capabilities that groups of students develop in carrying out and presenting the collective task. The civic engagement[6] throughout the curriculum in *Grande École* is also an opportunity for students to demonstrate that they have skills other than purely academic, whether sporting, artistic, managerial, educational, political or moral.

The analysis of the evolution of merit thus shows a dimension specifically related to the construction of self in school during the *Grande École* years. It is striking how students categorize themselves according to their capacity for self-growth, borrowing from English (nobody) the term 'nobods' to describe some of their peers who seem to 'be nobody' because they have little social life in the school and fail at demonstrating to others their possession of non-academic skills. In this sense, the model a number of the *Grandes Écoles* offer to their students is inspired in part at least by the Anglo-Saxon model of the well-rounded elite (Kingston and Lewis 1990) rather than only by the education-based meritocratic model. The importance of this new dimension of personal construction in assess-ing the merit of individuals, however, varies from one school to another. Considered a prerequisite in schools highlighting vocational merit like HEC or Sciences Po which practice motivational or personality interviewing as part of the entrance exam, it is much more implicit in schools such as the École Normale Supérieure where academic merit still prevails. At the ENS in fact it seems that this personal construction is much more independent of the curriculum and the institution and is not the subject of any specific evaluation. The school which most formally institutionalizes this personal training in the curriculum is the École Polytechnique where human and military training gives rise to an assessment done under military supervision.

The interviews also revealed that the model of academic merit instilled by the prep schools cannot be erased so easily and that the acceptance of this new 'meritocratic contract' tends to create divisions among the students. If the institutions are doing everything possible to neutralize the pre-existing hierarchies between students, these hierarchies are recreated quickly. At the beginning of their schooling in each *Grande École*, the students construct and use fine distinctions between different types of merit within a single institution or between institutions thus breaking the outward appearance of unanimity that the institutions strive to maintain.

First of all, the existence of various access routes to *Grandes Écoles* tends to maintain an implicit hierarchy between students. There are indeed in each institution alternative tracks which allow specific categories of students (mainly students from French universities and international students) to be recruited without passing the general and traditional *concours*. They will instead be recruited under specific conditions which are perceived by some students as more flexible and less rigorously selective.[7] Indeed, the students accepted by entry routes other than that of the competitive exam remain more or less permanently regarded by many of their peers as 'second rank' students in the order of academic merit. It is then the various access channels to the competitive exam which implicitly determine the degree of merit among students and consequently their greater or lesser legitimacy as a student of the institution. Furthermore, the academic aspects of the competitive exam tend to be more highly regarded and valued because they are viewed as more oriented towards abstraction and thus more demanding and discriminating than another aspects of the exam. Even if there is then a tacit contract between students, encouraged by the institution, to sweep under the carpet these hierarchies inherited from the competitive exam, they structure nevertheless the perception that students have of their respective merit and value.

Among the specific categories of students, international students appear to be twice 'outsiders' (Elias and Scotson 1965). As foreigners and as aliens to the French *Grandes Écoles* and prep school system they are usually not familiar with the French education system and its meritocracy norms and rules. Consequently, their experiences and perceptions offer some different and useful insights into the formal and informal integration processes in the *Grandes Écoles* and can thus serve to highlight the specificity of the French definition of merit.

The Perception of the Merit of Foreign Students in French Elite Institutions and Their Own View on Merit

Alternative non-traditional access procedures – which include the admission procedures for international students – have a tendency to be devalued by those who have passed the traditional entrance examination, for different reasons. First of all, the students who are consecrated by the *concours* suspect these alternative modes of recruitment to be less rigorous and to have lower requirements. A second reason is, to some extent, the opacity of the selection criteria.[8] Foreign students, taking the full *Grande École* track, also pass competitive exams, but these exams are adapted to their prior *curriculum* experience. The degree and forms of adaptation varies nevertheless across the institutions. On the one hand, state schools such as the École Normale Supérieure or the École Polytechnique where merit is still tightly related to academic achievement have somehow 'translated' and adjusted their traditional competitive exams, preserving as much as possible the academic content and the existing criteria of assessment and selection. Nevertheless, other criteria, less official or explicit, can play a role in the process of selection for specific countries, depending either on curriculum compatibility or on historical ties – namely colonial history.[9] On the other hand, private or semi-private *Grandes Écoles* like HEC or Sciences Po have developed two different strategies regarding the competitive exam. At Sciences Po the choice was made to circumvent the exam altogether and to admit international students through a different application procedure based on files and interviews, while in HEC students are assessed through standardized tests like GMat or Tage-Mage (Darchy-Koechlin 2012). A third reason for the 'insiders'' suspicion of the legitimacy of the presence of international students is that their recruitment exempts them from attending the demanding *classes préparatoires* track.

> There is a big and absolute contempt of the students directly admitted. Because they actually think that when you're directly admitted, you made no preparation. And that they really merit because they have done a prep school and it was super hard.
>
> (Noémie, HEC)

Thus, if the rite of institution, that constitutes success in the traditional or 'first' competitive exams, consecrates the majority of students of the studied *Grandes Écoles*, it actually tends to marginalize international students as well as those national students, less numerous, who enter by other specific routes. The very notion of consecration seems dubious in their case. The creation by the *Grandes Écoles* of various parallel admission procedures for the admission of a growing number of international students or national students who have not passed the first competitive exam (post-baccalaureate or post-prep schools) creates heterogeneous status groups inside these schools, established on the basis of differences between fully legitimate students whose enrolment and presence based on examination is seen as self-evident, whereas others are only 'admitted', which implies that their presence is 'unnatural' and a challenge to the traditions and purpose of the institution (Darchy-Koechlin and Draelants 2010). Concomitantly, it is therefore not surprising that these students do not necessarily perceive the exam as consecration.

The marginalization of 'parallel admission' students is also created through subtle terminological distinctions that schools themselves operate among students according to their mode of admission. For example, at the École Polytechnique the exclusive title of *Polytechnicien* is denied to foreign students by certain French students who believe that they should be called 'Foreign student, EV2 of the École Polytechnique' (EV2, meaning *élève de la voie 2*, that is students that were recruited through the international procedure and not through the *concours*). The same is true for students of the ENS who do not afford foreign graduates the prestigious title of 'former student of the École Normale Supérieure'. The traditional employers of the graduates of these schools, moreover, represent yet another obstacle to a greater opening of these schools to foreign students. In fact, with the sole exception of the HEC (École des Hautes Etudes Commerciales), historically an important mission of these schools has been to train the high officers of state. These careers, being as they are specifically French, are either unattractive or inaccessible to foreign students.

When they enter these *Grandes Écoles*, most international students have no idea of their perceived meritocratic status among the French student community. Their lack of knowledge of the *Grandes Écoles'* meritocracy scale is due to the limited influence and reputation of these institutions on the international scene, except in some highly specialized milieus. Their modest size (a few hundred students for most of them) render them less visible compared with much larger 'global' institutions such as Stanford, Harvard or Princeton in the United States. Besides, the very specific nature of these schools, where the challenge of producing a state elite, which is partly meant to provide a cadre of civil officers for the country, serving the French Republic (the common mission of these schools, with the exception of HEC) is often misunderstood in the international arena. The *Grandes Écoles* are indeed intimately tied to a history that is above all national. Moreover, the very specific, homogeneous, and Malthusian nature of their recruitment, their slow adaptation to and use of international standardized exams and admission policies have not helped to heighten awareness of these schools outside France.

International students, however, gradually discover their meritocratic inferiority in the eyes of their French peers as well as in the distinction *Grandes Écoles* make among the student body. Most of them tend to internalize this stigma, which thus jeopardizes their social and academic integration. They have then to develop coping strategies to overcome the obstacles and difficulties they meet (Darchy-Koechlin 2012). We will now look as some of these strategies.

The first type of adaptive response may lead the international students to assume their role as a *Grande École* student and play the game of socialization and integration in trying to understand the institutional rules and master the culture and its codes. Integration is then assumed by social acceptance and participation in festive and associative forms of socialization in the school. This adaptation relies on the adoption and mastery of social codes that may seem anecdotal or folk, but which have a decisive function, as for example the jargon of the schools or various rites of integration organized by students (traditional, sometimes secret, induction ceremonies in the student community). Being a foreign student considered a stranger does not always make things easy and most international students experience a double externality, as non-native speakers and immigrants, that of the language of the host country and that of the initiatory language of the institutions. Typically international students try to make efforts to adapt while developing nonetheless at the same time forms of linguistic resistance. Some international students may hyper-identify with the role of *Grande École* student: they express during the interview a strong sense of belonging to their *Grande École* and full adherence in the model of selection, training, socialization and consecration. Such students feel almost members of the French elite. They then carry the official word of the institution.

Some of the *Grandes Écoles'* international students, including many Asian students in particular, internalize the rules of a scholastic game that fits, by its academic standards and competitive aspects, in the continuity of preparatory classes for the *Grandes Écoles*. Confronted with the competition with their peers, they take full account of the acquired benefits the French students enjoy. Those indeed who are insiders have a more intimate and direct knowledge of the curriculum and its requirements. Asian students tend then to invest heavily or exclusively in school work, in order to 'catch up' on the curriculum and the school advantage that the prep' school years gives to the French students. Yet the effects of this adaptive response characterized by over investment can be very uncertain, mainly due to the evolution of the definition of merit in the *Grandes Écoles* as described above.

A second adaptive strategy is 'exit', which is manifested by refusal to enter the academic game. Such a strategy is evident among a small number of international students who face difficulties in coping with academic requirements and also risk academic burn-out and losing face in relation to school competition. Many such students retreat from the double bind in which they find themselves: they are not being recognized as legitimate in the academic competition by national students because of their foreigner status, which is a depreciated status but not enough to justify any form of affirmative action. They then resign themselves to their lower status position, finally accepting that their foreigner status entitles them to no particular attention, neither solidarity nor empathy.

Conclusion

The meritocracy that characterizes French society is a meritocracy based on titles, ranks and prestige, shaped by the French Revolution but also inherited from the *Ancien Régime*.[10] Through the analysis of the perception of merit by national and international students, we have highlighted the centrality of merit in the French model of elite education and more specifically in the identity of higher education institutions (and their academic and intellectual traditions) and in the identity of students who enter these sites of elite formation. This work therefore indirectly demonstrates that very competitive entrance examinations, relying strongly on academic skills remains the cornerstone of the French republican ideal of meritocracy and of the egalitarian passion that animates it, even if this ideal operates primarily as a founding myth (McNamee and Miller 2004) for the resulting academic hierarchies or perhaps as a 'necessary fiction' (Dubet 2004).

International students in these *Grandes Écoles* are selected through entrance examinations which are supposed to ensure their legitimacy. Nevertheless their status is not perceived as being equivalent to that of French students. This may seem counter-intuitive in relation to the republican meritocratic imagination, but the acceptance of equivalence would mean giving less importance to the traditional entrance examination system and to the terms and conditions of its implementation (competitive and highly codified written and oral exams to test a well-defined preparatory programme).

Therefore the question of the evolution of the national entrance exams system is raised, along with that of the harmonization of recruitment procedures in order to adjust the French definition of meritocracy to the new context of the *Grandes Écoles* as international institutions of Higher Education. Should the specificity of national entrance examinations be maintained and should international selection procedures be drawn closer to national selection procedures? Or, on the contrary, should the national selection be opened to more international forms of selection likely to ensure a better measure of equity and diversity in the profiles of the chosen candidates and attract more international students?

In that respect, the recent policies aiming at the international opening of higher education in France stress the need to reflect on entrance exams and the republican meritocratic model, even more so because the French selection system and training of its elites is questioned by international evaluations such as PISA.[11] The French system is therefore facing competition from other national models that appear to be more efficient and more equitable in selecting and training a less Malthusian and more diversified elite.

The perception of merit by national and international students has consequences for students and their identities as elite students. It produces also significant effects on the institutions and on the system of elite education as a whole and more specifically on the identity of higher education institutions and the identity of the French elite higher education system. These higher education institutions, based on an *esprit de corps* in which merit is the keystone – dependent on success in the competitive entrance exam – are weakened by the differentiation of national and international students, which create social and cultural divisions within institutions. As Bourdieu put it:

> The influence of highly integrated groups [. . .] stands for a large part to the fact that they are linked by a collusion in the *illusio*, a fundamental complicity in the collective fantasy which ensures each member experience an exaltation of self, the principle of a solidarity rooted in adherence to the group's image as enchanted self-image. Indeed, it is this feeling socially constructed of being from a superior essence which, with the solidarity of interests and affinities of *habitus*, contributes the most to create what we must call an *esprit de corps*.
>
> (Bourdieu 2004, p. 19)

France continues to want to protect the *Grandes Écoles*, considered as a French exception in the global space of higher education, but the international opening up of these elite institutions inevitably raises questions about the French definition of meritocracy, and about the future role of the *Grandes Écoles* nationally and internationally.

Notes

1 Contrary to most OCDE's higher education systems, in France universities are not the main higher education institutions preparing for the core of elite professions: the main channel for education in Engineering, Management and Politics goes through *Grandes Écoles* and their preparatory classes. Whereas the university is open to every holder of the *baccalauréat*, *Grandes Écoles* are selective higher education institutions. There is first a selection for entry into the preparatory class, on the basis of application files, and then the competitive examination for entry into the *Grande École*. The *Grandes Écoles* and their preparatory classes enrol about 5 per cent of an age class (or one in ten students, knowing that there is about 50 per cent of an age cohort in higher education).

2 With the notable exception of HEC presented for several years in the *Financial Times* ranking as the best business school in Europe and one of the top business school in the world.

3 In 2006, in the ARWU ranking established by the Shanghai Jiao Tong University, the ENS reached the 99th place, the École Polytechnique was classified beyond the 200th place and the École des Mines for its part ranked beyond the bar of 300. In response, the École des Mines established a rival ranking based on the measurement of career success rather than on criteria of scientific production, as is the case for the Chinese university ranking. In the ranking of the École des Mines (September 2007 edition), the methodology consisted in counting the number of each institution's alumni reaching number one positions in the 500 largest companies. Consequently, five major French schools (Polytechnique, HEC, Sciences Po, ENA and Mines) appear in the top ten, along with Harvard, Stanford and MIT. We bring to attention that in the last editions of the Shanghai and Times rankings, some French *grandes écoles* have somehow improved their scores but remain far from the world's top twenty (in the 2013 ARWU, the ENS is 71st, Polytechnique 201–300th and Mines 401–500th and in the 2014 Times ranking, the ENS is 65th, Polytechnique 70th and Mines 193rd).

4 This research was directed by Agnès van Zanten and funded by the Agence Nationale de la Recherche (ANR). Its complete results will be published in 2015 (van Zanten *et al.* 2015). Our case studies are not representative of all of French *Grandes Écoles*. 'Prestigious among the prestigious' (Euriat and Thélot 1995), their recruitment process is the most competitive in their respective field of training (engineering, humanities and sciences, business, human and social sciences). The uniqueness of the social composition of these institutions is clear, not only in relation to the entire French population, but compared with all students enrolled in French selective higher education. Although recent data are lacking, the information gathered during our research suggests that working-class students remain significantly under-represented in these institutions (less than 10 per cent while there were on average 21 per cent in other GE according to statistics published in 2002 by the association which federates and represents the vast majority of French *Grandes Écoles*. The proportion of international students in the studied *Grandes Écoles* varies from 10 to 35 per cent with their level of international openness.

5 Namely, two or three years of full-time investment for the prep-school students with most of their social life put into parenthesis (Darmon 2013).

6 Civic engagement consists in community service (for example within an association).

7 At the École Polytechnique, 10 out of 400 admissions existing for French candidates are reserved for students coming from universities. International admissions target 100

candidates. At the École Normale Supérieure, the number of admissions for students preparing the degree is not predefined (180 students were admitted in 2009), almost as much as the 194 students recruited through the competitive exam. The international selection recruits annually 20 foreign students. In HEC, direct Master admissions targets 50 candidates, whereas 380 places are reserved for CPGE competitive entrance exam; 500 students altogether are welcomed on the campus. At Sciences Po, the number of admitted students varies each year. In 2009, among 1,224 admitted students, 381 were admitted because they were holders of the highest honours at the *baccalauréat*, 415 through the competitive entrance examination, 126 through the '*Convention Éducation Prioritaire*' (a special procedure reserved to students from disadvantaged *lycées*, a main element of the institution's equality of opportunity program) and 302 through international enrolments.

8 This opacity of selection criteria goes together with their reluctance to provide data on the national status and social profile of foreign students.

9 First of all *curriculum* compatibility with some countries, like Morocco for example where schools still teach the traditional mathematics curriculum of the French *lycées*, or Vietnam, where the French influence is also present as well as that of the Mandarin Chinese system. The same process has been observed within the section of literature and humanities of the *École Normale Supérieure*, where strong links with Eastern European countries can be observed due to the importance attributed to high cultural capital in the school curriculum of some of them as well as to historical links between France and Romania. Colonial history as well as the influence of French language and culture in some countries is frequently the central factor here as well as geopolitical strategies, financial issues and the search for excellence through symbolically rewarding partnerships.

10 *Ancien Régime* refers to the pre-revolutionary era where the ruling class was the nobility. From this point of view, the Republic introduced a radical change by giving the school a central role in access to dominant positions, thus creating a 'state nobility' (Bourdieu 1989), based on scholastic achievement and '*esprit de corps*' and transforming the essence of social distinction.

11   The Programme for International Student Assessment (PISA) is a triennial international survey organized by the Organisation for Economic Co-operation and Development (OECD) which enables the comparision of education systems worldwide through a test of the skills and knowledge of 15-year-old students and the characteristics of their family and their school (http://www.oecd.org/pisa/aboutpisa/).

References

Bourdieu, P. (1989) *La noblesse d'état. Grandes Écoles et esprit de corps*, Paris: Minuit; trans. Lauretta C. Clough (1998) *The State Nobility: Elite Schools in the Field of Power*, Stanford, CA: Stanford University Press.

Bourdieu, P. (2004) *Esquisse pour une auto-analyse*, Paris: Raisons d'agir; trans. Richard Nice (2008) *Sketch for a Self-Analysis*, Chicago: The University of Chicago Press.

Bourdieu, P. and Passeron, J.-C. (1964) *Les heritiers. Les étudiants et la culture*, Paris: Éditions de Minuit; trans. Richard Nice (1979) *The Inheritors: French Students and Their Relations to Culture*, University of Chicago Press.

Bourdieu, P. and Passeron, J.-C. (1970) *La Reproduction. Éléments pour une théorie du système d'enseignement*, Paris: Editions de Minuit; trans. Richard Nice (1977) *Reproduction in Education, Society and Culture* (Theory, Culture and Society Series), London: Sage Publications.

Clark, B. (1960) 'The "cooling-out" function in higher education', *The American Journal of Sociology*, 65: 569–576.

Cuche, D. (1988) 'La fabrication des "Gadzarts". Esprit de corps et inculcation culturelle chez les ingénieurs Arts et Métiers', *Ethnologie Française*, 1: 42–54.

Darchy-Koechlin, B. (2012) 'Les élites étudiantes internationales face au modèle d'excellence des Grandes Écoles françaises', unpublished thesis, Paris, Sciences Po.

Darchy-Koechlin, B. and Draelants, H. (2010) 'To belong or not to belong? The French model of elite selection and the integration of international students', *French Politics*, 8: 429–446.

Darchy-Koechlin, B., Draelants, H. and Tenret, E. (2015, forthcoming) 'La perception de la méritocratie dans les classes préparatoires et dans les Grandes Écoles', in A. van Zanten *et al.* (eds), *La formation des élites*, Paris: PUF.

Darmon, M. (2013) *Classes préparatoires. La fabrication d'une jeunesse dominante*, Paris: La Découverte.

Draelants, H. and Darchy-Koechlin, B. (2011) 'Flaunting one's academic pedigree? Self-presentation of students from elite French schools', *British Journal of Sociology of Education*, 32: 19–36.

Dubet, F. (2004) *L'école des chances. Qu'est-ce qu'une école juste?*, Paris: Seuil, La République des idées.

Duru-Bellat M. (2006) *L'inflation scolaire, les désillusions de la méritocratie*, Paris: Seuil, La République des Idées.

Elias, N. and Scotson, J.L. (1965) *The Established and the Outsiders: A Sociological Enquiry into Community Problems*, London: Cass & Company, Social surveys.

Euriat, M. and Thélot, C. (1995) 'Le recrutement social de l'élite scolaire en France: évolution des inégalités de 1950 à 1990', *Revue Française de Sociologie*, 36: 403–438.

Faguer, J.-P. (1991) 'Les effets d'une "éducation totale"', *Actes de la Recherche en Sciences Sociales*, 86: 25–43.

Harfi, M. and Mathieu, C. (2006) 'Classement de Shanghai et image internationale des universités: quels enjeux pour la France?', *Horizons Stratégiques*, 2: 100–115.

Iribarne (d'), P. (2006) *L'étrangeté française*, Paris: Seuil.

Karabel, J. (2005) *The Chosen: The Hidden History of Admission and Exclusion at Harvard, Yale, and Princeton*, Boston, MA: Houghton Mifflin Harcourt.

Kingston, P.W. and Lewis, L. S. (Eds.) (1990) *The High-Status Track: Studies of Elite Schools and Stratification*, Albany, NY: SUNY.

McNamee, S.J. and Miller R.K. (2004) *The Meritocracy Myth*, Lanham, MD: Rowman & Littlefield.

Parsons, T. (1951) *The Social System*, Glencoe, IL: Free Press.

Tenret, E. (2011) *L'école et la méritocratie*, Paris: PUF.

van Zanten, A. (2015, forthcoming) *La formation des élites. Selection et socialisation*, Paris: PUF.

Weber, M. (1971) [original edition 1922] *Economie et société*, Tome 1, Paris: Plon.

Young, M. (1958) *The Rise of the Meritocracy*, London: Thames & Hudson, Penguin Books.

11 Globalizing Femininity in Elite Schools for Girls

Some Paradoxical Failures of Success

Jane Kenway, Diana Langmead and Debbie Epstein

Introduction

Girls from elite schools appear to have everything – wealthy and well-connected families, regular international travel to study, play and shop, and seemingly limitless ability, confidence and poise. They are high achievers in all school activities – academics, sports and the arts. They are school leaders running student executives, clubs and societies. They serve good causes too, for example working in soup kitchens for the poor or travelling to villages in 'third world' countries to provide 'service'. Their futures are predictably top rung – top universities, prestigious and influential careers, partners in the upper tiers of society and expensive lifestyles. It seems that their propensities for success are endless; that they have infinite agency and worthiness.

Their expensive, exclusive and socially segregated schools like to take much of the credit for such girls' accomplishments. After all, they groomed them. And one possible inference from this is that these schools provide models for emulation around the world; that they are the inspirational pinnacle in the education of all girls. This is one of the reasons why these 'A1' girls (McRobbie 2009) and the A1 schools they attend are of interest.

Many elite schools for girls around the world have been modelled on the elite schools for girls that were established in England in the second half of the nineteenth century. Such schools helped pave the way for major reforms in the education and social role of girls and women. Two of the initiators of the reform agenda in the private girls' schools of England were Dorothea Beale and Frances Mary Buss (Kamm 2010): their aim was to ensure that the privileged girls at their schools acquired a worthwhile educational and career trajectory. Buss's North London Collegiate School for Ladies catered for 'daughters of retired gentlemen, doctors, artists, clerks and the more "respectable" tradesmen' (Kamm 2012 [1958]: 41). Beale's The Ladies' College catered for the 'daughters and young children of Noblemen and Gentlemen ... in Cheltenham' (ibid: 51).

At the time, privileged single women's social position was in flux (Vicinus 1985) as changes in the economy were reflected in new configurations of social relationships. These new schools for girls, and the educational philosophies that informed them, disputed conventional, upper class-based modes of femininity and, thus, gender relations at the apex of society. To some extent, these schools eventually helped to pave the way for girls from other classes to receive school and university education. Further, the goals they set travelled internationally via teachers trained at the institutions set up by these women and, therefore, heavily influenced the similar girls' schools that emerged in various British colonies in the late nineteenth and early twentieth centuries. Consequently, it can readily be argued that these schools played an important feminist role in the education of girls over time and place in that period.

Today, A1 schools for girls present themselves as continuing and updating this historical legacy and, thus, they enjoy the gloss of feminist progressivism. They present themselves as miniature utopias for all sorts of girls and claim to prepare them exceptionally well for their post-school lives. And, as such, the implication is that they continue to play a leading role in the education of girls. But is this so? Are they rising to the challenges of contemporary times of flux? Since, it seems, the complex contours of globalization have meant that social relationships are fluid and fixed simultaneously, how have the schools responded and coped and how have they prepared their girls for this brave new world?

In this chapter, we question the schools' utopian discourses and their proclamations that they produce successful, well-adjusted, globally competent young women. We argue that the hothouse environments within which girls are so vigilantly groomed for 'success' are oppressive. Elite girls' schools are now admitting girls from other countries and, also, grooming girls for the global. They, thus, believe that they are appropriately equipping their girls to operate successfully on the global as well as the national stage. But, again, this is open to question.

A Few Words on Method

We draw here from two girls' schools, Greystone School in South Africa and Highbury Hall in England, both part of our five-year study, *Elite independent schools in globalizing circumstances: a multi-sited global ethnography* (2010–2014).[1] The study includes one school in England and one each in Australia, Barbados, Hong Kong, India, Singapore, South Africa, Cyprus and Argentina (all former formal or informal British colonies). The project is exploring the extent to and manner in which these elite schools in countries with different colonial and postcolonial histories respond to globalizing circumstances and to changing elite formations. Our selected schools all draw their inspiration from the post-Arnoldian British public school model, are over 100 years old, have produced many influential people and have many powerful connections. Their records illustrate considerable success in end-of-school exams and prestigious university entrance and they have excellent reputations. Most are independent of government control (although not necessarily of influence and funding) and charge high fees. Most are very well resourced in comparison with the majority of other schools in the national education system that they are part of. Two are single-sex schools for girls; one is a single-sex school for boys; another is a single-sex school for boys up to year 10 (16 years old); the rest are co-educational (all are anonymized here).

Our method includes three weeks per year over three consecutive years of field-work in each school. Whilst in each school, two or three members of our research team generate data through conventional ethnographic techniques including intensive observations of various institutional practices, events, documents and its semiotic ecology (including websites, promotional materials), interviews and focus group discussions involving students, teachers, school principal and leading members of the school's governing body, alumni and parents' associations and informal conversations with members of the school (Epstein *et al.* 2013). Intensive case studies of 10 students in each school have been conducted through in-depth interviews during their final two years of school and their second year out of school. In this chapter, we draw on our intensive case studies of students in Greystone and Highbury Hall, using our data from and about them as illustrative examples of our argument.

Grooming for the Global

There is a burgeoning body of feminist scholarship which focuses on what are variously called 'top girls', 'Cosmo girls', 'A1 girls', 'can-do girls' and 'global girls', all defined as assured, accomplished, exemplary, empowered, adaptive and productive (see, for example, Allan and Charles 2013; Forbes and Weiner 2008; Maxwell and Aggleton 2010; McRobbie 2009, 2011). Such studies tell us much about the contemporary constitution of femininity amongst the more, and the most, privileged and powerful sectors of our national and, increasingly, global social worlds. But they do not address the globalizing world of work and its implications for such women.

Highbury Hall produces many 'A1 girls' who are led by the school to believe that they should become leaders. Indeed, in a recent media interview, a prominent staff member at Highbury Hall[2] said that the school has a mandate to teach the girls to push their intellectual boundaries. They must learn to lead and be well prepared for their future in positions of power and influence. Similar discourses abound at Greystone.

Many girls in all our schools expect to gain top-level employment in their own right, even if, due to family wealth, they have no financial need to be in paid work. Only the best universities will do and their proposed work will be of the sort considered proper for girls of their class, the higher-order professions, business (family or their own), banking, finance and senior management or management consultancy, leading roles in the culture, creative and fashion industries, the senior public service, politics or diplomatic posts.

Take the example of Maryam. Her mother is from the Middle East and came to the UK with her family at the age of seventeen to escape revolution in her own country. Maryam's father is British, in business. Maryam had an academic scholarship, won on the basis of merit, to Highbury Hall. She was very conscious of the need to do well academically:

> And you take the entrance exam … – you get in, so there's the band that gets in and then there's the top band – the very top band. They get called back

for a scholarship. ... And so I was awarded an academic scholarship. But the thing is with that you need to – they do expect you to keep up academically ... they expect you to get good grades.

(2010)

In 2010, she wanted to become a doctor, a consultant, probably a psychiatrist. In 2014, two years after finishing school, she was a second-year student in a high-status medical school in London, still planning to become a consultant and, she added, to do a PhD. She is highly ambitious and sees no barriers to her career success.

But the question arises, how well prepared are these girls for contemporary and future workplaces, let alone for leading them? Almost all such work, these days, is constituted globally. It involves global connections and expectations and, often, various forms of global mobility. This is the case, even though some such work 'places' are very clearly trans- or multi-national, while others are more nationally (domestically) based. Work in the latter, nonetheless, still has global components and responsibilities (such as overseeing international operations and business networks abroad). Hutchings *et al.* (2012: 1,765) point out that:

> organisations are increasingly utilising alternative forms of international assignments, including fly-in/fly-out project work, commuter assignments or domestic-based jobs with international business travel, virtual international assignments or teleworking, and short term international assignments of a few weeks or months.

No doubt, the dedication, hard work and self-sense of supreme capability learnt through elite schools are basic requirements for such work (Merilainen *et al.* 2004). So, too, are the so-called 'soft skills' of communicating and collaborating that girls' schools claim to specialize in. As Wardman *et al.* (2010) show, elite schools for girls claim not only to produce 'well-rounded' 'empowered' girls but, at the same time and equally, they validate the very 'feminine' virtues of caring, loyalty, contributing and responsibility for others – and it could be argued that Maryam's early preference for psychiatry might be demonstrating just such feminine virtues, alongside her very evident academic success.

But, such globally oriented workplaces have raised the stakes and demand a great deal more than 'soft skills'. It is in relation to such workplaces that these girls are incited by their schools to learn various languages, to develop international mindedness and cross-cultural awareness. The increasingly multicultural, multiracial and multinational membership of their schools is seen to help in this regard, as do the numerous opportunities the schools provide for international travel and for making connections with other, like-minded schools and students around the world (Kenway and Fahey 2014). The lessons they learn through this top-notch, intersectional, social positioning can be applied, it is believed, across multiple settings. In short, girls are expected to become classy cosmopolitans who can skate, with effortless efficiency, across the privileged surfaces of their working worlds and who can engage with total ease and grace their counterparts from other cultures and locations.

Blake might be thought of as in this way. Her family is originally from mainland China. However, she was brought up and educated in Hong Kong until aged sixteen, coming to Highbury Hall for the last two years of schooling. She explained that her mother knew that:

> since I've been [to school] in Hong Kong for several years, my math and my science and like those basic techniques that I have to excel in, science subjects – it's there. What I need is something that can broaden my mind and make me think. Because I can't really analyze politics or current issues back there. … And then she wants me to mingle with students abroad – like not just British girls but maybe like girls from India and girls from other cities so that eventually I will meet them. Like meet people from different countries when I grow older. So if I can get used to like talking with different people when I was young it's going to be easier for me in the future.
>
> (2010)

Blake went on to a prestigious London university where, in 2014, she was studying politics. She agrees with her mother's view that it is necessary to be fluent not only in Mandarin (her first language), Cantonese and English, but also in the cultural ways of the West: 'At least if even if … I don't work how Westerners would, I can understand [them]'. She is, in fact, well on the way to personifying ease and grace in her engagement with people from other countries.

But let us take a reality check with regard to the idea that such girls from elite schools have learnt to lead in the contemporary world of work. Despite all the schools' proclamations about leadership, and despite all the opportunities to lead that the schools provide, it is never made clear where, what and who the girls are supposed to lead. These A1 girls are highly unlikely to go on to occupy, through their work, the inner circles of the national/global power elite. Images of 'Davos man' at Davos conferences make this eminently clear: the first rule to becoming a member of the 'super-class' is '*Be born a man*' (Rothkopf 2008: 289). While women's increased education, power and money are certainly associated with escalating success in leading companies and, in rare cases, countries, overall they have not risen to lead 50 per cent of the 99 per cent let alone of the 1 per cent. And, at less than 0.07 of the ruling, hyper-wealthy 1 per cent, women are immensely under-represented in the global elite (ibid. 2008). It seems that women's options are remarkably restricted and regulated amongst the very rich and powerful and that this is rarely problematized by their male counterparts (Freeland 2012: 86–7).

No doubt, many women from elite schools will seek to join the outer circles of the global elite, travelling along its global routes. As such, they will be subject to the associated gendered expectations and relationships. But, what exactly are these? Research on related issues is sparse but, predictably, these will involve gender-based perceptions of their expertise, capability and authority in comparison with their male counterparts, they will face various organizational and cultural barriers in selection, and family commitments will be likely to restrict their mobility.

Speaking of the experiences of Highbury Hall's alumni with regard to such high-power work, the principal told us: 'They didn't want what would come with [such work] because it would be too high a cost, in their assessment of the balance of their lives' (2011). In 2014, Blake seemed aware of this, talking about her desire for children and the difficulties this might cause for her high-powered career.

In international management, for example, Hutchings *et al.* (2012: 1,765) argue that, 'Women continue to be an under-utilized source of talent globally as they remain under-represented relative to their male counterparts'. They believe that 'there is discrimination against women in selection for global assignments'. The barriers to women's global work, they contend, are:

(1) complexities of prejudice in the foreign location,

(2) long-standing corporate resistance,

(3) misperceptions about disinterest among female managers, and

(4) a lack of support (organisational, network or social/family) and work–family conflicts.

(ibid.: 1,765)

The principal echoed this last point: '[Working in international] hedge fund-y type of stuff, [an ex-student] found that, as a profession, it was completely incompatible really, in terms of progression, with having a family. Completely. [Leaving her feeling] disillusioned and lost, as an identity' (2011).

In light of these observations, we suggest that the grooming-for-the-global curriculum of elite girls' schools is not necessarily up to the job of preparing these girls for the workplaces that they will enter. It may well be doing them a disservice. Its bland, superficial and apolitical notions of international mindedness and cross-cultural competence leave them poorly prepared for dealing with the complexities of the gendered prejudice they are likely to experience. The smooth sailing they are taught to expect in their lustrous post-school lives leaves them unprepared for the male resistance they are likely to encounter in the corporate workplaces they will enter. Even so, the feminist tropes used to motivate students (and to market the school) construct such workplaces as primary sites and symbols of success, despite their uncongenial working conditions. Darlene (teacher 2011) worries that:

we make the girls think that they can have it all and I don't think that we always address ... how you balance having a family, how to balance relationships ... their role models of women are ones that pretend they don't have families.

As Walkerdine (2003) points out, the liberal feminist agenda, one so beloved of elite girls' schools, has transmogrified into a neoliberal, faux feminist agenda. And Highbury Hall's faux feminism means that these girls have few discourses at their disposal through which to understand these matters and no community of feminist agitators with whom they might work to try to effect change.

But, if they do go on to take up leadership positions in business, industry, politics and the professions and exert influence over the lives of people right across the social spectrum, then their schools' practices of social segregation are of consequence. Like their male counterparts, their school-based social cocooning means that such girls have little lived sense of life in wider society, let alone real life on the 'bottom rungs'. Such schools can be thought of as 'purified spaces . . . cleansed of variety and difference . . . tame, sanitized'. Missing from such schools is 'the plurality and multi-vocality of the life setting' (Bauman 2000: 99). Yet a large number of the girls at and young alumni of these schools told us that they expected to become high-powered, high-status 'consultants' or movers and shakers in the financial industries. Indeed, Blake explained that at her university, employers recruiting at careers fairs were virtually all from international consultancy, accounting and financial corporations – so the general expectation was that these young people, most of them with virtually no experience outside the cocoon, would be able to offer advice to public services and smaller firms.

Trophy Girls and Failure Phobia

This neoliberal, faux feminist agenda has placed such young women under enormous pressure to succeed across all the registers of success implied in our opening paragraph. Some will go to extraordinary lengths to be the best of what they consider the best, nationally and, in some cases, worldwide. But, no amount of grooming and of striving can ensure that *all* girls will reach the apex of contemporary neoliberal feminist achievement.

Many, not all, girls are, in effect, trophy daughters who are propelled to, and often do, gratify the ferocious ambitions of their parents. Our conversations with alumnae and parents indicate that the failure phobia this can engender in the daughters intensifies across generations of Highbury Hall girls. The daughter, now mother, not only dreads failing to produce a successful daughter but, at the same time, she develops a similar, obsessive fear that her daughter will fail. So, commensurate with her intense determination that her daughter must succeed, she is terrified she might not. And, mothers who had been miserable students at the school themselves, nevertheless sent their daughters there in order to ensure (or reassure themselves of) the success of their daughters. The next generation, then, inherits an internalized, inherent fear of failure. This is amplified when they are, also, seen as trophy students for the school; as proof positive of their school's superiority. Beset from all directions, their greatest responsibility is to shine, shine, shine – especially if, like Maryam, they are scholarship students.

A chain of expectation of perfection links the school, the teachers, parents and girls. It pressures the girls with a constant reminder that, as members of the elite, they can, and must, 'star'. The girls are burdened with ever-mounting levels of work that exhausts them mentally, while they forfeit sleep and recreation to be the best. 'Perfectionist' girls' sense of low achievement leads them to take on more and more work and, because they take such work, they are given even more, spinning them towards accreditation and exhaustion. Those who meet the outward measures of success are rewarded publicly and profusely at Highbury Hall, where a corrosive culture of reward lavishes cups, awards and certificates on them, emphasized by the rolling slideshow of success on the screen in the entrance lobby and items in the local and national press, reminding the 'winners' that all they do is noteworthy, leaving the remaining two-thirds anxiously awaiting songs of praise for their efforts. All, then, expect ongoing acknowledgement wherever they go, whatever they do.

Lacey, a young alumna, tells us how putting 'a lot of perfectionist, high achieving girls somewhere that rewards performance' leads to high numbers of 'casualties' with what she calls 'disordered eating' and mental illness (focus group, 2012). And, indeed, the school has a reputation locally of being 'Anorexia Hall' and we observed how, at lunch times, many thin and worried girls spent the time pushing their food around their plates without eating. Highbury Hall, unsurprisingly, encourages perfectionist traits and its ineffectual responses to the casualties hide the side-effects of maintaining the façade of the blithely brilliant.

The girls, ever conscious of how much work their peers are doing, never seem to reach a point where they can say: 'I've done enough' – they work until they 'fall in a heap', stressing about whether they are as good as everybody else. 'Naughty students', when they relax and have fun, feel anxious and guilty because, as Patsy (staff leader) says, no Highbury Hall girl is content with failure. Given the endless support and resources at home and school that their privilege provides, failure is relative and redefines what others might consider mere disappointment. Patsy uses the term 'Asian fail', by which she means marks below 90 per cent. Such marks give rise to paroxysms of fear not just amongst the 'Asian' girls but, also, the wider student population.

This fear of failure worries Highbury Hall's new principal who feels responsible for preparing students for a time when school support is no longer available. She hopes to help them find ways to 'celebrate the creativity of failing' (interview 2011) without feeling inadequate, by developing 'a mental elasticity and resilience that is not coupled to one's self esteem and self-belief levels'. Highbury Hall will, then, reframe 'failure' as creative opportunity and successful situation management and use the girls' privileged circumstances to cushion their disappointments in their futures.

Of course, notions of success and failure are relative and the girls in our schools only seriously compare themselves with those who they judge as worthy comparators; girls like them in schools like theirs. And, typically, they only compare 'up', looking to emulate those they perceive as the top of the top, those at the apex of achievement and worthiness.

Tense and Toxic Mobilities

There has been a recent flow into certain elite schools in the so-called West of girls from various countries in Asia, particularly India, Hong Kong and mainland China

(Fahey 2014). In such countries, the quest for educational success is at fever pitch (Kenway *et al.* 2013). The presence of such girls in our elite schools in England has added a whole new layer of competitive intensity to the grooming curriculum.

Along with this, elements of international racism have arisen. For example, girls from Hong Kong pride themselves on their ability to outshine their white, English peers at Highbury Hall. Indeed, they claim that the school actually depends on their success for its reputation. In contrast, their English peers argue that the school is being so swamped by 'Asians' that its English-boarding-school-ness is at risk. It can be inferred they think keeping it English (read white) will protect them from the unwanted extra competition from these very high-achieving, exceedingly ambitious girls from Asia.

This is but one example of the tensions existing within elite girls' schools. We have found that, beneath such schools' smooth serene surfaces, such tensions can be explosive, torrid and, even, toxic or they can involve slow-burning antipathies that seldom surface. One set of tensions relates to changing configurations and formations of class, particularly those associated with globalization. For, as the tensions between the English and Asian girls demonstrate, international mobility is interfering with the educational and social order from which these precocious and privileged English girls have, hitherto, benefited exclusively. They want their class citadel to stay white.

International tensions are experienced differently in Greystone School in South Africa. The boarding house at Greystone includes girls from many different countries of sub-Saharan Africa, all of them former British colonies, with much smaller numbers of South African girls from other cities and local girls whose parents find it convenient to board them. The rest of the school's student population is largely white, though there are some Indian, coloured and African girls.[3] The small boarding house student population is, almost exclusively, black.

Those from outside South Africa collectivize themselves as non-South African. They do this to find a 'place' for themselves in the new environment where there may be few or none from their home country, so they look for commonalities, indeed, for affective communities who can, and eventually do, substitute for absent families. But, they, also, collectivize because they feel that 'local' students do not accept or respect them and, indeed, look down on them, not because of their social class (most come from highly privileged circumstances) but because of the national hierarchies they adopt and an associated practice of classing countries and attributing degrees of civilization. Their home countries are seen to be way down the hierarchy, even though few South African girls know much about such countries.

All the non-South African girls we spoke with commented on the lack of knowledge that the South African girls have, and their lack of interest in learning, about their home countries and, basically, their lack of respect for them. This is despite the fact most of their home countries have close links, politically, historically, economically and geographically, with South Africa. As Deka pointed out, 'Some South Africans don't even know where Namibia is', and Aziza (2012) commented that she is frequently asked whether the majority in Zambia is black.

Neema (2012) sums it up when she says: 'I get really tired when they speak about other African countries and ... look down on them and they put stereotypes onto the countries'. Day girls, who are primarily white, also notice this: 'Most black people in the school are from Africa. I don't think people care to know about those people's cultures and what those people believe' (Nina 2012). South Africa, then, becomes separated from 'Africa' in Nina's imagination and is seen as Western and developed in comparison with countries further north. The girls from other African countries recounted different learning experiences at home, 'In Namibia, we're brought up from grade one learning about what South Africa does, what Angola does, what Botswana and Zimbabwe and Zambia, all those Southern African countries do' (Deka 2012).

In a sense, these girls are objectified. Kristeva explains:

> [A]bjection is elaborated by a failure to recognize its kin ... hence before they are signifiable – [the subject in question] drives them out ... and constitutes his own territory edged by the abject. A sacred configuration. Fear cements his compound ....
>
> (Kristeva 1982: 6)

The South African girls split the schoolgirl population into 'compounds' of those worthy and not worthy of recognition. This can be read, in Kristeva's (1982: 6) terms, as a protective territorial strategy arising from fear of the outsider whose very presence threatens the compound's sacredness and security. This strategy includes a refusal to let a population become fully recognizable, in all its complexity, within the 'compound'. It can be understood as an attempt at spatial purging and purification in order to preserve the white South African-ness of the day school by quarantining the black, non-South African girls to the boarding house.

One of the boarding house girls' responses is to form their own 'compound' in which they mock their abjectification. They mock it by taking up a mode of girl-hood that is, largely, considered grotesque in this elite, predominantly white, school. They become 'uncivilized', extra loud and boisterous and adopt, what they call, a 'rural accent'. 'It makes us sound, like, uneducated and terrible, but that's just how we speak to each other as a joke ... like we're our own country [in the board-ing house]' (Deka). In effect, they adopt a form of 'abject agency', 'taking up an abject position,' (Cowlishaw 2004: 158) mocking and exaggerating it through defi-ance and disrespect, and hurling it back at the original perpetrators in order to confound, disconcert and embarrass them. In this way, they seek to defeat attempts at their humiliation.

It is, then, something of an irony that many of the non-South African girls do not plan to return to home after completing their education. Indeed, some adopt the very practices of abjectification to which they have been subject. And, here, we see a conflation of nation, class and opportunity. For instance, Helena's career plans are structured around the class-based opportunities available in South Africa as compared with her home country of Tanzania:

Well Tanzania is not really a … high-class kind of country … it's not as good as South Africa. South Africa's way beyond it and Tanzania is way at the bottom. There are not a lot of job opportunities, there would be … a job but … I wouldn't be … a top person. If I wanted to study, like build a magazine, I wouldn't be top I'd just be like the rest of the people.

(Focus group 2011)

Helena's expectations have shifted to align with those of her inhospitable host school and country. This is her way of ensuring that her international mobility secures her social security.

Not all girls are quite so ready to abandon their abjectified home country and, by association, the families they have left behind. But Fortune's story (2010) is one of several examples where their families and their attendant obligations and responsibilities are now read through a class lens, which the school seems to have helped foster. Fortune's uncles live 'in a poor society' [in Nigeria] and Fortune's father (who works for the UNHCR) has long financially supported her uncles and their families. Fortune is very dismissive of these families, 'they don't think before they do things' (such as having children they cannot afford). Here, she draws a clear connection between their class and their lesser ability to behave rationally. This is, clearly, a privilege-based reaction that does not incorporate empathy for those with fewer resources. Despite this, or perhaps because of her perceived 'superiority' by class and privilege, Fortune factors into her future plans a responsibility of sharing her father's obligation and, by implication, she is, thus, also adopting the familial responsibilities appropriate to her home country.

It is, perhaps, ironic, given how black the girls are in South Africa that, on return visits to their home countries, the girls are again seen as Other. Deka explained that: 'when we go home, everyone sees us as different because they know [we've been] in South Africa', while Lulu said:

When I go back home, people would [call me] *unzungu*, which means white person … because of the way I act, the way I dress … the local people [will say] oh look at that *unzungu*, she's speaking the *unzungu* language …. Even if you're black … they'll still see you as a white person.

It is more poignant for those few black South African girls to experience similar Otherness in their own country. Thandi is a gifted artist, able to attend Greystone because her mother was teaching there. Unlike other girls, when there was money required to go on trips or for other expensive activities, she had to raise it herself. She did not apply to do fine arts at university because she knew she would only get a scholarship for a more vocational course. In 2014 she was on a scholarship at a prestigious South African university studying architecture, where, she explained, virtually all the students were from schools like hers and most were white. She was aware of her own changed accent and embodiment: 'I find as a person who came to this school when I go back to the [black township] people go 'oh you're a coconut'. Because I speak differently and I notice I carry myself differently. 'Oh coconut" (Interview 2011).

In many ways, Thandi was more aware of her privilege than either the (rich) white South Africans or the (rich) African boarders. But, like Fortune, she had a strong sense of familial responsibility that led to her choice of degree. Being seen as Other because of her race/ethnicity at school and because of her privileged education amongst her local peers meant that, while benefiting from her elite education, and on her way to joining the emergent black upper professional class, she was never quite 'at home' (see also Epstein 2014).

Conclusion

To conclude, many feminist issues remain with regard to these girls and these schools which suggest that the schools are no longer in the position to claim they lead the way in the education of girls. There are a number of issues at stake here. First, there is the paradoxical failure of success. The expectations and anxieties produced by failure phobia are not sustainable or defensible as 'success'. Ironically, these schools are held up as exemplary. Government schools are supposed to learn from and emulate them while beneath the surface lie a mass of contradictions.

We have shown how the grooming for global success in the cocoon of the elite school does not actually prepare the girls for the challenges they will meet or the well documented misogyny and sexism of the corporate world. Their confidence that they can become internationally successful 'consultants', despite little experience or knowledge of the world outside school, is a case in point. Nevertheless, they are in a position to go to prestigious universities, do high-status courses, and gain employment at some level in, at least, the financial industries and the professions and some may, in the future, achieve the kind of success on the global stage of which they dream.

We have drawn attention, too, to some of the differences between being at such a school in the UK and its equivalent in South Africa. In both cases, class (local and global) is nuanced and impacted by intersections with nation and race, at the very least. Privilege is to be protected and defended, but it has become impossible to hold it to one imperial nation or one overweening school.

Finally, we have drawn attention to the soft underbelly of the elite school. Marketing and advertising themselves as progressive and (faux) feminist, they are productive of anxiety and offer no guarantee of the success they promise.

Notes

1 Funding: Australian Research Council (DP1093778) and our respective universities. Researchers: Jane Kenway, Johannah Fahey (Monash), Fazal Rizvi (Melbourne), Cameron McCarthy (Illinois), Debbie Epstein (Roehampton), Aaron Koh (NIE Singapore) and PhD students; Matthew Shaw, Howard Prosser (Monash) and Mousumi Mukherjee (Melbourne).

2 We cannot source this media report as it will identify the school.
3 These categories from the apartheid era are extant and monitored as part of the process of transformation.

References

Allan, A. and Charles, C. (2013). 'Cosmo girls: configurations of class and femininity in elite educational settings'. *British Journal of Sociology of Education*, 35(3): 333–532. doi: http://dx.doi.org/10.1080/01425692.2013.764148

Bauman, Z. (2000). *Liquid Modernity*. Cambridge: Polity Press.

Cowlishaw, G. (2004). *Blackfellas, Whitefellas and the Hidden Injuries of Race*. Malden, MA: Blackwell.

Epstein, D. (2014). 'Race-ing class ladies: lineages of privilege in and elite South African school'. *Globalization, Societies and Education: Special Issue on Elite Schools in Globalizing Circumstances*, 12(2): 244–61. http://dx.doi/pdf/10.1080/14767724.2014.890887

Epstein, D., Fahey, J., and Kenway, J. (2013). 'Multi-sited global ethnography and travelling biography: gendered journeys'. *International Journal of Qualitative Studies in Education*, 26(4): 470–488. doi: http://dx.doi.org/10.1080/09518398.2013.765613

Fahey, J. (2014). 'Privileged girls: the place of feminiinity and the femininity of place'. *Globalisation, Societies and Education,* 12(2): 228–243. doi: http://dx.doi.org/10.1080/14767724.2014.888307

Forbes, J. and Weiner, G. (2008). 'Under-stated powerhouses: Scottish independent schools, their characteristics and their capitals'. *Discourse: Studies in the Cultural Politics of Education*, 29(4), 509–525. doi: http://dx.doi.org/10.1080/01596300802410235

Freeland, C. (2012). *Plutocrats: The Rise of the New Global Super-Rich*. London: Penguin.

Hutchings, K., Lirio, P. and Metcalfe, B.D. (2012). 'Gender, globalisation and development: a re-evaluation of the nature of women's global work'. *The International Journal of Human Resource Management*, 23(9): 1,763–1,787. doi: http://dx.doi.org/10.1080/0958 5192.2011.610336

Kamm, J. (2010 [1965]). *Hope Deferred (Routledge Revivals): Girls' Education in English History*. Taylor & Francis e-library.

Kamm, J. (2012 [1958]). *How Different from Us: A Biography of Miss Beale and Miss Buss*. London: Routledge.

Kenway, J. and Fahey, J. (2014). 'Staying ahead of the game: the globalising practices of elite schools'. *Globalisation, Societies and Education*, 12(2): 177–195. doi: http://dx.doi.org/10 .1080/14767724.2014.890885

Kenway, J., Fahey, J. and Koh, A. (2013). 'The libidinal economy of the globalising elite school market'. In C. Maxwell and P. Aggleton (eds), *Privilege, Agency and Affect: Understanding the Production and Effects of Action*. Basingstoke: Palgrave Macmillan.

Kristeva, J. (1982). *Powers of Horror*. New York: Columbia University Press.

McRobbie, A. (2009). *The Aftermath of Feminism: Gender, Culture and Social Change*. Los Angeles, CA: Sage.

McRobbie, A. (2011). 'Top Girls – (Un) doing feminism'. Online. http://www.angelamcrobbie. com/2011/11/top-girls-un-doing-feminism/ (accessed 2011).

Maxwell, C. and Aggleton, P. (2010). 'The bubble of privilege: young, privately educated women talk about social class'. *British Journal of Sociology of Education*, 31(1): 3–15. doi: http://dx.doi.org/10.1080/01425690903385329

Merilainen, S., Tiernari, J., Thomas, R. and Davies, A. (2004). 'Management consultant talk: a cross-cultural comparison of normalizing discourse and resistance'. *Organization*, 11(4): 539–564. doi: http://dx.doi.org/10.1177/1350508404044061

Rothkopf, D. (2008). *Superclass: The Global Power Elite and the World They are Making*. New York: Farrar, Straus and Giroux.

Vicinus, M. (1985). *Independent Women: Work and Community for Single Women, 1850–1920*. Chicago: University of Chicago Press.

Walkerdine, V. (2003). 'Reclassifying upward mobility: femininity and the neo-liberal subject'. *Gender and Education*, 15(3): 237–248. doi: http://dx.doi.org/10.1080/09540250303864

Wardman, N., Hutchesson, R., Gottschall, K., Drew, C. and Saltmarsh, S. (2010). 'Starry eyes and subservient selves: portraits of "well-rounded" girlhood in the prospectuses of all-girl elite private schools'. *Australian Journal of Education*, 54(3): 249–261. doi: http://dx.doi.org/10.1177/000494411005400303

Part IV

Elite Institutions, Elite Positions and Elite Jobs

The chapters in this part focus on how the training received in elite institutions shapes access to elite positions and jobs. Specifically, this part offers an analysis of both objective and subjective trajectories of elite students and how the particular knowledge and skills they acquire in elite institutions can be successfully used in a range of positions in both the public and private sectors.

Paul Wakeling and Mike Savage examine processes of elite reproduction in Britain. Drawing on the BBC'S Great British Class Survey (GBCS) they demonstrate how attendance at specific British universities facilitates access to particular socially advantaged positions. Strong processes of internal stratification are identified; notably the emergence of a small group of universities that can be considered as 'super-elite'. Hierarchies between elite institutions are shown to be linked to both economic and cultural capital, but in particular to the former. These patterns of institutional stratification, though specific to the British case, fit with Bourdieusian theories of reproduction and with the effectively maintained inequality hypothesis.

Jules Naudet's chapter stresses how, despite similar levels of social mobility in France and the United States, there is a strong discrepancy in the way mobility is experienced in these two countries: Americans are shown to frequently minimize the differences between their social class origin and their new socio-economic location, while French elites reflect on their experience of mobility as something that has been affectively challenging. Naudet argues that the reasons for this discrepancy can be found in the specificities of pathways to elite status in these countries. The architecture of educational system in France is characterized by 'sponsored mobility', whereas a system of 'contest mobility' seems to prevail in the United States.

Marte Mangset's chapter offers another comparative perspective – this time on British, French and Norwegian administrative elites. Mangset argues that very similar general skills are required to be successfully recruited into these elite administrative positions across all three countries, reflecting a certain degree of decoupling between the kind of knowledge and skills implicitly valued in the selection process to civil service elite positions and the formal training required to be eligible for such positions. She also shows, however, that the socio-historical context and configurations of these countries is crucial for understanding subtle differences in how these civil servants talk about merit and the kind of work they do.

The final chapter in this part by Brown, Lauder and Sung analyses competing definitions of 'talent' and how they contribute to the (re)stratification of higher education. The chapter emphasizes the significant mismatch between the structure and historical purposes of national education systems and the global labour market, through using Singapore as an example. In order to reduce the numbers of highly skilled foreign workers employed in the country, the Singaporean government has promoted the expansion of higher education in the belief that this will increase the supply of indigenous talent. Employers of transnational firms, however, embrace an idea of talent as 'soft skills' that they associate with training in specific 'world-class' institutions.

12 Elite Universities, Elite Schooling and Reproduction in Britain

Paul Wakeling and Mike Savage

In his influential studies of the relationship between cultural capital and social inequality, Pierre Bourdieu (1984) famously argued in the French case that as educational opportunities increased, so the goalposts were moved to ensure that it was only a selective group of universities that conveyed access to true elite positions. He thus directed attention away from general analyses of higher education and society towards a more differentiated and nuanced account of the symbolic power of specific institutions. It is striking that despite increasing interest in elite formation, and extensive anecdotal and journalistic interest in the power of elite education to play key consecrating roles in elite formation in Britain, this issue has hardly been examined systematically. This is partly because we currently lack large-scale data and analysis which permit us to unpick how exclusive and significant such processes might be. Here we use the BBC's *Great British Class Survey* (GBCS) to provide a uniquely granular account of the impact of attendance at specific British universities in facilitating access to socially advantaged positions. We show that attending elite educational institutions at either secondary or higher education level increases the likelihood of entering elite positions. We further show, on the basis of our analysis of the GBCS, that there are clear and quite wide differences in economic outcomes within the elite group of universities. We see this as endorsing the broad spirit of Bourdieu's (1984) arguments regarding the 'changing goalposts' implicated in the expansion of higher education. However, we also note that entry to elite positions is not monopolized by graduates of elite institutions, nor does an elite education guarantee an elite outcome.

Our chapter proceeds by reviewing the different literatures on the relationship between universities and elite recruitment. We show that currently there is little bridging ground between (a) studies using national survey data which have insufficient sample size to break down particular university effects; and (b) specific studies of the institutional effects of particular universities. We also outline, briefly, the salient structural features of the British education system.

We subsequently address our key issues. First, we examine the gross patterns of association between attending specific universities and different indicators of advantage, including measures of 'economic', 'social' and 'cultural' capital, and entry to NS-SEC class 1, and the 'Elite' class defined by Savage *et al.* (2013). Here we show systematic, and considerable, inter-university differences within the elite

'Russell Group' of institutions. This is strong, prima facie evidence for internal stratification between even the most prestigious universities. We then investigate path-dependent progression from origin class to destination class, as mediated by type of educational institution attended at secondary and tertiary levels.

Finally we note that, despite the strong influence of elite educational pathways on elite entry, there remain routes into the elite which do not rely on educational credentials.

Universities and Social Advantage

The power of educational qualifications to convey social advantage is unquestioned, but hitherto the way that elite universities are associated with elite formation at the top of British society has been little studied. This is partly due to the focus on educational advantage via school effects, and especially the different prospects of children from independent and different types of state schools in attaining middle- and upper-class positions (see, notably, Halsey *et al.*1980). However, as the school leaving age was raised, and as the proportion of young people going to universities rose, there was increasing recognition that the later stages of educational attainment are becoming decisive (e.g. Roberts 2010).

The role of higher education in generating advantage in terms of status, occupational entry and earnings in the UK is now widely attested to in survey analyses in the political arithmetic tradition (e.g. Breen and Jonsson 2005; Halsey 1993) and by education and labour market economists (e.g. Machin and Vignoles 2005; Macmillan and Vignoles 2013). The focus within this tradition to date has been on the simple contrast between graduates and non-graduates – with the partial exception of the comparative research on 'institutional stratification' (Shavit *et al.* 2007), where in the British case the data (Cheung and Egerton 2007) is quite old and with insufficient sample size or detail to distinguish individual universities or even groups of institutions.

Studies in the discipline of higher education increasingly recognize inequalities and diversity within the field of universities, both in the UK and internationally (Marginson 2006; Marginson and van der Wende 2007). These attest to differences in funding, status, and the qualifications and background of students. Such differences are reflected in, and arguably (re)produced by performance measures such as league tables and metrics (Burrows 2012). In the UK, recognition of these differences has inspired research on the nature of unequal entry to universities, especially amongst the Elite (Boliver 2011, 2013). Those studies which focus on particular institutions have tended to be smaller in scale, using one or two universities as case studies (e.g. Bathmaker *et al.* 2013; Mullen 2010; Reay, David and Ball 2005; Stevens 2010; Zimdars 2010).

There are considerably fewer studies which move away from looking at *entry* to elite universities to examine how attending particular universities affects graduates' later prospects. In the UK this is principally due to difficulties in finding adequate, granular data which would allow these effects to be assessed in any detail. Conventional large-scale British surveys such as the Labour Force Survey and cohort studies such as the 1958 National Child Development Survey do not contain sufficient detail about the university attended and would be subject to large sampling error in any case. Researchers have been limited to studies which examine differences in outcomes using data on graduates' early careers, typically six months to three years after graduation (e.g. Brooks 2006; Macmillan, Tyler and Vignoles 2013; Purcell *et al.* 2012).

Our investigation of the differences in outcome for graduates according to the type of higher education institution (HEI) and the specific HEI they attended thus contributes to the field in two ways. First, it provides a more detailed and granular analysis of institutional effects on outcomes than has been attempted with British data. Second, it allows us to look beyond graduates' early labour market experiences to investigate the longer-term effects on outcomes associated with particular institutions and types of institution at both secondary and tertiary levels.

Data and Analysis

In this chapter we take advantage of the BBC's Great British Class Survey. This was a web survey, launched in January 2011 which obtained 161,000 responses by the summer of 2011, when it was delivered to the research team to analyse. It focused on developing detailed questions to map cultural and social capital, alongside some questions on economic capital (see the general discussion in Savage *et al.* 2013).

The GBCS is a unique database containing over 85,000 UK-based graduates.[1] It contains information not only on the specific universities attended, but also the fields of study, and the kind of schools that respondents attended. Because of the very rich information in the GBCS on cultural, social and economic capital, it allows unprecedented ways of linking university attendance to a range of sociologically pertinent outcomes. However, because of the sample skew (which is discussed in more detail in Wakeling and Savage 2015), we should be cautious in using GBCS to compare all UK universities. Any differences we might find between universities perceived as higher or lower in prestige, for instance, might reflect the different response rates between them, and the possibility that respondents from lower-ranking universities are less typical of their peers than those from the high-status institutions. However, we can, cautiously, use the GBCS to compare differences amongst prestigious institutions since response rates from this set of universities differ less.

In our analysis below we define the 'Elite' social class using the terms developed by Savage *et al.* (2013), where it is seen as the most privileged class according to its stocks of economic, cultural and social capital. It is marked by unusually high household income, residential property values and savings; by strong interests in highbrow cultural capital; and has extensive social networks, especially relative to other Elites. This is therefore a more sociological framing of an Elite class which is more restrictive (at about 6 per cent of the population) than competing conceptions of the service class. However, for the purpose of comparison, we also use an occupationally based measure of social class, the UK's official NS-SEC schema, which was developed from the Erikson–Goldthorpe–Portocarero schema (Rose and Pevalin 2001).

Key Features of the British Education System

The four UK nations – England, Scotland, Wales and Northern Ireland – have formally separate educational systems, although there is much similarity between them. National divergence is relatively recent, tied in with political devolution. From the late 1960s, schools moved gradually from the selective three-track 'tripartite' system to a non-selective 'comprehensive' system (Wakeling 2010). Latterly there has been a diversification of school forms, especially in England, although most of the GBCS respondents analysed here will have left school before these changes. Around 6–7 per cent of school pupils attend independent or private schools which are not under state control and typically charge substantial tuition fees. A minority of these schools are residential. There is substantial variation in the status of independent schools, with some of the most elite being world famous (Eton, Harrow, Rugby) and with an (inter)national intake, whereas others have a more local clientele (Walford 2013). On the whole though, independent education is seen as having higher prestige and there is evidence of lasting social advantage in attending an independent school (Power *et al.* 2003).

The British higher education system is also formally unitary. The binary system of universities and polytechnics established in the 1960s ended in 1992 with the conversion of all of the latter into universities. There have been further conversions of higher education colleges to universities in the period since (Wakeling 2010). British universities are unofficially arranged into a status hierarchy which is strongly related to institutional age. 'Oxbridge' – the ancient universities of Oxford and Cambridge – is typically held to be the most prestigious, and together with certain older London-based universities such as University College London and Imperial College London makes up the 'Golden Triangle'. All these institutions are members of the self-selected 'Russell Group' of 24 universities, typically those with the largest research incomes. Other self-organized 'mission groups' exist;[2] these have no official status but have a popular currency in the media and public discourse. Higher education entry is competitive – there is a *numerus clausus* in operation, with grades in school-leaving qualifications influencing the likelihood of entry. Except for Scottish students in Scottish universities, most students in the UK are liable for tuition fees, with many paying £9,000 per year. There are clear links between attending an independent school and attending the most prestigious institutions and similarly between social class background and entry to Russell Group ('RG') institutions (Boliver 2013). Whilst status hierarchies in British higher education are long-standing (Halsey 1992), it is suggested they have intensified as the system has expanded (Raffe and Croxford 2014), in line with the expectations of the effectively maintained inequality thesis (Lucas 2001). However, there is little hard evidence on how these status hierarchies translate into different outcomes for graduates over the longer term. We turn now to our findings from analysis of GBCS data to address this gap in the literature.

Entry into Elite Positions

Let us now explore how the structuring of higher education may be associated with entry to elite positions. In the large GBCS survey, 22 per cent of those with undergraduate degrees and 27 per cent of those with postgraduate degrees are in the Elite, substantially more than in a smaller, nationally representative survey, carried out by the market research company GfK to calibrate the sample (see Savage *et al.* 2013). Let us begin our analysis of whether there are specific university effects by considering how scores for measures of Bourdieu's economic and cultural capital are associated with attendance at particular RG universities. The patterns are revealing. Table 12.1 shows a sharp gradient in all the measures of economic capital amongst the top RG universities. This pattern is largely predictable but striking even so, with graduates from the top university, Oxford, reporting a 50 per cent higher household income than the 23rd-placed University of York. The gradient for house prices and savings is even steeper. This is prima facie strong evidence about the significance of internal differentiation amongst even the 'elite' RG universities.

Oxford is identified as clearly the strongest institution on all measures, and interestingly Cambridge is eclipsed by several of the London colleges for household income. By contrast, Table 12.2 shows that cultural capital varies little by institution and it is difficult to find clear institutionally specific patterns. This having been said, Oxford, University College London, Kings College London, the London School of Economics and the University of Cambridge stand out insofar as their graduates are more likely to possess highbrow cultural capital than other universities. Thus, a distinctive highbrow institutional group seems evident amongst a few HEIs located exclusively in the Golden Triangle. Once again, it is interesting that Oxford is well ahead of Cambridge (which is also behind King's College and University College London) on these measures.

The story for 'emerging cultural capital' is somewhat different. This measure captures *savoir faire* in newer cultural forms (think of the *avant garde* and 'cool'), a cosmopolitan cultural capital more typically associated with younger urban groups (Prieur and Savage 2011). Here Oxford, Cambridge and University College London are well below the means. Only the London School of Economics also predisposes its graduates to emerging, as well as highbrow cultural capital. The two universities registering the highest scores are Nottingham and Newcastle, both cities known to have particularly lively music and student cultures. This is intriguing evidence of a differentiation between attendance at different kinds of university in registering pre-dispositions towards highbrow and emerging cultural capital.

Having recognized the significance of these intra-group differences, let us now consider how Elite recruitment appears linked to university attendance. Figure 12.1 provides details of the association between university type and Elite membership. Here we can see that graduates of Russell Group and non-UK institutions are considerably more likely to be found in the Elite class and in its closest comparator in the NS-SEC schema, Class 1 (higher managerial, administrative and professional occupations) than graduates from other institutions. We can also see that non-British universities score highly in this ranking, indicating the possible role of 'cosmopolitan cultural capital'. Moreover, with the exception of the non-university institutions, the ranking across mission groups is consistent across the Elite and NS-SEC1.

Table 12.1 Reported economic capital for graduates of RG institutions – institutional means, GBCS

Mean household income	£	Mean house value	£	Mean household savings	£
University of Oxford	75,900	University of Oxford	243,000	University of Oxford	64,000
London School of Economics	74,400	King's College London	237,000	University of Cambridge	61,400
King's College London	70,200	University of Cambridge	232,000	Imperial College London	57,100
Imperial College London	69,300	Imperial College London	232,000	University of Bristol	54,100
University of Cambridge	68,000	University of Bristol	227,000	King's College London	49,800
University of Bristol	66,900	University of Southampton	222,000	London School of Economics	48,800
University College London	64,100	University College London	218,000	University College London	45,800
University of Exeter	63,000	London School of Economics	216,000	University of Manchester	44,200
University of Durham	62,600	University of Exeter	214,000	University of Birmingham	43,200
Queen Mary, University of London	62,000	Queen Mary, University of London	212,000	University of Southampton	42,300
University of Warwick	61,200	University of Birmingham	207,000	University of Edinburgh	42,100
University of Nottingham	60,100	University of Manchester	205,000	Queen Mary, University of London	42,000
University of Southampton	58,400	University of Nottingham	202,000	University of Nottingham	41,900
University of Birmingham	58,200	Newcastle University	198,000	University of Exeter	40,200
Newcastle University	58,000	University of Durham	198,000	University of Liverpool	40,000
University of Manchester	57,800	University of Liverpool	198,000	University of Durham	39,500
University of Edinburgh	57,200	University of Edinburgh	194,000	Newcastle University	39,400
University of Liverpool	56,500	University of Warwick	189,000	University of Warwick	38,400
University of Leeds	55,600	University of Leeds	188,000	University of Leeds	36,800
Cardiff University	54,300	Queen's University Belfast	181,000	Queen's University Belfast	35,700
University of Glasgow	53,800	Cardiff University	180,000	University of Glasgow	34,700
University of Sheffield	52,900	University of Glasgow	176,000	Cardiff University	33,100
University of York	50,200	University of Sheffield	174,000	University of Sheffield	32,800
Queen's University Belfast	49,800	University of York	158,000	University of York	29,200

Table 12.2 Mean cultural capital scores for graduates of RG institutions, by institution, GBCS

Highbrow cultural capital		z	Emerging cultural capital		z
University of Oxford	15.2	2.06	Newcastle University	19.0	1.60
King's College London	15.1	1.98	University of Nottingham	18.9	1.45
University College London	14.8	1.50	University of Exeter	18.8	1.10
University of Cambridge	14.8	1.38	University of Sheffield	18.7	0.92
London School of Economics	14.6	1.14	London School of Economics	18.6	0.73
University of Durham	14.5	1.00	Cardiff University	18.6	0.70
University of Edinburgh	14.3	0.61	University of Leeds	18.6	0.68
University of Bristol	14.2	0.48	University of Manchester	18.5	0.57
Imperial College London	14.0	0.10	University of Warwick	18.5	0.48
Queen Mary, University of London	14.0	0.03	University of York	18.5	0.46
University of Exeter	13.8	−0.23	University of Edinburgh	18.4	0.32
University of Leeds	13.7	−0.37	University of Bristol	18.4	0.18
University of Glasgow	13.6	−0.51	University of Durham	18.3	0.10
University of Birmingham	13.6	−0.55	University of Birmingham	18.3	0.06
University of York	13.6	−0.56	University of Glasgow	18.2	−0.19
University of Liverpool	13.6	−0.56	University of Southampton	18.2	−0.22
University of Manchester	13.6	−0.62	University of Liverpool	18.2	−0.24
Newcastle University	13.5	−0.78	Queen's University Belfast	18.2	−0.32
University of Warwick	13.5	−0.78	University College London	18.0	−0.62
University of Southampton	13.5	−0.82	King's College London	17.9	−0.88
Queen's University Belfast	13.4	−0.98	Imperial College London	17.9	−0.91
University of Nottingham	13.3	−1.03	Queen Mary, University of London	17.7	−1.35
Cardiff University	13.2	−1.22	University of Oxford	17.4	−2.06
University of Sheffield	13.2	−1.27	University of Cambridge	17.2	−2.57
SD (all GBCS)	0.59		SD (all GBCS)	0.44	
mean (all GBCS)	13.9		mean (all GBCS)	18.3	

Note: z scores are standardized around GBCS grand mean, not mean for RG institutions only.

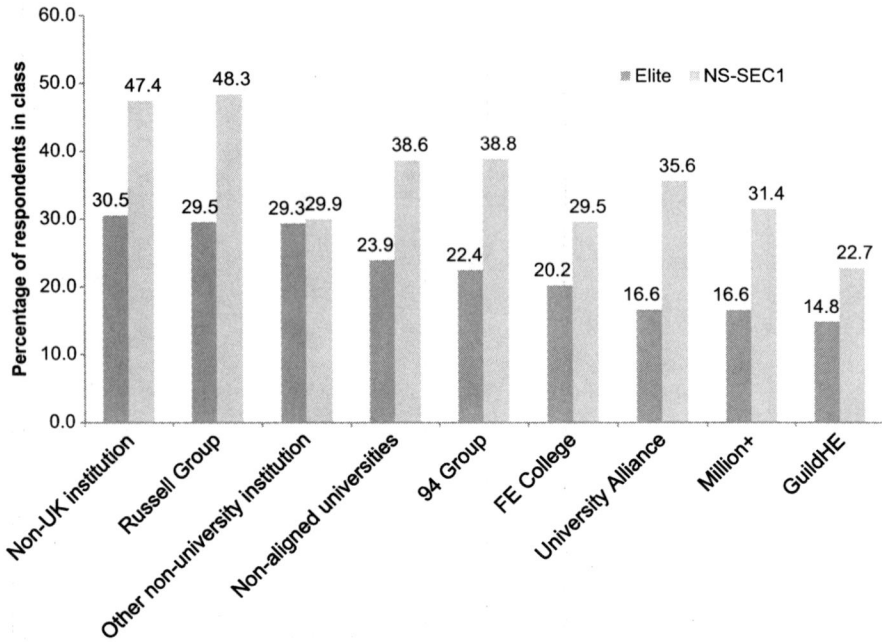

Figure 12.1 Percentage of graduates in NS-SEC1 and Elite by university 'mission' group/
type, GBCS (respondents aged 25–65 only).

Figure 12.2 examines the differences between graduates of RG universities in being in the Elite and NS-SEC1. Here, there is a predictable and very marked 'pecking order' with the traditionally most prestigious universities dominating the top positions. Comparing Elite with NS-SEC 1, there is an intriguing pattern: whilst the 24 RG institutions differ little according to the proportion of their graduates in GBCS found in NS-SEC1 (the range is 41–59 per cent), they differ considerably according to membership of the Elite. Here the proportion in the Elite at Oxford is more than twice that of Glasgow, Queen's Belfast, Cardiff, Sheffield and York. There is a strong southern England skew to the distribution, with Oxbridge and the London 'Golden Triangle' featuring heavily among the most Elite. This suggests that a more sociologically elaborated definition of an Elite class allows us to better detect the power of a small cluster of top-ranking universities in conveying advantage at the top end of the social hierarchy.

Pathways to Elite Universities

The GBCS dataset allows us to trace pathways from class of origin to class of destination via different kinds of educational institutions. We should be clear at the outset in noting that the GBCS is a cross-sectional survey, not a cohort study and has a known skew towards the more highly educated (Savage *et al.* 2013). The findings presented in this section must be viewed with those warnings in mind:

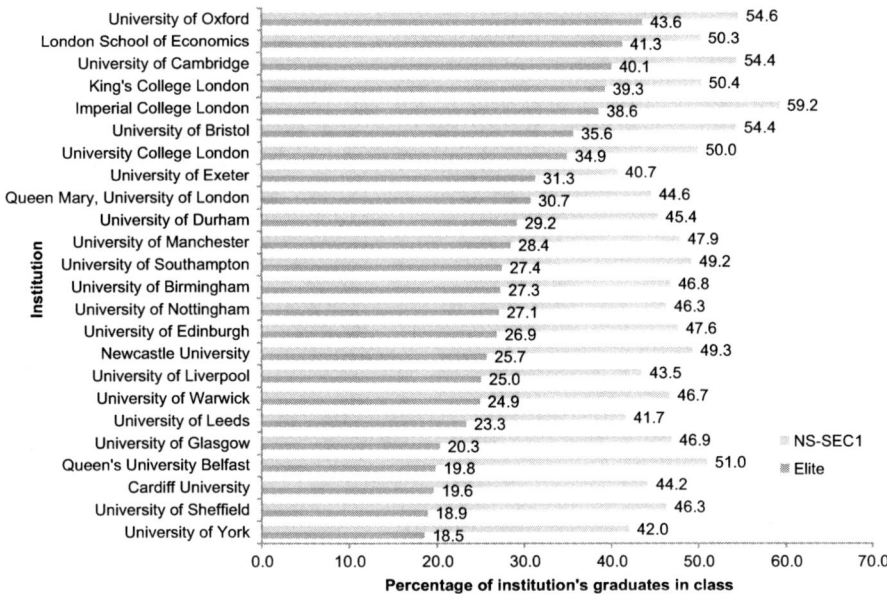

Figure 12.2 Percentage of RG graduates in NS-SEC1 and Elite by institution, GBCS.

we do not claim that they are statistically representative. Nevertheless, they provide strong indications of the structuring of social and educational pathways to the Elite in the UK which are not possible to investigate using other large-scale datasets.

Figure 12.3 shows the relationship between type of secondary school attended and Elite/NS-SEC1 membership. Around two-fifths of those who attended independent schools ended up in the Elite in our dataset, compared with less than one in five of those who went to comprehensive state schools. Having attended a selective state school increases the chance of Elite membership, but not to the same extent. As with higher education, there is a sharper gradient between types of institutions in entry to the Elite (measured using economic, social and cultural capitals) than there is into the occupationally based top category, NS-SEC1. Whilst numerous studies have shown a link between private education and very specific destinations in the British Elite such as the judiciary, membership of Parliament, journalism and others (Sutton Trust 2009), there is little research since the seminal Nuffield studies of social mobility (Halsey *et al.* 1980) showing the general extent of this connection. Here we need to recall that independent education accounts for only around 6–7 per cent of school pupils and the nationally representative GfK survey placed less than 6 per cent of respondents into the Elite group. Among those in the GfK who were independently educated, fully one quarter were categorized as Elite. Of all those categorized as Elite, 15 per cent were independently educated, more than three times the expected number based on the proportion of independently educated respondents in the GfK sample.

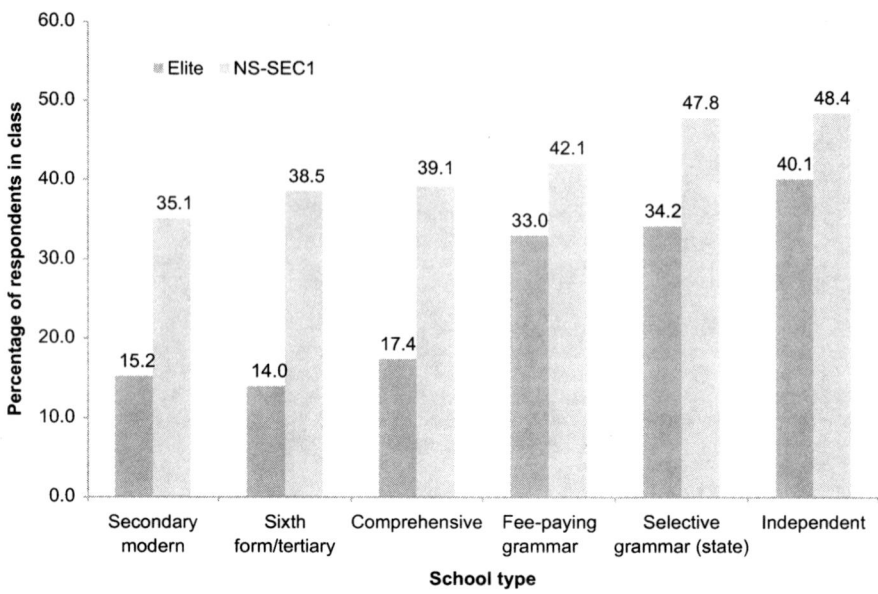

Figure 12.3 Percentage membership of Elite/NS-SEC1 classes by category of school last attended, GBCS.

Both type of school and type of university attended appear strongly to condition outcomes in the UK, based on our exploratory analysis of the GBCS dataset. Whilst, as noted, the GBCS is not a cohort study, it does allow us a retrospective glimpse of the processes leading to Elite membership. It is possible to trace an individual's pathway from natal class, through secondary and (where applicable) tertiary education to a destination class. This gives us a view, albeit one compromized to some extent by the nature of our data, of the 'origin–education–destination' relationship which shapes much of the literature in this area (Goldthorpe and Jackson 2008). However, it provides a level of detail about institutional identities and types not available elsewhere.

Figure 12.4 presents a view of the pathways from class of origin (based on reported paternal occupation) to class of destination as mediated by secondary and tertiary education. We focus on those aged 30–49 as a group who will have experienced a relatively stable secondary education system and who will have reached a settled social class destination. For ease of presentation and interpretation, we look only at those from 'service class'[3] and 'working class' origins (defined as 'Senior manager or traditional professional' and 'Semi-routine or Routine' occupations respectively).[4] We also contrast only two school types – independent school and comprehensive school – and two broad university groupings (non-graduates are not shown). The parameters shown on each pathway denote the proportion of respondents from the previous category who make the transition to the next category. For instance, 23 per cent of those from service-class origins attended an independent secondary school; 48 per cent of that group attended a

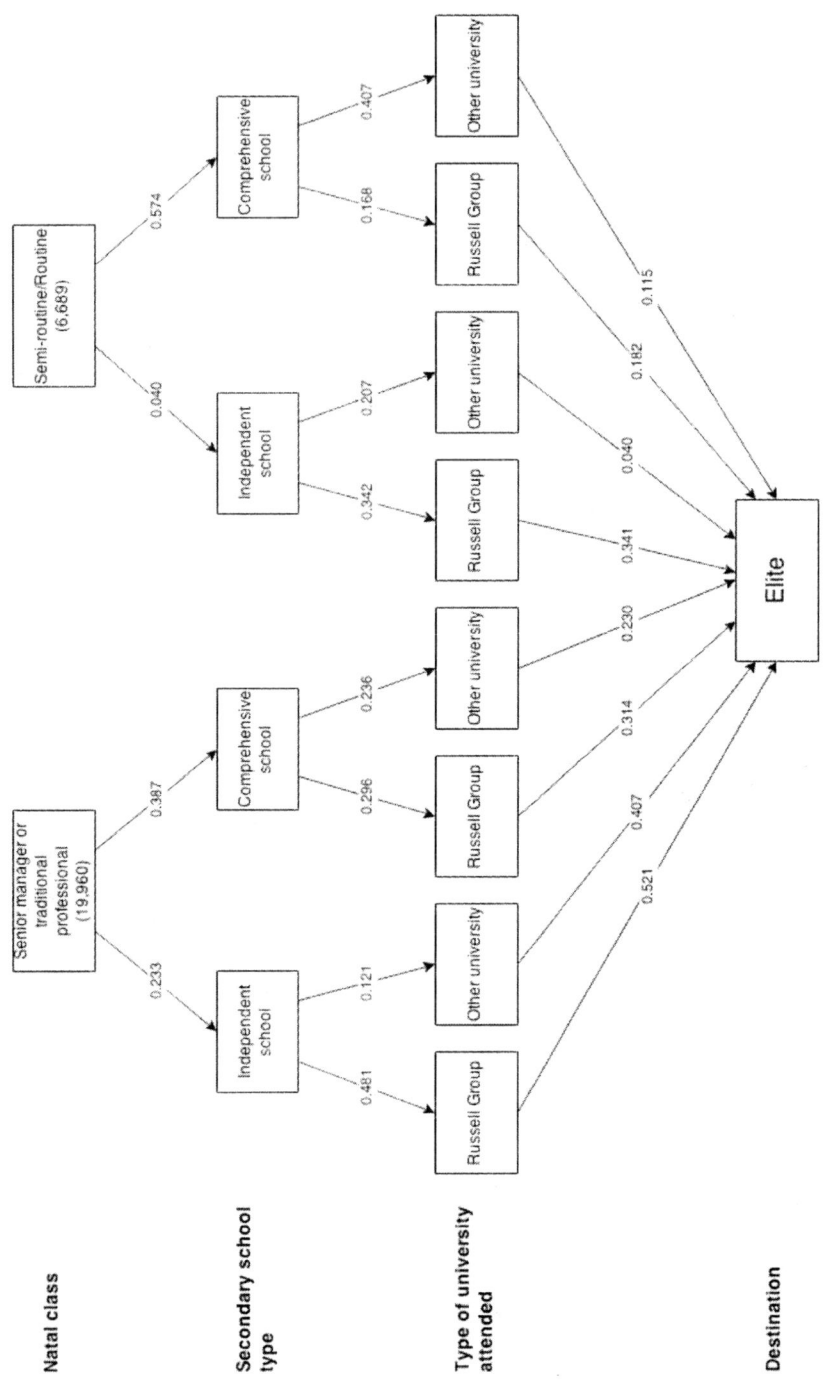

Figure 12.4 Pathways to the Elite for GBCS respondents aged 30–49 (selected categories only).

RG university; and 52 per cent of those graduates were assigned to the Elite social class. Thus $0.233 \times 0.481 \times 0.521 = 0.058$ of those born in the service class took the most 'elite' educational pathway, compared with $0.040 \times 0.342 \times 0.341 = 0.005$ of those born in the working class.

The pathways illustrate various layers of social and educational advantage. Natal class conditions entry to elite secondary education, such that those from a service-class background were much more likely to enter independent education.[5] At the next stage, former independent school pupils are more likely to enter RG universities than former comprehensive pupils. However, the extent of this advantage is greater among those from service-class backgrounds. After higher education, both independent education and natal class appear to show lingering effects. So whilst RG graduates are generally more likely to achieve an Elite destination than other graduates, the extent of this advantage declines as one moves rightwards across the diagram and is lower for those who previously attended a comprehensive school. The likelihood of achieving an Elite destination for a RG graduate from working-class, comprehensive origins are lower than those taking the pathways shown from a service-class background. Particularly interesting here is the difference between former independent school pupils from service- and working-class backgrounds who attended non-RG universities where the likelihood of Elite membership varies substantially (0.407 as against 0.040 respectively).

Table 12.3 focuses in further on university pathways. Here we can see even more clearly the effect of different pathways. We separate out Oxford, as the most 'elite' institution identified in the previous section; the other three Golden Triangle universities; the remaining RG universities; other HEIs and non-graduates. The majority of those from service-class backgrounds who attended independent school and a Golden Triangle university in the GBCS sample end up in Savage *et al.*'s Elite class. Indeed almost two-thirds of those taking the 'royal road' from the service class, via independent education and Oxford reach the Elite. This is a topical issue in the UK since the Prime Minister, David Cameron, and many of his cabinet followed this exact route. At the opposite extreme, only one in fourteen of those from a working-class background who went to comprehensive school and did not attend higher education attain an Elite destination. For each combination of social class background and secondary schooling, attending Oxford and to a lesser extent another Golden Triangle university denotes advantage. These effects are clearly different from attending a RG university. However, an independent education is particularly effective in social reproduction it seems, as those of service-class origin with no degree are as likely to enter the Elite, at least among our respondents, as working-class, comprehensive-educated Oxford graduates. It may be that those from service-class origins attend the more prestigious independent schools (not differentiated in our dataset).

In general terms, there appears to be a straightforward educational hierarchy at both secondary and tertiary levels. Graduating from a Golden Triangle institution trumps other RG institutions, which in turn offer more advantage than other institutions. Not attending university is the least trodden pathway to the Elite. We should note, however, that elite educational institutions do not have a monopoly on Elite entry and be wary of a deterministic interpretation of our results.

Table 12.3 Elite membership by social/educational pathway for GBCS respondents aged 30–49 (selected categories only)

Natal class	Secondary school type	University attended	Elite membership
Senior manager or traditional professional	Independent	Oxford	0.639
		Other Golden Triangle	0.539
		Other Russell Group	0.487
		Other university	0.407
		None	0.392
	Comprehensive	Oxford	0.494
		Other Golden Triangle	0.370
		Other Russell Group	0.290
		Other university	0.230
		None	0.194
Semi-routine/Routine	Independent	Oxford	0.357
		Other Golden Triangle	0.294
		Other Russell Group	0.350
		Other university	0.175
		None	0.091
	Comprehensive	Oxford	0.393
		Other Golden Triangle	0.317
		Other Russell Group	0.157
		Other university	0.115
		None	0.072

Conclusions

This chapter has used the unusually large sample size of the Great British Class Survey to consider how far we can detect distinctive university and school-type effects in generating advantage at the higher levels of British society. In the absence of other datasets large enough to have sizeable samples of graduates from specific universities and types of secondary school alongside measures of social, cultural and economic capital, this represents a potentially important contribution.

We need to repeat our caveats regarding the representativeness of the GBCS sample. Our analysis should be read as tentative and suggestive, but nevertheless points to some potentially important findings which bear further investigation.

We point to clear differences which emerge between operationalizing Elite positions using an occupationally derived measure of social class, and through using the multi-dimensional approach of Savage *et al.* (2013). Type of secondary school attended and type of university attended show an association with entry both to the Elite and to NS-SEC1. However there is a steeper hierarchy in entry to the Elite, particularly when looking at inter-university differences in outcome across the Russell Group of institutions. These hierarchies appear across indices of both economic and cultural capital, but are especially sharp within the former. A small group of universities, comprising Oxford, Cambridge and a select few current and former University of London colleges, emerges as a kind of super-elite. Although the patterns of institutional stratification reported here are specific to the British case, they fit with the general predictions of both Bourdieusian reproduction theory (Bourdieu 1996; Bourdieu and Passeron 1979) and the effectively main-tained inequality hypothesis (Lucas 2001). Global trends for increased status awareness and competition between universities (Marginson 2006) suggest simi-lar hierarchies will emerge and strengthen, both nationally and internationally, as access to higher education expands.

However, our findings remind us not to neglect the continued influence of social class background and secondary schooling in structuring social and educa-tional pathways. We have shown that private secondary education offers lasting advantages to former pupils, as does a service-class origin, in many cases off-setting a lack of higher education credential. This shows the importance of investigating the fine detail of origin–education–destination pathways as we strive to remove barriers to equality both in the UK and elsewhere.

Notes

1   The total number of GBCS respondents with a higher education qualification is almost 103,000. However, due to a technical error in the merging of the first and second batch of GBCS Wave 1 records, details of the institution attended are missing for all second batch records (approximately 11,000 cases). Wave 1 second batch records are omitted from the analyses presented here. Details are missing through item non-response for around a fur-ther 7,000 cases in the first batch. Further details of how sample selection issues affect the analysis of university effects on social mobility are available in Wakeling and Savage (2014).
2   Those used in the analysis are the 94 Group (now defunct) of smaller, research-intensive universities; million+, a group composed mainly of former polytechnics; GuildHE, com-prising mainly former colleges of higher education which now have university or university college status; University Alliance, a mixed group of new and older universities; and a catch-all group of non-aligned institutions, which do not belong to a mission group.
3   We use an approximation to the service class, based on father's occupation.
4   The skew in the sample is notable here, with many more service-class than working-class respondents.
5   We could reasonably expect the result for working-class entry to independent education to be an over-estimate, since the highly educated are overrepresented in the GBCS sample.

References

Bathmaker, A.-M., Ingram, N. and Waller, R. (2013) 'Higher education, social class and the mobilisation of capitals: recognising and playing the game', *British Journal of Sociology of Education*, 34 (5–6): 723–743.
Boliver, V. (2011) 'Expansion, differentiation, and the persistence of social class inequalities in British higher education', *Higher Education*, 61 (3): 229–242.
Boliver, V. (2013) 'How fair is access to more prestigious UK universities?', *British Journal of Sociology*, 64 (2): 344–364.
Bourdieu, P. (1984) *Distinction*, London: Routledge.
Bourdieu, P. (1996) *The State Nobility: Elite Schools in the Field of Power*, Cambridge: Polity.
Bourdieu, P. and Passeron, J-C. (1979) *The Inheritors: French Students and Their Relation to Culture*, Chicago: The Chicago University Press.
Breen, R. and Jonsson, J. O. (2005) 'Inequality of opportunity in comparative perspective: recent research on educational attainment and social mobility', *Annual Review of Sociology*, 31: 223–243.

Brooks, R. (2006) 'Young graduates and lifelong learning: the impact of institutional stratification', *Sociology*, 40 (6): 1019–1037.

Burrows, R. (2012) 'Living with the h-index? Metric assemblages in the contemporary academy', *Sociociological Review*, 60 (2): 355–372.

Cheung, S.-Y. and Egerton, M. (2007) 'Higher education expansion and reform: changing educational inequalities in Great Britain', in Y. Shavit, R. Arum and A. Gamoran (eds) *Stratification in Higher Education: A Comparative Study*, Stanford, CA: Stanford University Press.

Goldthorpe, J. H. and Jackson, M. (2008) 'Education-based meritocracy: the barriers to its realization', in A. Lareau and D. Conley (eds) *Social Class: How Does It Work?*, New York: Russell Sage Foundation, pp. 93–117.

Halsey, A. H. (1992) *The Decline of Donnish Dominion: The British Academic Professions in the Twentieth Century*, Oxford: Clarendon Press.

Halsey, A. H. (1993) 'Trends in access and equity in higher education: Britain in comparative perspective', *Oxford Review of Education*, 19 (2): 129–140.

Halsey, A. H., Heath, A. F. and Ridge, J. (1980) *Origins and Destinations: Family, Class and Education in Modern Britain*, Oxford: Clarendon Press.

Lucas, S. (2001) ' Effectively maintained inequality: education transitions, track mobility and social background effects', *American Journal of Sociology*, 106 (6): 1642–1690.

Machin, S. and Vignoles, A. (2005) *What's the Good of Education? The Economics of Education in the UK*, Princeton, NJ/Oxford: Princeton University Press.

Macmillan, L. and Vignoles, A. (2013) *Mapping the Occupational Destinations of New Graduates*, London: Social Mobility and Child Poverty Commission.

Macmillan, L., Tyler, C. and Vignoles, A. (2013) Who gets the top jobs? The role of family background and networks in recent graduates' access to high status professions, Working Paper No. 13-15, Department of Quantitative Social Science, Institute of Education, University of London.

Marginson, S. (2006) 'Dynamics of national and global competition in higher education', *Higher Education*, 52 (1): 1–39.

Marginson, S. and van der Wende, M. (2007) 'To rank or be ranked: the impact of global rankings in higher education', *Journal of Studies in International Education*, 11 (3–4): 306–329.

Mullen, A. L. (2010) *Degrees of Inequality: Culture, Class and Gender in American Higher Education*, Baltimore, MD: The Johns Hopkins University Press.

Power, S., Edwards, T., Whitty, G. and Wigfall, V. (2003) *Education and the Middle Class*, Buckingham: Open University Press.

Prieur, A. and Savage, M. (2011) 'Updating cultural capital theory: a discussion based on studies in Denmark and Britain', *Poetics*, 39 (6): 566–580.

Purcell, K., Elias, P., Atfield, G., Behle, H., Ellison, R., Luchinskaya, D., Snape, J., Conaghan, L. and Tzanakou, C. (2012) *Futuretrack Stage 4: Transitions into Employment, Further Study and Other Outcomes*, Coventry: Warwick Institute of Employment Research, University of Warwick.

Raffe, D. and Croxford, L. (2014) 'The iron law of hierarchy? Institutional differentiation in higher education', *Studies in Higher Education*. doi: 10.1080/03075079.2014.899342.

Reay, D., David, M. E. and Ball, S. J. (2005) *Degrees of Choice: Social Class, Race and Gender in Higher Educaiton*, Stoke-on-Trent: Trentham Books.

Roberts, K. (2010) 'Expansion of higher education and the implications for demographic class formation in Britain', *Twenty-First Century Society*, 5 (3): 215–228.

Rose, D. and Pevalin, D. (2001) *The National Statistics Socio-economic Classification: Unifying Official and Sociological Approaches to the Conceptulisation and Measurement of*

Social Class, Chelmsford: Institute for Social and Economic Research, University of Essex.

Savage, M., Devine, F., Cunningham, N., Taylor, M., Li, Y., Hjellbrekke, J., Le Roux, B., Friedman, S. and Miles, A. (2013) 'A new model of social class: findings from the BBC's Great British Class Survey experiment', *Sociology*, 48 (1): 219–250.

Shavit, Y., Arum, R. and Gamoran, A. (2007) *Stratification in Higher Education: A Comparative Study*, Stanford, CA: Stanford University Press.

Stevens, M. (2010) *Creating a Class: College Admissions and the Education of Elites*, Cambridge, MA: Harvard University Press.

Sutton Trust (2009) *The Educational Background of Leading Lawyers, Journalists, Vice-Chancellors, Politicians, Medics and Chief Executives*, London: The Sutton Trust.

Wakeling, P. (2010) 'Education and the state, 1850 to the present', in J. Arthur and I. Davies (eds) *The Routledge Education Studies Textbook*, London: Routledge.

Wakeling, P. and Savage, M. (2015, forthcoming) 'Entry to elite positions and the stratification of higher education in Britain', *Sociological Review*.

Walford, G. (2013) 'The development of private and state schools in England', in A. Gürlevik, C. Palentien and R. Heyer (eds) *Privatschulen versus Staatliche Schulen*, Wiesbaden: Springer.

Zimdars, A. (2010) 'Fairness and undergraduate admission: a qualitative exploration of admissions choices at the University of Oxford', *Oxford Review of Education*, 36 (3): 307–323.

13 Paths to the Elite in France and in the United States

Jules Naudet

The comparative study of the experience of social mobility in France and in the United States seems to confirm the most common representations of the United States as the country that values success and of France as a society with impermeable social boundaries (Naudet 2012).[1] Indeed, Americans' discourse is marked by a tendency to deny that social mobility involves a radical self-transformation, whereas the experience of mobility in French discourse is significantly more associated with suffering, isolation, and the feeling of not belonging to any group.

Quantitative studies on social mobility in these two countries have amended these representations, and the most recent works have shown that the levels of social mobility in France and the United States are in fact fairly close. For instance, in *The Constant Flux*, Erikson and Goldthorpe (1992) underline the similarity of the levels of social fluidity in French and American society. These works, relying on the criterion of intergenerational economic (rather than social) mobility, show that mobility proves to be slightly stronger in France than in the United States. Overall, these results tend to call into question the myth that American society is characterized by its very high level of intergenerational (social or economic) mobility. On the contrary, nothing allows us to say that American society is more "fluid" than French society.[2]

This chapter therefore intends to revisit this disjunction between the objective reality of the levels of mobility and the subjective experience of social ascension by questioning the ways in which the ideologies and representations of social mobility develop in a manner relatively independent of the reality of the levels of social fluidity. In this regard, our reflection is included in what Leslie McCall calls "theories of tolerance" (McCall 2013), that is, the line of works that seek to understand how individuals in the United States are able to tolerate high levels of inequality. Taking a view somewhat opposed to the theories of exceptionalism, the economists Alberto Alesina and Edward Glaeser claim that the true American exception does not rest on economic and social structures but rather on ideological foundations, with Americans believing that a person's situation is the fair recompense for his or her efforts while Europeans think that a person's situation is the consequence of the milieu into which he or she was born (Alesina and Glaeser 2004).[3] We intend to contribute to this debate by defending the idea that taking account of the hiatus between subjective experience and objective reality requires questioning the routes that make the most extreme mobilities possible. It is not so much the quantitative importance of these mobilities that counts as the conditions that make them possible.

The analysis of interviews conducted in France and the United States offers a first line of approach for making sense of the differences in the experience of social mobility.[4] If we attend to the individual trajectories of persons experiencing strong social mobility, we see that in the United Sates the frequent congruence between familial and dominant ideologies within the new group favor the representations of a classless society, whereas in France the gap between the familial and professional spheres is much more pronounced. Second, we defend the idea that Ralph Turner's (1960) proposed distinction between "contest mobility" and "sponsored mobility" helps make sense of these differences. We will therefore make use of two different analytical registers. We will first draw on a comprehensive approach centered on the individual trajectories of persons experiencing strong mobility in France and the United States, and then second, we will opt for a more structural approach, taking up and defending Turner's thesis while discussing the differences in the paths to the elite in France and the United States.

Upward Social Mobility and Representations of Class Boundaries[5]

Narratives of Mobility and the Ideology of Success in the United States

As stated in the introduction, the narratives about success that we collected in the United States show a strong tendency to minimize the differences between the originating group and the new group (Naudet 2012, chapter 4). The narratives recounted by many interviewees indeed suggest there are no deep differences in the way a worker and a manager think. The image of a classless society united around common, strongly integrative values gradually emerges from these narratives.

This image of a classless society is notably embodied in discourses that prioritize parents' moral values and that insist on the idea of a very strong continuity between parental values and the values of success. These discourses frequently aim at validating parents' life-projects. In France, parents' work-related suffering is often presented as the consequence of relations of class domination and thus as profoundly unfair, whereas Americans insist much more on the sense of suffering and on the denial of their parents. What sets their discourse apart from their French counterparts is the absence of a denunciation of the conditions experienced by their parents. This acceptance of their parents' condition of being dominated – in some ways legitimated *ex post* by their personal success – is inscribed in the continuity of an intergenerational conception of the ideology of the American dream. Success will therefore be more often experienced as a family "inheritance," as a *transgenerational* realization of the American dream.

This inclination to measure success on the yardstick of the parental project is also present in France, but this motif is noticeably stronger in the interviews conducted in the United States, where the discourses depend more often and much more explicitly on a family-centered ideology.[6] When the French mention the role played by their family in their success, they insist more on the fact that their parents provided them with important resources such as self-confidence, determination, a taste for a job well-done, the desire to learn, etc.[7] But this familial involvement is described as belonging to the past, as being circumscribed by the time spent living with their parents; their parents played a "role" in their success but do not have direct responsibility in the finally realized "project" of success. Success is seen more as a personal construction beyond family influence, and consequently, parents are more often presented as strangers in this new universe, unable to understand it. In contrast, Americans make much more effort than the French to mention parental influence at every stage (including the most recent) of their success narrative.[8]

Political opinions, values, or positions on "social questions" often constitute a means to trace a filiation with the family. By its content, opinion serves to situate the legitimacy of the claim for connection with the originating milieu. Religious practices are thus one of the themes most often used to emphasize the fact that familial ideology was preserved despite the transformations that the trajectory of mobility could have brought. Americans' childhood stories regularly mention the importance of family attendance of the local church, and continuous membership in the parish community indirectly illustrates the idea that the path of mobility did not require a radical transformation. Religious practices constitute the reflection of "essential" moral values. Therefore, not calling them into question despite the change in social status can be taken as evidence that what truly matters has not been affected: what is essential to the mode of life and the values inherited from the originating milieu can be preserved. The rest – all the transformations in the mode of life – would be only marginal adjustments to the practical constraints that every change in social status involves.

Unsettled Success Stories in France

In contrast, in France, the tendency to represent social boundaries as rigid and impermeable constitutes a backdrop against which diverse strategies for adapting to the tension between the originating milieu and the milieu of arrival will be developed. Unlike the Americans, who have a stronger propensity to express a continuous vision of the social space, the French are more spontaneously inclined to consider social space as divided into classes that are quite distinct from one another. For them, mobility necessarily supposes the crossing of a "barrier" and access to a "level" (Goblot 1925). Their life stories are thus perceived as more chaotic, less coherent, and are often characterized by the dissociation of two narrative frameworks that are alternatively mobilized and that intersect only with difficulty: the framework of "public" history, that is, of the academic and professional trajectory, and the framework of "private" history, that is, of the familial history and the evolution in the feeling of belonging to a social class. This dissociation (less evident in the American narratives) is never more obvious than in the narratives emphasizing a feeling of isolation or a double-absence. In these narratives, the description of the feeling of being "between two worlds" often goes together with the story of a brilliant academic or professional trajectory, as if this should compensate for their feeling of being profoundly different from the majority of those with a social status similar to theirs. These persons seem to have been able to find their place in their professional universe, but not able to acquire the lifestyle shared by the majority of their professional peers. Such a configuration is far more frequent in France than it is in the United States.

In this light, the importance of the logics of distinction in France constitutes a particularly important fact. The French discourses are often marked by the narration of a trajectory of mobility accompanied by a quest for the mastery of "codes," which is itself often accompanied by a "work of deculturation, of rectification, and correction, which is necessary to correct the improper effects of apprenticeship" (Bourdieu 1979: 77–78). These "codes" – a sort of euphemism designating the most legitimate and distinguished behaviors or dispositions – seem to be the secret key that one must have at any price in order to gain the legitimacy necessary to feel at home within this new group. This obsession for the "codes" is very specifically French and although we find this theme in the Americans' discourse, it never occupies the central place that it does for the French. The French discourses are distinguished by the frequent evocation of a process of deculturation and acculturation whose principal stakes are the mastery of schemes of action and of perception that the academic institution does not teach and does not expressly require. Many interviewees thus recount how hard they struggled to master this "hidden agenda" and how relieved they felt once they managed to "crack the codes." As Teresa gleefully puts it: "Today I have the codes! I no longer call to mind the daughter of a manual worker!" But, unlike Teresa, many others refer to their daily difficulties to master the "etiquette" when invited to formal dinners or, more simply, when interacting with upper-class colleagues. They constantly fear they are being judged for their improper body language, clothing, way of speaking, cultural practices, etc. Our findings thus concur here with a central aspect of the comparative literature that often evokes this weight of cultural literacy and of social distinction as being more important in France than in the United States (Clark 1979; Lamont 1995).

Contest Mobility and Sponsored Mobility

After having briefly discussed the modalities of narrating social mobility in France and in the United States, we would now like to open some lines of approach on the institutional and structural conditions that will allow us to make sense of such differences in the experience of social mobility. We will notably be defending the idea that Ralph Turner's thesis (1960) on contest mobility and sponsored mobility offers a particularly heuristic framework for making sense of the specificities of these two countries and of the paradox mentioned in the introduction.

Turner's Thesis

Turner seeks to describe "two ideal-typical normative patterns of upward mobility." Although this article has been widely criticized,[9] the analyses that it proposes nevertheless seem to open some fecund avenues of reflection that we will not hesitate to extend. Turner explains that the "system of contest mobility" aims at winning the loyalty of the underprivileged classes by relying on "by a combination of futuristic orientation, the norm of ambition, and a general sense of fellowship with the elite" (Turner 1960: 859). This is why it is possible to consider that the basic principle of the system of contest mobility is to "avoid absolute points of selection for mobility and immobility" (Turner 1960: 859).

This principle is embodied in other aspects of the system of contest mobility. The elite are in a relatively strong position of insecurity: "each success, rather than an accomplishment, serves to qualify the participant for competition at the next higher level" (Turner 1960: 860). The educational system of a society based on contest mobility therefore has certain characteristic traits such as "keeping everyone in the running until the final stages" (Turner 1960: 863).

In contrast, in the system of sponsored mobility,

> the elite or their agents, deemed to be best qualified to judge merit, choose individuals for elite status who have the appropriate qualities. Individuals do not win or seize elite status; mobility is rather a process of sponsored induction into the elite.
>
> (Turner 1960: 857)

Such a system of mobility therefore

> depends upon a social structure that fosters monopoly of elite credentials, [a monopoly that] is typically a product of societies with well entrenched traditional aristocracies employing such credentials as family line and bestowable title which are intrinsically subject to monopoly, or of societies organized on large-scale bureaucratic lines permitting centralized control of upward social movement.
>
> (Turner 1960: 858)[10]

In this regard, the particularly selective and elitist French academic system corresponds well to the ideal-typical situation presented by Turner. Although formally subject to the republican principle of equality of opportunity, it is also characterized by the very selective and quasi-monopolistic distribution of elite positions effected through the system of the *Grandes Écoles*. The sociology of French education shows that access to the *Grandes Écoles* is strongly linked to academic trajectories. Entrance into one of the *Grandes Écoles* is generally conditioned on having taken the most prestigious preparatory classes, and entrance to these preparatory classes is itself conditioned on having gone to the most prestigious high schools.[11]

The Architecture of Academic Systems

In order to discuss the pertinence of Turner's thesis, it is important to consider the architecture of the two educational systems. Numerous comparative studies

(Allmendinger 1989; and for a review of relevant literature, see Van de Werfhorst and Mijs 2010) have noted that the American education system is characterized by its "standardization" that is the fact that the architecture of the system ensures that a large number of students have access to the highest levels of secondary teaching.[12] This standardization would leave students with a broad range of choice at the end of secondary education. Social selection is not inexistent, but is masked by the very strong autonomy of schools unequally preparing access to the most prestigious institutions. In contrast, the French educational system is characterized by a very early selection of students who are able to claim access to the most prestigious courses of study (i.e. the preparatory classes for the *Grandes Écoles*) and of students who are relegated to the least-valued courses as early as middle school (on this, see notably Palheta 2012). The judgment determining the students' academic future is thus made much earlier with no apparent possibility of appeal; transfers to more prestigious courses are very limited when one is engaged on the path of vocational education.

The existence in the United States of transfers between the least and the most legitimate courses of study (even if the latter are not so frequent) thus play an important role in understanding the interiorization of the idea of a classless society. This has been suggested notably by Brint and Karabel's work on the American educational system (Brint and Karabel 1989a, 1989b). Revisiting the hypothesis of an "American exception," these two authors recall that one of the great specificities of the American academic system is to have developed "comprehensive high schools," wherein vocational and academic disciplines are taught under one roof. According to them, this particularity contributes to distinguishing the United States from Europe where, as Weber already noted, the cultural ideal of the "cultivated man" rests on an implicit recognition of the cultural superiority of the elites over the masses. In contrast to the segmented educational system in Europe, the unitary system of the comprehensive high school would tend to reduce the social distance between classes. If some French *lycées* sometimes gather students from both vocational (*filières technologiques et professionnelles*) and so-called "general" tracks, their interactions are extremely limited. The social and institutional boundaries between the students of the different tracks are very clearly drawn. As a general rule, the French secondary school system is indeed extremely segmented. To take one example, the transition from secondary schooling to higher education in France is highly conditioned by the type of specialization one has chosen two years prior to passing the *baccalauréat* (the French high-school certificate). If, theoretically, the holder of any type of *baccalauréat* can enroll in any public university or *classe préparatoire*, in practice, many combinations of baccalauréat and university courses are extremely rare. To be sure, students from a *baccalauréat professionnel* (vocational) will never manage to get admission in a *classe prépartoire* preparing to the best *Grandes Écoles* specializing in management or engineering.

The characteristic of the American academic system on which Brint and Karabel focus the most is nevertheless the community college (or junior college). The principle of these institutions is to offer two (rather than four) years of higher education and, like the comprehensive high schools, to provide both vocational and academic education. The community college thus avoids an overly strong segmentation between the different institutions of higher education. Although the junior college constitutes the lowest level within an extremely stratified system of higher education, it remains connected to the most prestigious institutions by means of a system of university credit transfer. Even though very few students are concerned, according to Brint and Karabel, this system plays a very important role in promoting the idea of American society as a classless society. Making use of a French example, they contend that this system functions as if there were transfers between the École Normale Supérieure and the Instituts Universitaires de Technologie (IUT). Today things have somehow improved in France and students often pursue B.A. studies (and sometimes even M.A.) after graduating from an IUT, even though these studies are generally pursued in universities and not in elite and prestigious *Grandes Écoles*.

By avoiding an early selection and by offering not one but several occasions to succeed, the American academic system appears to play a very strong role in the dissemination of a meritocratic ideology. The academic system is seen as offering multiple possibilities for success to those who have the talent and those who work hard, but this then leads to legitimating the idea that failure is above all the consequence of individual shortcomings. Brint and Karabel recall, however, that this is essentially a representation, and that the American university system actually remains deeply marked by class inequality and by the prevalence of the logics of reproduction.[13] The openings displayed in the American academic system thus primarily fill – and this is the most important point – a role in legitimating social inequalities and participate in the construction of the illusion of a classless society.

The Links Between Credentials and Jobs, and the Possibilities of Intragenerational Mobility

A second process seems to go in the same direction as the distinction proposed by Ralph Turner: the links between academic degree and employment. The weakness of these links can help understand why certain people think that their talents as a competitor could allow them to succeed professionally despite a lackluster start to their career. Access to employment is not exclusively linked to academic degree. Although the academic degree remains decisive for accessing employment in all postindustrial societies, several comparative works show that the relationship between academic degree and employment is weaker in the United States than in other countries. More specifically, these studies show that the degree of differentiation of educational systems (understood as the importance that educational systems grant to the differentiation of students – the number of different existing courses of study, the age at which students are oriented towards specific courses of study, etc.) and the degree of vocational specialization of the education provided have a strong impact on the importance of the academic degree in the job market (Van de Werfhorst 2011; Andersen and Van de Werfhorst 2010; Wolbers 2007; Shavit and Müller 1998). In this regard, the comparison between France and the United States clearly shows that the American academic system is both less differentiated and less professionalizing that the French system (see Figure 13.1).

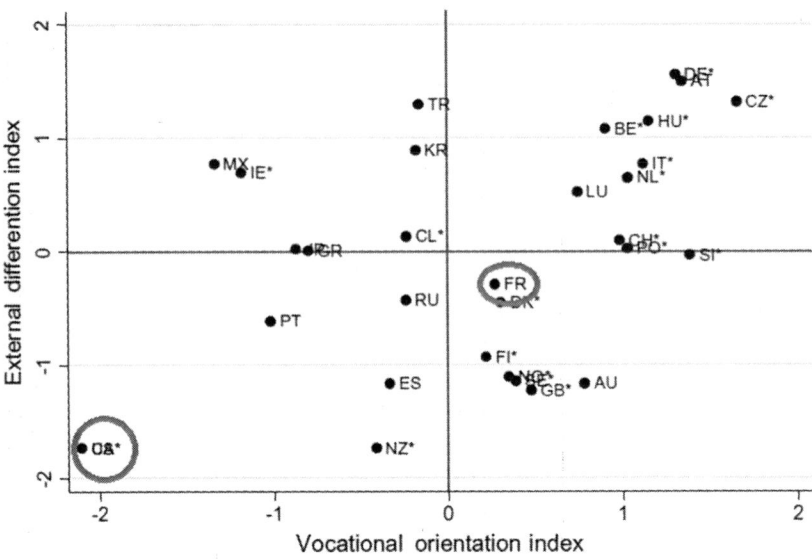

Figure 13.1 Indices of differentiation of the academic courses of study (external differentiation) and vocational specialization of education (vocational orientation index) for the educational systems of 31 countries (Van de Werfhorst 2011). The index of "external differentiation" rests on three criteria: the age at which the first selection is effected, the number of different courses of study available to 14-year-old students, and the number of years that each course lasts related to the total number of years of primary and secondary instruction. The index of professional specialization refers to the number of students enrolled in vocational education.

Likewise, one of the rare comparisons of intragenerational social mobility in France and the United States, undertaken by Haller *et al.* (1985), showed that career evolution in the United States and France present strong differences. In France, there is a very strong barrier between blue-collar employment and white-collar employment, whereas in the United States, passage from one sector to the other is frequent, which suggests that initial educational credentials are less decisive for the rest of the career. The most notable specificity of the class structure in the United Sates compared with France is thus that there are wide avenues of intragenerational mobility permitting access to managerial positions regardless of the starting position at the outset of the career (Haller *et al.* 1985: 598–99).[14]

If the links between credentials and employment are less important in the American system than in the French system, we can thus hypothesize that the attribution of professional positions is not effected merely on the basis of university degrees. Even without putting forward explanations for the relative weakness of these links in the American context,[15] we can nonetheless contend that it constitutes a factor likely to increase the feeling that educational credentials are not the only magic key to success and that success cannot be based solely on one's academic and university laurels. We once again find here the conception of the self-made man defended by Abraham Lincoln for whom education should not constitute the chief path to professional success (Brint 2006: 164; DeVitis and Rich 1996).

This dimension is particularly well illustrated by the narratives we collected from both French and American interviewees. As noted elsewhere (Naudet 2012), Americans tend less to assimilate their social success to their academic success than do the French. Significantly, Americans' narratives about professional careers are characterized by the precise attention paid in the narrative to various promotions and the means used to get them. This very clear difference in the narratives about career, this concern with explaining how each rung has been climbed, testifies to the fact that Americans have a greater tendency to view each promotion as the fruit of sustained efforts. The expression "they called me," frequently used by the highest ranking French bureaucrats to explain their rise to prestigious posts, demonstrates in a particularly striking manner the difference from their American peers, and exemplifies, almost to the point of caricature, the opposition between a system of sponsored mobility and a system of contest mobility, in which it is hard to conceive of "being called." This is most certainly the result of France being a much smaller country, where elite networks are structured by a very centralized system of education and by the geographical concentration around Paris of major firms and central administrations. Studying in a *Grande École* in Paris offers the possibility to accumulate a strong social capital that often proves decisive for the rest of one's career.

Access to the Elite: Sponsorship in France and Contest in the United States

It is equally interesting to note that elites', notably economic elites' modes of recruitment in the United States, favor the representation of persons from different academic institutions, whereas in France the number of institutions offering access to the most prestigious positions is much more limited. If we focus on the most important CEOs and business leaders, those whom we hypothesize are the object of particular media attention and who play a particularly important role in the construction of representations, we will note a relatively clear difference between France and the United States.

In the United States, the educational trajectories of the CEOs of the largest firms are extremely varied. Ivy League schools are the most frequently listed universities where the directors of the largest groups studied, but nevertheless represent only a small fraction of the total number of universities listed.[16] Thus, between 1999 and 2008 the percentage of CEOs of the 500 largest American groups (according to Standard and Poor's) attending Ivies oscillates between 9 percent and 11 percent.[17] This percentage does not change if we narrow our focus more specifically to the directors of the first 100 groups. We thus see that in 2001, nearly half of the directors of the first 100 groups received their diploma from a public university and only 10 percent at an Ivy League university (Cappelli and Hamori 2005). By relying on a larger sampling, the work of a team of Harvard Business School professors shows that between 1950 and 2003, 22.8 percent of the CEOs of the largest American groups came from the Ivy League, and 34.82 percent from the 100 most prestigious universities (Mayo *et al.* 2006: 142). Around 57 percent of the most important directors come from the 108 most prestigious

Table 13.1 Distribution of the directors of CAC 40 by type of training in 2007

Most prestigious Grandes Écoles[a]	Other Grandes Écoles	Universities	Other higher education degrees	No higher education	Total (N = 585)
67%	16.6%	13.5%	1.2%	1.7%	100%

Source: Dudouet and Joly (2010).

Note: a They group here the 13 most selective *Grandes Écoles*: Polytechnique (X), Centrale Paris, Mines de Paris, Ponts, les Télécoms, and Supélec for engineeering; HEC, ESSEC, and ESCP for business schoools; ENS for science and literature; IEP – Paris (Sciences Po) and ENA for specific competitive exams; and finally, INSEAD for MBAs.

institutions in the country, already a very large pool, but one that still leaves room for the recruitment of more than 40 percent of directors from less well-regarded institutions.

In contrast, the 585 directors of businesses listed in French CAC 40 came from a more restricted number of institutions. According to François Xavier Dudouet and colleagues, three institutions (ENA, HEC, and X) have trained nearly half of the directors of the 40 largest French groups (46 percent to be precise; Dudouet *et al.* 2011). Moreover, 67 percent of the directors graduated from the *Grandes Écoles*, that is, from only 15 institutions (see Table 13.1).

Once again we find similar differences in the modes of recruitment of the administrative elites. In the United States, entrance into the most prestigious positions in the public sector is not, as in France, conditioned by a competitive national examination. On the contrary, access to the highest positions reveals a diversity of possible trajectories. There is not any regularity in the university and professional trajectories of high-ranking administrators, whereas the ways to access the highest positions in the public sector in France are very narrow (Naudet 2013).

A strong contrast between the mode of recruitment of economic or administrative elites in France and in the United States emerges from this rapid comparison. In one case, access to dominant positions is very strongly structured by the academic institutions where individuals studied, whereas in the other, the prestige of the institution is much less important. Here again, Turner's thesis helps make sense of these national variations.

An Explanation by the Institutionalization of a Second Chance

A last avenue of reflection allows us to substantiate Turner's thesis a bit more empirically: the institutionalization of the second chance principle in the United States. In this country, the idea indeed prevails that it is always possible to succeed and that everything is not played out at the outset of higher education.

The most obvious evidence of this institutionalization of a second chance is certainly the fact that a prestigious university diploma earned later will have a value on the job market relatively similar to the same diploma earned earlier on. The same proposition is far from being true in the French case, and very rare are the *Grandes Écoles* that offer training to people who have already undertaken a professional career, with the notable but very specific exception of MBAs. The few comparative works interested in the question of adult students emphasize the extent to which the United States is at the forefront in this domain (Schuetze and Slowey 2002, 2000). A significant indicator of the massive character of late access to higher education is that in 2000, 43 percent of undergraduate students were more than 24 years old (Berker *et al.* 2003). Moreover, 69 percent of this group of late students were more than 30 years old.

This importance of adult access to higher education is the result of specific aspects of the history of the American educational system (Goldin and Lawrence Katz 2009; Kasworm *et al.* 2000; Maehl 2004). The concern for adult university education had been asserted very early, starting with the Morrill Land Grant Act of 1862 and the Smith-Lever Act of 1914, which already aimed at facilitating access to higher education for all. But it is above all the creation of the GI Bill after the war that allowed for a true massification of adult access to higher education. The expansion of the General Education Development (GED) Test granting a high-school diploma equivalency in order to access the university, as well as the massive development of community colleges in the 1960s allowed for the development of this already well-established tendency.

Conclusion

The different themes that we have explored to make sense of the salience of the idea of the United States as a classless society are not in any way exhaustive and must be read above all as a contribution to the much more vast and ongoing intellectual task of objectivizing the sociological mechanisms that make possible the existence of a discrepancy between the objective reality of social classes and the way they are subjectively experienced. For that purpose, the comparison of French and American systems proves particularly heuristic and allows us to grasp how a similar situation of overall weak levels of social mobility is accompanied by very different experiences of social ascension.

France and the United States are very clearly distinguished by the way in which this mobility plays out. The expression "system of sponsored mobility" forged by Ralph Turner nicely summarizes the quasi-monopolistic system that the French *Grandes Écoles* have developed in order to distribute entry tickets into the elite. In contrast, the "system of contest mobility" condenses the principal aspects of the system that prevails in the United States, where the paths for entering the elite are more varied and where it is not necessary to possess a diploma from elite universities in order to access the most prestigious positions. In France, in order to "enter into the elite," it is quasi-imperative to have a diploma from a *Grandes École*, a diploma that generally requires faultless academic trajectories, most often facilitated by graduating from the most well-regarded high schools and preparatory classes. In contrast, in the United States, attending an Ivy League college immediately upon graduating from high school is not an absolute imperative, even if it definitely constitutes a career accelerator.

These elements allow us to understand why Americans are more inclined to claim that their success is the victorious outcome of a long contest. But we must understand that these differences in the experience of mobility do not signify that social mobility is higher in the United States than in France. The concepts of sponsored and contest mobility only provide an idea of how access to the most prestigious places is determined, and the United States is not a more egalitarian society than France. In the two cases, social mobility is weak and the strategies of social reproduction structure access to the most prestigious courses of study for higher education. We therefore conclude that these two societies are characterized by different mechanisms of distribution of positions as well as by different mechanisms of exclusion and social reproduction. Different mechanisms can thus produce similar effects, and it is precisely this variation of mechanisms at work that allows us to make sense of the distinct systems of representation that prevail in France and in the United States. The question is therefore to know if it this "American exceptionalism" will be able to be maintained despite the constant and continuous increase of inequalities since the beginning of the 1980s. Leslie McCall's work (2013) suggests that Americans' view on equality has changed and is marked by a growing concern for the question of inequalities, a concern for which the recent movement Occupy Wall Street constitutes one of the most emblematic figures.

Notes

1   This work has been conducted on the basis of a collection of a hundred life stories from people who have known an extremely strong upward social mobility.
2   For more detail on this point, see Naudet (2012: 44–53).
3   Alesina and Glaeser see the explanation for this phenomenon in the racial and ethnic diversity of the United States as well as in the institutional and cultural history of the country. The work of Jérôme Bourdieu, Joseph Ferrie and Lionel Kesztenbaum (2009) comparing social mobility in the United States, France, and Great Britain allows us to consolidate this idea according to which the roots of American ideological exceptionalism are to be found in the nineteenth century. If the levels of social mobility are relatively similar in Great Britain, France, and the United States from 1880 to the twentieth century, the same is not true for the period from 1850 to 1880, during which social fluidity was much more important in the United States. It is therefore possible to hypothesize that the American ideological referents submit to an "effect of hysteresis": the dominant representations in the United States would not be adjusted to the contemporary socio-economic structures but rather to those that prevailed in the nineteenth century. The institutional and cultural bases posited in that period would have thus been extended to today.
4   The analysis presented in this chapter draws on in-depth, semi-structured interviews conducted with upwardly mobile people in France and in the United States as part of a doctoral research. Ninety-three interviews were conducted between 2004 and 2009 in the United States and France. All the respondents, aged between 30 and 65 years of age, had achieved prominent positions in the private sector, in public service and in academia (researchers and faculty members). Their parents had occupied professions ranging from menial work to low clerical positions. (For more details, see Naudet 2012a, chapter 2.)
5   For a more detailed analysis, we refer the reader to the chapters on France and the United States in the book *Entrer dans l'élite* (Naudet 2012a: chapters 4 and 5). The national

variable is not the only variable allowing us to make sense of the experience of upward social mobility (Naudet 2013). We nevertheless discuss here the experience of mobility by focusing on the most salient differences between France and the United States.

6 For a critical approach to family-based ideology in the United States, see Stacey (1996) and Coontz (1998, 2000).

7 Moreover, the French, whose relation to the family most closely approaches what we describe as frequent in the American context are, as we will see in the following chapter, characterized by very particular trajectories. In contrast, in the American context, this type of discourse does not seem so clearly linked to specific trajectories.

8 It is a matter here only of differences in narrative strategies, and this does not in any way mean that the parents of American interviewees are less "foreign" to the new group of their child than are the parents of French interviewees.

9 Alan Kerkhoff is probably the sociologist who pushed the discussion of Turner's thesis on mobility the furthest. Initially won over by his theory, he then developed a specific and rigorous critique of the weakness of Turner's thesis (Kerckhoff 1993, 1995, 2001). Following Edward Warren Noel (1962), he argues that the characteristics of the two systems of mobility are just as present in England as in the United States (and in our case, we could add that they are just as present in France as in the United States).

10 This citation from Turner directly echoes the theses defended by Pierre Bourdieu analyzing "state nobility" as a kind of structural inheritance from the noblesse of the *Ancien Régime* (Bourdieu 1989).

11 On access to the *Grandes Écoles*, see Ablouy and Wanecq (2003), Bourdieu (1989), and Euriat and Thélot (1995). On the strategies of the upper classes to place their children in the best schools and on the incapacity of the popular classes to access these same institutions, see Oberti (2007) and van Zanten (2001, 2009).

12 For a discussion on this point, see also Amable (2003: 207–219).

13 On the social and racial inequalities in access to the university and to the most prestigious courses of study in the United States, see Alon (2009), Espenshade and Radford (2009), Hout *et al.* (1993), Lucas (2001), Massey (2006), Massey *et al.* (2003), and Roska *et al.* (2007).

14 These results have unfortunately not been updated since this article was published in 1985.

15 A probable explanation is that being unable to judge the academic degrees, employers are more attentive to the institutions from which they have been obtained (Van de Werfhorst 2011: 1089).

16 Numerous articles in the economic or general press regularly take up this idea that it is not necessary to have studied at a prestigious university in order to become a CEO of a large business. See for example "Any college will do: Nation's top chief executives find path to the corner office usually starts at a state university," *Wall Street Journal*, September 18 2006; or "You can be the CEO of a Top 500 company without a Harvard degree," *Forbes*, 29 October 2012; or "Where CEOs at America's largest companies went to college," *Business News*, November 15 2010.

17 "2008 route to the top," Spencer and Stuart's report, prepared by Meghan Feicelli and Spencer Stuart, November 5 2008 (http://content.spencerstuart.com/sswebsite/pdf/lib/2008_RTT_Final_summary.pdf)

References

Albouy, V. and Wanecq, T. (2003) "Les inégalités sociales d'accès aux grandes écoles," *Economie et Statistique*, 361: 17–47.

Alesina, A. and Glaeser, E.L. (2004) *Fighting Poverty in the US and Europe: A World of Difference*, Oxford: Oxford University Press.

Allmendinger, J. (1989) "Educational systems and labor market outcomes," *European Sociological Review*, 5 (3): 231–250.

Alon, S. (2009) "The evolution of class inequality in higher education: Competition, exclusion, and adaptation," *American Sociological Review*, 74: 731–755.

Amable, B. (2003) *The Diversity of Modern Capitalism*, Oxford: Oxford University Press.

Andersen, R. and Van de Werfhorst, H.G. (2010) "Education and occupational status in 14 countries: the role of educational institutions and labour market coordination," *The British Journal of Sociology*, 61: 336–355.

Berker, A., Horn, L., and Carroll, C.D. (2003) "Work first, study second: Adult undergraduates who combine employment and postsecondary enrollment," Postsecondary Educational Descriptive Analysis Reports, available at http://nces.ed.gov/pubsearch/pubsinfo.asp?pubid=2003167

Bourdieu, J., Ferrie, J.P., and Kesztenbaum, L. (2009) "Vive la différence? Intergenerational mobility in France and the United States during the nineteenth and twentieth centuries," *Journal of Interdisciplinary History*, 39 (4): 523–557.

Bourdieu P. (1979) *La Distinction: critique sociale du jugement*, Paris: Les Editions de minuit.

Bourdieu P. (1989) *La noblesse d'Etat: Grandes Écoles et esprit de corps*, Paris: Les Editions de minuit.

Brint, S. (2006) *Schools and Societies*, Stanford, CA: Stanford University Press.

Brint, S. and Karabel, J. (1989a) "American education, meritocratic ideology, and the legitimation of inequality: the community college and the problem of American exceptionalism," *Higher Education*, 18 (6): 725–735.

Brint, S. and Karabel, J. (1989b) *The Diverted Dream: Community Colleges and the Promise of Educational Opportunity in America, 1900–1985*, Oxford: Oxford University Press.

Cappelli, P. and Hamori, M. (2005) "The new road to the top," *Harvard Business Review*, 83: 25–32.

Clark, P.P. (1979) "Literary culture in France and the United States," *American Journal of Sociology*, 84 (5): 1057–1077.

Coontz, S. (1998) *The Way We Really are: Coming to Terms with America's Changing Families*, New York: Basic Books.

Coontz, S. (2000) , *The Way We Never were: American Families and the Nostalgia Trap*, New York: Basic Books.

DeVitis, J.L. and Rich, J.M. (1996) *The Success Ethic, Education, and the American Dream*, Albany: SUNY.

Dudouet, F-X., and Joly, H. (2010) "Les dirigeants français du CAC 40: entre élitisme scolaire et passage par l'Etat," *Sociologies pratiques*, 21 (2): 35–47.

Dudouet, F-X., Grémont, E., Joly, H., and Vion, A. (2011) "Radiographie des comités exécutifs du CAC 40 au 31.12. 2009," *Les Analyses de l'OpesC*, 14.

Euriat, M. and Thelot, C. (1995) "Le recrutement social de l'élite scolaire en France. Evolution des inégalités de 1950 à 1990," *Revue Française de Sociologie*, 36 (3): 403–438.

Goblot, E. (1925) *La barrière et le niveau: Étude sociologique sur la bourgeoisie française moderne*, Paris: Alcan.

Goldin, C.D. and Katz, L.F. (2009) *The Race Between Education and Technology*, Harvard, MA: Harvard University Press.

Erikson, R. and Goldthorpe, J.H. (1992) *The Constant Flux: A Study of Class Mobility in Industrial Societies*, Oxford: Clarendon Press.

Espenshade, T.J. and Radford, A.W. (2009) *No Longer Separate, Not Yet Equal: Race and Class in Elite College Admission and Campus Life*, Princeton, NJ: Princeton University Press.

Haller, M., König, W., Krause, P., and Kurz, K. (1985) "Patterns of career mobility and structural positions in advanced capitalist societies: A comparison of men in Austria, France, and the United States," *American Sociological Review*, 50 (5): 579–603.

Hout, M., Raftery A.E., and Bell, E.O. (1993) "Making the grade: Educational stratification in the United States, 1925–1989". In Shavit, Y. and Blossfeld, H.P. (eds) *Persistent Inequality: Changing Educational Attainment in Thirteen Countries*, Boulder, CO: Westwiew Press, 25–48.

Kasworm, C.E., Sandmann, L.R., and Sissel, P. (2000) "Adult learners in higher education". In Wilson, A.H. and Hayes, E.R. (eds) *Handbook of Adult and Continuing Education*, San Francisco, CA: Wiley & Sons, 449–463.

Kerckhoff, A.C. (1993) *Diverging Pathways: Social Structure and Career Deflections*, Cambridge: Cambridge University Press.

Kerckhoff, A.C. (1995) "Institutional arrangements and stratification processes in industrial societies," *Annual Review of Sociology*, 21: 323–347.

Kerckhoff, A.C. (2001), "Education and social stratification processes in comparative perspective," *Sociology of Education*, 74: 3–18.

Lamont, M. (1995) *La morale et l'argent: les valeurs des cadres en France et aux Etats-Unis*, Paris, Éditions Métailié.

Lucas, S.R. (2001) "Effectively maintained inequality: Education transitions, track mobility, and social background effects," *American Journal of Sociology*, 106 (6): 1642–1690.

McCall, L. (2013) *The Undeserving Rich: American Beliefs about Inequality, Opportunity, and Redistribution*, Cambridge: Cambridge University Press.

Maehl, W.H. (2004) "Adult degrees and the learning society," *New Directions for Adult and Continuing Education*, 103: 5–16.

Massey, D.S. (2006) "Social background and academic performance differentials: White and minority students at selective colleges," *American Law Economic Review*, 8 (2): 390–409.

Massey, D.S., Charles, C.Z., Lundy, G., and Fischer, M.F. (2003) *The Source of the River: The Social Origins of Freshmen at America's Selective Colleges and Universities*, Princeton, NJ: Princeton University Press.

Mayo, A.J., Nohria, N., and Singleton, L.G. (2006) *Paths to Power: How Insiders and Outsiders Shaped American Business Leadership*, Boston, MA: Harvard Business School Press.

Naudet, J. (2012) *Entrer dans l'élite: Parcours de réussite en France, aux Etats-Unis et en Inde*, Paris: Presses Universitaires de France.

Naudet, J. (2013) "Par-delà les spécificités nationales: comprendre les expériences de mobilité sociale en France, aux Etats-Unis et en Inde," *Sociologie du travail*, 55 (2): 172–190.

Noël, E.W. (1962) "Sponsored and contest mobility in America and England: A rejoinder to Ralph H. Turner," *Comparative Education Review*, 6 (2): 148–151.

Oberti, M. (2007) *L'école dans la ville: Ségrégation – mixité – carte scolaire*, Paris: Presses de Sciences Po.

Palheta, U. (2012) *La domination scolaire: Sociologie de l'enseignement professionnel et de son public*, Paris: PUF.

Roska, J., Grodsky, E., Arum, R., and Gamoran, A. (2007) "United States: Changes in higher education and social stratification". In Shavit, Y., Arum, R. and Gamoran, A. (eds) *Stratification in Higher Education: A Comparative Study*, Palo Alto, CA: Stanford University Press, 165–194.

Schuetze, H.G. and Slowey, M. (eds) (2000) *Higher Education and Lifelong Learners: International Perspectives on Change*, London: Routledge Falmer.

Schuetze, H.G. and Slowey, M. (2002) "Participation and exclusion: A comparative analysis of non-traditional students and lifelong learners in higher education," *Higher Education*, 44: 309–327.

Shavit, Y. and Müller, W. (eds) (1998) *From School to Work: A Comparative Study of Educational Qualifications and Occupational Destinations*, Oxford: Clarendon Press.

Stacey, J. (1996) *In the Name of the Family: Rethinking Family Values in the Postmodern Age*, Boston, MA: Beacon Press.

Turner, R.H. (1960) "Sponsored and contest mobility and the school system", *American Sociological Review*, 25 (6): 855–867.

van de Werfhorst, H.G. (2011) "Skill and education effects on earnings in 18 countries: The role of national educational institutions," *Social Science Research*, 40 (4): 1078–1090.

van de Werfhorst, H.G. and Mijs, J.B. (2010) "Achievement inequality and the institutional structure of educational systems: A comparative perspective," *Annual Review of Sociology*, 36: 407–428.

van Zanten, A. (2001) *L'école de la périphérie: Scolarité et ségrégation en banlieue*, Paris: PUF.

van Zanten, A. (2009) *Choisir son école: Stratégies familiales et médiations locales*, Paris: PUF.

Wolbers, M.H.J. (2007) "Patterns of labour market entry: A comparative perspective on school-to-work transitions in 11 European countries," *Acta Sociologica*, 50 (3): 189–210.

14 Contextually Bound Authoritative Knowledge

A Comparative Study of British, French and Norwegian Administrative Elites' Merit and Skills

Marte Mangset

Those holding senior civil service positions may be defined as elite in that they occupy formally defined positions of authority while heading powerful institutions (Giddens 1972). According to Max Weber, the power of this elite derives from its legitimate authority based on hierarchical position and competence in meritocratic institutions: candidates should be recruited to civil service on the basis of their educational achievements and be promoted to more senior positions on the basis of the quality of their work in office (Weber 1992 [1922]). Those occupying the top positions in public administration should hence be the very best. However, if these people have reached their positions of power through a meritocratic selection system, what kind of knowledge and which skills are they supposed to excel in? Is it simply a question of putting the best in command and letting expertise serve the democratically elected politicians? Is the same kind of expertise required in all countries?

Based on qualitative interviews with 81 senior civil servants (from the level of deputy director/*chef de bureau*/*underdirektør* and above) in the ministries of finance and culture in Britain, France and Norway,[1] this chapter will analyse the knowledge and skills that contribute to the legitimation of these elites' power in different contexts. It will show that on the one hand, there is a significant variation between the educational profiles favoured in each country, but that on the other, the interviewees' descriptions of the knowledge and skills required for being recruited to top positions are strikingly similar across countries. This spurs the analysis of how varying types of educational institutions, somewhat regardless of the disciplinary or professional profiles they may train, serve as guarantors for meritocratic administrative elites in different countries.

Three Different Educational Paths to Elite Administrative Positions

When examining the educational routes to top administrative positions in France, Britain and Norway, one can wonder whether it is really the same profession: the French top bureaucrats have typically attended the French national school of administration, *École nationale d'administration* (ENA), and consider themselves to be generalists in administration. The British usually have university bachelor degrees in anything from literature to physics: they consider themselves generalists *period*. The Norwegian top bureaucrats most commonly have university post-graduate degrees in economics, law or political science and present themselves as specialists.

Training Generalists in Administration in France

French top bureaucrats are most commonly recruited from four elite educational institutions (*grandes écoles*): *École polytechnique, École nationale de statistiques et d'administration économique* (ENSAE), *Sciences Po Paris* and *École nationale d'administration* (ENA). The graduates from ENA constitute the most dominant group (Eymeri 1999; Gally 2012; Kessler 1978). The French system of governing is often characterized as an *énarchie*, since the graduates from ENA – often called *énarques* – tend to occupy leading positions in politics, public administration and business (Birnbaum 1994; Chevènement 1967). I shall focus on these *énarques*.

Whereas the other schools prepare for other careers as well, ENA was established in 1945 solely to educate candidates for top public administration. The great majority of ENA students attended *Sciences Po* beforehand, where they studied a range of subjects within the humanities and social sciences, with an emphasis on law, economics and public administration. The curriculum at ENA is also dominated by law, economics and public administration (Biland and Vanneuville 2012; Eymeri 1999). All students follow the same curriculum. There is no specialization in any particular discipline or field. The students are thought to study these disciplines as applied to real professional situations, not as academic disciplines *per se*. ENA defines itself as an '*école d'application*' (professional school). The teaching staff consists of top civil servants coming in to teach for a few hours in order to share their professional experience and knowledge of real life in top administration (Mangset 2003).

ENA graduates often describe their training as mainly being about one key assignment that they complete every week: they are presented with a question or problem drawn from a real civil service situation, a load of documents and five hours to write up a brief note. They are assessed on their ability to grasp the essentials of the information and to formulate a clear and convincing argument for decision-making within the time frame. This is an assignment that is supposed to be very close to the work they will actually be doing as senior civil servants: the writing of submissions with advice to political staff (interviews with French top bureaucrats 2011; Mangset 2003).

ENA graduates are supposed to be able to enter any ministerial department, any division within these, and be ready to switch recurrently and easily between administrative units, themes and tasks. Those with top grades will enter positions such as *adjoint de chef de bureau* in a top division at a prestigious administrative unit, such as the Ministry of Finance, and often reach the level of *chef de bureau* within six years (interviews, French Ministry of Finance 2011; Mangset 2003; Eymeri 2001). They generally spend only two years in a position before moving on to another and tend to occupy positions in several different administrative units. This is part of the generalist ambition of this education and of the public administration human resource policy: the fact that the top bureaucrats have one and the same schooling and that they circulate between different parts of the administration through their career is supposed to secure a good communication between and a strong cohesion within the different parts of the civil service (Eymeri 1999; 2006; Kessler 1978).

Cultivating One's Mind Through University Liberal Education in Britain

As in France, British top civil servants tend to have a rather homogeneous educational background. Most commonly, they come from one out of a handful of prestigious educational institutions. The most successful ones are often Oxford and Cambridge humanities graduates (Barberis 1996; Dargie and Locke 1999; Drewry and Butcher 1991). As in France, the educational landscape is clearly hierarchically structured, but instead of a special school in administrative studies, there are two ancient universities, first and second in the UK university rankings,[2] that educate candidates for elite positions in all sectors of society (Mangset 2009). A range of reforms has been instigated to diversify the types of candidates recruited and their social and educational background. Yet, young Oxbridge graduates have continued to dominate the British bureaucratic elite (Drewry and Butcher 1991; Hood and Lodge 2004; Richards 1996).

University graduates wishing to enter the British civil service must pass a common entry exam that is not specific to any discipline; it tests broader knowledge and skills, notably numerical, verbal and logical skills (Bryon 2010; The UK Civil Service 2012). At this moment, the distinction is first made between future *top* bureaucrats and ordinary ones: thus, on initial recruitment, the best ranked embark on a fast stream programme that can enable them to reach the top echelons of the system (Pyper 1995). Young Oxbridge graduates with an honours degree in the liberal arts (history, literature, philosophy and particularly courses such as Oxford's PPE (philosophy, politics and economics)) are the ones who tend to succeed in these entry exams (Bogdanor 2006: 151–153). This is despite the fact that the entry exams do not test knowledge and skills that are specifically related to these disciplines.

The lack of focus on specific disciplinary knowledge and skills is consistent with the liberal education ideal of British university teaching: the specialized training within a sub-field in a discipline provided by a university is considered a way of training the mind so that the student later can apply it to any subject or task, rather than representing specialized knowledge in that area. This ideal was already formulated in 1852 by the Oxford academic John Henry Newman, author of *The Idea of a University*:

> This process of training, by which the intellect, instead of being formed and sacrificed to some particular purpose, some specific trade or profession, or study or science, is disciplined for its own sake, for the perception of its own

proper object, and for its own highest culture, is called Liberal Education; [...] a cultivated intellect, because it is good in itself, brings with it a power and grace to every work and occupation it undertakes, and enables us to be more useful, and to a greater number.

(Newman 1982 [1852])

This ideal of general education as both the most advanced and useful form of knowledge provided the foundation of the nineteenth century civil service reforms. In their crucial report from 1854, Sir Stafford Northcote and Sir Charles Trevelyan advocate that in order to secure the recruitment of the best candidates to the civil service without regard to other aspects than their merit, the most suitable recruitment form would be an examination in general knowledge (Northcote and Trevelyan 1854: 9–10). The ideal of the generalist civil servant seems to have survived the numerous reforms of the British civil service and its recruitment practices (Gally 2012).

Following Specialized University Studies in Norway

The Norwegian educational system distinguishes itself from France and Britain by its lack of explicit hierarchical structure and its high degree of specialization: there is no single elite institution training candidates for top positions across labour market sectors (Bleiklie *et al.* 2000). There is also no explicit elite institution at which top bureaucrats tend to be trained. If one type of higher education institution enjoys more prestige than another, it would be the universities. Those applying for and recruited to the Norwegian civil service tend to be university graduates, although the Ministry of Finance also recruits regularly from the Norwegian school of economics. Compared with Britain and France, there is a greater variety in the disciplinary and institutional backgrounds of Norwegian civil servants. However, jurists, economists and political scientists are more predominant than other disciplinary groups (Christensen *et al.* 2001).

The relatively greater variety in the Norwegian civil servants' educational profiles must be seen not only in relation to the absence of clear hierarchies in the educational sector, but also in relation to the civil service recruitment system: in contrast to the French and British systems, whose common entry exams operate as a gatekeeper for the entire civil service across sectors, ministries and sub-units, in Norway, each administrative division recruits its own candidates. Each position is treated as an individual case. This system favours more specialized candidates: the recruiters search for candidates with a profile for their specific department and the specific position that needs to be filled.

Although both the British and the Norwegian civil service recruit university graduates, the difference between the two types of graduates is substantial: whereas the British most often have a bachelor's degree in a discipline without connection to their future profession, the Norwegians commonly have a postgraduate degree in a discipline and subject directly relevant to their job tasks. Norwegian university training is commonly about doing an in-depth academic study on a narrowly defined topic. Academic ideals such as critical sense, independence, methodological expertise and theoretical subtleness are valued (Mangset 2003; 2009). Recruiters in Norwegian administration say they prefer candidates with such specialized academic knowledge of the subject they will be working on (interviews with Norwegian Ministries of Finance and Culture 2012; Mangset 2003). In line with existing literature on professional ideals in the Norwegian civil service (Grønlie and Flo 2009; Jacobsen 1960; Lie and Venneslan 2010), the Norwegians interviewed for this study insist that their strength as bureaucrats is their disciplinary expertise (*faglighet*) (Mangset 2014).

Common Required Competences: A Combination of Personal Qualities and Generalist Skills

The tangible differences between the educational routes to leading positions in the central administration in these three countries makes one wonder whether it is really one and the same profession across countries. Are the French administrative generalist from ENA, the British liberal education generalist from Oxbridge and the Norwegian postgraduate in economics good at the same things? When a deputy director in a tax division in the British Treasury is a history graduate from Oxford, and a deputy director in a tax division in the Norwegian Ministry of Finance is a specialized tax economist, does that mean that they do different things in their jobs? The varying educational backgrounds suggest that they are valued for bringing rather different kinds of expertise to the table. However, when the bureaucrats are asked about the kinds of knowledge and skills that are required in order to reach the top echelons of the central administration and what kind of competence they actually need to succeed in their job, they disclose a more homogeneous picture. In all three countries, the interviewees insist on the significance of a set of common qualities and skills: intelligence, confidence, rhetorical skills, rapidity and ambition.

'Intelligence'

In all three countries, the interviewees argue that in order to reach the senior level in their department, you would have to be quite intelligent:

> I don't mean to be pretentious when I say this, but I really think it is impressive the amount of grey matter that you have on a square centimetre here in Bercy [the French Ministry of Finance]. It is really impressive.
>
> (France, Finance 8)[3]

> We have very bright young people [in the Treasury]. We are all very bright in fact.
>
> (Britain, Finance 7)

> These people that are hired here, fresh from the Norwegian school of economics, great grades, really clever, sympathetic people. You have to be rather smart to work here.
>
> (Norway, Finance 1)

Interviewees from all three countries seemed to have a firm belief in their intelligence's superiority and in how that helped them acquire and master the job they held. They used a range of terms like bright, clever, smart, analytically strong, etc., and they talked about it in a broad sense, i.e. not distinguishing between innate qualities and acquired skills. In none of the three countries was this required intelligence qualified as specific to a discipline or an area of expertise. It was described as a general kind of intelligence, as a capacity of the mind, for example in terms of a certain level of IQ:

> There are three things you need to be good at, I think, one is that kind of problem solving ability. So I've got a lot of that, I've got a ..., you know, I'm intelligent, I've got a very high IQ. I've got the kind of mind that can see complicated problems and see how to resolve them.
>
> (Britain, Culture 1)

However, they often described it as some kind of real-world intelligence. They considered their educational background a guarantor for their mind's quality, but still often contrasted the kind of intelligence required in their job with a more academic kind. Two of the British interviewees used the term *nous*, originally a Greek term, which in modern English defines a commonsensical, practical kind of intelligence.[4]

Also, the Norwegian top bureaucrats, who at some points in the interviews talked about how important their disciplinary expertise was, at other points claimed that it was a question of possessing certain analytical skills regardless of disciplinary background:

> So, [the ones that we recruit] have ... that *analytical level* that you need to have to be a good civil servant. They might ... they have very different backgrounds, and ... well, I'm not the kind of leader that needs to have jurists, political scientists, that needs to have economists ... I think you can use anything if they only have that level of thinking.
>
> (Norway, Culture 2)

So, in all three countries, the interviewees considered that in order to reach elite positions in public administration, you had to be simply generally smart.

Confidence

As we saw in the previous section, the interviewees from all three countries were quite confident in their own intellectual capacities. The British senior civil servants saying 'I have a very high IQ', or 'we are all very bright', certainly express confidence. And confidence is in itself brought up by several interviewees as a necessary quality in order to succeed in their profession. Confidence is often understood as a necessary condition for a certain kind of behaviour: they speak of how they are expected to display pleasant personality traits in interaction with others. They were particularly concerned with the manner of speaking:

You must also be able to speak out – in French or in English – in a meeting. To have a certain …, I don't know, charisma. […] There are people whom you can tell will be able to handle things, you can send them anywhere, and it'll work out. And then there are others whom you consider really brilliant, but too shy, or who express themselves poorly.

(France, Finance 2)

The interviewees describe how they are often required to interact with politicians, leaders in public or private organizations or their own subordinates and are expected to be convincing, concise and efficient. In order to accomplish that, they ought to perform such interactions, and their job in general, with *ease*:

When I was interviewed [for this position] […] you really had to show a certain energy, be comfortable, somewhat sure of yourself, but not too much either. Right. Here [at the Ministry of Finance] they really like people who are very much at ease, very forceful, very go-ahead.

(France, Finance 12)

The Norwegian top bureaucrats also expressed that such confidence, ease or charisma was a necessary quality in order to perform well in their job. It became a significant advantage in the competition for top positions:

I think [the recruiters appreciated that] I have better leadership skills than [the other candidate for this position had]. I have a natural authority when in a meeting. I have opinions about how to do things, and I communicate them clearly.

(Norway, Finance 9)

Such ease and confidence might very well be acquired in an educational institution (Cookson and Persell 1985a, 1985b; Khan 2011). The interviewed candidates educated at all these varying educational institutions seem to have succeeded by acquiring – or already possessing (Bourdieu 1979, 1989) – knowledge of how to interact professionally with ease. It is argued that those brought up in families (typically upper middle class) where asking questions, providing arguments and interacting confidently with adults and professional authorities is encouraged and rewarded (Lareau 2011) will in elite educational institutions also be rewarded for this behaviour. It is often part of elite educational institutions' objective to prepare their students for leadership by teaching them how to interact effortlessly, pleasantly and with authority. However, these qualities or related skills might be more or less explicitly transmitted as the purpose of the training. They are further not directly connected to any disciplinary specialization. There is great variation regarding the degree to which such skills are made explicit as part of the curriculum or the selection criteria for success at the educational institutions the British, the French and the Norwegian top civil servants have attended.

Rhetorical Skills

The capacity for talking pleasantly and convincingly in meetings was not presented purely as a question of confidence. It was also presented as a question of possessing rhetorical skills. In all three countries, the interviewees defined one of their most central skills as a capacity for argumentation – both in oral and in written form:

> [What we need to master is] the technique, after all. [Which] is to be lucid and clear. To be crystal-clear both in written and in oral form. That is, the more you muddle, the less people will listen. The less people will read you. So, the idea is to lay out your case, to make your argument, but always simple things. Few points, simple, but which make things move forward. Right. That is very important.
>
> (France, Culture 4)

The interviewees in all three countries and all six departments described their key task as reviewing and improving their subordinates' writing of *submissions*: brief texts intended to inform the politicians on some issue and to provide them with the necessary information in order to make a decision. The ability to translate complex expertise into concise and comprehensible language for politicians, who are short on time, was presented as a difficult task requiring excellent argumentative skills. Both the French and the British top bureaucrats explicitly argue that a generalist profile is an advantage for doing this translation work from expertise language into lay people's language well. Too much expertise was considered a risk for going into too much detail and not being clear.

> The thing where I'm adding most value most of the time, given that lots of people who work for me are either kind of professionals, i.e. statisticians, or you know a sort of good economists, is making sure that they're able to communicate those ideas sufficiently clearly to the chancellor, who, you know, doesn't have the time nor the inclination to try and understand bad writing. So I do quite a lot of that, actually.
>
> (Britain, Finance 1)

Although the Norwegian top bureaucrats do not explicitly argue in favour of a generalist profile, they too talk about their work and their competence as leaders as being about arguing precisely and clearly:

> So, I have a pretty good disciplinary background. As an economist. I did well in university. So I have the disciplinary background, which without doubt is important in the Ministry of Finance. But in addition to that I generally manage to deliver the job on time, and make sure that it goes to my bosses and to the politicians in a way that they understand. One must be able to explain something in a simple and comprehensible way, even if it is difficult and complex. I think that is an important quality.
>
> (Norway, Finance 20)

Despite the Norwegian top bureaucrats' relatively stronger focus on disciplinary expertise, they too argue that the civil servants who reach the top tend to be the ones who also hold such rhetorical skills: to be able to translate vast and complex expertise information into short, precise and clear advice.

Rapidity

Another skill that the top bureaucrats in all countries agreed was absolutely central to the mastery of their profession, was the ability to do things quickly:

> The third point is somewhat linked to the summarising, it's the rapidity. And to be fast, there too I think … I'm not saying that one should skim through the issue, one tries not to skim through the issue. But you know that at some point you have to stop with the technical expertise. You can't go as far as you would have wanted. You have to do things rather quickly.
>
> (France, Finance 3)

So, this is about being able to write the submissions mentioned before very rapidly, but also about being able to understand things rapidly:

> I think the strengths that I've brought to the job are: I can understand and grasp quite quickly what ministers want, and what the permanent secretary wants. So I kind of understand what the point of the job is quite quickly and can deliver it.
>
> (Britain, Culture 4)

Although the Norwegian bureaucrats expressed a stronger identification with academic skills and specialized knowledge than the British and the French, they too underscored how the bureaucratic profession is far more time-sensitive than the academic profession; it requires a quite different sense of urgency, and thus different skills. The value of disciplinary in-depth knowledge was put into perspective:

> And then there is something about being able to work under pressure and being able to handle short deadlines. Some people don't fit personality-wise to this division, because they like to work thoroughly on things. You can't […] So some get frustrated by short deadlines and never being able to delve into the discipline.
>
> (Norway, Finance 2)

Several of the interviewees compare their own work with academic work and bring up the shorter time frames as one of the contrasting points. They want to convey that the ability to work under such time pressure is a distinguishing feature of their own profession, and they often take great pride in mastering just that. The education provided to the French top bureaucrats at ENA does actually bear some resemblance with the kind of time frames they meet in real work life (Eymeri 2001; Mangset 2003). At British universities, it is not quite the same. Yet, the pedagogical tradition of weekly essay writing, which is central to bachelor's degrees at Oxford and Cambridge, probably comes closer to such administrative time frames than does the Norwegian university tradition (Mangset 2009; Palfreyman 2001). The capacity of handling time pressure is one of the key competences required from these top bureaucrats in all three countries, although the degree to which there is any focus on this in their education varies a lot.

Ambition

The interviewees from all three countries also insisted on the importance of ambition. In order to become a top bureaucrat, you would have to *want* to become a top bureaucrat. Your own eagerness to perform well and to reach the senior levels of the administrative system matters. One of the key issues that the interviewees regularly brought up as a reason for their success was their willingness to put in a significant number of hours at work:

> [In order to reach the position where I am], I was prepared to work a lot, you know. This is a division where you work a lot. It depends, there are different periods. Globally, we come in the morning at a normal time, between 8.30 and 9.00. And in the evening, we leave rather late. After 21.00. So, between 21.30 and 22.00, right.
>
> (France, Finance 3)

Particularly, the French insisted on the strain of the working hours and the difficulty of reconciling this work with family life. One interviewee said she was a mother of a toddler and therefore had to leave 'early' two nights a week, that is, at 19.30. The other nights she worked until 22.00 or 23.00. But that was worth it, and she was proud to have reached such a high position at a very young age (France, Finance 7).

The French interviewees also told stories of how they had to make sacrifices concerning their personal and family lives and accommodate their superiors' demands in order not to risk falling out of a bureaucratic elite career track. Two interviewees had been stationed abroad for a period of time and had settled down there with their family for a couple of years. Then, a year or so into that stay, they had suddenly been called home to enter a leading position back in a ministerial department on short notice; it could be a matter of days. Either they had to accommodate to these shifting demands and set all personal considerations aside, or they would no longer be in competition for leading positions (interviews France, Finance 4 and 9). These and the other French interviewees described how ambition, understood as encompassing adaptability and willingness to sacrifice, was necessary in order to stay on a career track for leadership.

The British interviewees seldom brought up such a conflict between work and family life, nor did they talk about ambition in terms of sacrifice. However, they did talk about ambition. They considered that those who were apt for leading positions in the civil service were those who demonstrated some sort of drive:

> You're also looking for a certain amount of commitment, appetite, as well. So I think more and more we're looking for people at all levels who are able to take responsibility within the areas that they're responsible for, to operate reasonably autonomously. People who've got initiative, who are able to think a bit sort of imaginatively, creatively […] a sort of 'can do'-approach.
>
> (Britain, Culture 6)

By 'can do'-approach we should probably also understand a certain degree of adaptability. This 'can do'-understanding of ambition, and the other generic skills and qualities that I analyse in this chapter, resonate with the skills or qualities that Phil Brown and Anthony Hesketh find that British employers of high-skill labour say they are looking for in their candidates: suitability, proactivity and acceptability (Brown and Hesketh, 2004). They describe them as generic skills that are largely performative and aesthetic in nature.

Like the French, the Norwegian interviewees mentioned the willingness to work hard as a requirement of top bureaucrats. But this down-to-earth interpretation of ambition is not the only one pointed out by the interviewees. Norwegian culture is often described as valuing modesty and sanctioning those who stick their head out. However, the Norwegian interviewees in this study clearly stated that willingness to stick one's head out was important. Explicitly aiming for leadership was certainly one of the central requirements to the ones entering top positions. Many of the Norwegian interviewees had through life, as students and at work, constantly showed such willingness. They thought that influenced their recruiters' positive evaluation of them:

> I do work hard – I mean, I spend loads of time at work – and that is appreciated […] I kind of respond to the responsibility that is given me […] And I have – through the years – gotten some management experience, some leadership experience. Through the military where I was squad leader and then troop leader. That was during regular military service and then during a supplementary year. That is, training for officer. And I've had some leading positions in student associations and that sort of things. And I've been a leader in a few joint-stock companies […] so I had, before I became a leader [in the civil service], an understanding of what that is, and I was confident that I too can be a good leader.
>
> (Norway, Finance 1)

Thus, whereas the formal education required from the Norwegian civil servants is specialized disciplinary education without explicit training in leadership skills, the interviewees indicate that informal training in such skills through extra-curricular activities and activities outside educational institutions is valued in the selection process. Having showed ambition or willingness to take on a role as leader in extracurricular settings is an advantage in the recruitment process for administrative elite positions. This is in line with prior research on elite education and on how elite educational institutions tend to facilitate extracurricular activities and communicate to their students the value of engaging in such activities (Cookson and Persell 1985b). However, the different educational institutions attended by the British, the French and the Norwegian civil servants vary regarding the degree to which they explicitly encourage such activities as part of the educational preparation for leadership positions. Whereas the institutions where French and British top bureaucrats are trained are defined as providers of training in generic skills and formers of character, the Norwegian institutions are not.

Contextually Bound Guarantors of Meritocracy

Do the similarities between the qualities and skills favoured in the three countries' central administrations' top layers imply that it is really irrelevant which educational institution a candidate for top bureaucracy attends? Does it not matter whether the formal training acquired by top bureaucrats is specialized disciplinary training or training in general skills? Are the educational institutions empty shells whose educational programmes are merely decorative?

My point is not to say that the top bureaucrats in these three countries do not actually possess somewhat different competences. Norwegian central administration does favour more specialized profiles among their top levels than the French and the British do. However, at the senior level, the Norwegian civil service also values such general qualities and skills as described in this chapter: intelligence, confidence, rhetorical skills, rapidity and ambition. In contrast to the French and British contexts, the significance of these general skills is often implicit in Norway and stands in stark contrast to the self-perception the Norwegian top bureaucrats have as specialized experts. When the British and French top bureaucrats are asked what their competences are, they immediately answer that they are generalists. They have an explicit professional identity as generalists. This identity is underpinned by formal documents such as the UK Civil Service Competency Framework (The UK Civil Service, 2012), and university ideals and practices promoting general skills (Newman 1982 [1852]; Palfreyman 2001). But when the Norwegian top bureaucrats are asked what their competences are, they first speak of disciplinary expertise. It is only after a while during the interview, when asked follow-up questions, that they start to relativize the importance of specialized expertise and bring up the significance of general skills.

Although they then speak of these general skills as crucial, as a way of distinguishing the best from the merely good ones, their primary identity is as specialists. This identity is underpinned by an educational system focusing on disciplinary and specialized training. General skills such as rhetorical skills, which certainly are important in order to succeed in the Norwegian university system, are rarely part of the explicit curriculum. In contrast to the Oxbridge tradition of weekly essay writing and the French ENA students' weekly writing of administrative notes, Norwegian students have little explicit training and guidance in how to write well (Mangset, 2009). Thus, although general skills count in the selection of the Norwegian bureaucratic elite, their importance is more implicit than in the case of the selection of French and British bureaucratic elites. Not verbalizing the importance of certain competences in recruitment and promotion processes represents a challenge to meritocracy.

Further, it is not my point to say that the explicit curricula in these educational institutions are irrelevant and that only hidden curricula matter. The central administrations in these three countries do probably value somewhat different types of knowledge and skills when they recruit administrative generalists, liberal education generalists and disciplinary specialists, respectively, for their top positions. However, my point is that these differences are not so much about French, British and Norwegian central administrations actually needing very different competence profiles because their civil servants are doing very different things in their daily work. Rather, it is related to how different perceptions of legitimate and authoritative knowledge prevail in these countries: the intellectual, educational and political debates as well as the institutional developments that through history have shaped the educational landscapes in each of these countries also influence the perceptions recruiters have of what are considered the necessary and optimal kinds of knowledge and skills for their particular profession.

In France, the universities were once seen as connected to the *Ancien Régime*, and since the Revolution, a different type of educational institutions, the *grandes écoles*, were considered the most legitimate holders and disseminators of knowledge (Musselin 2001; Ringer 1992; Zeldin 1967). These schools, on which ENA is modelled, were often tightly connected to the state. They were not primarily research institutions, and they were supposed to train candidates for leadership. Competences perceived as necessary for leaders were early on part of the explicit curricula.

In Britain, the industrial revolution and the requirement for new and more 'useful' knowledge and for new types of universities pushed the intellectual protagonists of the ancient universities to reformulate their academic ideals in a manner that made them acceptable to their challengers. Newman's formulation of liberal education as the most *useful* kind of knowledge ought to be seen in that context (Newman 1982 [1852]). The formulation of this general liberal education ideal as the best way to distinguish the best young candidates generally, and the best civil servants specifically, should also be seen as part of the ancient universities' attempt to protect their own role as a selection system for positions of power (Rothblatt 1997; Rothblatt and Wittrock 1993).

When the Norwegians established their first university in 1811 as part of their struggle for independence from their Nordic neighbour states, it was the German research university that had greatest influence (Collett 1999). The 400 years of foreign dominance and the lack of Norwegian nobility is relevant to the lack of traditional elite educational institutions teaching 'gentlemanly qualities' such as general skills (Bleiklie *et al.* 2000: 165; Vanneuville 1999). Rather, when this first university was established, indeed to independently educate a new national elite, it was important to its founders, to the political elites and in public debate that this institution be scientifically (*wissenschaftlich*) oriented (Collett 2011). Since then, and through the different waves of massification of higher education, the university – with its research identity – has remained the most prestigious educational institution.

Conclusion

These very briefly sketched socio-historical contextual configurations[5] are crucial to both candidates' and recruiters' perception of which educational institutions perform a fair selection of elite candidates for elite positions in the civil service. Thus, although the bureaucratic elite might need many of the same skills in all three countries, quite different educational institutions providing training in quite different knowledge and skills play the role as providers of excellent candidates and guarantors of meritocratic selection. One can thus speak of a certain degree of decoupling between the kind of knowledge and skills implicitly valued in the selection process to civil service elite positions and the formal training required to be eligible for such positions. The requirements to formal education and explicit professional identity in each country is based on the kinds of knowledge which historically has been constructed as authoritative knowledge in each society, and which institutions that have been perceived as legitimate providers of such knowledge. In order to understand how knowledge and education legitimizes elite power in different contexts, and in order to understand the mechanics behind various forms of meritocratic selection systems in education, one ought to take such contextually bound perceptions of knowledge and institutions into account.

Notes

1 All interviews were conducted in 2011 and 2012 by the author in English, French and Norwegian. The interviews lasted generally between 60 and 90 minutes and were taped and transcribed *in extenso*. The interview guide was constructed with open-ended questions and was the same in all three countries and six ministries.
2 http://www.theguardian.com/education/ng-interactive/2014/jun/02/university-league-tables-2015-the-complete-list
3 In order to protect the anonymity of the interviewees while letting the reader know whether the same or different interviewees are quoted, each interviewee is identified with his or her country affiliation, ministerial affiliation and a number. Interviewees from the ministries of finance are quoted somewhat more often than the interviewees from the ministries of culture because the former expressed what was discussed in both types of ministries in somewhat more succinct ways. However, the quotes are representative for what was said in both types of ministries.
4 *Oxford English Dictionary:* http://www.oxforddictionaries.com/definition/english/nous?q=nous, retrieved 27 May 14
5 A more comprehensive outline of the intellectual and institutional developments of French, British and Norwegian higher education can be found in Mangset (2009).

References

Barberis, P. (1996) *The Elite of the Elite: Permament Secretaries in the British Higher Civil Service,* Aldershot: Dartmouth.

Biland, É. and Vanneuville, R. (2012) 'Government lawyers and the training of senior civil servants: Maintaining law at the heart of the French state', *International Journal of the Legal Profession*, 19(1): 29–54.

Birnbaum, P. (1994) *Les sommets de l'État: Essai sur l'élite du pouvoir en France*, Paris: Seuil.

Bleiklie, I., Høstaker, R. and Vabø, A. (2000) *Policy and practice in higher education*, London: Jessica Kingsley.

Bogdanor, V. (2006) 'Oxford and the mandarin culture: The past that is gone', *Oxford Review of Education*, 32(1): 147–165.

Bourdieu, P. (1979) *La distinction*, Paris: Éditions de minuit.

Bourdieu, P. (1989) *La noblesse d'Etat: grandes écoles et esprit de corps*, Paris: Editions de minuit.

Brown, P. and Hesketh, A. (2004) *The Mismanagement of Talent: Employability and Jobs in the Knowledge Economy*, Oxford: Oxford University Press.

Bryon, M. (2010) *How to Pass the Civil Service Qualifying Tests: The Essential Guide for Clerical and Fast Stream Applications*, London: Kogan Page.

Chevènement, J.-P. (1967) *L'énarchie, ou Les mandarins de la société bourgeoise*, Paris: La table ronde.

Christensen, T., Lægreid, P. and Zuna, H. R. (2001) *Profesjoner i regjeringsapparatet 1976–1996. Økende heterogenitet: effekter og implikasjoner*, Oslo: Makt- og demokratiutredningen 1998–2003.

Collett, J. P. (1999) *Historien om universitetet i Oslo*, Oslo: Universitetsforlaget.

Collett, J. P. (2011) *1811–1870: universitetet i nasjonen*, Oslo: Unipub.

Cookson, P. W. and Persell, C. H. (1985a) 'English and American residential secondary schools: A comparative study of the reproduction of social elites', *Comparative Education Review*, 29(3): 283–298.

Cookson, P. W. and Persell, C. H. (1985b) *Preparing for Power: America's Elite Boarding Schools*, New York: Basic Books.

Dargie, C. and Locke, R. (1999) 'The British senior civil service', in E. Page and V. Wright (eds) *Bureaucratic Elites in Western European States*, Oxford: Oxford University Press.

Drewry, G. and Butcher, T. (1991) *The Civil Service Today*, Oxford: Blackwell.

Eymeri, J.-M. (1999) 'Les gardiens de l'État: Une sociologie des énarques de ministère', unpublished thesis, University of Paris 1.

Eymeri, J.-M. (2001) *La fabrique des énarques*, Paris: Economica.

Eymeri, J.-M. (2006) 'Comparer les hauts fonctionnaires en Europe: Variations sur le thème de la carrière', in F. Dreyfus and J.-M. Eymeri (eds) *Sciences politique de l'administration. Une approche comparative*, Paris: Economica.

Gally, N. (2012) 'Le marché des hauts fonctionnaires: Une comparaison des politiques de la haute fonction publique en France et en Grande-Bretagne', unpublished thesis, Sciences Po Paris.

Giddens, A. (1972) 'Elites in the British class structure', *Sociological Review*, 20(3): 345–372.

Grønlie, T. and Flo, Y. (2009) *Sentraladministrasjonens historie etter 1945. Den nye staten? Tiden etter 1980*, Bergen: Fagbokforlaget.

Hood, C. and Lodge, M. (2004) 'Competency, bureaucracy, and public management reform: A comparative analysis', *Governance: An International Journal of Policy, Administration, and Institutions*, 17(3): 313–333.

Jacobsen, K. D. (1960) 'Lojalitet, nøytralitet og faglig uavhengighet i sentraladministrasjonen', *Tidsskrift for samfunnsforskning*, 4: 231–248.

Kessler, M.-C. (1978) *L'ENA: La politique de la haute fonction publique*, Paris: Presses de la FNSP.

Khan, S. R. (2011) *Privilege: The Making of an Adolescent Elite at St. Paul's School*, Princeton, NJ: Princeton University Press.

Lareau, A. (2011) *Unequal Childhoods: Class, Race, and Family Life*, Berkeley: University of California Press.

Lie, E. and Venneslan, C. (2010) *Over evne: Finansdepartementet 1965–1992*, Oslo: Pax.

Mangset, M. (2003) 'Selvreflekterende reformatorer eller retoriske racere? En sammen-lignende studie av byråkratutdanninger i Norge og Frankrike', unpublished master thesis, University of Oslo.

Mangset, M. (2009) *The Discipline of Historians: A Comparative Study of Historians' Constructions of the Discipline of History in English, French and Norwegian Universities*, Bergen: Universitetet i Bergen.

Mangset, M. (2014) 'Hva er det toppbyråkrater er så flinke til?', in N. R. Langseland (ed.) *Politisk kompetanse. Grunnlovas borgar 1814–2014*, Oslo: Pax forlag.

Musselin, C. (2001) *La longue marche des universités françaises*, Paris: Presses universitaires de France.

Newman, J. H. (1982 [1852]) *The Idea of a University*, Notre Dame, IN: University of Notre Dame Press.

Northcote, S. H. and Trevelyan, C. E. (1854) *Report on the Organisation of the Permanent Civil Service, Together with a Letter from Rev. B. Jowett*, London: George E. Eyre and William Spottiswoode.

Palfreyman, D. (ed.) (2001) *The Oxford Tutorial: 'Thanks, You Taught Me How to Think'*, Oxford: Oxcheps.

Pyper, R. (1995) *The British Civil Service: An Introduction*, Hemel Hempstead, UK: Prentice Hall.

Richards, D. (1996) 'Appointments to the highest grades in the civil service: Drawing the curtain open', *Public Administration*, 74: 657–677.

Ringer, F. (1992) *Fields of Knowledge: French Academic Culture in Comparative Perspective, 1890–1920*, Cambridge and Paris: Cambridge university press and Editions de la Maison des sciences de l'homme.

Rothblatt, S. (1997) *The Modern University and Its Discontents: The Fate of Newman's Legacies in Britain and America*, Cambridge: Cambridge University Press.

Rothblatt, S. and Wittrock, B. (eds) (1993) *The European and American University Since 1800: Historical and Sociological Essays*, Cambridge: Cambridge University Press.

The UK Civil Service (2012) *Civil Service Competency Framework*, London.

Vanneuville, R. (1999) 'La référence anglaise à l'école libre des sciences politiques: La forma-tion de "gentlemen" républicains 1871–1914', unpublished thesis University of Grenoble 2.

Weber, M. (1992 [1922]) *Economy and Society*, Berkeley, CA: University of California Press.

Zeldin, T. (1967) 'Higher education in France, 1848–1940', *Journal of Contemporary History*, 2(3): 53–80.

15 Higher Education, Corporate Talent and the Stratification of Knowledge Work in the Global Labour Market

Phillip Brown, Hugh Lauder and Johnny Sung

Introduction

This chapter will provide a sociological analysis of competing definitions of 'talent' and elite employability in understanding the (re)stratification of knowledge work and its relationship to higher education. It describes how the signifiers of talent may be defined differently depending on occupational and labour market context. Consequently, the study of elite education and its relationship to the global labour market raises important theoretical and policy issues rarely addressed in the literature on elite education and social reproduction.

The chapter is divided into two sections followed by a conclusion. In the first section we argue that the management and business discourse on 'talent' and 'talent management' (which mirrors the rhetoric of the 'world class university' and global rankings within higher education) is central to understanding a growing 'legitimation crisis' in respect to widening inequalities in opportunities and incomes. Here we explain why knowledge work, covering many areas of professional, managerial and technical employment, is being realigned and (re)stratified, as part of a process of workforce differentiation. Two related points are developed to explain this: first, the twentieth century model of bureaucratic expertise linked to a hierarchy of educational achievement is not sustainable in an age of mass higher education. Second, many of the assumptions about the demand for knowledge workers in today's global economy have been found wanting, given a lack of conceptual understanding of the dynamics of knowledge capitalism. We argue that knowledge capitalism is consistent with the standardization of various forms of knowledge work and show how the restructuring of high-skilled work relates to corporate models of talent management. Rather than this leading to employer concerns over the underutilization of talent, it has led to a discourse of 'talent wars' premised on a belief that talent is in limited supply at the same time becoming more important to business success.

The second section examines how the development of talent within national education systems plays out in the global labour market. We draw on recent research on transnational companies (TNCs) with high-end operations in Singapore, given that inward investment from TNCs has played a major role in the country's economic development. It is also highly ranked for its business environment and competitiveness and regularly achieves high grades in educational league tables (e.g. PISA). Until recently it has embraced 'foreign talent' as a major driver of economic growth, encouraging TNCs to recruit the 'best' talent, regardless of whether local or foreign. But increasing political pressure on the Singapore government to reduce the numbers of highly skilled foreign workers has led to a further expansion of higher education in the belief that this will increase the supply of indigenous talent that can be used to replace foreign labour. However, this study points to a significant mismatch between the national education system and the global labour market. While the nurturing and management of national talent is used to justify unequal treatment and rewards within national systems of education, the 'talent' discourse is used by transnational companies in ways that are often inconsistent with national assumptions, given different priorities and perceptions of elite employability.

In conclusion, we examine the theoretical and policy implications of this analysis. The intersection of national and global fields of elite (re)production in education and the labour market highlight the complexities involved in theorizing the changing relationship between education, employment and the labour market. It also highlights the limitations of methodological nationalism and demonstrates the difficulty of developing national policies for fairer access to education and social mobility when elite reproduction (signified by being part of a global talent pool) may require more of the signifiers of talent than nation systems of education can provide, leading more prosperous families to augment, if not opt out of, the public education systems.

It also highlights issues of how TNCs are evaluating 'talented' candidates, and the quality of their educational experiences (including university status), developed in different national contexts. An intriguing aspect of this discussion in relation to Singapore is that in international tests it performs extremely well, but the education system is seen by many of the companies we interviewed to be failing to develop the managerial and professional talent that would lead them to recruit more Singaporeans, rather than recruit foreign graduates. In turn, it raises the issue of how a 'talented elite' are being (re)defined in respect to education, knowledge and performance.

Knowledge Economy Versus Knowledge Capitalism

Bell's (1973) classic account of the coming of post-industrial society attached great importance to scientific knowledge and the role of universities, as they acquired a 'quasi-monopoly in determining the future stratification of the society' (p. 410). Since its publication there has been flood of economics, management and policy literature, proclaiming the need for a larger proportion of the workforce to be up-skilled in preparation for the intellectual rigours of the modern workplace (Drucker 1993; Cortanda 1998). In economics, the focus has been on the role of skill-biased technological change driving up the demand for graduate labour (Acemoglu 2002; Goldin and Katz 2008). This intellectual *zeitgeist* around the importance of knowledge and technology to modern capitalism is reflected in policy narratives in which widening access to higher education constitutes a 'win–win' scenario in which increasing positions at the top of the occupational hierarchy offer greater equality of opportunity and higher rates of intergenerational social mobility.

In highlighting the dominant role of knowledge and skills, however, there has been a failure to understand the implications of what we call 'knowledge capitalism' rather than the 'knowledge economy', with different implications for the relationship between higher education and the future of knowledge work. Conflict over the 'capitalization' of knowledge by individuals, classes, companies and nations, is inherent to knowledge capitalism. Although, this is a far cry from the source of class conflict represented in Marxist accounts of the uprising of the urban proletariat, it does remain a conflict over capital, as the capitalization of human knowledge lives in a state of dynamic tension in which employers can frequently capitalize on labour more than labour can capitalize on their own education, talents, and abilities (Piketty 2014).

Moreover, if knowledge has become a key economic asset, the task of business is to capture and control as much of it as possible without undermining the organization's capacity to innovate and compete in global markets. Protagonists of the rise of the knowledge worker have neglected that 'the loss of control over production violates the profit-making objectives of a firm' (Holzl and Reinstaller 2003).

This reframing of how we understand the role of knowledge within today's economy takes on added significance given advances in global value chains (GVC), linked to rapid innovation in information and communication technologies (ICTs). These GVCs offer transnational companies new ways of sourcing high-skilled labour and of knowledge management, resulting in the (re)stratification of knowledge work, and changing the relationship between higher education and an increasingly global labour market.

The Creation of a Global Auction for High Skills

Transnational companies have played a decisive role in the construction of global labour markets. According to UNCTAD (2013), they now account for some 25 per cent of global employment. The role of TNCs has assumed added significance because their GVCs no longer divide the world between 'head' and 'body' nations (Rosecrance 1999). This essentially Western view foresaw a world in which the developed nations would do the thinking for the world at the same time that emerging economies could enter the global economy by competing on the basis of low-skilled and low-cost manufacturing. However, what we have witnessed is the rapid globalization of high skills through the expansion of higher education and rising quality standards around the world, offering TNCs with far greater choice of where to locate high-skilled operations, including emerging economies such as China, India and Brazil.

This is giving rise to a new international division of labour creating global skill webs that transcend national boundaries. It has also resulted in a global auction for high-skilled work contributing to the (re)stratification of knowledge work (Brown *et al.* 2011). The result is not a wholesale decline in the value of knowledge, because companies want the best ideas delivered at the lowest cost. The global auction is a dual auction. For a minority, their education, knowledge and skills will deliver rising living standards in a Sotheby's-style auction because they will continue to be highly valued by employers as high potential 'talent'. At the same time, many other college-educated graduates will struggle to achieve the trappings of a middle-class lifestyle, with shrinking pay-cheques, longer working hours, inferior retirement provision, reduced health care coverage, declining career prospects, and greater job insecurity. In this cut-price competition of brain-power, workers will be forced to do more for less. The same mixed fortunes are even more pronounced in those countries such as China and India, who may be thought to be winners in the global jobs auction.

The Role of New Technology in the (Re)stratification of Knowledge Work

These changes in the global division of labour also rest on advances in ICT that have enabled companies to align business practices across global operations. They are also contributing to the (re)stratification of knowledge work through the transformation of knowledge management within organizations. In much of the policy literature it is assumed that new technologies are skill-biased requiring an expansion of higher education in anticipation of a growing demand for employees given 'permission to think' for a living. However, advances in digital technologies are enabling companies to develop new business models that reduce the demand for knowledge-intensive roles (Brynjolfssen and McAfee 2014). The key to understanding the way IT technology restructures work is digital Taylorism (Brown *et al.* 2011).

If the twentieth century brought what can be described as mechanical Taylorism characterized by the Fordist production line, where the knowledge of craft workers was captured by management, codified and re-engineered in the shape of the moving assembly line, the twenty-first century is the age of digital Taylorism. This involves translating knowledge work into working knowledge through the extraction, codification and digitalization of knowledge into software prescripts that can be transmitted and manipulated by others regardless of location (ibid. p. 72). The ability of companies to leverage new technologies to globally align and coordinate business activities has also brought to the fore a different agenda involving the standardization of functions and jobs within the service sector, including an increasing proportion of technical, managerial and professional roles. The consequence is that the processes of digital Taylorism are rising up the value chain, reducing the anticipated demand for knowledge workers with high levels of workplace autonomy, discretion and opportunities for creative innovation.

The War for 'Talent' and the Rise of the 'Super' Manager

These trends in corporate restructuring, when combined with the rise of mass higher education, are transforming the relationship between higher education and the graduate labour market. The realities of knowledge capitalism require companies to introduce new ways of hiring, organizing and rewarding graduate employees. Companies may continue to use a bachelor's degree to screen candidates at an initial stage of the hiring process but there is no automatic premium attached to being a 'graduate' as distinct from other categories of less qualified employees.

Today, workplace inequalities in treatment and rewards are less likely to be based on a distinction between graduates and non-graduates and more on signifiers of talented performance (Brown 2013). The need to create a new model of employee stratification by singling-out talented performers also reflects a growth in income inequalities, where a larger proportion of corporate profits has been paid through the remuneration packages of senior managers and executives – the corporate elite. Thomas Piketty (2014) charts the rise of the super salary.[1] He shows how there has been a sharp increase in top decile salaries alongside returns to capital (e.g. dividends, rent) since the early 1990s. Indeed, the new class of super rich include those who have benefited most from remuneration packages awarded in executive pay deals. He also calculates that such trends are not restricted to the financial sector as 80 per cent of top earners are to be found in other industries.

Justifications for wage hikes at the top of the jobs pyramid rest on the idea that corporate competitive advantage depends on a talented elite – which remains in short supply despite the expansion of higher education. McKinsey & Co., a leading global consultancy company, has played a leading role in propagating the idea of a 'war for talent'. Michaels and his colleagues at McKinsey argue that reliance on talent increased dramatically over the last century:

> In the 1900s, only 17 percent of all jobs required knowledge workers; now over 60 percent do. More knowledge workers means it's important to get great talent, since the differential value created by the most talented knowledge workers is enormous.
>
> (Michaels *et al.* 2001, p. 3)

In other words, some knowledge workers are far more productive than others, and it is these talented workers that need to be identified, nurtured and rewarded as they have the knowledge and skills to drive the business.

It follows that when treating and rewarding 'talented' employees differently from other staff becomes normalized, special attention is given to the reproduction of the next generation of top performers. It is, after all, a form of personal flattery to current executives that they need to have equally 'talented' highly paid young executives to follow in their footsteps: a gilded form of succession planning.[2] Here the global ranking of universities has contributed to the talent management strategies of TNCs. League tables offer a comparative assessment of universities across global operations, along with rankings within national contexts where they have operations. This offers circumstantial evidence of where to search for global and domestic talent, given a widely held view that the best students go to the best universities because they have gained entry through competitive examination.

Hence, although academic performance is not necessarily a good indicator of managerial or employment potential, those who go to elite schools, colleges and universities are often seen to develop the cultural and social capital that companies are looking for in hiring high-potential candidates, leading to the reproduction of social inequalities as elite universities are over-represented by those from elite backgrounds and from Western universities, especially from the United States, that dominate world rankings. In the second section we highlight considerable ambiguity in the way talent is defined and understood (Brown and Hesketh, 2004). However, despite these difficulties all the TNCs we interviewed had introduced global talent management programmes that were applied to their recruitment and promotion criteria in Singapore.

The Singapore System of Talent Construction

How does the development of 'talent' within a national education system play out in the global labour market? Here we draw on recent research on transnational companies with high-end operations in Singapore, given that it is often viewed as a model of educational and economic development. It is one of the most open and prosperous economies in the world, embracing foreign direct investment (FDI) and attracting 'foreign talent' as a route to economic growth. It is highly ranked in global league tables on educational performance and economic competitiveness. A longstanding commitment to developing the skills of the workforce, as part of an active industrial strategy, has also been at the heart of Singapore's rise from an *entrepot* economy in the late 1960s (Sung, 2006). Beginning with low-skilled jobs in manufacturing, it has established itself as a major location for research, financial services and high-end manufacturing.

If Singapore maintains its position at the top end of the PISA league table and continues to expand its university system, it could plausibly be argued that it will result in a significant reduction in the numbers of 'foreign talent', an issue that has become of increasing political importance following concerns that Singaporeans are being locked out of senior and executive positions in foreign transnational companies.

In the era of Lee Kuan Yew, who believed in a natural aristocracy of talent, the education system was based on an elite model of 'meritocratic' competition, including the early selection and ranking of students. This commitment to early selection in a high-stakes competition for access to Singapore's leading universities has largely been maintained at the same time that it is committed to creating a high-skills workforce (Gopinathan 2012). Indeed, the more Singapore has become a high-cost location, engaged in a greater range of high-value activities, the more companies want 'talented' employees for which they are willing to pay a premium. Today, this emphasis on high-potential and high-performing employees is even more important given growing regional competition as countries including China, India, Malaysia and Thailand have expanded their capacity for undergraduate and postgraduate study.

As part of a study of global value chains and their implications for skills, knowledge and employment, we examined how TNCs viewed Singapore's workforce and whether its education system was developing the people who could replace foreign talent. We conducted 62 face-to-face interviews over a nine-month period in 2013, with managers and executives in leading TNCs in Singapore. The research focused on four sectors of strategic importance to Singapore: financial services, pharmaceuticals and medical technology, aerospace and electronics.[3] It was based on a purposive rather than a representative sample and the following discussion should be treated as indicative rather than conclusive.

It was widely acknowledged by participating companies that Singapore has been successful at creating jobs at the top end of value chains. This has resulted in more demand for 'talented' employees, capable of world-class performance. This cadre of employees defined as 'high potentials' or 'top performers' are not only defined by high-level technical skills or expertise. Many of the roles filled by those defined as 'talented' are believed to require a broad range of other skills and behavioural competences that cannot be captured in the distinction between low, intermediate and high-skilled work.

Despite its PISA ranking there was clear evidence of what companies viewed as a 'talent mismatch' or 'talent deficit'. Global companies, with high-end activities in Singapore, typically argue that they are only interested in recruiting the 'best of the best' regardless of what passport they hold. Singaporean candidates were expected to compete according to global standards of behavioural competence applied to all categories of high potential and senior appointments. This was highlighted by a company in the electronics sector, which was planning to recruit 20 people but only recruited 12 because 'we couldn't find another eight brilliant people'. The same senior HR manager explained, 'I would try and take in more Singaporeans ... but at the end of the day, I would only recruit on merit.'

However, the corporate executives we talked to, including heads of HR, have a major problem in defining what they mean by organizational 'talent'. In a previous study when asked how talent was defined in a major German corporation we were told 'there is no common understanding of what is talent ... I think that's a hype word now. Everybody is doing talent management not really kind of knowing what to do'.

If companies find it difficult to define talent (and its relationship to skill), the reality of a 'talent deficit' in Singapore is also difficult to assess. However, this study was focused on what corporate managers think, and regardless of the realities of the situation, their views have real consequences. It's clear that in most cases it is not a lack of technical knowledge (hard skills), as Singaporeans are often judged to be 'book smart' and 'numerically literate'. It's the assessment of their soft skills that seem to be at issue. But again the exact nature of soft skills is not always discernable from employer interviews as they tend to get bundled together under various labels including communication skills, problem-solving skills, emotional intelligence ('EQ'), resilience, self-assurance, 'the gift of the gab', 'well rounded', the 'wow' factor.

The problems companies have in defining talent and hiring people on a fair and rational basis are illustrated in the following discussion with a senior executive from a transnational bank. When asked how issues of talent are understood in the bank we were told:

> So the very first layer that we assess is really academic results. Yes, so really top students and then besides the academic it's how well rounded they are, what sort of activities do they take? We want to see demonstration of very early leadership. Well at least in … activities that they would have proven in terms of the interviews, we assess their thought leadership and how far do they think ahead …. One is their EQ, their social skills, the ability to connect in terms of talking about global activities in the financial world and just general understanding of things.

The 'wow' factor was also viewed as something that distinguished top graduates from others, but along with this they were required to be academically strong, to demonstrate emotional intelligence, to be quick learners and show team leadership qualities:

> I think for the local graduates, it would be a wow factor. If we can get someone who looks at a very global landscape and have that perspective, but for the local grads, definitely academically strong, very strong and besides that is EQ, good sense of EQ, ability to learn very quickly on the job and also if there's any team leadership qualities that they have exemplified, we pick that up.

But for this bank, being good is not good enough if you're a local graduate, as the real stars of the future are being educated elsewhere:

> Actually, quite frankly to a large extent, we will be very much guided by the Ivy League schools. So when we go out, if we pick somebody from a Brown University, from Georgetown and duh duh duh, we just assume that they are like higher grade. Quite frankly within this room and that's how we actually make the distinction of global graduate versus somebody from NTU (National Technological University) or SMU (Singapore Management University).

This response not only raises the issue of where and how 'true' talent is to be found and nurtured, but also the issue of cultural prejudice. This was commented on in two interviews, again with companies in the financial sector. The HR director of a North American bank thought that the qualities of Singaporeans were not always recognized:

> I would like to say something that there is a tendency for people like us to under-recognise the quality of Singaporean or local talent because we think

our world experiences, and I'm being very general here, but we think our world experiences are much broader. But in reality, my experience of my colleagues here in Singapore, and those who are really successful is, it's just a different perspective and so it's my job to learn the perspective, not to assume that my perspective is better as I think you hear a lot of this noise, but very, very bright, very capable, very intelligent, sharpest people going are Singaporeans, and they buy and sell quite nicely but we don't tend to recognize that as good.

In another interview with a female Singaporean head of HR at a different bank, we were told that there was a degree of prejudice in the way foreign managers within the company viewed Singaporean managers:

> There must be a push for … making management more and more aware that we really need to service local talent. I can tell you I'm not proud to say…I don't have a lot of local talents …. When the manager is a foreigner, they pick a foreigner to be a talent, not a local. So that is the problem …. Because they are so familiar with them. These are their colleagues from overseas.

Having said this there was also a recognition that foreigners have 'an edge' over 'locals' because 'I think it boils down to the gift of the gab … the NQ [networking quotient] … because when you network, you network with your bosses, you make your presence felt'.

The view that Singaporeans were less likely than other foreign managers and professionals to put themselves forward or to make their 'presence felt' – leading them to hit a 'glass ceiling' in the competition for senior managerial roles – was highlighted in other interviews, although most evident in the financial services sector. In aerospace, a major company reported a high degree of satisfaction in terms of the skills of Singaporean technicians. However, while Singapore was believed to be well placed in terms of skills for 'purely engineering and technology because it's always upgrading itself', there is a problem in respect to leadership skills. This regional CEO observed that in his company there are very few Singaporean leaders in their senior management team or in key positions around the world. Again, this was described as a 'cultural' issue:

> There's something about leadership and how we can develop that leadership. And it's probably cultural … and wanting to deal with a different culture. And probably learning to deal with a culture that's less polite, and more brash, and requires a bit more of "a front", definitely. And that definitely doesn't sit too well … [here, but] … I'm always really impressed with the leadership in Singapore. It's absolutely blessed with amazing leaders especially in the political front. But for some reason, and that is a company thing as well, we're not bringing that to the fore and developing in a global context.

The issue of putting oneself forward as a necessary condition for being recognized as managerial talent is a key issue in all sectors but in the pharmaceutical industry we were also told that although Singaporean students were 'book smart', students from the West had an advantage when it came to problem solving skills:

> [W]hat we find in Singapore are people which are numerically highly literate with people who can really handle complex data, integrate and analyse data. That you will find more regularly than anywhere else. Now what you also find in Singapore, people are incredibly "book smart", they are able to recite entire textbooks. What you find less is when you put them some problems and ask them to tackle that, that is where they struggle. That is where students from the West have the edge, they are thinking more in terms of "how I can solve the problem", "what do I need", "how can I break this down and tackle it?" But that is a generalization, but I mean there is a certain tendency of that.

These 'tendencies' can have a considerable impact in corporate hiring decisions that are based on global standards of behavioural competence. The identification of talent depends on an assessment of individual qualities judged through individual interviews, psychometric tests and group exercises. This process typically involves a self-assured performance, where ideas are presented and judged on what the candidate actually contributes. If they offer little in discussion, it is interpreted as having little to contribute. This is seen by some to put Singaporean candidates at a disadvantage. A stark example is again taken from a Singaporean senior manager in financial services: 'I think the main thing is, I'm sure you've heard it again and again, is their ability to be more vocal or more interactive, more communicative, that's really that stumbling block.' As a result:

> Every time when I go out to talk to the grads from NTU and so on and so forth versus some of the grads from the other universities, forget about the Ivy Leagues, just good universities from China or India, they lose out. They lose out in their ability to interact. If you put them together like a small roundtable discussion and then throw a subject, they're the quietest, they might have all the brains here and it just doesn't come out and you need to literally draw them out. It's very tiring and then so you have very little window of opportunity, they just lose out and they always fall behind.

The view that some students from China and India may present themselves as more employable than Singaporean candidates was often related to the importance of overseas experience, noted in a number of interviews that raise questions about the role of the education system. Many of those we interviewed where impressed with the country's performance in education league tables but thought that the system may not be geared towards creating a larger pool of employable talent:

> So I think there's a great amount of talent in Singapore up to a certain level … and I think it's starting to change. But I think education is geared

towards, 'this is the right way to do something', 'this is the defined way to do something', you learn how to do it and that's what you do. With those skills, that way of learning, they work really well up to a certain point in a person's career.'

This was also identified as an issue within higher education. In an interview with a global pharmaceutical company, an executive distinguished between 'somebody who can think a bit more how to tackle problems' required for more senior positions, as distinct from:

> an army executing it. I exaggerate it a little bit but that is how it looks to me in the Singaporean university when you walk around and it feels sometimes that you have kids standing at the bench ... being directed to take a certain direction.

For another senior manager, the concerns described in this section start at an early age due to an emphasis on performance and academic selection, making it difficult for the majority of students to develop a sense of self-assurance and self-worth:

> I think it starts with the educational system. I think it's more opportunity for them, for kids to talk. I mean like the first one to four years, we do so much to encourage them to walk, to do things and to be more confident. Give mummy that, go get it, it's okay, mummy's watching, go do that. They are developing and then suddenly they go into a class where they are really asked to, it's very sort of performance based, you get, I think it's the self worth, self-assuredness we don't develop enough of. It gets academic per- formance based at such a young age, even in kindergarten that if you're a slow starter, or not even slow, you're just a playful kid, you're not in that top tier anymore and then that's where you look at yourself like that and you go through the system, you just plough, plough, plough, through. Your self- worth, your self-assuredness is not there for you to say I'm different, this is how I think.

The issues identified here support a longstanding recognition of the need for educational reform, but as Singapore seeks further reforms of its education system it confronts increasing competition within Asia.

Conclusions

Several significant issues arise from this chapter. The first is that the competition for elite jobs has changed in fundamental ways. The twentieth century model, where there was a tightening bond between educational achievement and entry into higher-level bureaucratic careers, no longer holds. Educational achievement remains important but it is not enough to gain access to elite jobs. In part this is because the nature of knowledge work is itself being restructured, as have the selection criteria for entry into elite positions. The concept of 'talent' is a key signifier of elite employability, but although employers find it difficult to define, it is real in its consequences. Wrapped up in judgements about talent is a veritable mix of cultural assumptions about educational status, social class background, ethnicity and nationality as contributory factors in assessing elite employability.

However, our sociological understanding of issues of social mobility and justice, also need rethinking. We can no longer view the competition for elite work within the confines of national boundaries: that is to commit the error of methodological nationalism (Wimmer and Glick Schiller 2002). If there is a fundamental lack of correspondence between some national education systems and elite recruitment into TNCs, then we need to reconsider the way we understand issues of educational socialization and selection within national and global labour market contexts. In particular, this study points to changes in the role of educational credentials. Despite Singapore's success in the PISA studies, it appears to have a 'talent deficit' at least from the perspective of employers interviewed in this study. Ideas around corporate talent are being used by transnational companies in ways that are inconsistent with national assumptions about educational excellence, given different priorities and perceptions of elite employability. When we consider the comments of TNC executives, they see the intense system of testing and examinations in the Singapore system nurturing employees who are 'book smart' in contrast to the behaviour competences that signify global talent.

Arguably, this observation extends beyond Singapore. As education systems embrace the kind of league table competition exemplified by PISA, we observe a form of competitive isomorphism in which many countries interpret the PISA results as a need to engage in the repeated testing of students. The implication from the views of the executives in this study is that this is not the route to creating students that can occupy elite positions. Finally, in choosing to recruit 'talent' from globally elite universities, TNCs intensify the positional competition for educational credentials in national systems of higher education, intensifying the status competition between universities, students and families. Here, it may be that we are seeing an emerging correspondence between the stratification of knowledge work and the stratification of higher education sectors, as non-elite universities become more directive in their pedagogy and learning assessment (Naidoo and Jamieson 2006), thereby reducing student autonomy suited to demonstrator or technician roles within digital-Taylorized workplaces (Lauder and Brown 2011).

If what we are witnessing is the reconstruction of education in the light of changes in the global labour market, then we can also expect wealthier families to opt out of state systems of education. The alternative available to them is the old and new forms of private education within the international school system (Ball 2012), through which global elites can gain access for their children to elite universities (Brown 2000) and the cultural bonuses they can offer. In turn, such trends exacerbate the problems of seeking to construct a fair competition for credentials and jobs.

Acknowledgement

We would like to thank the Centre for Skills, Performance and Productivity, Institute of Education/Workforce Development Agency in Singapore for funding the research fieldwork for this chapter. We are especially indebted to Angeline Lim for her expert administrative support.

Notes

1 While it is important to recognize differences in corporate models, it is difficult to justify executive salaries in terms of individual productivity, as it is rather the exercise of market power by those in senior managerial and executive positions. However, it is not just their pre-tax salaries that have been constructed out of self-interest but also their post-tax incomes. It is quite clear that lobbying by the rich has enabled them to slant the tax on incomes and wealth in their favour (Hacker and Pierson 2010; Schlozman *et al.* 2012).

2 Thomas Piketty (2014) argues that the recent explosion in salaries of 'super managers' reflects 'the illusion of marginal productivity' (p. 330). It is an illusion for two reasons: the compensation packages for managers in comparable positions in different countries vary considerably, suggesting that there are other factors at work in the creation of high compensation packages. A further reason is that:

> Once we introduce the hypothesis of imperfect information into standard economics models ... the very notion of 'individual marginal productivity' becomes hard to define. In fact, it becomes close to pure ideological construct on the basis of which a justification for higher status can be elaborated.
>
> (Piketty 2014: 331)

The measurement of marginal productivity, he argues, is more applicable in standardized jobs but once job functions are seen as close to unique it is difficult to assess. Hence the productive contribution of talent is, in reality, difficult to assess. This is a view supported by Mats Alvesson (2001) who argues that,

> the ambiguity of knowledge and the work of knowledge-intensive companies means that "knowledge", "expertise" and "solving problems" to a large degree become matters of belief, impressions and negotiations of meaning. Institutionalized assumptions, expectations, reputations, images, etc. feature strongly in the perception of the products of knowledge-intensive organizations and workers.

In this context, it could be argued that what counts as 'talented' is the talent to engage effectively in impression management.

3 This also includes a small number of interviews with Singaporean policy-makers. It should be noted that a minority of the TNC executives interviewed were Singaporean of heritage but they were exceptions.

References

Acemoglu, D. (2002) 'Technical change, inequality and the labor market', *Journal of Economic Literature*, XL: 7–72.

Alvesson, M. (2001) 'Knowledge work: Ambiguity, image and identity', *Human Relations*, 54(7): 863–886.

Ball, S. (2012) *Global Education Inc.*, London: Routledge.

Bell, D. (1973) *The Coming of the Post-Industrial Society*, New York: Basic Books.

Brown, P. (2000) 'The globalization of positional competition', *Sociology*, 34(4): 633–653.

Brown, P. (2013) 'Education, opportunity and the prospects for social mobility', *British Journal of Sociology of Education*, 34(5/6): 678–700.

Brown, P. and Hesketh, A. (2004) *The Mismanagement of Talent: Employability and Jobs in the Knowledge Economy*, Oxford: Oxford University Press.

Brown, P., Lauder, H. and Ashton, D. (2011) *The Global Auction: The Broken Promises of Education, Jobs and Income*, New York: Oxford University Press.

Brynjolfsson, E. and McAfee, A. (2014) *The Second Machine Age*, New York: W.W. Norton & Co.

Cortanda, J. (ed.) (1998) *The Rise of the Knowledge Worker*, London: Routledge.

Drucker, P. (1993) *Post-Capitalist Society*, Oxford: Butterworth-Heinemann.

Goldin, C. and Katz, L. (2008) *The Race Between Education and Technology*, Cambridge, MA: Harvard University Press.

Gopinathan, S. (2012) *Education and the National State: The Selected Works of S. Gopinathan*, London: Routledge.

Hacker, J. and Pierson, P. (2010) *Winner-Take-All Politics: How Washington Made the Rich Richer and Turned Its Back on the Middle Class*, New York: Simon & Schuster.

Holzl, W. and Reinstaller, A. (2003) *The Babbage Principle After Evolutionary Economics*, MERIT-Infonomics Research Memorandum Series. At http://edocs.ub.unimaas.nl/loader/file.asp?id=812 (accessed 1 June 2014).

Lauder, H. and Brown, P. (2011) 'The standardisation of higher education and the global labour market', in King, R., Marginson, S. and Naidoo, R. (eds) *A Handbook of Globalization and Higher Education*, London: Edgar Allan.

Michaels, E., Handfield-Jones, H. and Axelrod, B. (2001) *The War for Talent*, New York: McKinsey & Co.

Naidoo, R. and Jamieson, I. (2006) 'Empowering participants or corroding learning?: Towards a research agenda on the impact of student consumerism in higher education', in Lauder, H., Brown, P., Dillabough, J-A. and Halsey, A.H. (eds) *Education, Globalization and Social Change*, Oxford: Oxford University Press, 875–884.

Piketty, T. (2014) *Capital in the Twenty-First Century*, Harvard, MA: The Belknap Press.

Rosecrance, R. (1999) *The Rise of the Virtual State: Wealth and Power in the Coming Century*, New York: Basic Books.

Schlozman, K., Verba, S. and Brady, H. (2012) *The Unheavenly Chorus: Unequal Political Voice and the Broken Promises of American Democracy*, Princeton, NJ: Princeton University Press.

Sung, J. (2006) *Explaining the Economic Success of Singapore: The Developmental Worker as the Missing Link*, Aldershot: Edward Elgar.

Wimmer, A. and Glick Schiller, N. (2002) 'Methodological nationalism and beyond: Nation-state building, migration and the social sciences', *Global Networks*, 2(4): 301–334.

Conclusion

Elites, Education and Identity
An Emerging Research Agenda

Stephen J. Ball

> Elite sociology is not a particular coherent realm of inquiry.
>
> (Khan 2012, p. 361)

In this conclusion to the *World Yearbook of Education 2015* my focus is primarily on what comes next. I look beyond the end of the book and attend to some of the absences, slippages and dissonances that are evident or implied across the collection as a whole and to some pointers and directions for future work. Taken together these chapters move us on; they are a useful and important resource for elite studies of education, but they also highlight in different ways what else needs to be done, empirically and conceptually and theoretically. As a whole the collection offers a sketchy outline map of global elites, a set of starting points, but it is a map on which there remain many blank spaces, and there is a lack of joining up between the points and a need for more signposts and a more widely shared language of description.

Educational researchers are, on the whole, not good at 'remembering elites'. For very good reasons the primary focus of educational research has always between 'downward', on social disadvantage, rather than what Aguiar and Schneider (2012) call 'Studying Up'. The downward focus has been organised around a commitment to greater equity and social justice but also has followed the predominant gaze of policy. Until recently, policy discourses and programmes have been primarily preoccupied with the management of the working class but the assertion of neoliberal rationalities has led to a much more explicit concern with the preoccupations of more advantaged social groups anxious about the social reproduction of those advantages. Educational researchers have been mainly concerned with explaining disadvantage rather than with understanding and explaining advantage, although again this has changed somewhat in the last twenty years with a spike of interest in 'studying across' to examine the 'middle classes' (Ball 2003; van Zanten 2003; Vincent and Ball 2006; Vincent et al. 2012; Savage and Butler 1995; Brantlinger 2003). Over and against this, Savage and Williams (2008, p. 2) refer to what they call the 'glaring invisibility of elites', although they do also acknowledge that there is a long history of 'traditional elite theory' (p. 3) within sociology (see Maxwell, Chapter 1 in this collection). And even in the relatively short time since their comments were written, there has been more remembering and greater visibility – in

234 Stephen J. Ball

no small part due to the efforts of Mike Savage and his colleagues at the ESRC Centre for Research on Socio-Cultural Change. The title of the Centre makes the point here – to a great extent the 'remembering' has been driven by, made necessary by, social and cultural, and economic changes to which research has needed to respond. Elites have been made more visible, through the attention of the media in particular, but also by virtue of increasing and glaring wealth and income inequalities (see Kahn's discussion of this in Chapter 4 of this collection), lifestyle flamboyance and public displays of excess. The OECD (2014) reports that the income of the richest 10 per cent of the population in OECD countries is about 10 times higher than that of the poorest 10 per cent.

At the same time the term *elites* itself has become increasingly widely taken up as a descriptor in a whole range of social fields, most obviously recently in relation to sport. Both in a technical and semantic sense the word elite is a problem for social researchers – what exactly do we mean when we use it? That problem is evident in a number of ways in this volume. There is clearly no single or agreed usage or definition of the term – the chapters slip between wealth (economic), lifestyle (culture), exclusivity (social) and power (political) as the basis for identifying elites. In part this signals the importance of differences in local and national histories and traditions – that is, elites are different and differently constituted and understood in different places – but it is also a matter of empirical focus and theoretical orientation. However, also empirically, despite the care and clarity brought to bear by Maxwell's chapter in this collection, there are inherent conceptual problems involved in distinguishing the elite from other relatively advantaged groups, and in identifying the commonalities and differences between elites of different kinds – cultural, political, economic and sporting. It is worth reiterating the disclaimer made by Savage and Williams in their introduction to the collection of papers *Remembering Elites*. They say:

> We are best off sidestepping the debate about precise definitions of elites, to pose the issue in a somewhat different way, where our attention is directed in the first instance, towards how the wealthy have prospered and regrouped in contemporary financialized capitalism.
>
> (Savage and Williams 2008, p. 9)

This particular formulation of the issue of how we know elites has a particular relevance to the concerns of this volume. Here we are concerned primarily with the contribution of education to access to and the social reproduction of elites and their exclusivity both locally and globally through education. That is, the relation of schooling and higher education to the formation and reformation of elite identities and as means of access to elite 'opportunities' in the labour market and elsewhere, although of course there remain routes into the elite which do not rely on educational credentials. That is, elite schools 'inculcate and certify economically valued cultured capital' (Kingston and Stanley Lewis 1990, p. xxviii). Students of elite schools gain their first rewards in the education system and later in high-status and highly paid occupations, 'where their social gifts are interpreted as natural ability and interest' (Kennedy and Power 2010); although as Kenway and colleagues point out in this collection (Chapter 11), attendance at an elite school does not always translate into elite roles in the economy – especially if you are female. However, again Kenway *et al.* (2013, p. 18) make the point that:

> Eliteness in schooling is an elusive quality but usually involves some degree of longevity, consistent and significant success in the end-of-school public exams and entry to prestigious universities and faculties; the on going production of influential alumni across government, industry, the professions and, in certain countries, the military ...

Education plays its part both in maintaining existing advantages and distinctions and creating new ones, which underlines the point that elites change. Savage and Williams argue, 'the continued rhetorical identification of elites with "old boy networks", the "establishment", or "inner circles" is deeply unhelpful' (2008, p. 15). Luna Glucksberg's research identifies two distinct branches of elites – those of the established elite and new elite groups.[1] An important cultural distinction is identified between these two groups – the new elite group she finds tend to be more preoccupied with material items and are acutely conscious of the potential for downward mobility, while the established elite tend to have less regard for material items and instead place greater value on high-culture pursuits and social connections. Elites are diverse and heterogeneous and elite research needs to be and to some extent has already become intersectional – that is, it needs to explore dynamically the interplay of wealth and power with gender, race and sexuality. Kenway and colleagues do this in consideration of the increasing ethnic diversity of elite girls' schools. Among others, Maxwell and Aggleton (2010) and Forbes and Lingard (2013) also attend specifically to the formation and reproduction of elite girls. These categories and their attendant identities play a role in shaping lived experience differently, even among elites. 'Eliteness' appears in a diverse array of constellations and spaces of practice.

However, latterly, Savage and others have made a sustained attempt to specify 'the elite' as a class more closely and have deployed traditional sociological sensibilities to establish a working definition. Wakeling and Savage, in this volume (Chapter 12) refer to the 'Elite social class':

> [U]sing the terms developed by Savage *et al.* (2013), where it is seen as the most privileged class according to its stocks of economic, cultural and social capital. It is marked by unusually high household income, residential property values and savings; by strong interests in highbrow cultural capital; and has extensive social networks, especially relative to other Elites. This is therefore a more sociological framing of an Elite class which is more restrictive (at about 6 per cent of the population) than competing conceptions of the service class.
>
> (p. 171)

In Lockwood's (1995) terms the issue is whether we can think about the elite as a 'well formed class', and as Maxwell points out he suggests that there are three key criteria to be addressed. First, that of structure: categories of class and the boundaries between them. Can we distinguish the elite from others? Second, that of culture: the specificity of classed lifestyles and behaviours. Third, that of identity: the sense that people have of themselves and others as of a class, the 'social structures in their heads' as Bourdieu puts it, and related to this their strategies of social reproduction. Despite the portability of Wakeling and Savage's attempt at a definition, and its relative looseness, questions still have to be asked about both its robustness in relation to Lockwood's criteria and its relevance to settings other than the UK.

Shamus Rahman Khan (2012) takes a rather different definitional tack; in his article he highlights some different and perhaps more broadly applicable characteristics of contemporary elites. He draws indirectly on Bourdieu to suggest that:

> Elites are those who have vastly disproportionate access to or control over a social resource. Such resources have transferable value – access or control in one arena of social life can result in advantages in other. This control over or access to transferable social resources provides elites with disproportionate social power and advantages; their decisions and actions influence and affect vast numbers of people. We can categorize elites by the kinds of resources they have access to or control. We might speak of "economic" elites, who have money or control over the economy; "political" elites, who influence or make decisions within the state; "social" elites, whose personal ties provide them with information and access to other resources; "cultural" elites, who influence social tastes, dispositions, and cultural development; and "knowledge" elites, who control or influence social knowledge.
>
> (p. 362)

Khan's (2011) book *Privilege: The Making of an Adolescent Elite at St. Paul's School*, examines a process of elite-making which is much more open in terms of gender and race than previously but which nonetheless contributes to the ramification of new inequalities. The young people in his study are very much at ease with their privileges and display a clear sense of entitlement and of the naturalness of difference, both in terms of material advantages and social fate. This is what Forbes and Lingard (2013) call *assuredness*. They do not question their privileges. Khan's research portrays an elite which is capable of crossing boundaries and participating in diverse cultural forms, they are aware of their status but also see the world as a playground of possibilities which can be enjoyed and leveraged.

The ghost of Bourdieu haunts the research on education and elites for obvious reasons, his tools (field, capital and habitus) are widely deployed, although not always well used. Many researchers fail to attend to Bourdieu's point that habitus, capitals and field are a method rather than a theory, and many others detach capitals from the other two, failing to recognise the fundamental interplay between the concepts in Bourdieu's thinking. Khan's study of St Paul's school points up the importance of working with all three together. However, working with Bourdieu has also perhaps led to an over concentration on the cultural dimensions of class at the expense of the material. That is, in the case of elites, or at least some sorts of elites, attention to the basic role played in their lifestyle, identity and social relations by the exclusive possibilities provided by great wealth. Elite schools cost a lot of money, as do elite universities. Khan attends to this in this collection (Chapter 4). Elite formation and reproduction rest heavily on the ability to pay; even elite sport is defined primarily these days in financial terms. We only occasionally glimpse the material aspects of the elite class in the pages of this collection but clearly elite membership and social identities are, as in the past, constructed in relation to certain forms of consumption – fashion labels, fast cars and exclusive eating. 'Taste' is not cheap.

Despite attempts at definitional clarity, deciding where elites begin and other social groups or classes end remains an intractable empirical problem. In some cases, in some locations, elite is elided with middle class or other categories and markers of distinction that make sense locally but make comparison across localities difficult. However, there is another side to the question of definition, as emphasised by the findings of Savage *et al.* (2013) and by Khan's chapter here. The elite class is increasingly dynamic in its structure. This raises new issues for research and Friedman's research for example (Friedman 2012) draws on Bourdieu's concept of habitus to explore the emotional experience of performing class. Friedman's study of movement into the elite classes addresses the emotional experience of mobility between classes and into the elite, and the symbolic baggage that people carry in the navigation of class. Kenway *et al.* (2013) take this a stage further by drawing attention to what they call 'the sale of affective flows' (p. 21). That is, the development of a market in elite 'desires' that links together anxiety, lifestyle and affect. Elite schools construct themselves as one such object of desire.

While, by definition, entry into the elite classes is highly skewed towards high-status groups, elites are now perhaps in some ways less impermeable than previous studies have indicated. This relative fluidity and dynamism poses certain perceived dangers for those in the elite class: there is a degree of churn or precarity, if that is the right word here, among even the top 1 per cent of income earners. Status and advantage have to be worked at and maintained, and done 'correctly' in order to ensure their preservation. Again, of course education plays a key role in this maintenance, and indeed 'access' work in families often focuses on choice of school and university as key sites in which economic assets can be translated into social and cultural assets which have high labour market and media value.

Clearly, as alluded to previously, in the introduction and the chapters in this collection, as in the field of elite research more generally, there are tensions between the conceptualisation of elites as a global as opposed to a local social formation. Perhaps indeed the chapters point up the need to distinguish elites spatially and within different circuits of social relations, social fields and educational settings. As in other areas of research, we have to be able to think both about structures and flows, and stability and mobility. Mobility also raises questions about identity or rather the extent of dis-identification by elite groups from local and national senses of 'belonging'. These might come together in a form of what Savage *et al.* (2005) call 'elective belonging' as against a 'diasporic identity'. That is to say, some elite fractions are involved in 'transnational practices' (Sklair 1991) and move between 'global cities' and might be understood as what Bauman (1991) calls *globals*, who he argues are literally 'not of this world'. Bauman also suggests that globals lead a precarious, liquid life and in this globalised, mobile and postmodern world the category of home is problematised. Drawing on Heller's essay on home (Heller, 1995), Bauman highlights the differences between those who are locally tied, who may experience their home as a prison, and those (the globally mobile) 'who can dissolve whatever constraints a real home may impose' (Bauman 1998, p. 91). It follows from this that these are people 'for whom the nation works less well as a source of resonance' (Hannerz 1996, p. 88) and for whom nation is replaced by transnational ties and 'such ties may entail a kind and a degree of tuning out, a weakened personal involvement with the nation and the national culture' (p. 89).

Over and against this, mobile elites, although continually travelling, find for themselves or build isolated and exclusionary private spaces – gated communities, exclusive hotels and restaurants, private islands. Elliott and Lemert (2006) write about 'global spaces, individualist lives' and a 'new age of individualism' within which 'people desperately search for self-fulfillment and try to minimise as much as possible inter-personal obstacles to the attainment of their egocentric designs' (p. 3) in the 'polished cities of the west', as they call them.

Elliott and Lemert go onto suggest that 'the conflict between globalisation and identity has led to the kind of "hollowing out" of people's emotional intimacies' (p. 7) and a sense of experience on the edge of 'a disappearance of context' (p. 13). In less grandiose terms, Savage *et al.* (2005) write about ambivalance, cosmopolitanism, diaspora and global reflexivity but also reassert the role of localities 'as sites chosen by particular social groups wishing to announce their identities' (p. 207). They also argue that 'the precise form and nature of global connections depends strongly on the precise field of practice that is being studied' (p. 207).

All of this suggests three imperatives for further research: the need, as highlighted already, for attention to differences within and between elites, especially differences in terms of localism as against cosmopolitanism and the different roles of education in identity formation in relation to these different orientations; the need to explore the complex relationships between the global education market and elite formation, differentiation and reproduction; and the need for research studies which 'get close' to the 'work' of social reproduction and the performance of eliteness within families and educational institutions. 'Studying up' in these ways can contribute to our understanding of growing inequality, economic polarisation and global social change. We also need to think about elites and elite formation and reproduction in relation to education policy, and the interests of state. As discussed in the introduction and evident in some of the chapters in this book, in China, France and Germany, in different ways, elite formation is in a sense a state project related to 'other' kinds of political interests – international competitiveness in the cases of China and Germany, political management and cultural leadership in the case of France.

What all of this indicates then is the need to bring what Beck (2006) calls a 'cosmopolitan sociology', to bear upon the issue of elites and education. This is, he says, a necessary condition for grasping the dynamics of an increasingly cosmopolitan reality. Over and against this, he argues that 'national sociology' is beset by 'a failure to recognize – let alone research – the extent to which existing transnational modes of living, transmigrants, global elites, supranational organizations and dynamics determine the relations within and between nation-state repositories of power' (Beck 2007). 'National sociology' is beset by the fallacy of what he calls '*Methodological nationalism*', that is, 'the standpoint of social scientific observers who implicitly or explicitly undertake research using concepts and categories associated with the nation'. That is very pertinent in relation to the definition of and research on elites. He goes on to argue: that this produces 'the zombie science' of the national that thinks and researches in the categories of international trade, international dialogue, national sovereignty, national communities, the 'nation-state' and so forth, a 'science of the unreal'. According to Beck (2007) 'a cosmopolitan sociology must develop conceptual and methodological resources for understanding the world that is undergoing a cosmopolitan transformation'. Research on the education of elites would have a substantive contribution to make to our understanding of the relationships between choice and social advantage but it would also contribute to the development of the conceptual and methodological resources for which Beck (2007) calls. *The World Yearbook of Education* is a very appropriate vehicle to begin to undertake such work.

Note

1   Her research explores elite spaces in and around London in order to account for the constitution, experiences and practices of inhabitants/members, and their interaction with and impact upon the urban space and communities within it. She draws on their desire to 'educate' her. She is currently working on 'Life in the Alpha Territory', an ESRC funded project on the changing nature of some of London elite neighbourhoods.

References

Aguiar, L. L. M. and Schneider, C. J. (2012) *Researching Amongst Elites: Challenges and Opportunities in Studying Up*, Farnham: Ashgate.

Ball, S. J. (2003) *Class Strategies and the Education Market: The Middle class and Social Advantage*, London: RoutledgeFalmer.

Bauman, Z. (1991) *Modernity and Ambivalence*, Oxford: Polity Press.

Bauman, Z. (1998) *Work Consumerism and the New Poor*, Buckingham: Open University Press.

Beck, U. (2006) *Cosmopolitan Vision*, Cambridge: Polity Press.

Beck, U. (2007) 'Cosmopolitanism', available at http://www.ulrichbeck.net-build.net/index.php?page=cosmopolitan

Brantlinger, E. (2003) *Dividing Classes: How the Middle Class Negotiates and Rationalises School Choice*, New York: RoutledgeFalmer.

Elliott, A. and Lemert, C. (2006) *The New Individualism: The Emotional Costs of Globalisation*, London: Routledge.

Forbes, J. and Lingard, B. (2013) 'Elite school capitals and girls' schooling: Understanding the (re)production of privilege through a habitus of "assuredness"', in C. Maxwell and P. Aggleton (eds) *Privilege, Agency and Affect*, Basingstoke: Palgrave.

Friedman, S. (2012) 'Cultural omnivores or culturally homeless? Exploring the shifting cultural identities of the upwardly mobile', *Poetics* 40(5): 467–489.

Hannerz, U. (1996) *Transnational Connections*, London: Routledge.

Heller, (1995) 'Where are we at home?', *Thesis Eleven* 41: 1–18.

Khan, S. R. (2011) *Privilege: The Making of an Adolescent Elite at St. Paul's School (Princeton Studies in Cultural Sociology)*, Princeton, NJ: Princeton University Press.

Khan, S. R. (2012) 'The sociology of elites', *Annual Review of Sociology* 38: 361–377.

Kennedy, M. and Power, M. J. (2010) '"The smokescreen of meritocracy": Elite education in Ireland and the reproduction of class privilege', *Journal for Critical Education Policy Studies* 8(2): 223–248.

Kenway, J., Fahey, J. and Koh, A. (2013) 'The libidinal economy of the globalising elite school market', in C. Maxwell and P. Aggleton (eds) *Privilege, Agency and Affect: Understanding the Production and Effects of Action*, Basingstoke: Palgrave.

Kingston, P. and Stanley Lewis, L. (1990) *The High Status Track: Studies of Elite Schools and Stratification*, New York: SUNY Press.

Lockwood, D. (1995) 'Marking out the middle class(es)', in T. Butler and M. Savage (eds) *Social Change and the Middle Classes*, London: UCL Press.

Maxwell, C. and Aggleton, P. (2010) 'The bubble of privilege: Young privately educated women talk about social class', *British Journal of Sociology of Education* 31(1): 3–15.

OECD (2014) *All on Board: Making Inclusive Growth Happen*, available at http://www.oecd.org/inclusive-growth/reports/All-on-Board-Making-Inclusive-Growth-Happen.pdf

Savage, M. and Butler, T. (1995) 'Assets and the middle classes in contemporary Britain', in T. Butler and M. Savage (eds) *Social Change and the Middle Classes*, London: UCL Press.

Savage, M. and Williams, K. (eds) (2008) *Remembering Elites*, Oxford: Blackwell.

Savage, M, Bagnall, G. and Longhurst, B. (2005) *Globalization and Belonging*, London: Sage.

Savage, M., Devine, F., Cunningham, N., Taylor, M., Li, Y., Hjellbrekke, J., Le Roux, B., Friedman, S. and Miles, A. (2013) 'A new model of social class? Findings from the BBC's Great British Class Survey Experiment', *Sociology* 47(2): 219–250.

Sklair, L. (2001) *The Transnational Capitalist Class*, Oxford: Blackwell.

van Zanten, A. (2003) 'Middle-class parents and social mix in French urban schools: reproduction and transformation of class relations in education', *International Studies in Sociology of Education* 13(2): 107–124.

Vincent, C. and Ball, S. J. (2006) *Childcare, Choice and Class Practices: Middle-Class Parents and Their Children*, London: Routledge.

Vincent, C., Rollock, N., Ball, S. and Gillborn, D. (2012) 'Being strategic, being watchful, being determined: Black middle-class parents and schooling', *British Journal of Sociology of Education* 33(3): 337–353.

Index

Note: *italic* page numbers indicate tables; **bold** indicate figures.

211 Project 118–19, 122; locations **120**
985 Project 119, 122; locations **120**

'A1 girls' *see* girls' education
Aarseth, H. 21
Abitur 82, 84, 85, 87
abjection 162–4
academic degrees, and employment 191–3
academic merit, and culture 5
academic requirements 7
access to higher education: adults 194–5;
   Brazil 71, 72; China 115–16; Germany
   82–3, 91; as 'win–win' scenario 219
Acharya, A. 126
activating resources 30–3
administrative elites: ambition 210–12;
   competences 205–12; confidence
   206–7; context and overview 201;
   educational routes, Britain 203–4;
   educational routes, France 201–3;
   educational routes, Norway 204–5;
   intelligence 205–6; meritocracy 212–14;
   rapidity 209–10; rhetorical skills 208–9;
   summary and conclusions 214; *see also*
   British elite workers; France
admission procedures 46; *Grandes Écoles*
   140–1; universities 66–8, 73–4
advantage, social and educational 180
affirmative action, Brazil 74–5
Aggleton, P. 20
Alesina, A. 185
alumni: networks 50–1; privileges 4
American exception 190, 196
Appadurai, A. 131
Argentina: alumni networks 50–1; Catholic
   vs. secular schooling 47; Colegio Nacional
   de Buenos Aires (CNBA) 47–51;
   context and overview 43; elite fragments

44–5; familiar environments 45–6; family
support 51; history of research 43–5;
institutional networks 44; kinship groups
45–6; lack of elite production system 44;
national schools 47–8; peer relationships
49–50; pupil selection 46; schooling and
family networks 46–7; social relationships
50; summary and conclusions 51–2;
traditional schools 45–7
Arnold, T. 102
Asia Rising: context and overview 126–7;
   India Shining 129; rise of Asia 127–9;
   summary and conclusions 137; *see also*
   Ripon College
Asian Century 128
assuredness 236
Attewell, P. 86–7
autonomy, children's 36–8

Ball, S.J. 23
Bauman, Z. 159, 238
Beale, Dorothea 153
Beck, U. 239
Bell, D. 218
belonging 46
Bender, W. 66
beneficence 101–2
Berman, E. 68
Bernstein, B. 114–15
Bhagwati, J. 130–1
big door 49
Big Society 104
bilingual schools 78, 85–6
Black movement 74
Bond, M. 20
book: focus 234; looking forward 233;
   overviews 9, 13–14, 57–8, 109–10, 167–8
Botana, N. 49

Bourdieu, P. 3, 5, 18, 21, 31, 33, 46, 49, 51–2, 114, 115, 140, 141, 149, 169, 173, 181, 236–7
Brazil: access to higher education 71, 72; admission procedures 73–4; affirmative action 74–5; college applications 73; context and overview 71–2; diversification of elites 72; enrollment 75; internationalization 77–8; private universities 72, 73, 75, 76; São Paulo 75–8; schools 73; segmentation 72–3, 75–8; social inclusion 73–5; summary and conclusions 78–9
Bretton Woods 112
Brewis, G. 104
Brezis, E.S. 18–19
Brint, S. 190–1
Britain, universities 213
British colonialism 129–30
British education system 172
British elite workers: advantage 180; context and overview 169–70; data and analysis 171; elite membership by social/ educational pathway **181**; entry to elite positions 172–6; membership of Elite/ NS-SEC1 classes by category of school **178**; social class origin to destination 178–80, **179**; summary and conclusions 181–2; universities and social advantage 170–1; university pathways 180–1; *see also* administrative elites
Brosius, C. 136
building on investment 33–6
Buss, Frances Mary 153

Caletrío, J. 23–4
capitals 17, 21
Carroll, W.K. 136
CEOs, educational trajectories 193–4
Charle, C. 49
Cheltenham Ladies' College 153
Chiang, T.H. 111, 112, 113, 115
child-rearing, and social class 114–15
children, parents' representations of 37
China: 211 Project 118–19, 122; 985 Project 119, 122; access to higher education 115–16; context and overview 111–12; economic development **118**; economic growth 117; Education Action Project 112; financial resource inequality 121–2; globalization 116–18; influencing elite universities 118–20; international competitiveness 112–13; modernization 116–17; national and local universities 121–2; Open Door

Policy 116; Special Economic Zones 117; students' expenditure **121**; summary and conclusions 122–3; top universities and economic regions 121; wealth 117–18
Chinese University Evaluation Report 119
choice of school 5–6, 33
choices, curricular 34–5
Chowdhury, K. 136
circulation of elites 18–19
civic engagement 144
Clark, B. 142
class boundaries, and social mobility 186–8
class formation 22; India 135–7; *see also* social class
classless society 186
co-curricular activities 104
codes, social mobility 188
Colegio Nacional de Buenos Aires (CNBA) 47–51
Coleman, T. 96–7, 105
Collaborative Research Centres (SFBs) 88–9
collective merit 144
collective strategies 51
college applications, Brazil 73
Collins, D. 96–7, 105
community colleges (US) 190–1
community engagement 7, 95; beneficence 101–2; explanations of 101–4; *Grandes Écoles* 144; political imperatives 103; schools' depictions of 98–100; summary and conclusions 105; themes 100–1; volunteering 101, 104
community partnerships 101
community service 101–2
competition, for elite jobs 227–8
concerted cultivation 32
consumption, Asia 127–8
contest mobility 186, 188–96
context, social 60
cooling out 142–4
cosmopolitan sociology 239
cosmopolitanism 8
cultivated man 190
cultural activities 32–3
cultural assets 5
cultural capital 5, 31–2, 35, 173, *175*, 234
cultural openness 7–8
cultural reproduction 114–15, 116
cultural understandings 65
culture: and academic merit 5; and leadership 225
curricular choices 34–5

Dahl, R.A. 18
Darchy-Koechlin, B. 142, 146

Das, G. 131
de-unionization 63
decision making, political and economic 16
degrees, value of 71
Deng Xiaoping 116–17, 128
deserving elites 39
deservingness 67
differentiation 21
digital Taylorism 220
distinction, process of 21
distinctiveness, features of 6–7
Dogan, M. 18–19, 23
Domhoff, G.W. 18
dominant agents 17, 21
Donner, H. 132
Draelants, H. 146
Dreze, J. 136
Dudouet, F.X. 194
Duru Bellat, M. 50

École nationale d'administration (ENA)
    201, 202–3
École Polytechnique 145
economic capital 173, *174*
economic decision making 16
economic development, China **118**
economic globalization 112–13
economic growth: Asia 127; China 117
economic inequality 114–15
economic resources 30–1, 35
education: British system 172;
    participation, Brazil 72
education choices 5–6
education systems: composition of 16;
    differentiation 191; professionalizing
    191; and recruitment into TNCs 228;
    and social mobility 189–91
educational apartheid 103
educational disadvantage, poverty 67
educational focus 7
educational inequalities, perpetuating 39
educational participation, Asia 127
educational strategies, overview 13–14
elite education, aims and effects 20
elite fractions 6, 22, 51–2, 237–8
elite fragments 44–5
elite girls 235; *see also* girls' education
elite institutions, access for non-elites 4
elite recruitment 173
elite schools, defining 59–60
elite status, claiming 51–2
elite studies: areas of further research 22–3;
    circulation of elites 18–19; context and
    overview 15; defining elites 16–18, 21,
    23–4, 171; elites as social class 21–3;

history 15–16; preparing for power
    19–21, 24; researching elites 16–18;
    summary and conclusions 23–4
elite trajectories, production of 19–20
elite workers, overview 167–8
eliteness 235
elites: boundaries 237; defining 16–18,
    21, 23–4, 171, 235–6; dynamism 237;
    established and new 235; nature of 13;
    research neglect 233; as social class 235–6;
    as social problem 15–16; use of term 234
Ellersgaard, C.H. 19, 23
Elliott, A. 238
embodied qualities 8
emerging economies 21
emotional capital 32
employment, and academic degrees 191–3
énarchie 202
enculturation 20
England 19; beneficence 101–2; community
    engagement themes 100–1; community
    partnerships 101; context and overview
    95; explanations of community
    engagement 101–4; political imperatives
    103; research methods 97–8; schools'
    depictions of engagement 98–100;
    spatial practices 95–7; summary and
    conclusions 105; volunteering 101, 104
entrance examinations 141–2, 143–4, 145
equilibrium 18
equity, and globalization 114–15
Erikson, R. 185
ESRC Centre for Research on Socio-
    Cultural Change 234
ethnicity 22–3
Eton College 20
Eurocurrency Market 112
excellence, conceptions of 7
excellence initiative, Germany 89–90
exceptionalism 185
external differentiation/vocational
    orientation **192**
externalization 37–8

Fachhochschulen (FH) 87–8
failure, fear of 159–60, 164
familiar environments, Argentina 45–6
families: enculturation 20; ideology 186–7;
    practices within 22
families study: autonomy 36–8; building
    on investment 33–6; context and
    overview 29–30; cultural activities 32–3;
    cultural capital 31–2; deserving elites
    39; economic resources 30; intimacy
    32; parental cultivation 35; parental

investment 36–7; parental strategies 36–8; participant families 30; research basis 29–30; resource activation 30–3; school choice 33; sources of influence 38; summary and conclusions 38–40
family strategies 13–14
family support 51
faux feminism 158–9, 164
fear of failure 164
femininity 156
feminist scholarship 155
Fernandes, L. 136
field of power 17
financialization, effects of 17
Flemmen, M. 19
Fordism 220
Foucault, M. 111
Four Modernizations 117
fragmentation 44–5
France 19; criticisms of 140–1; educational system 189–91; universities 213; *see also* administrative elites; families study; *Grandes Écoles*; social mobility
free competition 44
Friedman, T. 126
functional evolution 112
funding: China 121–2; Germany 88–9

Gandhi, R. 128
Ganguly-Scrase, R. 136
gender 22–3
gender disadvantage 157
gendered expectations 157–8
General Agreement on Tariffs and Trade (GATT) 112
geographical positioning 95
geographical segregation 30
geography, of income distribution 64
German Research Foundation (DFG) 88–9
Germany: access to higher education 82–3; allocation of university places 87–8; bilingual schools 85–6; context and overview 82–3; excellence initiative 89–90; *Fachhochschulen* (FH) 87–8; *Gymnasiums* 83–7; overcrowding 87–8; privatization 84, 85–6; research 88–9; selectivity in access 91; stratificatory differentiation 87–91; study programmes 90–1; summary and conclusions 91–2
GfK survey 173, 177
Giddens, A. 201
gifted pupils 85
Gini coefficient 64
girls' education: casualties 160; context and overview 153–4; expectations

155–7; feminist scholarship 155; gender disadvantage 157; gendered expectations 157–8; geography and race 161–4; influence 153–4; internationalization 160–4; mobility 160–4; preparation for life 156, 158; pressure to succeed 159–60, 164; research methods 154–5; social class 161, 164; stereotypes 161–3; summary and conclusions 164; template 153; trophy daughters 159–60; *see also* women
Glaeser, E. 185
global labour market: context and overview 217–18; educational systems and recruitment 228; high skills auction 219–20; knowledge economy vs. knowledge capitalism 218–22; research methods 223; summary and conclusions 227–8; super managers 220–2; talent construction, Singapore 222–7; technology and restratification 220–1; war for talent 220–2
globalization: China 116–18; and class formation 135–7; educational responses 133–5; effects of 17; and equity 114–15; and identity 238; India 130–1; international competitiveness 112–13; overview 109–10; preparation of girls 156
globals 238
Goldthorpe, J.H. 185
Good Neighbours 103
governing elites 18
graduate orientations 6
Gramsci, A. 16, 114
Grandes Écoles 190, 191, 195; changing definitions of merit 142–5; civic engagement 144; context and overview 140; entrance examination 141–2, 143–4, 145; entrance rituals 142–3; hierarchies 145; international students 145–8, 149–50; parallel admission 146–7; research methods 141; student perceptions of merit 141–2; student selection 140–2; student self image 144–5; student status 145–50; summary and conclusions 148–9; *see also* France
Great British Class Survey (GBCS) 169, 171–81
great divergence 62
great government 113
Guimarães, A.S.A. 74
Gymnasiums 83–7

habitus 114, 237
Haller, M. 192
Halperín Donghi, T. 43

Halsey, A.H. 170, 177
Hamid, M. 126
hegemony 16
high-status track 34
Holdsworth, C. 104
Holloway, S. 96
horizontal circulation 18–19
Howard, A. 102
Hua Ze 126
human capital, and international
    competitiveness 113
Hunter, F. 18
Hutchings, K. 156, 158

IDEALS of learning 134
identity, and globalization 238
identity construction 6–8
income distribution 60–4
income growth 62–3; Asia 127
income inequality 63, 111, 114
Independent–State School Partnership
    scheme 103
India: British colonialism 129–30; class
    formation 135–7; context and overview
    126–7; economic focus 130; educational
    responses to globalization 133–5; focus
    groups 132–3; global aspirations 131–3;
    globalization 130–1; middle class 131, 132;
    modernization 130; neoliberalism 131;
    Ripon College 129–31; summary and
    conclusions 137
India Shining 129
indirect rule, India 130
individual self-cultivation 68–9
individualism 238
inequality 114–15; concern for, US 196;
    legitimation crisis 217; responsibility
    for 69; universities 170; in workplace 221
inequality hypothesis 181
institutional cultural capital 31–2
institutions: roles of 20, 22; size of 6–7
intergenerational transmission 49
intergenerational transmission of status 23
internal rationality 112
internal social capital 33
International Baccalaureate (IB) 77
international capital 78
international competitiveness 112–13
international division of labour 219–20
International General Certificate of
    Secondary Education (IGCSE) 134–5
international schools: Brazil 77; Germany
    85–6
international students, *Grandes Écoles*
    145–8, 149–50

internationalism 95
internationalization 77–8; girls' education
    160–4; overview 109–10; Ripon College
    134–5
intragenerational mobility 191–3
Ivy League 65–6, 193

Jacques, M. 126
Jöns, H. 96

Karabel, J. 190–1
Kennedy, M. 234–5
Keqiang Li 112
Keynes, J.M. 113
Khan, S.R. 7, 17, 21, 64, 236–7
Kingston, P. 234
kinship groups, Argentina 45–6
knowledge capitalism 217
knowledge, economic role 219
knowledge economy, vs. knowledge
    capitalism 218–22
knowledge work 217, 220–1
Kristeva, J. 162
Krugman, P. 62

Lareau, A. 29, 32, 34–5
leadership, and culture 225
legislation, Brazil 74
legitimacy 7, 102, 113, 140
legitimation crisis 217
Lemann, N. 66
Lemert, C. 238
LeRoux, B. 17
liberal education 203–4, 213
liberalism 68
life expectancy, Asia 127
limited circle 18–19
literacy, Asia 127
Liu, Y.S. 116
local engagement *see* community
    engagement
location, importance of 30
Lockwood, D. 22, 236
Long Gilded Age 62
Luhmann, N. 112
lycées 190

managerialism 111
Marques, A.C. 50
marriage 20
Massey, D. 137
Maxwell, C. 20
Mayo, A.J. 193
McCall, L. 185, 196
McKinsey and Company 128, 130, 221

meaning, of schooling 51
merit: changing definitions of 142–5; collective 144
meritocracy 5, 19, 40, 49, 66–7, 69, 140, 142; administrative elites 212–14; Singapore 222
meritocratic contest 33
meritocratic mobility 36
Michaels, E. 221
middle-class America 62
middle class, India 131, 132
Mills, C.W. 15–16, 18
Misra, P. 126
Mitre, B. 48
mobility 62, 237–8; contest vs. sponsored 186; girls' education 160–4; São Paulo 75–8
modernization: China 116–17; India 130
moral superiority 46–7
Mosca, G. 15
motivation letters 35, 37–8
Multiple Correspondence Analysis 17
muscular Christianity 102

narratives 23
National Examination of High-School Education (ENEM) 77
national sociology 239
national systems, and elite formation 19
neoliberalism 111, 113; faux feminism 159; India 130–1
nepotism 66
networks 20; Argentina 46–7, 50–1; and power 22
new economic elite 21
new elites 20–1
new gilded age 64
Newman, J.H. 203–4, 213
non-elite students, in elite establishments 21
non-elites, access for 4
non-governing elites 18
normative dimensions 22
North London Collegiate School for Ladies 153
Norway 19, 21; universities 213–14; *see also* administrative elites
Norwood, C. 101–2
NS-SEC schema 171

OECD 113
Offe, C. 112
open days 35–6
Open Door Policy 117
openness 8

parental ambition 159–60
parental cultivation 35
parental investment 36–7
parental strategies 13, 29–30, 36–9, 51, 78, 86–7, 115
parentocracy 87
parents: representations of children 37; validation of values 186
Pareto, V. 15, 16, 18
Paris *see* families study
participation, Brazil 72
participation policies 4–5
partnerships 103
Passeron, J.C. 5, 114, 140
peer relationships 49–50
perfectionism 159–60
Piketty, T. 60, 61, 65, 219, 221
pillarization 86, 92
plural differentiation, Germany 86–7
political decision making 16
political imperatives 103
political rationalities, redefining 111
population growth, Asia 127
postcolonial confidence 126–7
poverty 60; Asia 127; educational disadvantage 67
power: measuring 17–18; nature of 22; Pareto's view 15; preparation for 19–21, 24; as resource 4–6; and social culture 114; visibility 23–4; as zero sum game 16
power elites 15–16
Power, M.J. 234–5
power relations 22
practices 24
preparatory classes, pupil selection 34–5
prestige 60
pretenders 30
private tuition 5
privatization, Germany 84, 85–6
privilege: elements of 43; as resource 4–6
Privilege: The Making of an Adolescent Elite at St. Paul's School 236
problem solving 226
processes of reproduction 20–1
pupil selection: Argentina 46; preparatory classes, France 34–5
pupil volunteering 101

quotas, Brazil 74

Rampell, C. 62
rational capital 115
Reay, D. 32
reference 112
relational dimensions 22

Remembering Elites 234
rentiers 18
reproduction processes 20–1
reproduction theory 180, 181; *see also*
    British elite workers
research agenda 233, 238–9
research, Germany 88–9
researching elites 16–18, 23, 24
residential segregation 59
resource activation 30–3
resource manipulation 5
resources, access and control 60
Ripon College 129–31; class formation
    135–7; class relations 133; educational
    responses to globalization 133–5; focus
    groups 132–3; ideological work 136;
    International General Certificate of
    Secondary Education (IGCSE) 134–5;
    internationalization 134–5; Principal
    134; reforms 131–3; self image 134;
    student and parent aspirations 131–3;
    summary and conclusions 137
rise of Asia 127–9
rite of consecration 141
Robinson, B. 136
Rouanet, H. 17
Round Square (RS) 134
Russell Group 172, 173; cultural and
    economic capital *174–5*

Saez, E. 61
São Paulo 75–8
Savage, M. 171, 173, 181, 234, 235, 236, 238
school choice 5–6, 33
school credentials, value of 71
schooling, meaning of 51
schools: admission procedures 46;
    bilingual 78; Brazil 73; changes in, US
    65–8; Germany 82–3; *Gymnasiums*
    83–7; membership of Elite/NS-SEC1
    classes by category of school **178**; as
    purified spaces 159; religious and
    secular 47; in social context 96–7; types
    attended and elite membership 177; *see
    also* universities
Sciences Po 20, 143, 144, 146, 202
Scott, J. 16, 21
Scrase, T. 136
second chances 194–5
segmentation, Brazil 72–3, 75–8
segregated democratization 44–5
segregation, Germany 85–7
selectivity in access, France 190
self-assurance 227
self-identity 6–8

self-worth 227
Sen, A. 136
seniority 46
sense of entitlement 33
Singapore 19, 217–18; local talent 224–7;
    regional competition 222; research
    methods 223; summary and conclusions
    227–8; talent construction 222–7
size, of institutions 6–7
skill-based technologies 63
Sklair, L. 135–7, 238
social and political theory 15
social capital, acquisition and possession 51
social class: cultural reproduction 114–15,
    116; elites as 21–3; girls' education 161,
    164; origin to destination 178–80, **179**;
    see also class formation
social class theory 22, 23
social closure 71, 140
social context 60
social inclusion, Brazil 73–5
social justice 102
social mobility 18, 177; academic systems
    189–91; access to elite 193–4; and class
    boundaries 186–8; codes 188; contest
    and sponsored mobility 188–96; context
    and overview 185–6; credentials and
    jobs 191–3; distribution of the directors
    of CAC 40 by type of training *194*;
    external differentiation/vocational
    orientation **192**; intragenerational
    191–3; second chances 194–5; success
    narratives, France 187–8; success
    narratives, US 186–7; summary and
    conclusions 195; Turner's thesis 188–9
social networks 20
social openness 8
social relationships, Argentina 50
social requirements 7
social selectivity: Brazil 76; Germany 89–90
sociology, levels of 239
soft skills 156, 223–4
space, use of 23
spatial practices 95–7; beneficence
    101–2; community engagement themes
    100–1; community partnerships 101;
    explanations of community engagement
    101–4; political imperatives 103; research
    methods 97–8; schools' depictions of
    engagement 98–100; summary and
    conclusions 105; volunteering 101, 104
spatiality 96, 237–8
Special Economic Zones, China 117
speculators 18
sponsored mobility 186, 188–96

stability, of elites 18
standardization, United States 190
Stanley-Lewis, L. 234
status, intergenerational transmission 23
stereotypes, girls' education 161–3
stratificatory differentiation, Germany
    87–91
student aid, Brazil 74–5
students' expenditure, China **121**
students, qualities 8
study of elites, background 3
Stuyvesant High School 59
super-elites 65
super managers 220–2
symbolic architecture 98

talent construction, Singapore 222–7
talent, defining 223–4
talent mismatch/deficit 223, 228
talent wars 217, 220–2
Taylorism 220
Teaching Schools 103
technology, and restratification 220–1
The Idea of a University 203–4
theories of tolerance 185
time, purchase of 31
Tiramonti, G. 44
trade liberalization 112
traditional schools, Argentina 45–7
transformations, American elite 60–5,
    68–9
transnational capitalist class 135–7
transnational companies (TNCs): context
    and overview 217–18; educational
    systems and recruitment 228; high
    skills auction 219–20; research methods
    223; summary and conclusions
    227–8; super managers 220–2; talent
    construction, Singapore 222–7;
    technology and restratification 220–1;
    war for talent 220–2
transnational practices 238
transnationality 20, 23
trophy daughters 159–60
Tunstall, J. 114
Turner, R.H. 33, 186, 188–9, 191
Turner's thesis 188–9, 194

Ullrich, H. 85
United States: changes in elite schools
    65–8; context and overview
    59–60; educational system 189–91;
    Gini coefficient 64; imperialism
    112; income distribution 60–4;
    professional composition of wealthiest

1% *61*; residential segregation 59;
    transformation of elite 60–5, 68–9;
    understanding 68–9; *see also* social
    mobility
universities: admission procedures 66–8;
    adult access 194–5; allocation of places
    87–8; Britain 213; changes in, US 65–8;
    commerce and markets 68; cultural
    and economic capital 173, *174–5*; and
    economic regions 121; elite pathways
    180–1; enrollment 75; entry to 170–1;
    France 213; graduates in NS-SEC1 and
    Elite **176**; inequalities 170; influencing
    through policy 118–20; national and local
    121–2; Norway 213–14; overcrowding
    87–8; pathways to elite universities
    176–81; RG graduates in NS-SEC1 and
    Elite **177**; São Paulo 75–8; and social
    advantage 170–1; status hierarchy 172;
    students' expenditure **121**; *see also* China
University of Oxford 20
urbanization, Asia 127
USA 19

values, parental 186
van Zanten, A. 20
vertical circulation 18–19
vertical stratification, Germany 86–7,
    90–1
volunteering 101, 104

Wakeling, p. 236
Walkerdine, V. 158
Wardman, N. 98, 156
wealth 60, 114; China 117–18; role of 20–1
wealth transfer 64–5
Weber, M. 140, 190, 201
Williams, K. 234, 235
Willis, P. 114
Wilshaw, M. 103
Wolff, E. 63
women: fear of failure 159, 164; gender
    disadvantage 157; middle class 132;
    single 153–4; *see also* girls' education
workforce differentiation 217
workplace inequality 221

Xu Youyu 126

Yang, D.P. 116

Zakaria, F. 126
Zeigler, S. 45
Zemin Jiang 119
Zimdars, A. 5